FUNDAMENTALS OF
COGNITIVE
PSYCHOLOGY

Cognitive Psychology Program

Senior Consulting Editor
James S. Nairne (Purdue University, USA)
Consulting Editors
Martin Conway (University of Leeds, UK)
Stephan Lewandowsky (University of Western Australia, AUS)
Elizabeth F. Loftus (University of California at Irvine, USA)
Mark A. McDaniel (Washington University in St. Louis, USA)
Hal Pashler (University of California at San Diego, USA)

SAGE Publications is pleased to announce a new, international program of titles in cognitive psychology—both textbook and reference—brought together by a team of consultant editors led by James S. Nairne: the **SAGE Cognitive Psychology Program**. Featuring books written or edited by world-leading scholars (or younger academics "on the rise") and infused with the latest research in the field, the program is intended to be a self-contained, comprehensive resource that meets all the educational needs of a cognitive psychology program including and beyond the introductory level.

The aim of the **SAGE Cognitive Psychology Program** is to offer both breadth and depth. Student textbooks are written by leading and experienced scholars in a style that is carefully crafted to be stimulating, engaging, and accessible. They are scholarly, comprehensive, and up-to-date, and boast the appropriate pedagogical devices and supplements—thus making them appropriate for building courses around a variety of levels. Reference works, including handbooks and encyclopedias, survey the landscape with an even broader sweep and should become benchmark volumes for years to come.

Existing and forthcoming titles:

- **Handbook of Cognition** (Koen Lamberts, *Warwick*; Rob Goldstone, *Indiana University*)
- **Cognitive Psychology, Second Edition** (Ronald Kellogg, *Saint Louis University*)
- **Fundamentals of Cognitive Psychology** (Ronald Kellogg, *Saint Louis University*)
- **Cognitive Psychology & Metacognition** [forthcoming] (John Dunlosky, *Kent State University*; Janet Metcalfe, *Columbia University*)
- **Attention: Theory & Practice** (Addie Johnson, *University of Groningen*; Robert Proctor, *Purdue University*)
- **Culture & Cognition: Implications for Theory & Method** (Norbert Ross, *Vanderbilt University*)
- **Rational Choice in an Uncertain World: The Psychology of Judgment & Decision Making** (Reid Hastie, *University of Chicago*; Robyn Dawes, *Carnegie Mellon*)
- **Handbook of Understanding & Measuring Intelligence** (Oliver Wilhelm, *Humboldt-University, Berlin*; Randall Engle, *Georgia Tech*)
- **Cognitive Science: An Introduction to the Study of Mind** (Jay Friedenberg; Gordon Silverman, both of *Manhattan College*)
- **Handbook of Implicit Cognition & Addiction** (Reinout Wiers, *Universiteit Maastricht*; Alan W. Stacy, *University of Southern California*)
- **Human Memory: Structures & Images** (Mary Howes, *SUNY–Oneonta*)
- **Prospective Memory** (Mark A. McDaniel, *Washington University*; Gilles O. Einstein, *Furman University*)
- **Cognitive Modeling** [forthcoming] (Jerome R. Busemeyer, *Indiana University*; Adele Diederich, *International University, Bremen*)
- **Handbook of Cognitive Aging: Interdisciplinary Perspectives** [forthcoming] (Scott M. Hofer, *Pennsylvania State University*; Duane F. Alwin, *University of Michigan*)

FUNDAMENTALS OF COGNITIVE PSYCHOLOGY

RONALD T. KELLOGG

Saint Louis University

SAGE Publications
Los Angeles • London • New Delhi • Singapore

For information:

Sage Publications, Inc.
2455 Teller Road
Thousand Oaks,
   California 91320
E-mail: order@sagepub.com

Sage Publications Ltd.
1 Oliver's Yard
55 City Road
London EC1Y 1SP
United Kingdom

Sage Publications India Pvt Ltd.
B 1/I 1 Mohan Cooperative
   Industrial Area
Mathura Road, New Delhi 110 044
India

Sage Publications Asia-Pacific Pte Ltd.
33 Pekin Street #02-01
Far East Square
Singapore 048763

Printed in the United States of America

Library of Congress Cataloging-in-Publication Data

Kellogg, Ronald Thomas.
Fundamentals of cognitive psychology / Ronald T. Kellogg.
    p. cm.
Includes bibliographical references and index.
ISBN 978-1-4129-3692-7 (pbk. : alk. paper)
   1. Cognitive psychology. I. Title.

BF201.K453 2007
153—dc22

2006102694

This book is printed on acid-free paper.

07 08 09 10 11   10 9 8 7 6 5 4 3 2 1

Acquisitions Editor:	Cheri Dellelo
Editorial Assistant:	Anna Marie Mesick
Associate Editor:	Deya Saoud
Production Editor:	Catherine M. Chilton
Copy Editor:	Diana Breti
Typesetter:	C&M Digitals
Proofreader:	Doris Hus
Indexer:	Diggs Publication Services
Cover Designer:	Michelle Kenny
Marketing Manager:	Amberlyn Erzinger

BRIEF CONTENTS

Preface   **xi**

Acknowledgments   **xiv**

   1. Introduction   1

   2. Perception   31

   3. Attention   63

   4. Memory Systems   93

   5. Remembering Events   125

   6. Memory Distortions   153

   7. Knowledge Representation   183

   8. Language   213

   9. Problem Solving   245

  10. Reasoning and Decision Making   279

Glossary   **311**

References   **325**

Index   **359**

About the Author   **375**

CONTENTS

Preface   **xi**

Acknowledgments   **xiv**

1. Introduction   **1**

  Scope of Cognitive Psychology   2
    Historical Perspective   2
    Defining Cognitive Psychology   3
  Core Concepts   7
    Mental Representations   7
    Stages of Processing   7
    Serial Versus Parallel Processing   8
    Hierarchical Systems   8
    Cognitive Architecture   9
    Memory Stores   11
    Consciousness   12
    Emotion   13
  The Brain   14
    Cerebral Cortex   14
    Parallel Processing   18
  Research Methods   19
    Behavioral Measures   20
    Physiological Measures   21
  Summary   29
  Key Terms   30

2. Perception   **31**

  Visual Consciousness   33
    Visual Pathways   34
    Visual Cortex   36
  Pattern Recognition   37

Agnosia	39
Top-Down Versus Bottom-Up Processes	42
Object Representations	45
Modularity	49
Holistic Versus Analytic Processing	49
Face Perception	51
Speech Perception	53
Summary	61
Key Terms	62

3. Attention **63**

Filter Theories	65
Early Selection	67
Attenuation	69
Late Selection	71
Capacity Theories	72
Mental Effort	73
Multiple Resources	75
Conclusion	76
Automatic Processes	76
Criteria of Automaticity	77
Practice and Automaticity	77
Genetics and Maturation	80
Visual Attention	81
Neural Basis of Selection	81
Executive Attention	83
Perceptual Binding	84
Subliminal Perception	88
Summary	89
Key Terms	91

4. Memory Systems **93**

Sensory Memory	95
Iconic Memory	96
Echoic Memory	98
Short-Term Versus Long-Term Memory	99
Serial Position Effects	100
Neurological Dissociations	102
Capacity	106
Duration	107
Other Distinguishing Criteria	111
Conclusion	117

	Working Memory	117
	Multiple Components	119
	Supporting Evidence	121
	Summary	123
	Key Terms	124
5.	**Remembering Events**	**125**
	Types of Long-Term Memory	126
	Declarative Versus Procedural Memory	126
	Episodic Versus Semantic Memory	130
	Criticisms of Multiple Systems	132
	Encoding and Storing Events	133
	Levels of Processing	135
	Transfer-Appropriate Processing	136
	Distinctiveness	137
	Relational Processing	140
	Retrieval Processes	141
	Retrieval Mode	142
	Encoding Specificity	144
	Summary	150
	Key Terms	151
6.	**Memory Distortions**	**153**
	Reconstructive Retrieval	154
	Reconstructing Laboratory Events	155
	Reconstructing Autobiographical Events	158
	Encoding Distortions	160
	Selection	160
	Interpretation	161
	Integration	162
	Source Monitoring	163
	Memory Illusions	166
	Confabulation	169
	Eyewitness Testimony	170
	Reconstructive Retrieval	170
	Selective Encoding	171
	The Misinformation Effect	172
	Implanted Memories	174
	Recovered Memories	176
	Summary	180
	Key Terms	182

7. Knowledge Representation   **183**

Representing Concepts   184
Rule-Governed Concepts   184
Object Concepts   185
Schemas   191
Meta-representations   192
Propositions and Images   193
The Nature of Images   196
The Nature of Propositions   202
Using Semantic Memory   205
Semantic Network Models   205
The Feature Comparison Model   208
Summary   210
Key Terms   211

8. Language   **213**

Defining Language   213
Origins of Language   214
Meaning, Structure, and Use   215
Contrasts to Animal Communication   220
Representations of Language   223
Universal Grammar   223
Neural Systems   225
Comprehension of Language   230
Word Recognition   230
Sentence Comprehension   233
Discourse Comprehension   237
Eye Movements and Comprehension   240
Summary   242
Key Terms   244

9. Problem Solving   **245**

Types of Thinking   246
Well-Defined and Ill-Defined Problems   246
Productive and Reproductive Problem Solving   249
Relations Among Terms   250
A General Model of Problem Solving   251
Representing Problems   252
Searching the Problem Space   255
Domain-Specific Knowledge and Metacognition   263

Creativity 267
    Historical Versus Process Creativity 268
    Stages of Creativity 268
    Creativity Blocks 270
    Sources of Creativity 274
    Creative Production 275
Summary 276
Key Terms 278

10. Reasoning and Decision Making **279**

Syllogistic Reasoning 280
    Syllogistic Forms 281
    Common Errors 284
    Cognitive Constraints 285
Conditional Reasoning 288
    Valid and Invalid Conditional Reasoning 289
    Common Errors 290
    Cognitive Constraints 290
Decision Making 295
    Types of Decisions 295
    Subjective Utility 296
    Emotion and Thinking 299
    Probability Heuristics 300
    Dual Process Theories 307
Summary 308
Key Terms 309

Glossary **311**

References **325**

Index **359**

About the Author **375**

PREFACE

Cognitive psychology has evolved over the past half century to become the dominant approach to virtually all aspects of human psychology. Its influence is strong in clinical, assessment, developmental, social, comparative, and physiological psychology, among other areas. Alternative approaches such as psychoanalysis, behaviorism, and humanistic psychology carry less force not only in psychology but in related fields as well. Linguistics, computer science, philosophy, anthropology, and the other sister disciplines of cognitive psychology are part of a remarkably encompassing and exciting enterprise known as cognitive science. During the early years of the twenty-first century, the cognitive approach has become so integrated into psychology it is invisible and taken for granted.

It is important, therefore, for all students of psychology to receive a solid introduction to the fundamental concepts of cognitive psychology. The aim of this book is to present a readable, relatively brief survey of the discipline. It is designed to meet the needs of instructors and students in introductory courses to the field. It is divided into 10 chapters that can readily be covered in a single term, even in a quarter system with less time available than in a semester system.

In the introductory chapter, *Fundamentals of Cognitive Psychology* prepares students to understand the exciting discoveries of cognitive neuroscience along with the history, scope, and methods of the discipline as a whole. Perception and then attention are covered in Chapters 2 and 3 as fundamental aspects of cognition. Chapter 4 introduces memory by covering the multistore model that has been the standard of the field for over 50 years. The working memory system that supports language production, comprehension, and thinking is then introduced by integrating the short-term store with attentional components. The architecture of the long-term system is described next in Chapter 5, distinguishing, for example, between declarative or explicit and nondeclarative or implicit components. Also, in Chapter 5, episodic memory—one kind of explicit memory—is treated fully. The ways in which memory can be distorted through forgetting and false recollection are discussed in detail in Chapter 6. Knowledge representation in semantic memory and concept learning are presented in Chapter 7. The treatment of language in Chapter 8 omits the topic of speech production. However, the chapter provides a thorough discussion of the nature of language; the ways in which language is represented, including its neurobiological substrate in the brain; and the means by which language is comprehended. Problem solving is covered in Chapter 9 and reasoning and decision making in Chapter 10. Perception, attention, memory in all its forms, and language are the platforms on which higher-order thinking processes unfold in problem solving, reasoning, and decision making.

As a text for an advanced undergraduate or graduate level course, my earlier book titled *Cognitive Psychology* (2nd ed.) is recommended instead of *Fundamentals of Cognitive Psychology*. The earlier book provides a deeper introduction to cognitive neuroscience with a separate chapter on functional neuroanatomy and connectionist modeling. It also provides a fuller treatment of language and higher level cognition, including coverage of intelligence, as well as a separate chapter on concept learning and the development of skills and expertise. These topics lie beyond the fundamentals of cognitive psychology.

As in *Cognitive Psychology* (2nd ed.), I seek here to provide a synthesis of cognitive psychology at its best rather than a chronicle of its arguments and conflicts. Certainly, the difficult struggle of cognitive approaches in psychology during the past 100 years deserves coverage, as do the many disagreements in contemporary theories and findings. But controversy can easily be overdone to the point of befuddling students. More advanced courses can dig deeper into the many controversies in the field, and students can consult the primary sources cited throughout the text or supplemental readings assigned by the instructor. Here, I seek to encapsulate the relevant background, theory, and research within each chapter. For example, details about the development of language, memory, and perception are covered in their respective chapters rather than culled and packaged as cognitive development.

Findings from cognitive neuroscience are frequently cited throughout the book. The methods of cognitive neuroscience, particularly neuroimaging of the brain as a person perceives, attends, learns, remembers, and thinks, are now fundamental concepts that are rapidly advancing the state of the science. With these new methods has come a focus on the relation between emotion and cognition, on how the bodily, visceral experiences of emotion color our memories and thoughts. Understanding cognitive psychology and, more broadly, cognitive science now requires a deeper understanding of the brain and emotion than was the case in the past. The approach taken here is that cognition cannot be understood without reference to both its development and its biological bodily substrate.

Applications of the fundamental concepts are also emphasized in this book. For example, research on the encoding and retrieval processes involved in false memories have important applications for eyewitness testimony in police and court proceedings. Applications are integrated into the narrative of the text itself, rather than set off in boxed material that students are tempted to ignore or regard as unnecessary detail. Another important pedagogical feature is the inclusion of margin notes. These notes summarize important concepts and are of great benefit in previewing and reviewing each chapter. Key terms are listed at the end of each chapter and each is defined clearly in the glossary at the end of the book. Each chapter is summarized to help students effectively integrate the material. In addition, an Instructor's Resource CD provides materials for PowerPoint presentations, interactive demonstrations, Web resources, suggestions for further reading, and test questions, and the Companion Student Study Site includes Internet exercises and Web resources, flashcards containing key terms and definitions, self-quizzes, and links to Sage journal articles. Visit http://www.sagepub.com/kelloggfcpstudy to access these materials.

ACKNOWLEDGMENTS

Fundamentals of Cognitive Psychology benefited from the useful suggestions by reviewers of both editions of my earlier work: Michael Anch; Terry Au; Lyle E. Bourne, Jr.; James Chumbley; Ira Fischler; Michael E. J. Masson; Thomas H. Carr; David C. Geary; Lewis O. Harvey; Paula Hertel; Donald Homa; Ken McRae; Akira Miyake; Lance Rips; Steven Sloman; John E. Taplin; and other anonymous reviewers. The proposal for the *Fundamentals* manuscript was reviewed by

Stacy Birch
State University of New York, Brockport

Tim Curran
University of Colorado at Boulder

Simon Farrell
University of Bristol

F. Richard Ferraro
University of North Dakota

Robin Flanagan
Western Connecticut State University

D. Kristen Gilbert
University of Montevallo

Holly Irwin-Chase
Point Loma Nazarene University

Michael J. Kane
University of North Carolina, Greensboro

Erica Kleinknecht
Pacific University

Trudy Kuo
University of Arizona

Tara T. Lineweaver
Butler University

Dr. Toby J. Lloyd-Jones
University of Kent at Canterbury

James Mazur
Southern Connecticut State University

Klaus Oberauer
University of Bristol

Julie Patrick
West Virginia University

Rayne A. Sperling
The Pennsylvania State University

Constance Toffle
West Virginia University

Mark Van Selst
San Jose State University

W. Richard Walker
Winston-Salem State University

Robert L. Widner
Minnesota State University, Mankato

Stuart Wilson
Queen Margaret University College, Edinburgh

I thank Becky Elliott for her help in preparing the manuscript for submission to Sage. The graphics in the book are the careful, artful work of Barry Burns. Barry's drawings are complemented by the charts and tables prepared by Nicholas Alexander. The final version of the manuscript benefited greatly from the skillful and thorough copyediting done by Diana Breti.

Jim Brace-Thompson at Sage Publications suggested the idea of *Fundamentals of Cognitive Psychology* to serve instructors seeking a condensed text for their courses. Cheri Dellelo took over the project when Jim moved to a different division at Sage. Both she and Deya Saoud were helpful in bringing the project to completion.

In memory of my mother, Patricia Elaine Johnson Kellogg

CHAPTER 1

INTRODUCTION

Cognitive psychology and its more inclusive partner, **cognitive science,** exert a strong influence on psychology as a whole and promise a scientific understanding of the human mind in all its complexity and significance. The discipline that you will study in this book concerns itself with the science of mental life, as defined by contemporary research methods, theories, and findings. The questions raised by cognitive psychology typically have ancient roots in the study of philosophy; the answers provided by the science of the mind are recent and undergoing continual refinement. Here you will learn how far we have come in one of science's grandest quests: the mind seeking to understand itself.

Cognitive psychology, neuroscience, developmental psychology, evolutionary biology, anthropology, linguistics, philosophy, computer science, and other research programs that together make up the broad interdisciplinary field of cognitive science are thriving. Discoveries beckon in understanding how humans perceive, remember, imagine, think, and create.

Consider the despair of a child who struggles in school because of an impairment in the ability to read written language, a disorder called dyslexia. Dyslexia is one of several learning disorders that cognitive psychologists study to understand the specific breakdowns in cognitive processes that are at fault. The concepts and theories of cognitive psychology assist educators to understand learning disorders and design interventions that help with reading and other learning problems in school-age children.

Or consider the anguish of family members who lose a parent to the confusion and memory loss of dementia of Alzheimer's type. This disease causes a progressive deterioration in cognition that in advanced stages leaves the victim with a complete loss of memory and self-identity. It affects primarily individuals over the age of 65, with the risk level rising to nearly 50% by age 85. Given that more people are living to advanced ages, Alzheimer's disease will, unfortunately, become increasingly common. Our ability to diagnose, prevent, and possibly even cure this tragic disease will depend on advances in cognitive psychology and its close relative, cognitive neuroscience.

SCOPE OF COGNITIVE PSYCHOLOGY

Historical Perspective

William James (1890) defined the whole of psychology as "the Science of Mental Life, both its phenomena and their conditions" in his classic book titled *The Principles of Psychology* (p. 1). More than a century later, the field of cognitive psychology has fulfilled James's vision. The cognitive approach to psychology pervades all areas of psychology today and even some of its neighbor sciences. The term surfaces often, as in cognitive development, social cognition, cognitive neuroscience, cognitive therapy, and cognitive anthropology.

This turn of events has been surprising given that for many decades, psychologists selected the study of behavior over the study of cognition. Behaviorism referred to an approach that tried to make psychology objective, like physics and chemistry. It tried to eliminate the discussion of consciousness and introspective reports on the contents of consciousness. It tried to reduce psychology to the study of observable behavior. Thus, research on classical conditioning and operant conditioning was in vogue because they depended solely on environmental stimuli and observable responses. Inferences about the cognitive operations that intervened between the stimulus and the response were unwelcome during the behaviorist era.

Behaviorism was a reaction to several schools of thought in psychology that emerged in the late nineteenth and early twentieth centuries (Boring, 1957). Structuralism aimed to describe the elemental components of consciousness, specifically sensations, images, and feelings. This school was based on the method of introspection pioneered by Wundt and developed by Titchener. The problem with this approach is that different observers too often gave different introspective reports in the experimental conditions arranged by the researchers. Also, cognition did not necessarily register in consciousness. For example, in judging which of two weights is heavier, an individual is conscious of numerous sensations. However, the decision process itself seems to occur unconsciously as a form of imageless thought. Functionalism arose as an alternative school of thought to deal with these problems. Angell, Thorndyke, and other functionalists studied the mental processes that mediated between the environment and the organism. Functionalism addressed what the mind is for, rather than its structural components. Today's cognitive psychologists are concerned with both the structural architecture of the mind and the mental operations that mediate between stimuli and responses.

Despite the accelerating pace of change in the discipline, James's *Principles of Psychology* remains worthwhile reading more than a century later. Numerous concepts and hypotheses first described by William James in 1890 remain viable today. He included discussion of the pioneering work of Hermann Ebbinghaus, who systematically studied his own ability to learn lists of nonsense syllables. Ebbinghaus selected material that was unfamiliar to him to control for the effect of past learning and meaning. Instead of measuring his ability to directly recall a list he had learned in the past, Ebbinghaus used an indirect method of measuring the time taken to relearn a list that had once been learned to perfection but was later forgotten to a degree. Ebbinghaus calculated the savings in the time needed to relearn a partially forgotten list relative to learning a control list from scratch. This so-called method of savings foreshadowed the contemporary interest in indirect ways of assessing memory performance, as will be discussed in Chapter 4.

Defining Cognitive Psychology

Cognitive psychology refers to the study of human mental processes and their role in thinking, feeling, and behaving. Perception, memory, acquisition of knowledge and expertise, comprehension and production of language, problem solving, creativity, decision making, and reasoning are some of the broad categories of such study. Experimentation lies at the heart of cognitive psychology, but as we will see, mathematical models and computer simulations also play a role. Cognitive psychologists measure behavior in laboratory tasks in order to reach conclusions about covert mental processes. As we will also see, the related discipline of cognitive neuroscience uses neuroimaging methods that try to relate activity in the brain to the behavioral measurements.

The discipline often portrays the human mind as first a processor of information: the mind computes answers to problems in a manner analogous to the software of a computer. A digital computer represents an arithmetic problem, such as 21 + 14, in a symbolic code of zeros and ones according to an agreed convention. Specifically, each digit is represented by eight bits of information, where each bit takes the value of either zero or one. Then, a software program processes those symbols according to the rules of addition, yielding the correct answer, 35. Similarly, as you read this problem and verified the answer, your mind interpreted the numbers and processed the information. The analogy between mental processes and computation has proved fruitful and provides what is called the *information processing approach* to cognitive psychology.

But the human mind does more than process information the way a computer would. Information technically refers to a reduction in uncertainty about events. For instance, consider the toss of a coin as an event with an uncertain outcome. If it comes up heads, then the uncertainty about the event has been reduced (one bit of information has been transmitted, to be mathematically precise). Information is transmitted in this example, but the event is meaningless. Now, suppose that the coin is tossed again, but this time heads means you lose $500 and tails means you win $500. Are you ready for the toss? The outcome again reduces uncertainty by one bit, but more important, the toss now has meaning. It refers to other events that are significant to you. Meaning, not information in the mathematical sense, provides the focus of human mental life (Bruner, 1990).

Throughout this book, the fundamental importance of meaningfulness will be plain. A simple illustration concerns your ability to remember the items from two different lists. The first list in Figure 1.1 contains meaningless trigrams; each set of three letters carries few natural associations (unless your initials are there by accident). The second list contains three-letter words, each of which refers to an object that you have experienced in the world and know well. Study the trigram list for 30 seconds and then try to recall the items without looking. Then, do the same with the word list. Undoubtedly, you will find the meaningful list much easier to memorize.

The mind lives and breathes through meaning. Our use of symbols to refer to objects, events, and other experiences; our efforts to understand why experiences occur as they do; and ultimately our hope to understand the purpose of our own existence all reflect the human need for meaning.

Finally, the discipline of cognitive psychology assumes that the mind and brain are systems that emerged through

Trigram	Word
WAQ	PIG
BEC	LIP
LOK	CUP
RIZ	BAT
TUZ	MAP
LUT	CAP
DOX	TAG
PEM	RIB
GAX	CAT
MIB	LOG

Figure 1.1 A demonstration of meaning in the cognitive function of memory.

evolution. They have adaptive functions that enable us to succeed as repro-ducing organisms. The structures of mind and brain must be related to these adaptive functions, just as the opposable thumb of primates is related to their ability to grasp objects. Systems for perceiving, remembering, and thinking have evolved in a manner that allows us to adapt to our environment. Understanding these systems in the context of neurophysiology and evolu-tionary biology provides another driving force in the discipline. The human mind did not emerge from the spotless laboratory of a computer scientist; rather, it emerged from the messy forces of biological development and sur-vival. Adaptations to the environment persisted in subsequent generations through natural selection.

To understand the mind from an evolutionary perspective, psychologists make comparisons of, say, memory functioning across different species. Another useful method is to study the cognitive development of memory in a single species, from infancy through old age. Functions that develop rapidly early in life are assumed to be genetically specified predispositions that were naturally selected in the history of the species. For instance, a predisposition to learn and use spoken language seems to be coded in the human genome, whereas the use of written language is not. Speech is learned early and rapidly during the first few years of childhood, whereas reading and writing are learned later and more slowly.

Cognitive science may be defined as the study of the relationships among and integration of cognitive psychology, biology, anthropology, computer science, linguistics, and philosophy (Hunt, 1989). It represents an interdisciplinary effort to address basically the same issues that confront cognitive psychology. How is knowledge represented? How does an individual acquire new knowledge? How does the visual system organize sensory experiences into meaningful objects and events? How does memory work? As shown in Figure 1.2, these are among the problems that cogni-tive science attempts to understand in terms that make sense to scholars from diverse backgrounds.

> Cognitive psychology is only one of the cognitive sciences. Others include behavioral and cognitive neuroscience, cognitive anthropology, and computer science.

Cognitive science is not a coherent discipline in and of itself but rather a perspective on several disciplines and their associated questions (Hunt, 1989). Researchers who regard themselves as cognitive scientists typically have educational backgrounds in at most one or two of the contributing dis-ciplines. Furthermore, they approach the issues of mind and brain with research methods unique to their disciplines. As Stillings and colleagues (1987), an interdisciplinary team of co-authors, explained in their pioneering text in cognitive science,

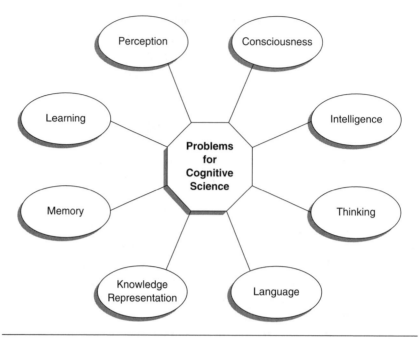

Figure 1.2   Eight critical areas of research in cognitive science and cognitive psychology.

Psychologists emphasize controlled laboratory experiments and detailed, systematic observations of naturally occurring behaviors. Linguists test hypotheses about grammatical structure by analyzing speakers' intuitions about grammatical and ungrammatical sentences or by observing children's errors in speech. Researchers in AI [artificial intelligence] test their theories by writing programs that exhibit intelligent behavior and observing where they break down. Philosophers probe the conceptual coherence of cognitive scientific theories and formulate general constraints that good theories must satisfy. Neuroscientists study the physiological basis of information processing in the brain. (p. 13)

This book focuses on the theories, methods, and results of cognitive psychology. On occasion, we encounter arguments and evidence that might constitute an entire section or chapter in a text of another branch of cognitive science. The book tries to provide you with enough context to grasp the matter at hand without assuming that you have had a course in, say, neuroscience.

CORE CONCEPTS

Mental Representations

The information processing approach is built on the assumption that an organism's ability to perceive, comprehend, learn, decide, and act depends on mental representations. A **mental representation** is an unobservable internal code for information. It is helpful to contrast a mental representation of an object with a physical external representation. Take a robin, for example. Your mental representation of a robin codes information about the bird's shape, size, coloring, and perhaps even its distinctive song. An artist's drawing of a robin is an external representation of the real thing. It, too, may convey properly the bird's shape, size, and coloring, but it would certainly lack its song.

Now, close your eyes and imagine a robin. You are using your mental representations of birds to create an image that only you can experience. Some mental representations can be consciously experienced as images that are similar to visual, aural, and other kinds of perceptions. Unlike the artist's sketch, they cannot be observed by anyone but you. Mental representations are private and are perceived, if at all, only by their owners. Not all mental representations are perceived as images, and their owners may not be conscious of them. Even with the new technologies for examining the brain, scientists cannot read your thoughts because they cannot process your conscious or unconscious mental representations. Observing patterns of neural activity is not the same as experiencing mental representations. Look again, in your mind's eye, at the robin. Can you hear its song? Perhaps, but you will hear the real song of a robin only if you have acquired a mental representation of how a robin sounds. If you confuse it with the song of a cardinal or sparrow, that is because your mental representation is in error.

> All perceptions, memories, flights of imagination, and dreams occur because of mental representations that code information.

Mental representations, then, provide the basis for all cognitive abilities. To perceive your environment, you must compute mental representations of the objects around you and the events that are taking place. To comprehend and learn from this book, you must mentally represent the information that is conveyed through language. All that you know about the world, and your only basis for acting on the world, is found in your mental representations.

Stages of Processing

Another basic concept of cognitive psychology is that processes modify mental representations in a series of stages (Massaro & Cowan, 1993). To see this point, it is easiest to consider a specific task, such as the memory task presented earlier. To remember the trigrams, you needed to first perceive or encode them, meaning you had to read the letter combinations on the page. The encoding stage could be made harder by dimming the lights in the room so that the letters are not as legible. Next, you needed to store the encoded items in memory. The words were much easier to store than the meaningless letter combinations. Next, the items needed to be retrieved from memory, which was also easier with the meaningful material. Finally, the retrieved items needed to be spoken or written during the output stage of processing. So, to be able to recall WZT, you had to compute a mental representation during encoding, store this representation as an item on the list, retrieve the representation when trying to remember, and then convert the representation to a spoken or written word. **Stages of processing,** then, refers to the steps required to form, modify, and use mental representations in a cognitive task.

Serial Versus Parallel Processing

A fundamental question is whether cognitive processes occur one at a time or simultaneously during a given stage of processing. To illustrate, consider the encoding stage of the memory task. Is each item on the list encoded one at a time, or are all of them encoded simultaneously? **Serial processing** refers to cases in which cognitive operations occur one at a time in series. Are the letters P-I-G perceived one at a time or simultaneously? **Parallel processing** refers to cases in which cognitive operations occur simultaneously in parallel.

> Multiple cognitive operations occur at once in parallel processing, or they occur one at a time in serial processing.

Hierarchical Systems

In biology, the body is divided into systems composed of many component parts. These parts are arranged hierarchically. The respiratory system, the muscular system, the cardiovascular system, and the nervous system all are organized this way. For example, the nervous system divides into the peripheral branch and the central branch. The peripheral branch further divides into sensory versus autonomic components. As you know, the autonomic branch must be further divided into the components of the sympathetic system, on the one hand, and the parasympathetic system, on the other.

In cognitive psychology, the mind is also viewed as a hierarchical system composed of many component functions. For example, the mind can be divided into branches of perception, memory, and motor output. Memory is further divided into a working or short-term system and a long-term system. The long-term system appears to be composed of further subsystems, an issue that we examine in Chapter 5. The mind can be best described as a hierarchical arrangement of functional components that can be analyzed and studied in isolation (Simon, 1969). A core task of cognitive psychology is to determine the number and organization of these functional systems. The related field of cognitive neuroscience attempts to specify the brain structures that support each functional system.

Cognitive Architecture

The design or organization of the mind's information processing components and systems is referred to as its **cognitive architecture.** The distinction between a working memory system and a long-term memory system is an architectural distinction. Another such distinction is the organization of components or subsystems of, say, long-term memory. As a third example, some theorists contend that the mind is built from independent processing modules, with each **module** specialized for a particular function such as perceiving faces or recognizing speech. An alternative point of view is that the building blocks of the mind are flexible, general-purpose mechanisms that perform many diverse functions. Long-term memory is one general purpose mechanism in that it stores representations of both faces and speech sounds from the past to enable recognition in the present and future.

A fourth and final example is the distinction between symbolic and connectionist architectures. **Symbolic models** assume that the mind is built like a digital computer. Pioneering work on computers by von Neumann (1958) provided the foundation for such models. They assume that mental representations are symbols that are serially processed by a set of rules, just as the data in a computer are processed according to the rules of a program. Simon (1990) argued that "a system will be capable of intelligent behavior if and only if it is a physical symbol system . . . capable of inputting, outputting, storing, and modifying symbol structures, and of carrying out some of these actions in response to the symbols themselves" (p. 3). This class of architecture posits a centralized control over the flow of information from sensory input, through memory, to motor output. Shown in Figure 1.3 is Atkinson and Shiffrin's (1971) influential model of the control of

> Symbolic models explain cognition in terms of simulations that operate like a computer program that encodes, stores, and manipulates symbols.

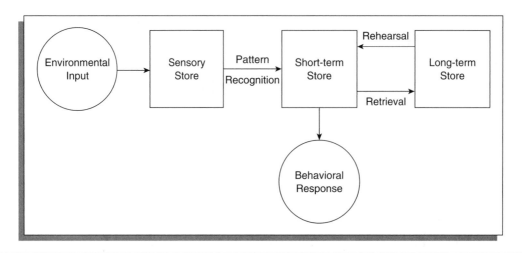

Figure 1.3   Cognitive architectures: Example of a symbolic model.

SOURCE: From Atkinson, R. C., & Shiffrin, R. M., The control of short term memory, in *Scientific American,* August 1971. Reprinted with permission.

short-term memory; it employs a symbolic architecture. Control processes, such as rehearsal, transfer information from a short-term memory store to a long-term store.

Connectionist models comprise an alternative class of cognitive architectures. Instead of looking to the digital computer, connectionist architectures try to use the structure of the brain itself as a model of the mind's structure. Instead of being based on a set of rules for operating on symbols, connectionist models are based on associations among numerous simple units called neurons. These are highly simplified units that bear scant resemblance to real neurons. However, the assumption is that a population of simple artificial neurons carries out computations that enable intelligent behaviors. Early connectionist models were proposed by McCulloch and Pitts (1943) and Hebb (1949). In connectionist architectures, there are no localized symbols to be processed. Instead, a mental representation is distributed over a population of neurons. Shown in Figure 1.4 is McClelland and Rumelhart's (1981) influential model of word recognition that uses a connectionist architecture. It employs three layers of units. The first layer represents visual features, the second represents letters, and the third represents words. Excitatory connections, shown by arrows, increase activation at a unit, whereas inhibitory connections, shown by dots, decrease it. Connectionist architectures are based on the spread of activation through local excitation and

> Connectionist models explain cognition in terms of simulations of simple neuron-like units arranged in complex networks.

inhibition. Control of the flow of information is not centralized as it is in symbolic architectures.

Memory Stores

Atkinson and Shiffrin (1971) described a short-term store that retains information just attended to for several seconds (see Figure 1.3). They distinguished this kind of memory from a long-term store that retains information over intervals of several minutes, hours, days, weeks, months, or years. Furthermore, additional distinctions may be drawn. For example, in Atkinson and Shiffrin's model, during perceptual processing, very brief storage of information takes place in the visual or auditory registers—what is called sensory memory. Over the past 30 years, it has become clear that sensory, short-term, and long-term memory are, by themselves, insufficient to describe the complexity of memory stores. Long-term memory, for instance, is further divided into subsystems, as is described later in the book.

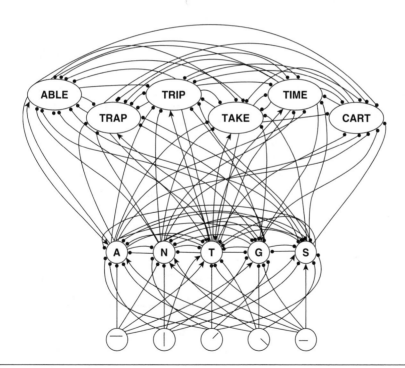

Figure 1.4   Cognitive architectures: Example of a connectionist model.

SOURCE: From McClelland, J. L., & Rumelhart, D. E. (Eds.). (1981). An interactive model of context effects in letter perception: I. An account of basic findings. *Psychological Review, 88,* 375-407. Copyright © American Psychological Association. Reprinted with permission.

Consciousness

Consciousness is certainly a core concept in cognitive psychology. But it has been a difficult one to investigate for many reasons, and progress has been slow. One major problem in studying consciousness is that the concept is not well-defined. People mean different things when they talk about consciousness, including the scientists who try to study it. Pinker (1999) explained that cognitive scientists often talk about consciousness as **self-knowledge**, even though this is not what the average person on the street means by the term at all. Self-knowledge refers to the capacity to represent the self mentally in addition to the objects, events, and ideas encountered in the external world. That is to say, included among the many kinds of knowledge that one has is knowledge about the self-concept. A human being can look in a mirror and recognize that she is viewing herself because she possesses knowledge about herself.

A second meaning of consciousness is **informational access,** the capacity to be able to report on mental representations and the processes that operate on them. Access consciousness includes the end products of our perceptual systems, allowing us to see, hear, smell, and touch the world around us and to feel the positions and tensions of our bodies. Some of these mental representations are attended to and maintained in short-term memory for several seconds. We seem to also have access to our emotional states and to our self-concept—an awareness of an executive, I, who interprets why things happen the way they do and makes decisions about how to behave in response. At the same time, many mental representations and the processes that operate on them are unconscious and unavailable for verbal report. Just as you do not have conscious access to workings of the cardiovascular system or the autonomic nervous system, you also do not have access to the processes that create vision or audition. For example, all of the processes that detect the lines that make up a single letter on this page, match the letter shape to a representation in memory, and specify where on the page the letter appears are unconscious. You have awareness only of the product—the perceived letters and words.

Finally, there is consciousness defined as **sentience,** the basic capacity for raw sensations, feelings, or subjective experience of any kind. How is it that a material object, the brain, can give rise to subjective experience? Trying to understand the relationship between consciousness as sentience and the brain has bedeviled philosophers and psychologists in what is known as the mind-body problem. A great deal is known about consciousness as self-knowledge and informational access. Despite mountains of books and articles on the problem, little if any progress has been made in understanding how, or even whether, the brain

> In cognitive psychology, the term *consciousness* can refer to self-knowledge, informational access, or sentience.

causes sentience. The positions on the mind-body issue are beyond our scope here; most of what you will learn about consciousness in this book concerns findings about self-knowledge and informational access.

Not all cognitive processing is accompanied by consciousness. Unconscious processes are fast, automatic, intuitive, and unreflective. These occur without the sentience, informational access, and self-knowledge associated with different aspects of consciousness. The cognitive processes that give rise to conscious awareness are, by contrast, slow, effortful, and deliberate. Many theories discussed throughout this book rely on a dual process of unconscious and conscious cognition. It is worth pointing out, however, that the unconscious processes posited in contemporary cognitive theories are not identical to the concept of the Freudian unconscious described in psychodynamic theory.

Emotion

The topic of emotion or affect has not traditionally been part of cognitive psychology. The information processing approach, and particularly the idea that the mind was a processor of symbols in a manner analogous to a digital computer, did not readily accommodate the study of fear, anger, sadness, happiness, and disgust. Instead, cognitive psychology focused on "cool" cognition and left the study of "hot" cognition—thoughts infused with emotion—to other areas such as social, personality, and clinical psychology (Phelps, 2006). However, the recent focus on cognitive neuroscience and on connectionist models that adopt the architecture of the brain as the basis for understanding the mind has placed emotion in the mainstream of cognitive psychology.

A fundamental debate centers on the basic structure of emotion. There is a long tradition of research suggesting that certain emotional states are genetically prewired categories of physiological and behavioral patterns. These affective states are universally experienced and recognized as social stimuli through facial expressions (Ekman, 1972). Human beings throughout the world can readily interpret the facial expressions of fear versus happiness, for example. Neuroimaging methods, introduced later in this chapter, have been used to try to capture the patterns of neural activation in the brain corresponding to each basic emotion. To illustrate, when an animal freezes when confronted with a threatening, fear-inducing stimulus, a group of neurons in a brain region called the amygdala become active (LeDoux, 2000). It has been proposed that the amygdala is part of a neural circuit that mediates the emotional state of fear in humans as well. Specifically, the amygdala seems to be involved in a fast, unconscious reaction to the fearful stimulus. Human beings may then follow this with a slower, deliberate, and conscious appraisal of the situation. This is one example of dual process theory applied to our understanding of human emotional responses.

An alternative theoretical framework suggests that categories such as fear, sadness, happiness, and so on are not the way nature carves up emotional life at all. Instead, these psychological categories are elaborate constructions from biologically simpler, more fundamental dimensions of affective valence (pleasure/displeasure) and arousal (high activation/low activation). From this affective dimension perspective, it may not be possible to identify a specific neural circuit for, say, fear. The response of freezing and the activation in the amygdala associated with it could be part of more than one emotional state. Researchers are currently looking to discover whether the brain circuitry of fear is distinct from the circuitry involved in, say, anger (Barrett & Wager, 2006). These emotions are similar in valence and arousal and, in fact, have brain regions in common. Of interest, then, is whether each emotional category has a specific "brain marker" that can be disentangled from others that share some, but not all, brain regions in common.

THE BRAIN

Cognition is assumed to be a function of the brain, just as breathing is a function of the lungs or blood circulation is a function of the heart. The human brain may well be the most complex structure in the known universe. Consider just a few of the brain's properties to understand this point (Sejnowski & Churchland, 1989). A neuron is one of about 200 different types of cells that make up the 100 trillion (10^{14}) cells of the human body. As shown in Figure 1.5, a neuron includes dendrites for receiving signals from other neurons, a cell body, and an axon for transmitting a signal to other neurons via a synaptic connection. This is an idealized illustration of one of several classes of neurons that vary in the size, shape, number, and arrangements of their dendrites and axons. The dendrites of a single neuron may receive as many as 10,000 synaptic connections from other neurons. The central nervous system is composed of 1 trillion (10^{12}) neurons of all kinds and about 1,000 trillion (10^{15}) synaptic connections among these neurons.

Cerebral Cortex

The outer neural covering or "bark" of the brain is called the cerebral cortex. It is the most recently evolved part of the brain and is, therefore, referred

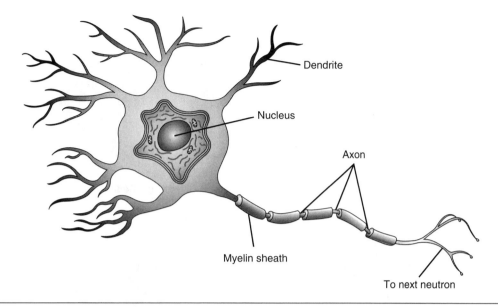

Figure 1.5   The basic components of a neuron.

to as **neocortex** to differentiate it from the more primitive, ancient types of cortex (e.g., the **limbic system**). The cerebral cortex is especially well-developed in primates, including human beings, and cetaceans, including dolphins and whales. The total surface area of the human cerebral cortex is 2,200 to 2,400 square centimeters, but most of this is buried in the depths of the *sulci* (Gazzaniga, Ivry, & Mangun, 1998). To pack that much neural tissue in the small space of the human cranium is no small challenge. The evolutionary solution to this problem was to fold the cortex, creating the convoluted surface seen in Figure 1.6. Each enfolded region is a *sulcus*. Cortical regions within these lobes have been mapped extensively based on the structure of the neurons in those regions and how they are arranged with respect to each other. The surface area of the cerebral cortex is made of gray matter, which consists of densely interconnected, unmyelinated neurons. Regions below the surface appear white in color because of the fatty myelinated fibers that insulate the axons of the neurons to speed their signal transmission (see Figure 1.5).

Shown in Figure 1.6 are the four lobes of the cerebral cortex from (a) a lateral view, (b) a medial view, (c) a dorsal view, and (d) a ventral view. These regions are separated, in part, by anatomical markers called the central sulcus, lateral fissure, and longitudinal fissure. The lobes of the cerebral cortex are divided into a left and right hemisphere by the longitudinal fissure. Large folds

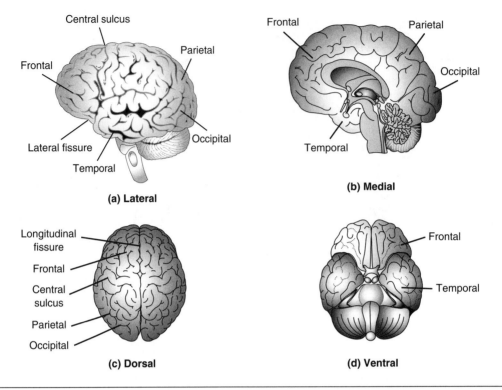

Figure 1.6   Four views of the lobes of the cerebral cortex.

in the cortex identify the boundaries of the four lobes of the brain. The **frontal lobe** extends from the anterior of the brain back to the central sulcus. The **temporal lobe** lies on the side of the brain, beginning below the lateral fissure. The **parietal lobe** extends toward the rear of the brain, beginning at the central sulcus. The **occipital lobe** lies at the rear base of the brain.

The two hemispheres look like similar structures, but they do not perform exactly the same functions. Instead, the left and right hemispheres have evolved to specialize to a degree in particular cognitive functions (Ornstein, 1997). For example, the left hemisphere specializes in producing and comprehending language. For its part, the right hemisphere specializes in recognizing faces and processing the spatial relationships among objects.

Underneath the lobes of the neocortex lies the limbic lobe, an evolutionarily old portion of cortex that mediates emotionally driven behaviors fundamental to survival, such as approach, attack, mate, and flee. These basic responses are found in primitive reptilian species such as the crocodile, where the limbic lobe analyzes olfactory or smell stimuli that are linked to these survival responses (Thompson, 2000). The limbic system consists of the limbic lobe and subcortical structures including the cingulate gyrus, fornix, **hippocampus**, and amygdala. Many of the components involved in emotion are shown in Figure 1.7. These regions are highly developed in mammals, so much so that the limbic system is sometimes referred to as the "mammalian brain" (MacLean, 1973). The primary function of the limbic system is regulation of motivational and emotional states. These range from rudimentary states of pleasure (reward) versus pain (punishment) to more complex motivational drives, such as hunger, thirst, and sex. The basic emotions of fear, sadness, anger, and happiness are also mediated by the limbic system, as perhaps are still more complex blends of emotions, such as jealousy.

Because the limbic system is so well-developed in mammals, animal models have been extremely useful for understanding the neural substrates of emotion and their role in cognitive functioning (LeDoux, 2000). For example, the hippocampus plays a critical role in learning and memory storage as well as in emotion.

The most primitive or ancient parts of the brain in terms of evolution are the brain stem and the spinal cord. The **brainstem** consists of the midbrain and the hindbrain, which includes structures called the medulla oblongata, pons, and **cerebellum**. Together these provide the basic life support

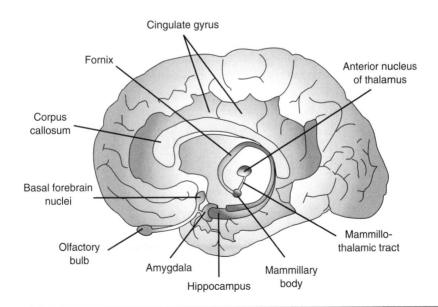

Figure 1.7   Brain structures involved in emotions.

SOURCE: From Beatty, J. (2001). *The human brain: Essentials of behavioral neuroscience.* Reprinted with permission of Sage Publications, Inc.

mechanisms of the body, such as regulating respiration, heart rate, and blood pressure. In primitive animals such as fish and amphibians, the hindbrain and midbrain are about the end of the story. The forebrain is hardly developed at all, totally unlike mammals, whose forebrain evolved into the large, complex structures of the limbic system and neocortex. The life support structures of the spinal cord, hindbrain, and midbrain, together with other ancient regions immediately surrounding the midbrain, are sometimes called the "reptilian brain" (MacLean, 1973). The human brain, therefore, evolved as a composite structure with the reptilian brain at its core, the mammalian limbic system surrounding this core, and the neocortex, in turn, surrounding the limbic system.

Parallel Processing

Another way the brain supports cognitive function is parallel processing. Many separate streams of data are processed to support a single cognitive function. Each parallel stream involves a series of stages of processing. Consequently, it is misleading to think of a cognitive function, such as recognizing your friend across a crowded room, as dependent on just one cortical region. Although it is known that certain regions in the temporal cortex of the brain are necessary for face and other object recognition, in a parallel data stream in the parietal lobe, the location of your friend in the room is computed simultaneously (Gazzaniga et al., 1998). As shown in Figure 1.8, a ventral or side pathway projects from the occipital lobe to the temporal lobe—the so-called "what" pathway. The dorsal or top pathway projects from the occipital lobe to the parietal lobe—the "where" pathway.

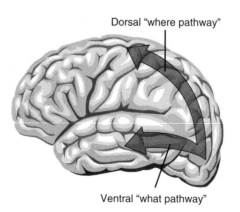

Dorsal "where pathway"

Ventral "what pathway"

Figure 1.8   The ventral "what" pathway versus the dorsal "where" pathway.

Shown in Color Plate 2 in the section of color plates are the results of a functional magnetic resonance imaging study in which the participants attended to the identity of a face (by matching it to another face) or attended to its location in a different matching condition. The red arrow marks the ventral pathway, and the green arrow marks the dorsal pathway. As may be seen, there was greater activation in the ventral pathway in the face matching condition and greater dorsal activation in the location matching condition (Haxby, Clark, & Courtney, 1997).

> Some functions are known to be localized in the neocortex, such as preliminary visual processing in the occipital lobe. However, visual perception depends on multiple regions of the brain carrying out processes in parallel, such as identifying an object using the temporal lobe while spatially locating it using the parietal lobe.

Although the brain uses parallel processing extensively, serial processing is also involved. For example, the streams of data corresponding to facial recognition and to identifying location both depend on an earlier serial stage of processing in the visual cortex of the occipital lobe. The occipital, parietal, and temporal lobes all are necessary for recognizing your friend. No one region is sufficient by itself, and both parallel and serial processing are necessary.

RESEARCH METHODS

Laboratory experiments that measure behavior form the methodological backbone of cognitive psychology. Measuring behaviors can inform us about cognitive processes. For example, counting the number of words correctly recalled from the list shown in Figure 1.1 would shed light on memory processes. Cognitive psychologists and neuroscientists also measure physiological indicators of brain activity. The neuroimaging methods, for example, are increasingly being used to understand brain structures that support a particular cognitive function. Cognitive psychologists typically try to isolate a particular component of cognitive functioning, such as working memory. They design a laboratory task that allows them to study the characteristics of this component by manipulating independent variables. For example, the digit span task calls for a research participant to recall a list of digits, such as 1-6-4-8-3-9-2, immediately after their presentation. The number of digits presented is an independent variable.

The independent variable causes changes in a dependent variable or measurement of performance in the chosen task. By manipulating the independent variable and measuring its effects, clear causal relationships may be established. In our example, the percentage of digits correctly recalled is the dependent variable. The percentage correctly recalled decreases once the number of digits exceeds about seven. Studies of this type are considered in

Chapter 4. Researchers commonly manipulate more than one independent variable at a time. For example, a researcher might vary both the number of digits presented and whether they are heard or seen by the participant.

Behavioral Measures

Typical dependent variables in cognitive psychology measure the speed and accuracy of human performance. Some tasks are so easy and automatic that few errors occur. For example, are these letter strings the same or different: WAQ, WAO? Now, try again with this pair: WAQ, BEC. **Reaction time,** the number of milliseconds to perform a task, provides a sensitive measure of the cognitive processes required. The participant is provided with two buttons and presses the one on the right if the letter strings are the "same" and the one on the left if they are "different." The first pair of letter strings in the example above requires identifying a single distinctive feature to make the correct "different" response, and the additional search time for this feature is easily detectable in reaction times measured with millisecond accuracy. Reaction times might range from 400 to 500 milliseconds in same-different judgment tasks, depending on the stimuli compared. Such times are much larger than the neural transmission time for inputting information from the eye to the brain and for outputting a motor response from the brain to skeletal muscles. Furthermore, reaction times vary in systematic ways as stages of processing are added to or subtracted from tasks (S. Sternberg, 1995).

The proportion of correct responses, or conversely the **proportion of errors,** provides another widely employed measure. For example, in a memory experiment such as the one demonstrated in Figure 1.1, the researcher might measure only the proportion of errors made in recalling the words or nonsense syllables. Suppose that instead of asking the participant to recall the words, a recognition test was given. Which of these two words appeared in Figure 1.1: PIG, DOG? Here, the researcher could readily measure not only the errors but also the time taken to reach a decision. Typically, the faster the reaction time in a task, the higher the proportion of errors. This relationship is called a speed-accuracy trade-off.

Lastly, **verbal protocols** or tape-recordings of people thinking aloud while they carry out a task provide a rich record of conscious processing. For example, suppose that you are presented with an arithmetic problem to solve. As you solve the problem, verbalize aloud your thinking. Remember to vocalize each thought you have as you solve the problem: $482 + 341 = ?$

Ideally, the research participant introspects and reports all that passes through consciousness without omitting any thoughts. Equally important, the process of thinking aloud ought not to change the processes used to perform the task. If providing verbal protocols distorts the processes normally used when thinking silently, then the validity of the method is compromised. Problem solving, reasoning, writing, and related tasks have been investigated extensively using verbal protocols. In such tasks, it is possible to identify many of the steps individuals work through in arriving at final solutions. The use of verbal protocols is justified so long as the processes required by a task are mentally represented in a verbal format or can be readily translated into words, phrases, or sentences (Ericsson & Simon, 1980). It is also necessary to demonstrate that thinking aloud is inert and does not react with and alter the processes that the researcher is trying to reveal (Russo, Johnson, & Stephens, 1989).

Physiological Measures

Besides behavioral measures, physiological measurements of bodily systems, including the brain, are also collected in experiments. These include continuous monitoring of eye movements and other muscular activity or changes in the autonomic nervous system such as heart rate, blood pressure, respiration rate, and skin conductance. Direct measurements of brain activity are also examined. The electroencephalogram (EEG) is a multichannel recording of the continuous electrical activity of the brain. It is measured with a multichannel recorder that detects voltage changes generated by large numbers of neurons below each of many electrodes placed on the scalp. The frequency and amplitude of these voltage fluctuations depend on whether the brain is awake and alert, drowsy and relaxed, or at various stages of sleep, including the well-known phase of rapid eye movement sleep.

An EEG signal that reflects the brain's response to the onset of a specific stimulus is called an **event-related potential** (**ERP**) or simply an evoked potential. To illustrate ERPs, consider the response of the brain to the presentation of a novel stimulus. An ERP called the P300 component (also known as the P3a) is the positive peak in the EEG signal that occurs 300 milliseconds after onset of an attention-getting stimulus, as shown in Figure 1.9. This component arises from an individual orienting to a novel stimulus and can be readily observed when recording from regions in the frontal lobe (Knight, 1996). Researchers use an "odd ball" task in which participants attend to and count an infrequent stimulus (e.g., red dot) while ignoring the frequent occurrences of another stimulus (e.g., green dot). In normal individuals, a novel red dot elicits a P3 ERP associated with detecting and remembering its occurrence. It turns out that this response is absent in alcoholics, however, even when they have quit drinking. Abstinent alcoholics display a diminished or delayed ERP in the odd ball task, reflecting a long-term impairment in the processing of novel information (Rodriguez, Porjesz, Chorlian,

Polich, & Begleiter, 1999). The effect does not reflect alcohol intoxication per se because the participant is sober when tested.

Moreover, the novelty deficit indexed by a P300 response might not even be related to the effects of chronic alcohol consumption per se. The children of alcoholics who have not yet consumed alcohol also show the same deficit in the odd ball task. Thus, this cognitive deficit may reflect a genetic predisposition to ignore novel stimuli rather than an alcohol-produced deficit. Of great importance, the ERP deficit can, in theory, be used as a marker of the genetic disorder. Children and adolescents who display this ERP deficit

> An ERP measures the activation of large numbers of neurons in a cortical region by detecting positive and negative voltage fluctuations on the scalp in response to a stimulus event. Multiple ERPs occur as time passes after the event is first registered.

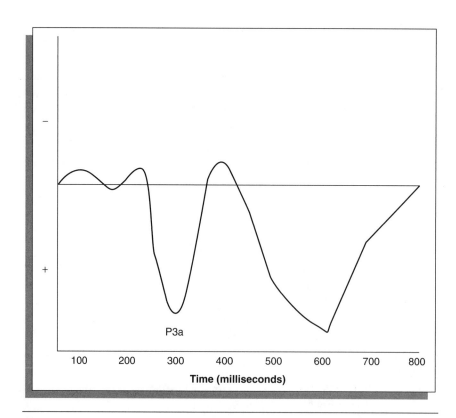

Figure 1.9   An idealized P3a ERP elicited 300 milliseconds after the presentation of a novel unexpected visual event. By convention, positive voltage changes are plotted below the x axis.

SOURCE: Adapted from Knight (1996).

are vulnerable to alcohol dependence and should avoid ever starting to drink.

Neurometric profiles can be developed that show how various stimuli and tasks evoke activities in different regions of the brain. Posner and his colleagues have developed a geodesic sensor net containing 128 electrodes for obtaining such profiles (Posner & Raichle, 1994). Each electrode, in the form of a tube containing saline solution, rests on a small sponge that makes contact with a carefully calibrated spot on the person's head. By averaging together the voltage changes that occur following the presentation of a stimulus, a waveform can be plotted at each of the locations.

EEG and ERP provide information about the temporal dynamics of neural activation in the millisecond range. Such electrophysiological measures of brain activity show excellent temporal resolution (see Figure 1.10). But it is not possible to identify the specific location, within a few millimeters, of the neuronal networks that generate the evoked potentials and fields. To pinpoint the location of neuronal activity, other methods are required.

Neuroimaging. Methods of neuroimaging measure the location of neural activation generated during a cognitive task. Two techniques now in wide use

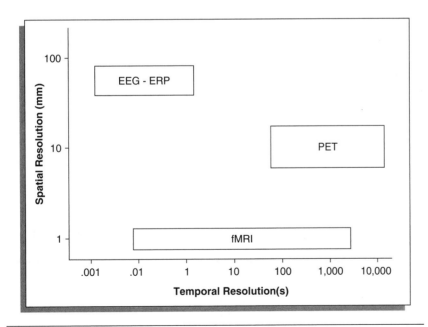

Figure 1.10   The spatial (*y* axis) and temporal (*x* axis) sensitivity of different neuroimaging techniques.

provide an indirect measure of more localized brain activity as compared with electrical scalp recordings. The first of these is **positron emission tomography (PET).** PET uses injections of radioactively labeled water (hydrogen and oxygen 15) to detect areas of high metabolic activity in the brain before the radioactive substance decays completely and is no longer radioactive (about 10 minutes). PET images require multiple scans and allow the reconstruction of a three-dimensional picture of activated regions.

The second technique is called **functional magnetic resonance imaging (fMRI).** With fMRI, a powerful magnetic field is passed through the head to reveal detailed images of neuronal tissue and metabolic changes reflecting the brain's cognitive activity. This technique extends the method of structural MRI that simply shows a detailed static image of the brain's structure. Both PET and fMRI are based on the principle that as areas of the brain increase their activity, a series of local physiological changes accompanies the activity and provides a way to measure it (Buckner & Petersen, 2000). PET works by detecting increases in blood flow in the vascular network that supplies a population of neurons; fMRI works by detecting changes in the concentration of oxygen in the blood—this is often referred to as the BOLD signal in fMRI studies, an acronym for blood oxygenation level–dependent. Thus, both PET and fMRI reveal how the brain supports behavior in a cognitive task by measuring local changes in blood properties.

> PET and fMRI provide neuroimages of the living brain as it processes information in a cognitive task. An increase in brain activity in a region is detected by increases in blood flow with PET and by increases in blood oxygenation with fMRI.

Because changes in blood flow and oxygenation take a few seconds to occur, the neuroimaging methods do not provide the temporal resolution found with evoked potentials (see Figure 1.10). The color plate section of the book includes several examples of PET and fMRI images. A person undergoing an fMRI scan is shown in Figure 1.11.

A high degree of neural activation in one region of the brain provides evidence that it is necessary for the cognitive process under investigation. It does not mean that the region is sufficient, all by itself, for the process in question. The brain processes multiple streams of data in parallel, and multiple structures are typically activated in any task. How are the regions of interest identified for a particular cognitive process?

The **method of subtraction** is used to isolate the properties of a single stage of cognitive processing. The method assumes that stages of processing used in a simple task are not modified in some way when a choice is added to the task. This is called the assumption of pure insertion. If a control task requires Stages 1 and 2 of processing and an experimental task requires Stages 1, 2, and 3, then pure insertion holds when the experimental task does

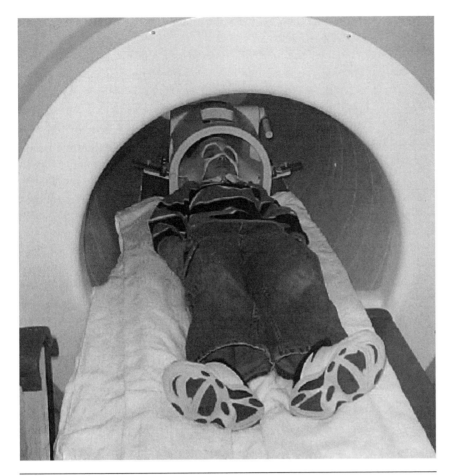

Figure 1.11   An fMRI scanner at the Washington University laboratory in
St. Louis, Missouri.

SOURCE: Courtesy of Steven E. Petersen, Washington University, St. Louis, MO.

not in any way alter the processes and time needed for Stages 1 and 2. In this
way, the extra time required by the experimental task can be assigned to the
demands of Stage 3 (S. Sternberg, 1969, 1995).

For example, suppose that researchers design two tasks for the participants that, in theory, demand exactly the same cognitive processes but for a
single process of interest. The researcher then obtains neuroimages during
both tasks and subtracts one from the other, leaving only the brain activity
related to the process under study. A classic PET study on how word names

are retrieved from long-term memory illustrates the method of subtraction (Posner, Peterson, Fox, & Raichle, 1988).

Participants in the study were presented with familiar nouns one at a time (e.g., *bottle*). The way the words were presented and the instructions regarding how to process the words were varied at different points during the experiment. The experiment was designed hierarchically, so that the processes engaged by one set of instructions provided a control condition for examining the brain regions activated by a condition higher in the hierarchy. The design is shown in Figure 1.12. In the fixation point only or control condition, brain activity associated with focusing attention on the task is measured. The activation pattern obtained in the "perceive fixation" condition is then subtracted from the activation levels found when words are perceived as the experimental condition. This subtraction isolates the processes involved in "word recognition." In the next experimental condition, participants repeated each word aloud. Now, the "perceive word" condition is used as a control, and its activation is subtracted from the "repeat word" activation. In so doing, the activation associated with "speech production" is isolated. Finally, the "repeat word" or experimental condition serves as the control for the task of generating functional uses of the words. For example, if presented with the word *bottle,* the participant might respond with *drink.* The "generate use" task requires that the meaning or semantic features of each word be processed, and the activation associated with this semantic processing is thus isolated.

The results are shown in Color Plate 1 in the section of color plates. Following convention, the relative degree of blood flow in a region is depicted in a different color. The highest to lowest levels of activation are coded by white, red, orange, green, blue, and purple, respectively. These show activation patterns resulting after subtracting the appropriate control activation patterns for each of the four tasks in the left hemisphere only. In the upper left scan, participants visually perceived each word. As shown,

Control	Experimental	Experimental-Control
Perceive fixation	Perceive word	Word recognition
Perceive word	Repeat word	Speech production
Repeat word	Generate use	Semantic processing

Figure 1.12   The method of subtraction used in neuroimaging studies of cognitive processes.

regions in the occipital cortex at the rear of the brain were activated in this condition. In the upper right scan, a similar passive perception condition is shown, except in this case the words were heard rather than seen. As a result, the auditory cortex in the temporal lobe was recruited into action. When participants repeated the words, PET revealed activation in the frontal motor areas of both hemispheres. Finally, generating a verb related to each word recruited extensive regions in the left prefrontal cortex, including Broca's area. This semantic processing also recruited regions in the temporal cortex that other research has suggested are involved in representing meaningful categories.

Brain Lesions. The oldest method of studying the function of the brain is to examine individuals who have suffered damage to brain tissue through accidents, strokes, and diseases of the brain such as Alzheimer's and Parkinson's disease. For example, in the nineteenth century, Paul Broca reported a case study of "Tan," a man with brain damage whose speech ability was reduced to saying the word "tan" repeatedly. Such tragic circumstances have provided the data for the field of clinical neuropsychology, which seeks to correlate specific lesions in the brain with specific kinds of behavioral and cognitive deficits. Lesions have also been experimentally created in rats, rabbits, monkeys, and other mammals to determine the function of the damaged area. With the exception of psychosurgery performed on psychiatric patients, for ethical reasons lesions have not been created in humans. Indeed, many have questioned the ethics of treating even severely disturbed psychiatric patients with lesions in the frontal lobe and limbic system.

Until recently, clinical neuropsychology was limited to verifying the exact location of a lesion only after the death of a patient through postmortem examination of the brain. For example, Broca discovered that Tan's brain was damaged in the left frontal lobe. This became known as Broca's area when it was discovered that additional patients with speech disorders also suffered from lesions there. Today, the use of structural as opposed to functional MRI scans allows identification of the brain regions injured by a stroke, aiding the process of using lesion case studies to understand how the brain supports cognition.

The case study method of research is a valuable tool in cognitive neuroscience. The behavior of a patient is related to the specific areas of the brain known to be damaged by a tumor, accident, or stroke.

In using single cases or group studies, the investigator attempts to find two tasks that discriminate between the performance of normal controls and patients with lesions in a particular region of the brain (Gazzaniga et al., 1998). The objective is to find evidence that one cognitive function is served by one brain region, whereas a different function is served by another brain region. To reach this conclusion, the investigator seeks double dissociations, in which the specific type of brain injury affects performance in two tasks in different ways.

In general terms, a **double dissociation** refers to situations in which an independent variable affects Task A but not Task B, and a different variable affects Task B but not Task A. One independent variable might be a lesion in the parietal cortex as compared with normal controls. A second independent variable might be a lesion in the frontal lobe as compared with normal controls. To illustrate, suppose that Task A measures planning in problem solving and Task B measures locating objects in space. If it can be shown that frontal lobe damage disrupts planning performance relative to normal controls but has no effect on locating objects in space, then a single dissociation has been demonstrated (see Figure 1.13). If, in addition, it can be shown that the parietal damage affects locating objects in space but not planning in problem solving, then a double dissociation has been established. The double dissociation isolates planning as a function of the frontal lobe and locating objects in space in the parietal lobe.

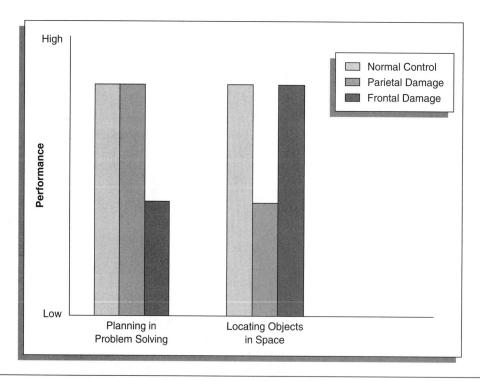

Figure 1.13 Hypothetical results of studies illustrating a single dissociation and a double dissociation.

SUMMARY

1. The beginnings of a scientific understanding of the human mind are taking shape in the fields of cognitive psychology and cognitive science. These fields connect with numerous areas of inquiry, as one would expect of a science of mental life. Cognitive psychology is the study of human mental processes and their role in thinking, feeling, and behaving. Cognitive science takes a mathematical perspective of the mind or brain as a computational device and draws insights and methods from psychology, biology, anthropology, linguistics, philosophy, and computer science.

2. Information must be mentally represented to be involved in perception, memory, or any other cognitive activity. It is through our mental representations that we know anything and everything. Mental representations are processed in stages such as encoding the information, storing it in memory, retrieving it when needed, and manipulating the information to arrive at a decision. Cognitive operations needed to, say, retrieve an item from memory may, in theory, occur in a series of steps or in parallel. Symbolic models and connectionist models are two alternative ways to describe the architecture of the information processing system.

3. Consciousness is another core concept of cognitive psychology that does not stem from information processing theory. It is necessary to distinguish between unconscious cognitive operations and those that give rise to the subjective qualities of consciousness. There are three senses in which the term *consciousness* is used in cognitive psychology. Self-knowledge means the capacity to represent the self mentally in addition to the objects, events, and ideas represented. Information access means being aware of and able to report on mental representations and cognitive processes. Finally, sentience means the capacity for feelings and other subjective experiences.

4. The human brain may well be the most complex structure in the known universe. The central nervous system contains on the order of 1 trillion neurons and about 1,000 trillion synaptic connections among these neurons. The outer layer of the brain—the cerebral cortex—is symmetrically divided into two hemispheres. Within each hemisphere, the frontal, temporal, parietal, and occipital lobes are distinguished. Regions within these anatomical structures support specific cognitive functions, such as speech or face recognition. The limbic system lies beneath the cerebral cortex and is important in emotion, learning, and memory. The organization of the brain is highly parallel, with many separate streams of data being processed to support a single function, such as the recognition of an object in a spatial location.

5. Cognitive psychologists measure behavior that provides information about cognitive processes (e.g., verbal protocols of thinking aloud). They also measure physiological indicators of brain activity, such as event-related potentials (ERP) and neuroimages (PET and fMRI). Lesions provide another way to study the cognitive functions served by the brain. A double dissociation refers to a lesion that disrupts performance on Task A but spares performance on Task B, whereas a different kind of lesion disrupts Task B but spares Task A. Double dissociation suggests that the two brain regions damaged by the lesions support different cognitive functions, as measured by Tasks A and B.

KEY TERMS

cognitive science

mental representation

stages of processing

serial processing

parallel processing

cognitive architecture

module

symbolic models

connectionist models

self-knowledge

informational access

sentience

neocortex

limbic system

frontal lobe

temporal lobe

parietal lobe

occipital lobe

hippocampus

brainstem

cerebellum

reaction time

proportion of errors

verbal protocols

event-related potential (ERP)

positron emission
  tomography (PET)

functional magnetic resonance
  imaging (fMRI)

method of subtraction

double dissociation

CHAPTER 2

PERCEPTION

The mind comes to know the world through sensing and perceiving the environment. As the three-store model of information processing showed in Chapter 1 (Figure 1.3), input from the environment first enters sensory memory, where it is held briefly. Sensation refers to the transduction of physical energy, such as sound waves or electromagnetic radiation, into an initial mental representation that can be further processed and transformed over time. Transduction means the conversion of one kind of energy into another kind. For example, in vision, electromagnetic energy is converted into an electrical signal in neurons. As a result of this processing, the objects and events that are present in the environment are perceived, in the sense of being detected. With still more processing, the objects and events are recognized, in the sense of being categorized as meaningful. Even to recognize your own mother involves a sequence of processing stages that is complex and can take as long as a half-second.

It is difficult to grasp that a process as rapid and effortless as perception involves multiple stages and transformations of mental representations. This point can be understood most easily when an illusion is perceived, that is, when perceptual processes construct a mental representation that does not accurately mirror the object in the environment. For example, examine the two creatures in Figure 2.1. The upper right creature appears larger than the lower left creature. Yet if you take a moment to measure them, you will find

Figure 2.1   An illustration of the constructive nature of perception.

SOURCE: From Shepard, R. N., *Mind sights,* copyright © 1990. Reprinted with permission from W. H. Freeman and Company.

them to be equal in size. This is an example of an illusion related to depth perception. Cues in the drawing, such as the background lines converging from the bottom to the top of the picture, contribute to a perception of distance. Normally, an object at a distance is perceived as small relative to an object identical in size viewed from close-up. In Figure 2.1, the creature higher in the picture is inferred to be farther away, and yet it is not smaller, as is usually the case in the real world. As a consequence, the size of the upper right creature is transformed, and the end result of this constructive activity is an illusory perception of a large creature in the distance chasing a small creature in the front.

Perception, then, is the result of processes that construct mental representations of the information available in the environment. Such representations draw on information stored in memory as well as present in the environment. The knowledge that a familiar object is supposed to appear smaller at a distance affects our perception of the creatures in Figure 2.1. As further examples will demonstrate in this chapter, perception is always driven in part by expectations of how the world ought to look or sound based on knowledge stored in long-term memory. In a nightly dream or in the waking hallucinations of a psychotic individual, bizarre perceptions may be fabricated out of whole cloth, secreted from memory alone.

Perception is a large subject that lies well beyond the scope of a chapter in a book on cognitive psychology. To focus the discussion, four related problems in perception are addressed. Why is it that you can see anything at all, regardless of its identity? Given that you can see something, how do you recognize it as a person instead of, say, a hat rack? Even more specifically, how do you recognize that you are perceiving the face of a person rather than the back or side of the person's head? Finally, how do you recognize what the person is saying to you as the person moves his or her lips, uttering familiar sounds? Visual sensation, object recognition, face recognition, and speech recognition will illustrate important concepts in perception that lay the foundation of cognitive psychology as a whole.

VISUAL CONSCIOUSNESS

Visible light is a narrow band of electromagnetic energy. The wavelengths of light that may be sensed by the human visual system range from 400 to 700 nanometers, where 1 nanometer = 10^{-9} meters. As shown in Figure 2.2, the full spectrum of electromagnetic energy dwarfs this tiny band of visible light. Ultraviolet rays, X-rays, and gamma rays are progressively shorter in wavelength and are not sensed by the visual system. The longer wavelengths of infrared rays, radar, radio waves, and AC circuits also go undetected. The visual system cannot construct a mental representation of an object without first transducing electromagnetic energy into a neural signal. It is sensitive only to wavelengths within the visible spectrum.

Visible light from the sun or other light sources, such as an indoor table lamp, is reflected off the objects in the environment. This light, in what is called the visual field, is structured in accordance with the structures of the objects themselves. Without structured patterns of light in the visual field, it

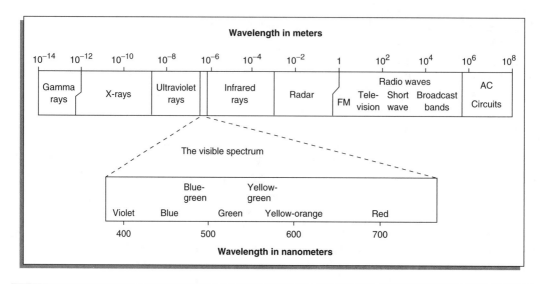

Figure 2.2 The spectrum of electromagnetic radiation includes a narrow band of visible light.

would be impossible to see in the sense of both detecting a stimulus and recognizing its identity. The detection process begins with the transduction of electromagnetic energy by photoreceptors in the retina of the eye. Photoreceptors are neurons specialized to convert visible light into electrical signals that may be propagated by the neurons of the visual system.

Visual Pathways

The cornea and the lens within the eye work together to bring the light reflected from an object into focus on the retina, the structure containing the photoreceptors. Failure to achieve a focused image is the cause of vision problems such as an inability to see a focused image of a close object (far-sightedness) or of a distant object (nearsightedness). The neural signals generated in the retina are sent via the optic nerve to a portion of the thalamus lying deep in the brain called the lateral geniculate nucleus, as shown in Figure 2.3. The thalamus receives inputs from auditory and other sensory channels in addition to vision. The pathway continues to the primary visual cortex in the occipital lobe.

The pathway from the optic nerve exiting the left eye projects to both the left and right hemispheres of the occipital lobe. Similarly, inputs to the right eye are also sent to and processed by both hemispheres. As shown in

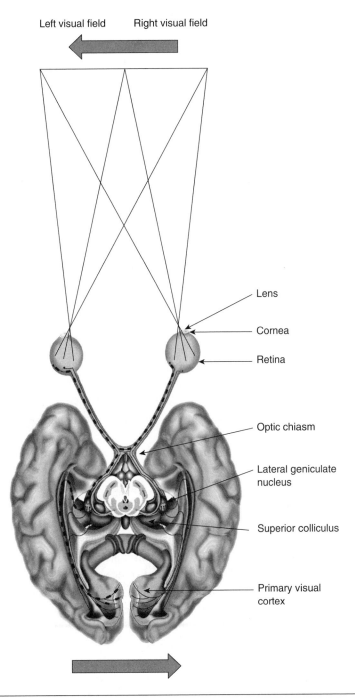

Left visual field Right visual field

Lens

Cornea

Retina

Optic chiasm

Lateral geniculate nucleus

Superior colliculus

Primary visual cortex

Figure 2.3   The visual pathways result in the representations of stimuli from the left visual field projecting to the right visual cortex and vice versa.

Figure 2.3, the axons of the optic nerve cross over to the opposite side of the brain at the optic chiasm. Here, the axons of the optic nerve from the inner, or nasal, half of each retina cross over to the opposite side of the brain. Those from the outer or temporal half remain on the same side of the brain. This arrangement results in a division of labor in vision such that the objects in the left visual field are processed by the right hemisphere and those in the right visual field are processed by the left hemisphere. Representations of stimuli presented to the left visual field project to the right visual cortex, whereas those to the right visual field project to the left visual cortex.

Although most signals follow the pathways just described, about 20% of the signals leaving the retina are projected to another structure lying at the top of the midbrain called the superior colliculus (Schiffman, 2000). This region controls eye movements. Importantly, then, there are signals from the retina processed by regions that do not terminate in the primary visual cortex. The significance of this pathway will soon become clear.

Visual Cortex

Seeing something rather than nothing depends on the processes that occur in the primary visual cortex (Crick, 1994). Visual consciousness hinges on more than a functional retina, an optic nerve, and a lateral geniculate nucleus. The occipital cortex must also function properly for one to be aware of an object in the visual environment. Two findings strongly support this conclusion.

Experiments on the development of the neurons in the visual cortex have shown that there are critical periods during which stimulation must be received for normal development. In cats, the critical period begins during the first few weeks of life and lasts about three or four months. In humans, the critical period may extend much longer to four or five years (Schiffman, 2000). To illustrate, Blakemore and Cooper (1970) raised kittens in an environment that restricted the kind of visual stimulation they received. The kittens were kept in darkness for all but about five hours a day. During this time, they lived in a restricted environment consisting only of horizontal lines for one group of kittens and vertical lines for another group. After about five months of this selective exposure, the kittens were tested for their visual awareness of horizontal and vertical lines.

Some tests used single-cell recordings from the primary visual cortex. The cortical cells responded to the orientation of lines received early in life. In the kittens that had been exposed only to horizontal lines, for example, the cells of the primary visual cortex fired at above baseline rates only to horizontal stimuli. Of critical importance, when a black bar was held horizontally, the kittens initially exposed to horizontal lines batted at the bar in play. Their behavior suggested that they could see the bar. By stark contrast, the kittens raised in the vertical line environment ignored the horizontal bar, which implied that the cortical cells were needed for visual awareness.

A second result from a neuropsychological case study confirms the conclusion that the cortex is necessary for visual consciousness. The patient known as "D. B." was a 34-year-old male who suffered from severe migraine headaches. All treatments failed, and the migraines became so severe that surgeons took the extreme step of removing part of his occipital cortex. The surgery was successful in reducing the intensity of the migraines, but it left D. B. blind in about a quarter of his visual field, specifically with respect to objects presented to his left. A test light was presented on a screen situated in front of D. B. The location of the target was varied from trial to trial in a random way, and D. B. was asked to point to its location.

As shown in Figure 2.4, when the target was presented to his normal sighted visual field to the right, D. B.'s pointing responses tracked the actual location of the target, producing a straight line for sight with awareness. Astonishingly, D. B. performed nearly as well when the target was presented to his blind left visual field. Although D. B. reported no visual awareness of anything on these trials, his pointing responses closely (but not perfectly) tracked the target (Weiskrantz, 1986). Despite his lack of conscious perception in these regions, when D. B. was encouraged to guess where the test light had occurred, he was remarkably accurate.

Vision without awareness as a result of lesions in the occipital cortex is called **blindsight.** It demonstrates the necessity of intact cortical regions for visual consciousness. Apparently, D. B. succeeded in the location task even in his blind field of vision by using information processed in the superior colliculus. This structure deep in the midbrain controls eye movements and seems to have allowed D. B. to identify the location of an object not consciously seen.

> Blindsight is vision without awareness that can be observed in patients with lesions in the occipital cortex.

PATTERN RECOGNITION

The term **pattern recognition** refers to the step between the transduction and perception of a stimulus in the environment and its categorization as a meaningful object. There is more to seeing or hearing than simply perceiving the patterns of light or sound available in the environment. It is necessary to

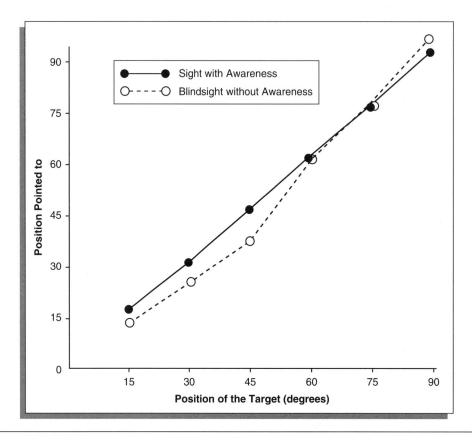

Figure 2.4   Blindsight enabled a patient to point to the location of a target unaccompanied by any visual awareness of it.

SOURCE: From Weiskrantz, L., et al., Visual capacity in the hemianopic field following a restricted occipital ablation, in *Brain: A Journal of Neurology,* copyright © 1974. Reprinted with permission of Oxford University Press.

categorize the object on the basis of its perceived features. Look at the drawings in Figure 2.5. Each drawing shows the same object from a different point of view. Although the visual information received by the retina in each case is quite different, the same object is easily recognized. The visual features are perceived and then used to categorize the object as a dog. For recognition to succeed, the mental representation of dogs, and Shelties in particular, must be retrieved and matched against the visual features that are perceived in the drawing.

> The ability to perceive depends on pattern recognition—categorizing objects and events detected in the environment by matching their preliminary representations with patterns stored in long-term memory.

Figure 2.5   An example of pattern recognition in which different features in each drawing are categorized as a Sheltie dog.

Agnosia

As a result of a neuropsychological condition called agnosia, a stimulus can be perceived and understood in terms of its properties but not recognized as a meaningful object. Patients suffering from lesions in certain regions of the brain can see objects but not recognize them at all. Such individuals are not blind; nonetheless, they fail to "see" in the fullest sense because for them, pattern recognition has failed.

For example, Sacks (1970) described a man identified as "Dr. P." who suffered from a massive brain tumor or degenerative disease that destroyed portions of his occipital cortex. Dr. P. taught music at a local school and appeared to Sacks as a cultivated man with great charm, humor, and imagination—certainly not someone suffering terribly from a serious brain disorder. However, on closer examination, it became clear that Dr. P. suffered from a form of visual agnosia, specifically an inability to recognize objects clearly from their shapes. For example, during a neurological examination, Dr. P. had removed his shoe as part of a reflex test. When asked to put his shoe back on, Dr. P. seemed baffled as he stared intently at his foot, put his hand to it, and said, "This is my shoe, no?" Stunned, Sacks replied, "No, it is not. That is your foot. There is your shoe." "Ah!" exclaimed Dr. P., "I thought that was my foot" (p. 9). The damage to Dr. P.'s brain had impaired his ability to pick up the concrete textures and other details of visual experience. Because the outline of his foot matched the outline of his shoe, he could not distinguish between the two. As Dr. P. prepared to leave the examining room, he "reached out his hand and took hold of his wife's head, tried to lift it off, to put it on. . . . He had apparently mistaken his wife for a hat! His wife looked as if she was used to such things" (p. 10).

Two kinds of visual agnosia have been documented, one resulting from damage to the right hemisphere and the other resulting from damage to the left hemisphere (Gazzaniga et al., 1998). In both cases, the primary visual cortex is intact and supports the ability to see objects in the visual field, but the objects cannot be recognized. Normally, humans can recognize an object despite wide variations in the details of how the object looks. A dog is a dog, no matter its distance, its orientation, or the angle of viewing. In the case of **apperceptive agnosia,** such ready object recognition fails as a result of difficulties in identifying the visual features that define a perceptual category.

K. K. Warrington (1982) discovered that patients with damage to the rear or posterior region of their right hemispheres made frequent errors in recognizing objects presented at unusual angles. In the example given earlier, a picture of a dog from the front, showing its head in relation to its body, was easily recognizable by all patients in the study. Yet when the picture was taken from behind, without the dog's face or feet in the picture, patients with posterior right hemisphere damage often made mistakes, as shown in Figure 2.6. By contrast, other patients with posterior damage in the left hemisphere were able to succeed on this test with a high level of accuracy. Other data showed that damage to the anterior regions of either hemisphere did not cause a problem on the unusual views test, leading to the conclusion that the right posterior hemisphere is critical for successful perceptual categorization.

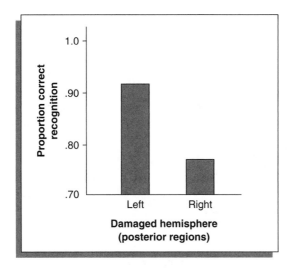

Figure 2.6   Perceptual categorization fails in apperceptive agnosia because of posterior right hemisphere damage.

SOURCE: From Warrington, K. K., Neuropsychological studies of object recognition, in *Philosophical Transactions of the Royal Society of London,* 298B (1982). Reprinted with permission.

In the case of **associative agnosia,** object recognition fails because of difficulties in identifying the functional features that define a semantic category. The problem is not at all perceptual in nature. Instead, the sufferer of associative agnosia cannot categorize objects successfully at an abstract level of meaning. The unusual views test that trips up patients with apperceptive agnosia fails to bother those with associative agnosia. By contrast, a test that requires matching objects in terms of semantic categories while ignoring their appearance causes problems for individuals with associative agnosia. For example, suppose that an individual is shown a cane, a closed umbrella, and an open umbrella and is asked to identify which two objects have the same function. An individual with perceptual agnosia has no difficulty in seeing the open and closed umbrella as representing the same semantic category. However, individuals with associative agnosia often fail to do so; they cannot see beyond the perceptual similarities of the cane and the closed umbrella.

These two kinds of agnosia demonstrate that the pattern recognition process involves two separate levels of categorization. The visual features of an object must first be matched against representations in long-term memory that identify perceptual categories. Variations in how an object looks (e.g., its orientation, the angle of viewing) must be ignored, whereas features that do matter (e.g., eyes, ears, fur, tail) are heeded. This perceptual level of categorization appears to be mediated by posterior regions in the right hemisphere and occurs prior to semantic categorization (E. K. Warrington, 1985).

> *Apperceptive agnosia* refers to a failure of pattern recognition caused by an inability to categorize objects at a perceptual level of analysis. *Associative agnosia*, by contrast, is caused by an inability to categorize objects at a functional semantic level of analysis.

As can be seen in patients with associative agnosia, it is possible to see two objects as alike perceptually (e.g., a cane and a closed umbrella) and to fail to see that they belong to different semantic categories and have different names. The functional features of an object must also be matched against representations stored in long-term memory to identify semantic categories and names. E. K. Warrington (1985) contended that this second stage is dependent on processes supported by the left hemisphere.

Top-Down Versus Bottom-Up Processes

A **schema** is a mental representation that organizes knowledge about related concepts. Imagine, for a moment, the classroom that you attend for cognitive psychology. In forming a mental picture of this particular environment, you activate a schema that represents what you know about classrooms in general and their relations to other types of rooms. The schema involves many concepts, such as those of a room, a desk, a table, a computer, an overhead projector, a projection screen, and a video recorder. In imagining each of these objects, you activate their conceptual representations, which represents what you know about the general characteristics of a category of objects, for example, tables. Organized knowledge representations or schemas direct exploration of the environment to sample features of the objects and events to be perceived.

As you walk into the building on campus containing your classroom, your mind unconsciously begins to anticipate the objects and events that will soon be seen and heard. These anticipations play a vital role in directing exploration of the environment (Neisser, 1976). The steps you take, the way you turn your head, the objects you reach for and grasp, and the eye movements you make are directed by your expectations. For example, the eye movements made to explore the environment are guided by your immediate goals (Yarbus, 1967). If you anticipate seeing a particular friend in the classroom, for example, then your eyes will quickly scan the faces of people to confirm your expectation. If expectations are violated by novel surprising events, then these are explored extensively. For example, suppose that a student brings his pet boa constrictor to class one day. People, desks, and books are expected in a classroom—but not snakes. The surprising object would be scrutinized immediately.

Top-down or **conceptually driven processes** reduce the need to sample all of the information available in the environment by providing the perceiver with expectations. Simultaneously, bottom-up or **data-driven processes** analyze the edges, lines, areas of light and dark, colors, sounds, and other physical features available briefly in sensory memory. These processes pick up the features needed to confirm or refute expectations. Through such simultaneous processing from both the bottom up and the top down, people can perceive the features of the environment with remarkable quickness and accuracy.

The contribution of each type of process depends on the perceptual circumstances (Shepard, 1984). Strong bottom-up activation occurs when perceiving under good viewing conditions. In poor, ambiguous viewing conditions, accurate perception depends more strongly on top-down than on bottom-up activation. Very strong top-down activation is responsible for the hallucinations experienced nightly in dreams. The lack of any significant external input during dreaming might be why it is experienced as real (Antrobus, 1991). Daydreaming, or imagining an event while awake and concurrently processing some external events, also depends on top-down activation, but it is less intense and is not experienced as real.

In the laboratory, several experiments have shown that the speed as well as the accuracy with which a person can identify an object depends on the context in which the process occurs (Biederman, Glass, & Stacy, 1973; Friedman, 1979; Palmer, 1975). One expects to see a cow in a farm scene or a fireplug in a city street scene. Putting the cow and the fireplug in the wrong scene measurably slows one's ability to recognize them by pitting top-down processes against bottom-up processes. Preventing the activation of a schema or frame—by removing or scrambling the context so that it looks incoherent— also hinders pattern recognition by requiring that all of the work be done from the bottom up.

Perceiving each word on this page as you read is conceptually driven, in part. Reicher (1969) presented a word (WORK), a nonword (ORWK), or a single letter (K) as a stimulus to participants. A mask (####) then appeared that stopped the processing of the original stimulus by filling the contents of iconic memory with irrelevant visual elements. Probe letters also appeared above (D) and below (K) the fourth element of the mask. The observers then guessed which of these had occurred earlier. Surprisingly, the letter K was correctly identified more often when it appeared in the word than when it appeared in isolation. The **word superiority effect** refers to a single letter being recognized faster in the context of a whole word

> Paradoxically, a single letter is identified faster when in the context of an entire word than when isolated. This word superiority effect is caused by top-down or conceptually driven expectations activated by the word.

than when presented as an isolated letter. The word activates conceptually driven processes that ease the recognition of each individual letter. The non-word stimulus fails to activate these processes and so supports the same level of identification accuracy as does the single letter.

Tulving, Mandler, and Baumal (1964) showed how varying amounts of context provided in reading speeds word recognition. They presented a target word either with no context (0 words), as the last word of a phrase (4 words), or as the last word of a sentence (8 words). The more context provided, the more conceptually driven processes should aid recognition of the target. As shown in what follows, the participant first read the context, if given, and then briefly viewed a target word such as "opponent":

opponent

challenged by a dangerous opponent

The political leader was challenged by a dangerous opponent

Tulving et al. (1964) also varied the exposure duration of the final word, "opponent," from 0 to 140 milliseconds. The longer the exposure, the more data-driven processes should aid recognition. Note that in the zero condition, only conceptually driven processes are at work, allowing perhaps a correct guess about the target word. As can be seen in Figure 2.7, with eight words of context, the proportion of correct recognition averaged nearly .20. The systematic increases with longer exposure durations show the role of making more data available from the bottom up. The differences among the eight, four, and zero word curves show the role of more precise expectations from the top down.

> Conceptually driven processes operate from the top down—from long-term memory to sensory memory—to identify the stimulus. Data-driven processes operate from the bottom up—from sensory memory to long-term memory—to achieve the same goal.

Another laboratory phenomenon that is at least partly explained by conceptually driven processes is **change blindness**. Suppose that as you spoke with a person, a different person were surreptitiously substituted. Would you notice? Suppose that in viewing a photograph of two people, the heads were surreptitiously exchanged as your eyes sampled features from one part of the picture to another. Would you notice that? People assume they would, but the results from experimentation show otherwise. Nearly 50% of observers missed these kinds of changes in the visual environment (Simons & Ambinder, 2005). Change blindness refers to the phenomenon that people fail to notice large changes in visual scenes. Limited attention and other factors probably are also involved, but it is clear that expectations that observers have about their visual environment play a major role in the features that

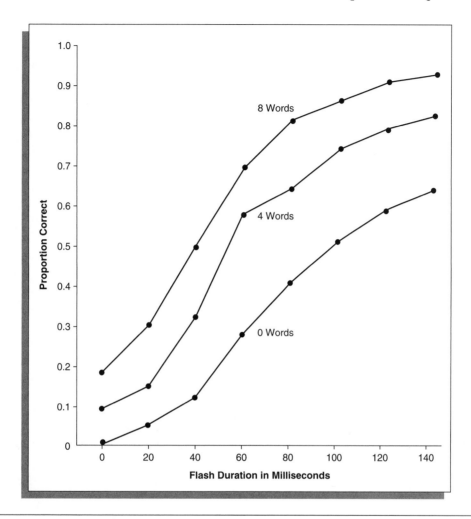

Figure 2.7   Word recognition varies with the amount of context provided.

SOURCE: From Tulving, E., Mandler, G., & Baumel, R., Interaction of two sources of information in tachistoscopic word recognition, in *Canadian Journal of Psychology, 18,* © 1964. Reprinted with permission.

they sample from the environment. Data-driven processes do not notice these changes because they are not expected.

Object Representations

If pattern recognition requires matching perceived information against perceptual representations stored in long-term memory, then what is the nature of these representations? Research into this question has examined several possibilities, but a firm answer to the question remains elusive. One possible solution is that perceptual concepts are stored as lists of **distinctive features**. For example, the distinctive features of block letters can be specified readily. Some features are straight lines at particular angles (e.g., E, M) and others are curves (e.g., O, C). A list of a relatively small number of distinctive features allows a complete specification of the printed alphabet (Gibson, 1969).

Feature Detectors. There is powerful evidence that the visual cortex of mammals is organized to detect the presence or absence of simple features. Hubel and Wiesel (1959, 1963) presented an edge, a slit of light, or a darkened bar at different orientations to the eyes of a cat or a monkey. At the same time, they recorded the neural activity in single nerve cells in the occipital lobe of the lightly anesthetized animal. Hubel and Wiesel discovered that the cells were tuned to respond maximally to bars of a particular orientation. For instance, some cells fired rapidly to a vertical bar, whereas others preferred a horizontal bar.

In human vision, evidence for feature detection can be seen in visual search tasks. Neisser (1963) asked for the participant to search for a particular letter among a long list of lines of printed letters. In one condition, the letter shared many features with the distractors such as searching for Z among T, L, K, M, V, and other letters with straight lines. In another condition, the target letter, say Z, stood out clearly from the distracters such as O, Q, P, B, D, and other rounded letters. The more rapid search times obtained by Neisser in the second condition, in which the target stood out, suggests that the human visual cortex analyzes stimuli in terms of simple component features. Note that if people compared each letter to a unique template in memory, then their search time ought to be the same for the straight and rounded distracters. This is one of several experimental results at odds with template theory (Hummel & Biederman, 1992).

> Distinctive features differentiate objects during pattern recognition. Neural cells in the occipital cortex are tuned to fire when stimulated by simple lines presented at a particular orientation.

Structural Descriptions. Other researchers have explored an additional problem with the feature detection theory of pattern recognition. Specifically, they have shown that the relations among features are as important to recognition as the features themselves. A letter Z is not simply three independent lines at certain angles. The lines must be structured in accordance with the rules for constructing the letter Z. A face, for instance, is not simply a collection of features positioned haphazardly—an eye here, a nose there, a mouth over there. The relations among features must conform to the rules that define the structure of the face. In other words, the whole object is not simply a list of independent features. The relations among features are equally important. One also needs a grammar or set of rules for how to put the features together properly (Reed, 1973; Sutherland, 1968). Several other studies have shown that people process the relations among features in perception (Hummel & Biederman, 1992; Reed, 1974; Reed & Johnson, 1975).

> Structural descriptions consider not just features, but also the relations among features, to facilitate pattern recognition.

Biederman (1987) proposed a set of 26 basic geometric features (geons) that, when put into proper structural relationships, constitute all visual objects. A sample of these is presented in Figure 2.8. A simple object, such as a cup, comprises the geons numbered 3 and 5. The telephone involves these geons and more that are related very differently compared with the cup.

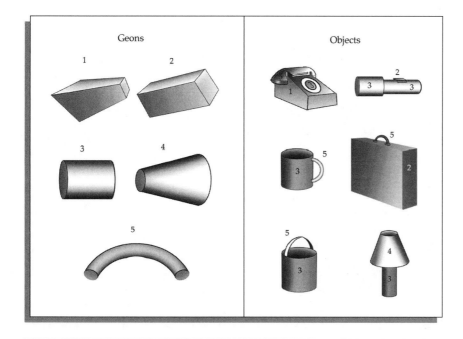

Figure 2.8   Examples of geons or basic sub-objects involved in scene perception.

SOURCE: From Biederman, I., Human image understanding: Recent research and a theory. *Computer Vision, Graphics, and Image Processing, 32*, 29-73. Copyright © 1985. Reprinted with permission.

An interesting prediction of Biederman's theory is that not only is relational information needed, but it may be more critical to perception than the features themselves. Biederman (1985) deleted 65% of the contours (features) from drawings of common objects, as illustrated in Figure 2.9. For example, the

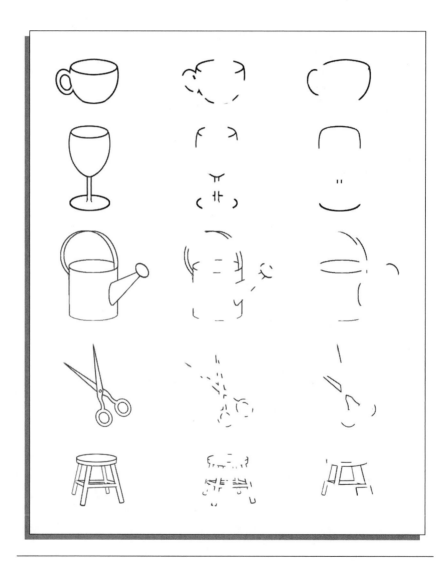

Figure 2.9   Perception of the object depends on the availability of structural relations at the vertices.

SOURCE: From Biederman, I., Human image understanding: Recent research and a theory. *Computer Vision, Graphics, and Image Processing, 32*, 29-73. Copyright © 1985. Reprinted with permission.

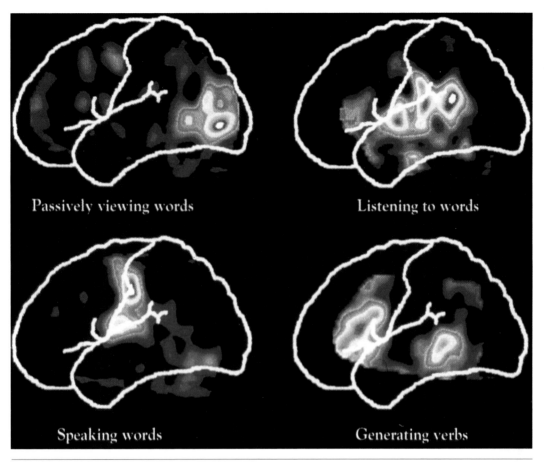

Color Plate 1   Different language tasks activate different brain regions, as isolated by using the method of subtraction in positron emission tomography (PET) neuroimaging; for example, the processes involved in actively generating and speaking verbs aloud are isolated, compared with the processes of simply speaking words the speaker has heard. Neural activation is inferred from blood flow detected by PET and is coded from high to low as white (high), red, orange, green, blue, and purple (low).

SOURCE: From Petersen, S. E., Fox, P. T., Posner, M. I., Mintun, M., & Raichle, M. E., Positron emission tomographic studies of the cortical anatomy of single-word processing, in *Nature, 333,* pp. 585–589, copyright © 1988. Reprinted with permission from the Nature Publishing Group.

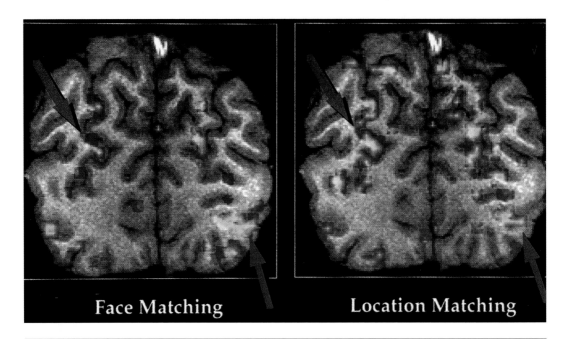

Face Matching　　　Location Matching

Color Plate 2 Attending to the identity of a face in a face matching task versus the location of a face in a location matching task, as revealed by functional magnetic resonance imaging (fMRI). These are coronal sections taken through the occipital cortex, showing how the brain looks when examined from the rear. Ventral lateral occipital areas are most activated by face matching (red arrow), whereas the dorsal occipital areas are most activated by location matching (green arrow).

SOURCE: From Haxby, J. V., Clark, V. P., & Courtney, S. M., Distributed hierarchical neural systems for visual memory in the human cortex. In B. Hyman, C. Duyckaerts, & Y. Christen (Eds.), *Connections, cognition, and Alzheimer's disease,* copyright © 1997. Reprinted with permission of Springer-Verlag.

Black	**Green**	**Yellow**	**Red**	**Blue**
Red	**Black**	**Blue**	**Green**	**Yellow**
Green	**Yellow**	**Red**	**Blue**	**Black**

Color Plate 3 Stimuli for the Stroop task. As rapidly as possible, name the color of the ink in which the words are *printed*.

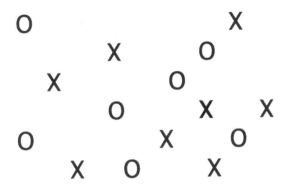

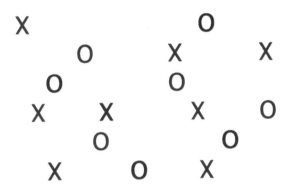

Color Plate 4   Stimuli used in the pop-out (a) and conjunctive (b) search tasks. Try to find a red X in each panel.

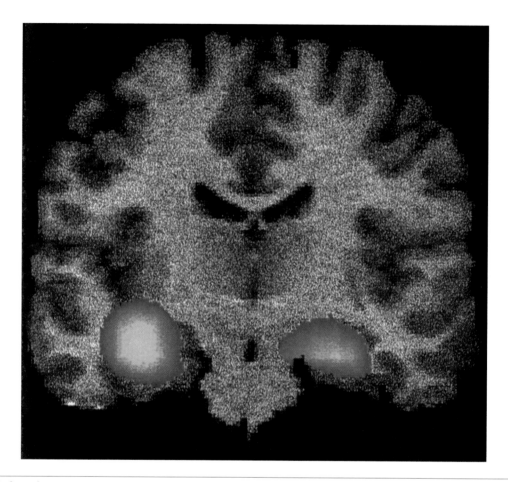

Color Plate 5　The temporal medial lobe, including the hippocampus, is activated by encoding pictures into memory. Shown here is bilateral activation of the hippocampus, using functional magnetic resonance imaging (fMRI).

SOURCE: From Martin, A., Wiggs, C. L., & Weisberg, J. A. (1997). Modulation of human temporal lobe activity by form, meaning, and experience. *Hippocampus, 7,* 587-593. Reprinted with permission of John Wiley & Sons, Inc.

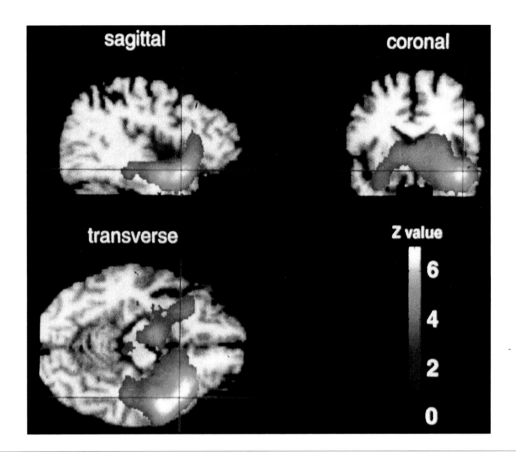

Color Plate 6 Retrieving an emotionally laden event from episodic memory activates regions in the right frontal and temporal lobes. Shown here are positron emission tomography (PET) results when an individual recollected a highly emotional episode that had occurred more than a year before.

SOURCE: From Fink, G. R., Markowitsch, H. J., Reinkemeier, M., Bruckbauer, J., Kessler, J., & Heiss, W. D. (1996). Cerebral representation of one's own past: Neural networks involved in autobiographical memory. *Journal of Neuroscience, 16,* 4275-4282. Reprinted with permission from the Society for Neuroscience.

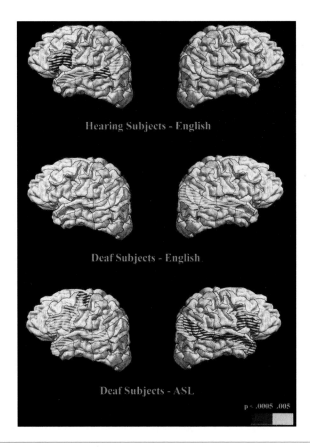

Color Plate 7   Left hemisphere activation is revealed by functional magnetic resonance imaging (fMRI) both in hearing participants reading English and in congenitally deaf participants viewing signs in their native American Sign Language (ASL). When congenitally deaf native signers read English (their second language), activation is seen primarily in the right rather than in the left hemisphere.

SOURCE: From Gazzaniga, M., *The New Cognitive Neurosciences, 2nd Edition,* copyright © The MIT Press. Reprinted with permission.

Example of the Four Types of Visual Stimuli

False fonts	Letter strings	Pseudowords	Words
ꓥꓮƎ	VSFFHT	GEEL	ANT
ꓘꟼꓘꓥ	TBBL	IOB	RAZOR
ꓤꓦꟼꓥ	TSTFS	RELD	DUST
Ⱶꓥ�	JBTT	BLERCE	FURNACE
ꓭꓥꓯꓴꓭ	STB	CHELDINABE	MOTHER
ꓘꓥꓷꓭ	FFPW	ALDOBER	FARM

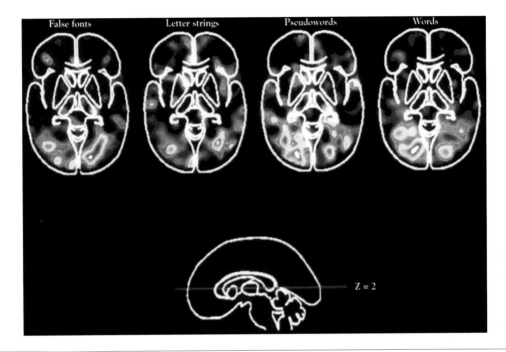

Color Plate 8 All four kinds of stimuli shown in the accompanying table activate regions in the visual cortex. Words and pseudowords that follow the orthographic rules of English activate additional language regions in the posterior left hemisphere.

SOURCE: From Petersen, S. E., Fox, P. T., Snyder, A. Z., & Raichle, M. E., Activation of extrastriate and frontal cortical areas by visual words and word-like stimuli. *Science, 249,* 1041-1044, copyright © 1990. Reprinted with permission of the AAAS.

cup on the left retains the vertices so that an observer can pick up the relations among the remaining contours. The cup on the right destroys this relational information by removing contours from the vertices. Biederman found that observers, after a brief 100-millisecond exposure, could accurately identify the left-hand cup 70% of the time as compared with only 50% for the right-hand cup. The color, texture, and other details that add such richness to our perceptual experience are less relevant to recognition than are the vertices. In support of this, Biederman and Ju (1988) found that schematic line drawings are indeed recognized as quickly as color photographs of objects.

MODULARITY

Thus far, it is clear that explaining how one is able to see and recognize a familiar object is a nontrivial problem. The visual system constructs a mental representation that allows the object in the environment to be both seen and understood as meaningful. The final two sections of this chapter show that particular kinds of pattern recognition invoke specialized processes. The evidence to date suggests that the perception of faces and speech each draws on processes that have evolved to cope with the particular demands of the task. A module refers to a set of processes that are automatic, fast, encapsulated apart from other cognitive systems, and instantiated in a localized area of the brain (Fodor, 1983). There may be several modules, each dedicated to the perception of an important class of stimuli such as faces or speech.

Social interactions are crucial to our survival and reproduction, and these depend on the ability to recognize faces and speech. So, perhaps it is not surprising that the cognitive system includes specialized modules for processing these categories of stimuli. Obviously, speech is central to communication between two or more humans. Less obviously, facial expressions provide a key means for communicating emotional states. Through body language and particularly facial expressions, humans communicate whether they feel happiness, sadness, or anger, for example. The role of **holistic processing** and modularity in face processing is presented next, and then the chapter concludes with a consideration of speech perception.

Holistic Versus Analytic Processing

Although the theorist can identify the features or parts that make up a whole object, an observer may perceive only the meaningful object. Several factors control the extent to which perception is dominated by the whole versus the parts, including the type of stimuli presented to the observer and the task required of the observer (Treisman, 1987). Holistic processing refers to perceiving the whole object; **analytic processing** refers to perceiving the features that compose the whole. Holistic processing, then, involves the spatial-relational aspects of the features of the whole face. Analytic processing targets the nose, the eyes, the lips, and other specific features instead of their relations. Faces, perhaps more than any other object, are perceived holistically rather than analytically. An intriguing demonstration of this fact comes from an illusion that occurs when the normal orientation of facial features is inverted (Thompson, 1980).

First, study the pair of faces in Figure 2.10 in the normal orientation. In the face on the left, the eyes and mouth have been turned upside down. As you can see, the face takes on a grotesque appearance as a consequence. Now, turn the book upside down and study the two faces again. Notice that when viewing the faces in an unusual orientation, the grotesqueness disappears. Both faces take on a normal appearance. This demonstrates that in the normal orientation, holistic processing heavily influences face perception. The individual features are encoded, but so, too, are their spatial relations that together compose the whole face. When the normal relations among the

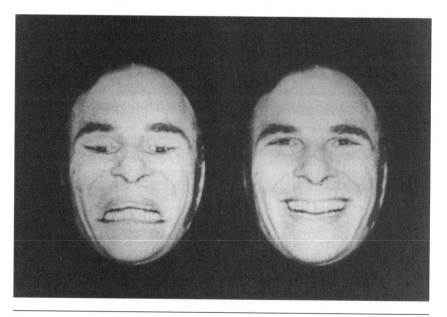

Figure 2.10   A demonstration of holistic processing of faces.

SOURCE: From Bartlett, J. C., & Searcy, J., Inversion and configuration of faces. *Cognitive Psychology, 25,* 281-316. Copyright © 1993. Reprinted with permission.

eyes, nose, mouth, and eyebrows are rearranged, the face looks grotesque. But the holistic processing of the face can be disrupted by inverting the face 180 degrees, a position that we rarely encounter in everyday perception. The face as a whole no longer dominates perception; the individual parts of the face are taken on their own terms and appear perfectly normal to the eye.

Several studies have shown that face perception is more vulnerable to inversion than is perception of other kinds of objects (Searcy & Bartlett, 1996; Valentine, 1988). Recently, Murray, Yong, and Rhodes (2000) found that as a face is rotated from 0 to 180 degrees, there is a discontinuity in its appearance. Up to rotations of 90 degrees, a normal face looks increasingly bizarre, whereas the distorted face looks less and less bizarre. Between 90 and 120 degrees of rotation, the distorted face begins to look fine and continues to do so on up to a complete, 180-degree inversion. This is not so with the normal face, which continues to look more bizarre as it is rotated up to 180 degrees. Try rotating the page of this book and notice what happens to the distorted face somewhere between 90 and 120 degrees. Inversion disrupts the holistic processing of spatial-relational information more than it disrupts the analytic processing of features.

> Perception of faces is unique in that it is more strongly influenced by holistic processing than by analytic processing.

Face Perception

Why is it that upright faces are perceived more holistically than analytically? Farah (1990, 1998) presented several lines of converging evidence pointing to the existence of a specialized module for face recognition. **Prosopagnosia** is a selective inability to recognize faces that does not involve other kinds of vision difficulties. A prosopagnosic patient cannot recognize the photographs of famous individuals, but when the patient is tested on other kinds of complex visual discrimination tasks, no deficit is found (MacNeil & Warrington, 1993). For example, a sheep farmer had no problem in distinguishing photographs of his own sheep from pictures of other sheep despite their close similarity in appearance. Yet his recognition of human faces was profoundly impaired.

Inverted faces are not, therefore, processed holistically the way normally oriented faces are. If the holistic processing of spatial relations in faces is driven by a specialized module, then what would happen if this module were damaged, as in prosopagnosia? Normal controls have more difficulty recognizing inverted faces as compared with upright faces because the module constructs an accurate representation of the test face. If damaged, the module would provide inaccurate information and disrupt performance.

Farah (1990) discovered that a prosopagnosic patient actually correctly identified more faces when they were inverted (72%) than when they were upright (58%). Normal controls showed the expected pattern of more correct identifications with upright faces (94%) than with inverted faces (82%). By inverting the face, the damaged module in the prosopagnosic was removed from play, thus improving performance.

Farah (1990) also discovered that damage to the occipital and temporal cortices, usually bilateral damage in both hemispheres, was correlated with prosopagnosia. A localized region of the temporal lobe seems to be crucial for face recognition. One way to demonstrate this localization is to examine other neurological disorders and compare their effects on different kinds of tests. Reading and face recognition tests both are complex visual tasks that reveal a double dissociation. There are a variety of kinds of lesions in the brain caused by head injuries or strokes that are collectively called *acquired dyslexia*. Relative to normal controls, dyslexic patients perform poorly on a reading test but show no impairment on a test of face recognition. By contrast, prosopagnosic patients show deficits on the face recognition test but not on the reading test, relative to normal controls. Because brain damage can be extensive, some of these patients had trouble recognizing objects of any kind. That is, they suffered agnosia in addition to prosopagnosia or dyslexia. However, patients rarely suffered from a combination of dyslexia and prosopagnosia. In short, prosopagnosia was uncorrelated with acquired dyslexia, suggesting that they are handled by different structures in the brain and can be selectively damaged.

Another source of evidence in favor of a face recognition module comes from normal college students in an object versus part recognition task. Participants learned the names of normal upright faces and objects during the first phase of the experiment. Next, they were asked to recognize the faces or objects in the whole condition. For example, they either were shown a face and asked "Is this Jim's face?" or were shown a house in the object condition and asked "Is this Jim's house?" In the part condition, they were tested on particular features of the studied faces or objects. For example, they might be shown a nose in isolation and asked "Is this Jim's nose?" or they might be shown a door and asked "Is this Jim's door?" Recognition was just as good for the parts of houses as for whole houses. However, recognition was substantially less accurate in the part condition than in the whole condition for faces. The participants had difficulty processing the faces in an analytic manner—zeroing in on, say, the nose by itself—during study or test. This outcome is understandable if faces are processed holistically by a specialized module.

> A specialized module is responsible for face perception. Other modules may exist for specific kinds of perception such as speech recognition.

The rapid speed of the face processing module enables one to extract enough information from even a very brief exposure to a face to form a first impression of the individual's personality. Willis and Todorov (2006) proposed that making inferences about personal traits—such as attractiveness, likeability, trustworthiness, and competence—are fast, automatic, intuitive processes. They found that with only 100 milliseconds' exposure to a face, participants' judgments about a face were highly correlated with the judgments made when participants were given an unlimited time to examine the face. Increasing the time up to 500 milliseconds did not change these correlations at all, although participants became more confident in their judgments, and their judgments of all the test faces became somewhat more negative with additional exposure time. Finally, doubling the exposure time from 500 milliseconds to a full second did little but increase confidence still further. This is not to say that slow, reflective, and conscious deliberation does not have a role in helping us to discriminate between individuals on the basis of, say, attractiveness versus competence. Also, conscious processes help build confidence, but the first impressions are mediated by unconscious processes.

The amygdala's role in the rapid, unconscious, and automatic sensing of fearful stimuli may be at work in the detection of threatening faces. Winston, Strange, O'Doherty, and Dolan (2002) discovered a higher degree of amygdala activation in viewers looking at faces rated as untrustworthy compared with the activation obtained for trustworthy faces. The mechanisms involved in face perception, then, play an important social function. Human beings rapidly and intuitively make judgments about whether an individual is friendly and approachable versus threatening.

Speech Perception

Another example in perceptual modularity may well be the most remarkable feat of pattern recognition performed by humans. Having recognized the face of a person standing before you, you then must decipher the sounds being emitted by the person's vocal tract. Spoken language and its comprehension is a vast subject that will be addressed in Chapter 8. The issue at hand here is how the complex, information-packed auditory signals of spoken language are perceptually recognized at an extraordinarily rapid rate, enabling you to hear the words spoken to you.

Consider that language uses basic speech sounds to distinguish words with different meanings. A speech sound or phonological segment that makes a difference in meaning is called a **phoneme.** Each phoneme is pronounced in a distinctly different manner from all others, and this difference in pronunciation signals a difference in the meaning. For example, pill and kill differ with respect to initial phoneme, and this signals a difference in the meaning of the two words. Now, consider that normal speech unfolds at a rate of about 12 phonological segments per second. The speech perception system handles this rate with ease and can, in fact, cope very well with speech artificially accelerated to 50 phonological segments per second (Foulke & Sticht, 1969). A listener can even understand a speaker who whispers a sentence, despite the fact that whispering alters not only the intensity of the acoustic signal but also its frequency. It has been estimated that the brain must process 40,000 bits of information per second to recognize the phonemes that are the building blocks of spoken language (Fodor, 1983). The fast automatic extraction of speech signals suggests that it is the work of a module dedicated to the task.

That everyday speech is riddled with noise and indeterminacy makes the task of speech perception all the more daunting (McClelland & Elman, 1986). Unless the speaker formulates complete sentences and articulates them clearly and slowly in a quiet setting, the speech signal is fragmentary. Yet, somehow listeners manage to understand speakers who rapidly utter incomplete sentences and even distorted words in noisy environments. A speaker might not articulate clearly, but the listener uses top-down recognition processes to fill in the gaps. For example, Warren (1970) presented listeners with tape-recordings of a sentence with a single phoneme deleted, for example, "The state governors met with respective legi*latures convening in the capital city." The asterisk marked the spot where the /s/ was removed and replaced with a cough lasting 0.12 seconds. Warren presented the recording to 20 listeners and asked them whether any sounds were missing. Only one individual heard a missing sound, and that person identified the wrong sound as missing. Clearly, the listeners had restored the missing phoneme. Even when the missing phoneme comes at the beginning of the word (e.g., *eel) and is disambiguated by a later word in the sentence (e.g., shoe), listeners rarely report any perception of a gap.

The module dedicated to speech perception is adapted to process a very complex series of acoustic signals arriving at the ears that do not correspond in a one-to-one fashion to the critical speech sounds. To see this, consider a **speech spectrogram**, which represents the physical acoustic energy of an utterance by plotting frequency in hertz or cycles per second on the y axis and time in milliseconds on the x axis. Examples are shown in Figure 2.11 for "bab," "dad," and "gag" spoken with a British accent (Ladefoged, 1975). The darker the band of energy at a particular frequency, the greater its amplitude. Notice that the energy clusters at low-, medium-, and high-level frequencies. These bands are called **formants.** The first formant is the lowest frequency band, the second formant is at the next higher frequency band, and so on. One might expect that the spectrum for, say, "gag" could be neatly divided into three time segments, with the early segment providing an invariant feature for the phoneme /g/ followed by one for /a/ and then returning to the one for /g/. It turns out that the three time segments of the speech spectrogram do not match up with the three phonemes /g/, /a/, and /g/.

Instead, each segment of the acoustic signal provides clues about the identity of more than one phoneme (Liberman, Cooper, Shankweiler, & Studdert-Kennedy, 1967). This is called **coarticulation.** As shown in Figure 2.12, each of the three phonemes of "beg" are being transmitted simultaneously. They are not separated in time, with /b/ followed by /ae/ and then /g/. Instead, the acoustic energy corresponding to the phonetic segment of /b/ overlaps that of the other phonemes.

Phrased differently, before you have articulated /b/, the vocal track already takes shape to articulate /ae/. Notice, too, from Figure 2.12 that you begin to articulate /g/ even before finishing the articulation of /b/. The key point about coarticulation is that multiple phonetic segments are being articulated in parallel at each point in time.

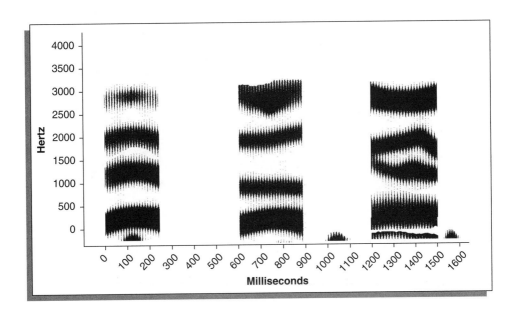

Figure 2.11   Speech spectrograms for (left to right) "bab," "dad," and "gag" spoken with a British accent.

SOURCE: From *Course in Phonetics, 2nd Edition,* by Ladefoged, P., 1982. Reprinted with permission of Heinle, a division of Thomson Learning: www.thomsonrights.com, fax 800-730-2215.

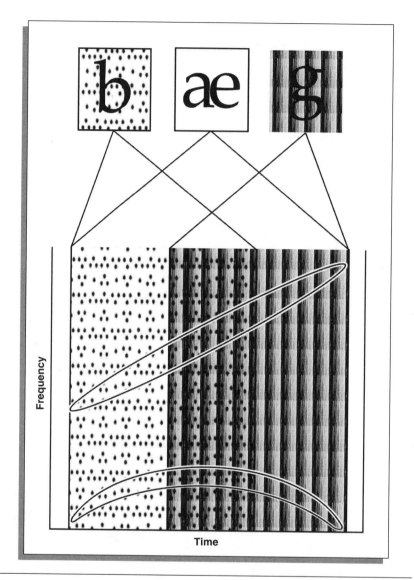

Figure 2.12 Coarticulation as parallel transmission of phonemes.

SOURCE: From Liberman, A. M., Cooper, F., Shankweiler, D., & Studdert-Kennedy, M. (1967). Perception of the speech code. *Psychological Review, 74,* 431-459. Reprinted with permission.

Moreover, the acoustic spectrum fails to reveal a distinctive invariant feature for a particular phoneme that stays the same in all contexts (Liberman et al., 1967). Phonemes lack invariant distinctive features. As illustrated in Figure 2.13, the spectrogram for /di/ versus /du/ reveals different formants for

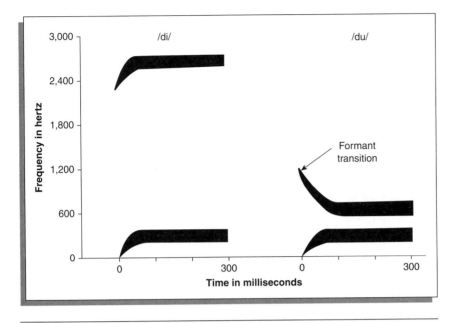

Figure 2.13   Spectrograms for /di/ and /du/.

SOURCE: From Liberman, A. M., Cooper, F., Shankweiler, D., & Studdert-Kennedy, M. (1967). Perception of the speech code. *Psychological Review, 74,* 431-459. Reprinted with permission.

the phoneme /d/ depending on whether it is followed by the phoneme /i/ versus /u/. The first formant is the same in each case. But look at the second formant containing the higher frequencies. As the speaker enunciates the /d/ phoneme, a remarkable change occurs at about 200 milliseconds; the formant turns to higher frequencies when followed by /i/ and to lower frequencies when followed by /u/. Consequently, a listener could not zero in on the acoustic spectrum and identify the phonetic segment of /d/ by matching it with a distinctive feature that remains the same in all contexts.

Both coarticulation and the lack of invariance imply that listeners must process the context in which a given acoustic signal occurs. The relations among features are just as critical as the features themselves. Recall that the same is true in understanding the recognition of visual objects; only a structural theory that specifies both features and their relations is adequate. In speech recognition, a remarkably large number of features and relations must be processed in a fraction of a second simply to identify a single phoneme. Furthermore, unlike the recognition of static visual objects, speech must be recognized over time. Both the sounds that precede a given phonetic segment and those that follow it influence perception (Salasoo & Pisoni, 1985). The contextual nature of the acoustic speech signal enormously complicates the job of the listener. To illustrate, a speaker can produce the phonemes /b/ and /p/ by changing only one feature during articulation. For the /p/ phoneme, the vocal cords do not vibrate, whereas for the /b/ phoneme, they do. The listener must detect this difference in discriminating words such as "pad" versus "bad." To do so, the listener must process 16 acoustic features that bear on the correct identification of /p/ versus /b/ (Lisker, 1986).

> Phonemes are coarticulated, meaning that each segment of the acoustic signal provides clues about the identity of more than one phoneme. As a consequence, the signal lacks an invariant feature for a particular phoneme that stays the same in all contexts.

Third, the acoustic signals composing the speech stream are virtually continuous throughout a sentence (Foss & Hakes, 1978). Few pauses occur, and astonishingly, the pauses that do occur generally fall in the middle of words, not between words. Pauses mark boundaries between words less than 40% of the time (Cole & Jakimik, 1980). This phenomenon is illustrated with a portion of the speech spectrogram for the sentence "John said that the dog snapped at him" shown in Figure 2.14.

Notice the pauses in acoustic energy between the /s/ and the /n/ and between the /p/ and the /t/. The listener hears pauses between the words and phrases of the sentence, but the acoustic energy fails to provide them. Instead, they are inserted by the speech recognition processes that categorize the acoustic input; they divide the sounds into the words, phrases, clauses, and sentences through top-down or conceptually driven recognition processes. Conversely, the pauses in acoustic energy that do not signal an important linguistic unit, such as those in the word "snapped," are not perceived by the listener.

It is easier to appreciate the role of conceptually driven processes in speech perception when listening to a foreign language. The continuous nature of the acoustic speech stream is perceived as it really is. The pauses that occur in the middle of a word are heard correctly. One word streams into another. The coarticulation effect discussed earlier applies across word boundaries as well as within word boundaries. Thus, the speaker is sending acoustic clues at any given moment about the identity of phonemes that belong to adjacent words. The true complexity of the stream, if analyzed solely from bottom-up or data-driven processes, can be readily heard when listening to a native speaker of a language that is foreign to us. But when listening to our own first language, we hear the speech stream as a sequence of neat and tidy packages of sound that specify meaning.

A critical function of the speech processing module is the categorization of speech input at the phonemic level, a phenomenon called **categorical perception.** Subtle variations in the acoustic signal are ignored unless they mark a boundary between one phoneme and another. For example, /b/ and /p/

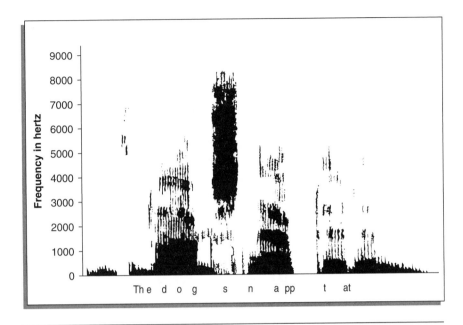

Figure 2.14   Portion of the speech spectrogram for "John said that the dog snapped at him."

SOURCE: From Foss, D. J. & Hakes, D. T., *Psycholinguistics: An Introduction to the Psychology of Language, 1st edition,* copyright © 1978. Reprinted with permission of Pearson Education, Inc., Upper Saddle River, NJ.

differ in terms of the amount of time that elapses between the release of the lips and the onset of voicing. The voice onset time for /b/ is immediate (0 seconds). For /p/, the voice onset time is 0.06 seconds. Within this narrow window of time lies the boundary between hearing one phoneme versus another.

Lisker and Abramson (1970) demonstrated the phenomenon of categorical perception by continuously varying voice onset time from −0.15 to +0.15 using computer-synthesized speech. For the 31 stimuli, the acoustic signal differed by 0.01 seconds in voice onset time, yet only two phonemes were heard. Listeners identified all sounds as /b/ over a large range of variation in the acoustic signal, from −0.15 seconds up to just over 0 seconds. As soon as the voice onset time slightly exceeded 0 seconds, the listeners began to hear /p/ instead of /b/ and continued to do so for all remaining stimuli. What matters, then, is not the degree of change in voice onset time; all variations of 0.15 seconds are heard as the same phoneme. Instead, what matters is whether the change in acoustic signal crosses a sharply defined boundary. There is, therefore, a sharp decision boundary that distinguishes the perception of one phoneme from the perception of another related one.

Although speech phonemes exhibit well-defined categorical boundaries, it is mistaken to conclude that the auditory system cannot sense the gradual transitions in voice onset time. Data-driven sensory processes plainly pick up these differences (Massaro, 1994). The sensory system detects continuous changes in the speech signal, but a decision process assigns the signal to one phonemic category or another. Repp and Liberman (1987) found that the boundary between two phonetic categories is flexible, to a degree. Precisely where a given listener locates the boundary depends on the context provided by other stimuli.

> Speech signals are assigned to phonemes on the basis of well-defined categorical boundaries. The continuous speech stream is heard as separate words and phrases as a result of conceptually driven recognition processes.

Despite the complexity involved in extracting phonetic segments from the speech stream, infants between the ages of one and four months can detect the acoustic features that distinguish one phoneme from another. Indeed, it appears that at this age, infants are prepared to identify not only the phonemes of their native language but virtually all possible phonetic segments used in human languages (Eimas, Miller, & Jusczyk, 1987). Such evidence is consistent with the idea that speech is perceived by a special processing module (Eimas & Miller, 1992).

Infants cannot, of course, report what they hear. Yet by ingeniously monitoring the rate infants suck on a pacifier, developmental psychologists can infer changes in attention to a stimulus. The sucking schema is well-established in a one-month-old infant. In fact, sucking is one of a small number of reflexes present at birth. This basic sensorimotor schema develops with experience in nursing and displaces the reflex. It turns out that infants suck faster when attending to a novel stimulus. With repeated presentations of the stimulus, the sucking rate slows down as the infant habituates to the stimulus. If the stimulus is abruptly changed in a way that is noticed by the infant, then dishabituation occurs (i.e., the sucking rate suddenly increases). The difference between preshift stimuli and postshift stimuli can be measured by the difference in rates of sucking.

Using this method, Eimas (1974) found categorical perception of speech by infants. The infants dishabituated when a change in the acoustic signal crossed a phonetic boundary. Subsequent research has shown that infants can, in fact, discriminate among the stimuli that fall within a phonemic boundary (Miller & Eimas, 1983). Like adults, however, infants appear tuned to pick up the critical differences that separate one phoneme from another and to process the context in which the acoustic signals occur.

Furthermore, infants are not born with full capabilities in categorizing speech. Newborns can detect differences among syllables that contain different phonemes, but their representations at this early stage of development might not be full-fledged phonetic segments (cf. Eimas & Miller, 1992). Instead, over the first one or two months of life, the infant may progress from a global representation of the syllable to the specific phonemic level representations (Bertoncini, Bijeljac-Babic, Jusczyk, Kennedy, & Mehler, 1988).

SUMMARY

1. Perception begins with the transduction of the physical energy of a stimulus into an initial neural representation of the stimulus. As a result, the objects and events that are present in the environment are perceived, in the sense of being detected. With still more processing, the objects and events are recognized, in the sense of being categorized as meaningful. Visual consciousness depends on representations being processed in the visual cortex. Patients with blindsight lack any visual awareness but are able to guess accurately about the actual locations of objects in space.

2. The ability to perceive depends on pattern recognition, that is, categorizing objects and events detected in the environment by matching their preliminary representations with patterns stored in long-term memory. A stimulus can be perceived and understood in terms of its properties but not recognized as a meaningful object—a neuropsychological condition called agnosia. Patients suffering from lesions in certain regions of the brain can see objects but not recognize them at all. Apperceptive agnosia refers to a failure of pattern recognition caused by an inability to categorize objects at a perceptual level of analysis. Associative agnosia, by contrast, is caused by an inability to categorize objects at a functional semantic level of analysis.

3. Schemas generate expectations about the objects and events that will be encountered. These expectations direct exploration of the environment in the form of eye movements and other bodily movements that pick up the information available. The sampled information either confirms or modifies the original expectations, which in turn leads to renewed exploration. Top-down or conceptually driven pattern recognition refers to the use of expectations to ease the process of finding a match between incoming stimuli and schemas that store our knowledge about the world in long-term memory. Bottom-up or data-driven pattern recognition refers to the use of the features picked up from the environment. Both the data and the expectations play a critical role in rapid, accurate, and adaptive perception.

4. The representation of objects in long-term memory has been viewed theoretically as feature lists and as structural descriptions. An object can be represented in terms of a list of distinctive features that discriminate it from other objects. The problem with this view is that two objects might include

the same features but differ in terms of their relationships. A structural description takes into account both the distinctive features and their relations.

5. Holistic processing refers to perceiving the whole object; analytic processing refers to perceiving the features that compose the whole. Perception of faces is unique in that it is more strongly influenced by holistic processing than by analytic processing. A specialized module is responsible for face perception. Face perception is automatic, fast, encapsulated from other cognitive systems, and instantiated in a localized area of the brain. Prosopagnosic patients suffering from damage to the module are unable to recognize faces despite intact object recognition in general.

6. Speech perception is challenging because the acoustic signal for the basic sounds of speech that communicate meaning—phonemes—is highly complex. Phonemes are coarticulated, meaning that each segment of the acoustic signal provides clues about the identity of more than one phoneme. As a consequence, the signal lacks an invariant feature for a particular phoneme that stays the same in all contexts. Speech signals are assigned to phonemes on the basis of well-defined categorical boundaries. Gradual variations in the acoustic signal are perceived categorically. Finally, the acoustic energy in speech is often continuous across word boundaries. The continuous speech stream is heard as separate words and phrases as a result of conceptually driven recognition processes.

KEY TERMS

blindsight	distinctive features
pattern recognition	holistic processing
apperceptive agnosia	analytic processing
associative agnosia	prosopagnosia
schema	phoneme
conceptually driven processes	speech spectrogram
data-driven processes	formants
word superiority effect	coarticulation
change blindness	categorical perception

CHAPTER 3

ATTENTION

Our sensory systems are continually bombarded by sights, sounds, smells, and other signals from the external environment. At the same time, we experience mental representations of events that just occurred seconds ago, events from the distant past, and events only imagined in the present or future. From moment to moment, one possible train of thought is taken to the exclusion of many others. Some internal or external events dominate consciousness, and others are barely noticed or not noticed at all. *Attention* refers to selecting certain stimuli from among many and focusing cognitive resources on those selected. William James (1890) described attention as "the taking possession by the mind, in clear and vivid form, of one out of what seem several simultaneously possible trains of thought. . . . Focalization [and] concentration of consciousness are of its essence" (pp. 403–404). Attention allows us to focus on what is important at the moment and to ignore the rest. Without attention, we would be overwhelmed by sensory information from the external world and our internal world would overwhelm us with memories or fantasies. When attention fails, we are left scatterbrained and unable to function.

Consider some everyday situations in which attention is important. When you carry on a conversation with someone, there are numerous irrelevant background stimuli. The sights and sounds of a nearby television, the distant roar of a commercial jet overhead, the songs of birds outside the window, the pressure of clothing on the skin, and the pain of a recently jammed finger all compete for your attention. The irrelevant thoughts must be ignored so that the demanding task of speech recognition takes precedence. In conversations, it is further necessary to divide attention or shift attention from listening, on the one hand, to speaking, on the other.

Now, consider carrying on your conversation on a cell phone while driving a car. Once again, it is necessary to ignore some distractions, such as the car radio and the sounds of traffic, in order to focus on speech production and comprehension. Yet at the same time, the task of driving also demands attention. Perceiving the road, other cars, and pedestrians is just part of what the task demands. Steering and braking can also demand attention, particularly when traffic is heavy. Thus, to drive a car and carry on a telephone conversation at the same time requires that attention be divided among multiple tasks, each of which can be highly demanding at a given moment in time. Not surprisingly, inattention is a leading cause of traffic accidents (Evans, 1991). If one gives too much attention to listening and speaking on a cell phone, then there is a risk of inattention to driving, even when both hands are on the wheel and one's eyes are on the road. In other words, the use of a hands-free cell phone does not eliminate the driving risk because cognitive limitations of attention underlie the problem, not just motor limitations. Cell phone-induced failures of visual attention have been documented in driving simulators (Drews, Johnston, & Strayer, 2003). Cognitive research on cell phones as a distraction should inform our public policy debates about whether they should be prohibited while driving in much the same way that alcohol use is prohibited. In fact, some research indicates that hands-free cell phone use impairs peripheral vision in a manner comparable to alcohol use (Holzner, Kopp, Langer, & Magnet, 2005).

When attention malfunctions, its importance to normal cognition and behavior is apparent. Attention deficit/hyperactivity disorder (ADHD) is a commonly diagnosed psychiatric disorder that occurs most often in children younger than seven. Children with ADHD are easily distracted and excessively restless and impulsive. This malfunction of attention disrupts children's ability to fit into social and academic environments and, later in life, into occupational settings. Behavioral symptoms of the disorder include making excessive careless mistakes; not following instructions or failing to finish tasks; avoiding tasks that require sustained effort; and showing signs of hyperactive fidgeting, talking, and impulsive behavior. ADHD is diagnosed when inattention, hyperactivity, and impulsivity are frequent and severe, beyond the range of normal behavior in young children (Shaywitz, Fletcher, & Shaywitz, 1995).

Theoretical accounts of attention are presented at the outset of this chapter. These theories are divided into two major camps. The first assumes that attention operates as a filter that blocks the processing of some stimuli and allows the processing of others. This camp addresses at what point selection takes place in the processing of information. The second assumes that the person actively chooses stimuli for further processing by allocating a portion of one or more limited pools of attentional capacity. This camp addresses how cognitive processes concentrate on particular stimuli. Filter theories and capacity theories have spawned impressive research on the nature of attention, and each class is considered in turn. Next, the distinction between automatic processes, which proceed without attention, and controlled processes, which require attention, is illuminated. The chapter then concludes with a discussion of visual attention in selection, effort, and perception.

FILTER THEORIES

Selective attention refers to the ability to perceive a particular stimulus of interest while ignoring numerous other stimuli. It is contrasted with **divided attention,** in which two or more stimuli share cognitive resources. For example, at a noisy party, you can carry on a conversation with one person while other people are carrying on conversations all around you. With selective attention, you focus on your conversation with the person in front of you and ignore the rest. With divided attention, you attempt to listen to an adjacent conversation while maintaining limited involvement in responding to the person before you.

An extraordinary example of selective attention can be found in the use of hypnosis to control pain. If one selectively attends to other stimuli and ignores pain signals, it is possible to experience analgesia, that is, relief from the pain. This phenomenon has long been investigated with highly hypnotizable individuals who experience a form of dissociated consciousness (Hilgard, 1986). Some individuals are able to carry out suggestions to feel no pain in a portion of the body so that normally painful procedures can be performed in dentistry and medicine without the administration of anesthetics. They selectively attend to pleasant thoughts and filter out the pain signals. Hilgard (1986) used the cold pressor method to induce pain by asking a person to leave his or her arm in a bucket of ice water for as long as the person could tolerate. After the arm is in the ice water for 20 to 30 seconds, the pain is immense. But under deep hypnosis, the same individuals can tolerate the pain without difficulty.

Filter theories were designed to explain how selective attention operates. The classic laboratory task for studying selective attention, called dichotic listening, simulated the party situation just described. In dichotic listening, both ears receive stimuli in synchrony and participants are asked to attend to only one ear or channel. This is enforced by using **shadowing,** in which the participant repeats aloud the stimuli presented to the attended channel and ignores the stimuli presented in the unattended channel. This is illustrated in Figure 3.1.

In a pioneering study with shadowing, Cherry (1953) found that people noticed and remembered little about the second unattended series. Specifically, they seemed oblivious to the meanings of unattended words, failing even to notice that on occasion the material shifted from English to German. However, while they missed the meaningful or semantic features, they did notice changes in physical or sensory features, such as when a low-pitched male voice changed to a higher pitched female voice. Thus, the first key finding to explain was that selective attention resulted in little, if any, processing of the semantic features of the unattended channel but did permit the processing of sensory features.

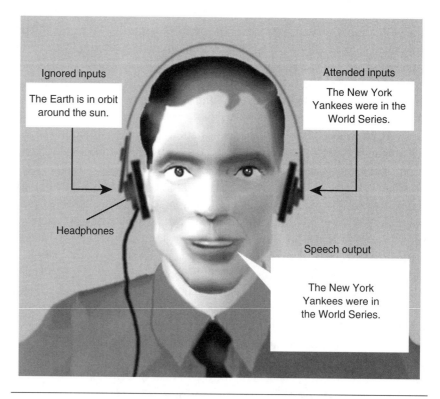

Figure 3.1   The shadowing task used to study selective attention.

Early Selection

Broadbent (1958) proposed a model to account for the findings with the shadowing task (see Figure 3.2). It postulated two stages of information processing to explain the phenomenon of selective attention. In the first stage, all information from the senses is processed, but only partially. Today, this stage is referred to as sensory memory. A selective filter then winnows the information to only the stimuli of interest, and these few items are fully processed in the limited capacity channel. **Early selection** refers to an attentional filter that operates after sensory processing but prior to meaningful semantic processing. The model also included a store of conditional probabilities about past events, what today is called long-term memory. Furthermore, a system for controlling behavioral output was described by Broadbent.

Broadbent (1957) examined how well a series of digits could be recalled under dichotic listening conditions. For example, suppose that the series 7-3-5 arrived at the left ear perfectly synchronized with the series 1-6-2 at the right ear, as shown in Panel (a) of Figure 3.3. Each pair was separated by only 500 milliseconds. When allowed to recall the digits in any order, the participants successfully recalled nearly two thirds of the digits. Interestingly, their successes came when they first reported from one ear and then the other (e.g.,7-3-5-1-6-2). However, when instructed to recall the digits in the order of their arrival (e.g., 7-1-3-6-5-2), they correctly reported less than one-fifth of the digits, on average.

Broadbent (1957) proposed a mechanical analogy to explain how an early selective filter might work to produce these findings, as shown in Panel (b) of Figure 3.3. The digits were briefly held in a sensory memory store

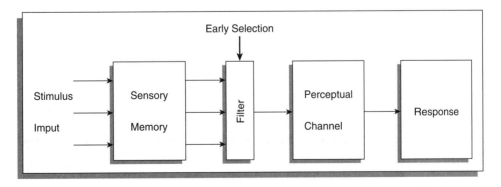

Figure 3.2   The early selection model of attention.

SOURCE: Adapted from Broadbent (1958).

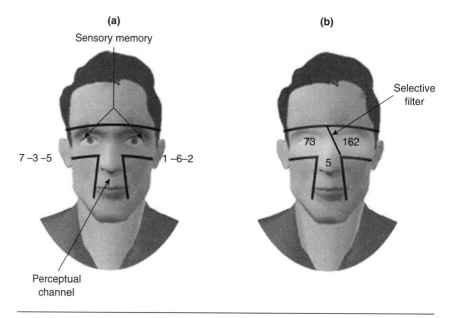

Figure 3.3   An early selection explanation of recall of dichotic input.

SOURCE: Adapted from Broadbent (1957).

specific to each ear. The perceptual analysis channel was limited in capacity relative to the sensory memory; thus, multiple stimuli had to be selectively filtered prior to perception. It was assumed that the limited-capacity perceptual channel could process only a single stimulus at a time. The selective filter precluded the passage of a stimulus from sensory memory into the perceptual channel. The filter could be switched so that it allowed passage from the left ear and then the right ear, or it could be held in place so that all digits were perceived first from, say, the left ear. Switching the position of the filter back and forth between ears was more difficult, and fewer digits were successfully remembered. Because the digits could be retained briefly in sensory memory, filtering first all digits from the right ear while the left ear digits were perceived and then allowing the right ear digits to pass led to the best recall.

Broadbent's (1957) model captured Cherry's (1953) findings in that only the shadowed channel benefited from full perceptual analysis at the deep level of semantic features. Shifts in languages should have gone unnoticed despite the fact that German was unintelligible to the English-speaking participants in the experiments. However, a sensory feature such as pitch should be identifiable at a very early stage of processing, the echoic store, even on the unattended channel. Identifying the pitch and storing it in echoic memory should occur simultaneously in both channels before the selective filter operates. Similarly, the model explained Broadbent's findings by assuming that with only 500 milliseconds between each dichotic pair of digits, the gate cannot be swung back and forth quickly enough to allow a correct report of digits in their order of arrival.

> Shadowing or repeating a message heard in an attended ear or channel results in selective attention; the meaning of a message heard at the same time in the other ear is ignored.

Successful recall should occur only by leaving the gate in one position until all three digits from one ear move through the perceptual channel, followed by those from the other ear.

Attenuation

Other studies showed that the early selection model oversimplified human attention. It turned out that if the participant's name occurred on the unattended channel, it sometimes received semantic processing and was reported (Moray, 1959). The participant did not divide attention between the two channels because the shadowing task is too demanding to allow a division. Nonetheless, even without attempting to divide attention between the two conversations, highly pertinent words such as one's name can still slip through the processes of selective attention. Moray's finding can readily be observed in any crowded, conversation-filled room. When you are engaged fully in one conversation, the words of an adjacent conversation are ignored—unless your name gets mentioned, and then attention shifts to the previously ignored conversation.

This phenomenon suggests that the semantic content of items in the ignored channel must be processed to at least some degree. Otherwise, how would one recognize a name in an ignored conversation? Other experiments explored the idea of unattended semantic analysis further in the following task. Treisman (1960) presented a sentence to the left ear to be shadowed and a different sentence to the right ear to be ignored. However, one word in the right ear sentence fit the context of the shadowed sentence. To illustrate, in the sentences below, the italicized words were those actually reported by the individual. Notice that the semantically appropriate "table" was perceived instead of the correct response of "three." The word from the unattended right channel, which fit nicely the meaning of the sentence being shadowed in the left channel, was perceived and repeated by mistake. An error in shadowing occurred because of a failure in selective attention.

Left: . . . *sitting at the mahogany* three *possibilities.* . . .

Right: . . . let us look at these *table* with her head. . . .

Such findings violated the assumptions of the early selection model. Processing the meaning of any item in the nonshadowed material should not occur if the filter selects only the shadowed items for complete pattern recognition. Perceiving "table" in Treisman's (1960) experiment or one's name in Moray's (1959) experiment refutes this claim. Clearly, an alternative theory is needed to explain such results.

One alternative to Broadbent's (1958) model again placed a filter early in the sequence of information processing, before pattern recognition. Instead of an all-or-none filter that allows only a single channel to undergo pattern recognition at a time, Treisman (1970) suggested a filter that attenuates the unattended channel, making its inputs less likely to be heard. **Attenuation** refers to an attentional filter that lowers the strength of the sensory signal on the unattended channel. Treisman's attenuation model is illustrated in Figure 3.4. The degree of perceptual analysis received by an item depends only in part on its signal intensity. The intensity threshold required for recognition also plays a part. A word is perceived if its stimulus intensity remains sufficiently high after the filter to exceed its recognition threshold; this is denoted by the long arrow reaching the perceptual channel in Figure 3.4. Other stimuli are attenuated too much to reach their recognition thresholds.

A word's recognition threshold depends on how important the word is or on how expected it is in a particular context. Thus, a weak signal intensity for one's name could exceed the threshold required and be responded to as the most pertinent stimulus. Similarly, because of top-down pattern recognition processes, there is an expectation and temporary low threshold for the word

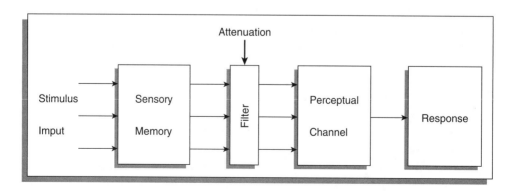

Figure 3.4   The attenuation model of selective attention.

"table" right after the word "mahogany" in Treisman's (1960) experiment. As a consequence, the expected word was perceived and remembered rather than the next word in the sequence presented to the attended ear.

Late Selection

Another alternative to Broadbent's (1958) model moves the position of the filter. Instead of assuming that selection takes place prior to perception, the late selection model holds that all stimuli are recognized but are narrowed to the most pertinent ones during response preparation. In other words, the late selection model designed by Deutsch and Deutsch (1963) and refined by Norman (1968) placed the filter after pattern recognition. Late selection refers to an attentional filter that operates after meaningful semantic processing but prior to response preparation. The words are fully perceived, but then the perceiver responds only to the most pertinent item (see Figure 3.5). In other words, according to late selection, a process similar to the one envisioned by Treisman (1970) during perceptual analysis occurs later but prior to response preparation. There is a bias to respond to the most pertinent word, such as one's name, because of conceptually driven processes activating the name in long-term memory. Despite the fact that inputs receive the same full semantic data analysis from the bottom up, only the most pertinent word is selected at the time of responding.

The late selection model accounts for the same findings as does Treisman's (1970) attenuation model. Perceiving one's name and repeating an anticipated word from the unattended channel occur because of their high pertinence values, not because only they received full semantic analysis owing to their low thresholds. The only way to distinguish which model best

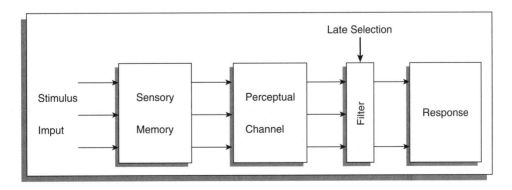

Figure 3.5   The late selection model of attention.

explains attention is to try to tell whether stimuli that are unattended and unselected for further processing actually receive full semantic analysis. Some experiments suggest that they do.

For example, MacKay (1973) had the person shadow a sentence in one ear such as "They were standing near the bank." In the other ear, MacKay presented either the word "river" or the word "money" at the same time. The results showed that the unattended and unselected word successfully biased the individual's interpretation of the sentence as referring to a "river bank" or a "financial bank."

Marcel (1983) adopted a very different methodology, backward masking, but reached the same conclusion. If a word is presented very briefly and is quickly followed by another visual stimulus, then the original word is masked backward in time such that the observer fails to perceive it consciously. Thus, the word is both unattended and unselected for further processing. Even so, Marcel found that the word primes the observer in a way that confirms the word had undergone semantic analysis. **Priming** refers to the presentation of a stimulus biasing how a subsequent stimulus is processed. Specifically, the time it takes to decide whether a subsequent string of letters is a word or not is speeded reliably if the original masked item is related in meaning. Lexical decision time, as it is called, is faster for, say, the word "ship" if the masked prime is "boat" as compared with "book." Remember that the observer claims no awareness of the prime itself, whether it is "boat" or "book." It seems as if the prime is perceived unconsciously.

> Selective attention may result from filtering of the unattended channel. The filter could occur at an early stage, just after sensory processing, or at a late stage, after semantic processing. A third possibility is that the unattended channel is attenuated rather than filtered entirely.

Results of the type reported by MacKay (1973) and Marcel (1983) hardly settled the matter in favor of a late selection model. First, some questioned whether the unreportable words fell totally outside the scope of attention and awareness (Cheesman & Merikle, 1984; Holender, 1986). Second, compelling evidence could be marshaled for either an early or a late location of the filter or bottleneck in information processing (Johnston & Heinz, 1978). It was as if the filter could move depending on the task at hand. Third, an alternative theoretical approach took hold that showed that filter theories of any sort fail to capture the full complexity of human attention.

CAPACITY THEORIES

Kahneman (1973) proposed that attention is limited in overall capacity and that our ability to carry out simultaneous tasks depends, in part, on how much capacity the tasks require (see Figure 3.6). For example, in the dichotic listening task presented earlier, the degree to which the secondary unattended channel is processed will depend on how much of the limited supply of attention is required by shadowing the primary channel. Because the shadowing task is highly demanding for most people, little, if any, capacity is left. If more capacity were available for allocation to the secondary channel, then the results would show a greater degree of processing. In principle, then, the results that seemed to support early or late selection could reflect the degree of capacity allocated to the secondary channel in shadowing tasks.

Mental Effort

The capacity approach conceives of attention as **mental effort**. The more a task requires of a limited pool of available capacity, the more mental effort the person exerts. For instance, try to solve these two arithmetic problems in your head:

$$a.\ 6 \times 6 = ?$$

$$b.\ 32 \times 12 = ?$$

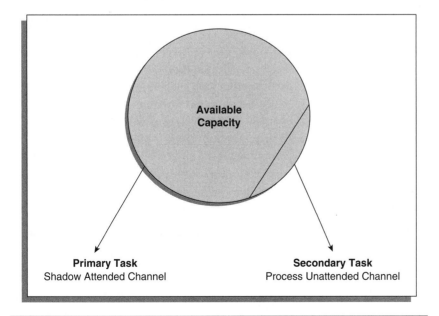

Figure 3.6   The capacity model of attention.

Clearly, Problem b demands more mental effort, that is, more of the capacity you have available for carrying out the task.

The central idea can be readily grasped by considering the dual task method of measuring mental effort. Suppose that while you solve a series of either easy [Problem a] or hard [Problem b] multiplication problems presented over headphones, you are given a secondary task of detecting the random appearance of a light on a panel in front of you. Your instructions emphasize focusing attention on the primary multiplication task while responding to the light with, say, a button pressed as rapidly as you can without disrupting primary task performance. The more effortful the primary task, the less capacity you will have available for rapidly detecting the light. The researcher can then compare your dual task reaction times with a simple reaction time, when light detection is the only demand on your limited attentional capacity. The more dual task reaction time increases over simple reaction time, the more effortful the primary task must be. In this case, your detection of the lights should slow down markedly more when you are doing the hard problems than when you are doing the easy problems.

> Mental effort increases as the proportion of available attentional capacity increases. One way to measure mental effort is through increases in reaction time to a secondary task that competes for limited attentional capacity with a primary task.

Enduring dispositions, momentary intentions, and evaluation of current demands on capacity shape the allocation policy. For example, when navigating a car on an interstate highway at, say, 65 miles per hour, the driver may be attending to music on the radio, reducing slightly the capacity available for driving. Far worse, the driver may dial a number on his or her cell phone and carry on a highly attention-demanding conversation, markedly reducing the capacity available for driving. If something unexpected happens on the road ahead—a tractor-trailer begins to swerve into the driver's lane—then a quick evaluation of the demands may, if all goes well, rapidly force all available capacity to steering and braking. If this shift to full attention to driving occurs too late or incompletely, then an accident is in the making. Fatigue or intoxication reduces the amount of attentional capacity available to the driver in the first place.

Johnston and Heinz (1978) extended capacity theory to account for the conflicting conclusions about whether the structural filter comes early or late in information processing. They proposed that, depending on the demands of the task, a person can flexibly employ either early or late selection, although the semantic processing of late selection comes at the cost of greater capacity use. The researchers studied dichotic listening in which the shadowed message could be identified by a sensory feature of pitch (male vs. female voice) or only by a semantic analysis (same voice but different categories, such as cities vs. occupations). They measured secondary task reaction times (detecting a light) during shadowing.

It took about 120 milliseconds longer to respond to the light while simultaneously shadowing using an early selection mode based on pitch, relative to simply detecting the light alone. Yet it took more than 170 milliseconds longer when shadowing required a late selection mode based on meaning. It would surely have taken even longer if the participants had managed to maintain accurate performance in the late selection case. As it happened, their error rate quadrupled when semantic analysis was needed. Thus, a capacity theory can subsume the findings of filter theories and explain further the nuances of human attention.

> Capacity theory assumes that attention is limited in overall capacity and that our ability to carry out simultaneous tasks depends, in part, on how much capacity the tasks require. Selective attention occurs because shadowing demands most of the capacity, leaving little, if any, for the unattended channel.

Multiple Resources

Further research has shown that a full accounting of the complexities of human attention requires that still finer distinctions be drawn than those seen in Kahneman's capacity theory (Navon & Gopher, 1979). Multiple resource theories account for how two simultaneous tasks will interfere with each other depending on the kind and level of resources they require. For example, C. D. Wickens (1980) proposed three dimensions of resources. First, he distinguished auditory versus visual perceptual modalities. Second, he distinguished perceptual-cognitive resources (consumed by the demands of tasks such as reading and mentally calculating) versus response resources (consumed by the demands of tasks such as speaking and moving one's hand). Third, he distinguished verbal versus spatial processing codes; speech and text illustrate verbal codes, whereas pictures and diagrams illustrate spatial codes.

Multiple resource theories attempt to explain how well two tasks can be done concurrently by specifying the capacity or effort demands, on the one hand, and the types of resources needed, on the other. For instance, attending simultaneously to speech and pictures should be more manageable than processing two channels of speech (Allport, Antonis, & Reynolds, 1972). Furthermore, attending to two channels of speech should be easier when the capacity demands of the task

> Multiple resource theories elaborate Kahneman's approach. The ability to perform two tasks concurrently depends not just on their respective demands on capacity but also on the specific kinds of resources required (e.g., perceptual vs. cognitive).

are low, as when the shadowed message can be identified by pitch, than when the demands are high, as in semantic analysis (Johnston & Heinz, 1978).

CONCLUSION

To summarize, filter theories evolved to explain the selective nature of attention. Experiments designed to test these theories showed the validity of assuming structural bottlenecks in the flow of information processing. However, they also showed the difficulty of specifying the exact location of these bottlenecks. Capacity theories built on the idea of bottlenecks but recognized that the location of the bottlenecks can vary from early to late stages in perception and cognition. Specifically, an individual can adopt either mode of selectivity in response to the demands of the current situation. Capacity theories also recognized that various dimensions of structural interference exist, such as the distinction between structures that use verbal versus spatial information. Last, and most important, capacity theories recognized the mental effort aspect of attention as well as the selective aspect. The degree of attentional resources demanded by a task became one focal point of further research, as explained in the next section.

AUTOMATIC PROCESSES

It has long been known that perceptual, cognitive, and motor processes may unfold automatically, without effortful control. Stroop (1935) devised an ingenious and somewhat diabolical test to study automatic reading (see Color Plate 3 in the section of color plates). The color terms occur automatically and effortlessly. The color terms (e.g., RED, GREEN, BLUE, YELLOW) are printed in an incompatible color of ink. The word RED appears in *green* ink, the word GREEN appears in *yellow* ink, and so on. The task is to say aloud the color of the ink while ignoring the meaning of the word itself.

The word recognition—one aspect of fluent reading—occurs automatically. That is, it is exceedingly difficult to ignore the meaning of the word RED when it appears in green ink. The correct response of GREEN competes with the habitual response of RED. Errors and delays in responding are the usual result. For more than 50 years now, the **Stroop effect** and variations on it have challenged theorists to account for the detailed patterns of errors and delays observed in experiments (MacLeod, 1991).

Word recognition illustrates one of many processes that have become automatic because of extensive practice, maturation, and skill development.

Walking, running, riding a bicycle, and typing on a keyboard are among the many motor skills that people automatize. Perceptual and cognitive skills also become automatic. Depth and object perception, as seen in Chapter 2, occur effortlessly despite the intensive computations that they require. Speech recognition, as will be seen later in the book, is one of the most complex perceptual tasks that we undertake. Yet by 5 years of age, a child effortlessly deciphers and comprehends spoken language.

Criteria of Automaticity

Posner and Snyder (1974, 1975) categorized a process as automatic if it met three criteria. First, an automatic process occurs unintentionally. Second, the process occurs unconsciously, outside the scope of even peripheral awareness. Third, the process operates without depleting attentional resources. The automatic process can carry on without interfering with processes that demand limited attentional resources. Put differently, **automatic processes** are often called preattentive. Whereas automatic processes are unintentional, unconscious, and undemanding of attention, **controlled processes** are intentional, conscious, and demanding of attention. This distinction is critical to understanding perception and attention (Schneider & Shiffrin, 1977), memory (Hasher & Zacks, 1979), language (Fischler, 1998), and higher order thinking skills such as reasoning (Stanovich, 1999).

Practice and Automaticity

Typically, a process or set of processes used in a particular skill, such as typing, becomes automatic only after extensive practice. Shiffrin and Schneider (1977) investigated the development of automaticity in a search task that has been investigated extensively by cognitive psychologists. The participants viewed a series of frames on a computer screen containing letters and digits. Their task entailed visually searching each frame for a target item while ignoring distractor items. The participants memorized the target items at the beginning of each series. Figure 3.7 shows two sample sequences for positive trials that contained a target. In the top case, the memory set consisted of two target items, the letters J and D. After memorizing the targets, a sequence of frames rapidly appeared on the screen, with one of the target items (J) occurring toward the middle of the sequence on positive trials. Besides target items, the frames contained either distractor items or nonmeaningful masks (dot patterns). The number of items in the memory set and the number in each frame of the sequence varied. The observers pressed

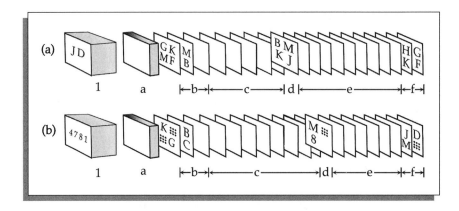

Figure 3.7   A visual search task for studying automatic and consciously controlled processing.

SOURCE: From Schneider, W., & Shiffrin, R. M., Controlled and automatic human information processing: Detection, search, and attention. *Psychological Review, 84,* 1-66. Copyright © 1977, The American Psychological Association. Reprinted with permission.

a button as quickly as possible on detecting a target. On negative trials, in which targets did not appear, the observers pressed a different button at the end of the sequence.

Schneider and Shiffrin (1977) examined two types of sequences, called varied mapping and consistent mapping. With varied mapping, the letters or numbers that served as targets on one sequence of frames could turn up as distractors on another sequence. These were letter-letter (or number-number) trials because in one sequence the observer might be looking for a particular memory set of letters while ignoring the distractor letters. Then, in a later sequence, the observer might be looking for the very letters that earlier had been distractors. Thus, to identify the targets accurately, the observer must carefully search each frame of the visual display and compare the items with the memory set on that trial. With consistent mapping, the memory set items (say, the numbers) never appeared as anything other than targets. The distractors were not used in the memory set across the trials of the experiment.

The participants practiced the search task for 10 hours beforehand and received further practice during the experiments. Schneider and Shiffrin (1977) manipulated the number of items in the memory set (1, 2, or 4) and the number in each frame of the sequence (1, 2, or 4). Shown in Figure 3.8 are the results for memory set size 4 on positive trials, when the target was present, as a function of the number of items in each frame. Although the time needed to detect the target increased substantially with frame size in the varied mapping condition, it remained at a low constant value for consistent mapping. Varied mapping produced an effortful, controlled search process. The observer had to consciously and deliberately match each item detected in a frame against each item held in short-term memory to decide whether a target appeared. By sharp contrast, the response times were fast and did not increase at all as frame size increased with consistent mapping, indicating an effortless automatic search process.

Spelke, Hirst, and Neisser (1976) reported that with extensive practice, even tasks that theoretically demand high levels of attentional capacity can be performed without interfering with each other. They trained two individuals to read short stories while simultaneously writing down words dictated by the experimenter. Spelke et al. managed to train their participants to take dictation of short sentences, which should require highly effortful semantic processing, while simultaneously reading. They found that after massive practice, people could accurately transcribe while reading with full comprehension. The authors

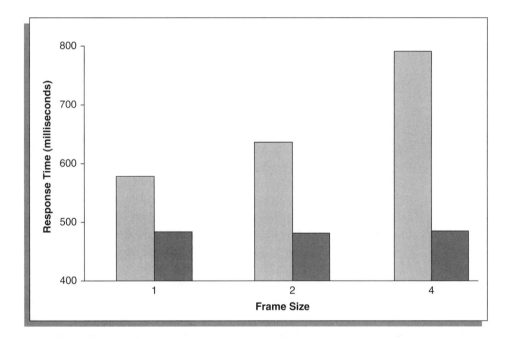

Figure 3.8   Automatic search is observed with consistent mapping and controlled search with varied mapping.

SOURCE: From Schneider, W., & Shiffrin, R. M., Controlled and automatic human information processing: Detection, search, and attention. *Psychological Review, 84,* 1-66. Copyright © 1977, The American Psychological Association. Reprinted with permission.

suggested that neither automaticity nor rapid alternation of attention accounted for the results. They contended that people split attention and simultaneously attended to both reading and dictation. Perhaps so, but it seems equally plausible that at least some of the component processes in reading, taking dictation, or both became automatized. The remaining component processes, then, could have been consciously controlled by a rapid alternation of attention.

Logan (1988) provided one explanation of how changes in the way a task is performed through practice lead to automaticity. Specifically, if a task can be restructured so that performance depends on retrieval from long-term memory, then automaticity occurs. Taking our example from earlier in the chapter, if you multiply 6 × 6, you do not need to carry out the **algorithm** because you can retrieve the answer, 36, from a memorized multiplication table stored in your long-term memory. The process is fast, effortless, and (most important here) different in nature from the alternative. If you must multiply 18 × 32, the only route available is to calculate the answer, unless perhaps you calculated the same problem just a few minutes before. Thus, as we learn to do a task automatically, it may be that the underlying processes change qualitatively by relying more on direct retrieval from memory.

Genetics and Maturation

Certain processes may be so basic for human learning and survival that they are genetically programmed to operate through maturation and interaction with the environment. Motor skills exemplify processes that achieve automaticity through genetic programming in addition to practice. Learning to crawl, walk, and run is not simply a matter of practice. At birth, there is a reflex to move the arms and legs in a crawling movement. This reflex typically disappears after about three or four months, with the ability to crawl appearing later, at about seven months (Gallahue, 1989). Whereas some species are programmed to walk moments after birth to ensure their survival, our species adopts a more leisurely pace, with the infant wholly dependent on the mother and father for survival. The effortlessness and automaticity that we see in the motor skills of an older child running while at play is only partly due to practice.

Basic cognitive processes may also be genetically programmed or hardwired in the nervous system (Flavell, Miller, & Miller, 1993). These should appear early in development and require relatively little learning to become fully operational. Moreover, individual differences in the functioning of these processes should be minimal if they are species-specific processes. Age, culture, intelligence, educational attainment, and other factors that strongly influence consciously controlled processes ought to be unimportant for innate automatic processes.

Hasher and Zacks (1979, 1984) proposed that humans innately and automatically process the frequency of occurrence of environmental features and events. They reported evidence that young children, as well as adults, keep track of stimulus frequencies, suggesting that the process undergoes little, if any, cognitive development. Individual differences in frequency processing also are minimal. Numerous studies have challenged the conclusion that frequency processing is entirely automatic. At times, the intention to keep track of frequency helps performance, and heavy concurrent demands on attention can hurt performance. Even so, the evidence strongly supports the conclusion that frequency processing operates automatically and innately, albeit less than optimally at times (Sanders, Gonzalez, Murphy, Liddle, & Vitina, 1987).

VISUAL ATTENTION

Besides the work on controlled versus automatic processing, researchers set about to map in detail the cognitive processes and associated neural structures involved in visual attention. The focus of attention in vision is sometimes likened to a spotlight, with ignored stimuli falling outside the beam (Posner, 1980). In selective attention, the diameter of the spotlight is highly focused on a central stimulus and adjacent stimuli are ignored. In divided attention, the beam is diffuse so that not only the central stimulus but also adjacent stimuli receive some processing. Researchers have asked an observer to focus attention on a centrally presented target letter and then examined the influence of flanker letters (Murphy & Eriksen, 1987). The logic of these experiments borrows from the Stroop effect. If the adjacent letters are associated with a wrong response or a different response from the target, then reaction time to the target slows down, just like in the Stroop effect. Alternatively, the response to the target is faster if the adjacent letters are associated with the same response. Murphy and Eriksen (1987) found that if the observer knew exactly where to focus attention, then the spotlight beam was concentrated. Any letter more than about one letter away from target had no impact on response time. By contrast, if a target could occur anywhere, then the spotlight was more diffuse. Adjacent letters often affected response times in this case.

Neural Basis of Selection

Recall that neurons in the occipital cortex act as feature detectors tuned to respond maximally to highly specific visual features, such as a line at a particular orientation. Moreover, the line must stimulate a specific area in the retina of the eye, which defines the receptive field for the neuron in question.

A group of cells in the retina—the receptive field—all map onto a specific neuron in the cortex that is "looking for" the feature to which it is tuned. Animal studies done on one of the areas in the visual cortex, called V4, reveal what seems to be the operation of an attentional spotlight narrowing in on relevant stimuli while ignoring others.

For example, the size of a receptive field apparently contracts in order to include a stimulus relevant to the task at hand while excluding an irrelevant stimulus. This occurs when both stimuli fall within the range of the original receptive field (Moran & Desimone, 1985). Furthermore, when the task requires a finer discrimination between, say, the orientation of two lines, the response of a neuron to a specific orientation becomes still more specific or more finely tuned (Spitzer, Desimone, & Moran, 1988). Thus, as Kinchla (1992) noted, "the contraction of receptive fields and the sharpening of tuning curves would seem to serve a selective or 'attentional' function" (p. 734).

The control of these changes in receptive fields lies in the thalamus, a structure deep in the midbrain that serves as a crossroad for an extremely large number of sensory pathways. Positron emission tomography (PET) scans with humans have revealed increased blood flow—implying increased neural activity—in a portion of the thalamus called the pulvinar thalamic nucleus when observers receive instructions to ignore an irrelevant but clearly visible stimulus (LaBerge & Buchsbaum, 1990). Equally telling is the clinical evidence with patients suffering damage to the pulvinar thalamic nucleus. Lesions in this area are associated with difficulties in directing visual attention (Rafal & Posner, 1987).

Posner and Peterson (1990) concluded from the relevant evidence that different areas turn the attentional spotlight off from its current focus and move it to a new focal point. The pulvinar thalamic nucleus, in their view, reads out the information available in the new focus of attention, and other regions control disengaging and shifting attention to a new location. A breakdown in the overall system of disengaging, moving, and reading out the new focus of attention may cause a disorder called **spatial neglect.** This disorder is characterized by a failure to attend to all areas of the visual field. Individuals with damage to the right hemisphere will neglect objects or events occurring in the left visual field. Although there is nothing wrong with their visual perception, they fail to attend to objects on their left. Spatial neglect can be seen in patients who read only the words on the right side of a paragraph presented to them or in those who draw only the right half of a picture they were asked to copy (McCarthy & Warrington, 1990). These patients seem to have trouble in voluntarily shifting the attentional spotlight to the neglected side (Posner, Cohen, & Rafal, 1982).

Executive Attention

Another kind of attentional circuit is involved in the executive control of mental processes. **Executive attention** refers to a supervisory attentional system that inhibits inappropriate mental representations or responses and activates appropriate ones. Its function is to control our thoughts and behaviors in adaptive ways. Imagine leaving a parking lot to drive home in the evening. If your usual routine is to drive straight home, then executive attention is needed to intervene and activate the thought of going first to, say, the grocery store. The automatic response of driving home must be inhibited or else it will control behavior. Norman and Shallice (1986) argued that executive attention is always needed when (a) planning or making decisions, (b) correcting errors, (c) the required response is novel or not well-learned, (d) conditions are cognitively demanding or dangerous, and (e) an automatic response must be inhibited and overcome.

The Stroop task provides an excellent way to study this region because there is a strong conflict between the automatic but incorrect response of reading the word name and the correct response of reading the color name. When participants perform the Stroop task in conditions that permit PET scans to be taken, a region in the frontal lobe shows strong activation. The **anterior cingulate gyrus** in the frontal lobe acts as a supervisory attentional system, inhibiting the automatic response and selecting the correct response. In reviewing the literature, Posner and DiGirolamo (1998) documented that several studies have shown increases in blood flow using PET in the regions of the anterior cingulate gyrus and the left frontal lobe in tests where there was a response conflict in a Stroop task (see Figure 3.9). Executive attention, together with short-term memory, plays a crucial role in all complex cognitive tasks, as is discussed in Chapter 4.

The disordered perception and thought of schizophrenia appears to be in part related to a breakdown in the normal processes of selective attention (David, 1993; Place & Gilmore, 1980). This possibly stems from a disorder in the inhibitory capacities of the prefrontal cortex (Cohen, Barch, Carter, & Servan-Schreiber, 1999). Without the ability to inhibit irrelevant information, schizophrenics experience problems in maintaining a representation of the context of their environment and their immediate task. If memories and hallucinations intrude at will, then the thought process disintegrates. A coherent stream of relevant task-related thoughts cannot be maintained if the inhibitory functions that normally enable such coherence break down.

> Executive attention refers to a supervisory attentional system that inhibits inappropriate mental representations or responses and activates appropriate ones. It is important in planning, decision making, and other complex cognitive tasks.

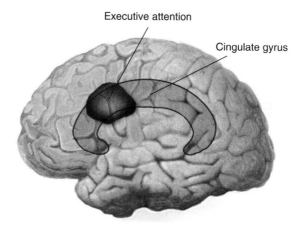

Figure 3.9   The cingulate gyrus serves an executive attentional function of inhibiting automatic incorrect responses.

Perceptual Binding

Another important line of work suggests that attention is necessary for object recognition (Treisman & Gelade, 1980). **Feature integration theory** posits that automatic preattentive processing of features must be followed by controlled attentional processing to bind the features into a whole object. An observer first scans a visual field preattentively, allowing the simultaneous parallel recognition of basic stimulus dimensions, such as color and shape. A further stage of processing requiring focused attention is then needed to integrate the specific stimulus features into a unitary object. To test their theory, Treisman and Gelade (1980) required observers to detect a target that differed from distractor items in terms of one dimension, such as color.

Following the logic of the set size effects discussed earlier, Treisman and her colleagues predicted that the number of distractor items should be irrelevant to speed of detection if the observer could automatically recognize all stimulus features in parallel. For example, finding a red X in a display with nothing but blue Xs and blue Os should be automatic (see the display at the top of Color Plate 4 in the section of color plates). As expected, the results showed that observers could detect such targets just as quickly in a display with 30 items as in a display with only 3 items (Treisman & Gelade, 1980; Treisman & Sato, 1990). This was referred to as a pop-out search because the target popped out at the observer (see Figure 3.10). When they required the observer to search for a unique conjunction of color and form, Treisman and her colleagues expected that focal attention would be needed to integrate the two features. For example, finding a red X in a display that includes red Os and blue Xs demands focused attention (see the display at the bottom of Color Plate 4). For a conjunctive search, she expected and found a strong set size effect; the more distractors, the longer it took to find the target.

Attention, then, can be thought of as the glue that binds together stimulus properties into the perception of a single object. As discussed earlier, different regions of the brain are responsible for processing the shape of an object (temporal lobe) versus its location (parietal lobe). Similarly, color, motion, and depth are distributed in different regions (Livingston & Hubel, 1987). The **binding problem** refers to how the features that are distributed in multiple brain regions are integrated to result in the perception of a single object. As you look at this book, you see an object at a specific location, color, and distance. Your perception is unified even though the mental representation of the book is known to be distributed.

Although the binding problem is not yet fully solved, one important part of the puzzle is that binding requires attention. A peculiar implication follows from this. If attention is not paid to an object, then it apparently is

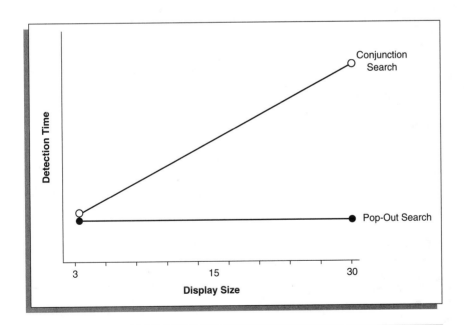

Figure 3.10   Detection time for automatic pop-out search and controlled conjunction search.

SOURCE: From Treisman, A. M., & Gelade, G., A feature-integration theory of attention. *Cognitive Psychology, 12,* 97-136. Copyright © 1980. Reprinted with permission.

not perceived, although its features are processed. Consider the experiment shown in Figure 3.11, reported by Mack and Rock (1998). The participant fixates on the cross-hair in the center but covertly attends to the large cross to the left. The mask that follows results in backward masking of all the information in order to prevent the use of sensory memory to mentally scan for other objects. On critical trials in the experiment, the fixation spot contains a small object, such as the diamond shown here. Note that this shape falls directly on foveal vision for 200 milliseconds, far more time than is normally needed to perceive an object when attention is paid to it. But remember that attention has been covertly shifted to the large cross, disconnecting it from the point of fixation. In this circumstance, between 60% and 80% of the observers failed to perceive the diamond. When asked "Did you see anything on this trial that had not been there on previous trials?" an astonishing large percentage of participants reported that they had not. The same result occurred whether the shape was a diamond, a circle, or a square and whether it was solid black or outlined.

> The binding problem refers to how the features that are distributed in multiple brain regions are integrated to result in the perception of a single object. Attention may be what binds the features together prior to conscious perception.

Mack and Rock called their discovery **inattentional blindness.** A superthreshold stimulus that is directly fixated for 200 milliseconds, a long leisurely glance when attention is (as usual) locked onto the fixation point, is simply not seen. Inattentional blindness provides a compelling, but disturbing, demonstration that attention is necessary for binding together features. Without attention and the binding that it supports, perception fails.

A similar phenomenon occurs when a series of stimuli are presented in rapid succession and the observer must attend to and report a target item (Shapiro, 1994). It turns out that any stimuli occurring within about 100 to 600 milliseconds after the target is heeded and reported are not attended and therefore not seen. For example, suppose that 500 milliseconds separates the presentation of a series of letters, as shown in Figure 3.12. If observers are instructed beforehand to detect the letter T, then they are likely to miss the letter E because it occurs too close in time to the letter T. It is as if they blink their eyes, but in reality the only blink is purely attentional. Their eyes are open, and all letters are registered by the visual system. They fail to report the

> Inattentional blindness and attentional blink are failures to perceive an object that is not attended.

letter E and fail to recognize it as having occurred. The interval of time after the target is presented when other stimuli in the series are not perceived is called **attentional blink.** This interval seems to be a refractory period following the encoding of the first stimulus that prevents attending to the second stimulus.

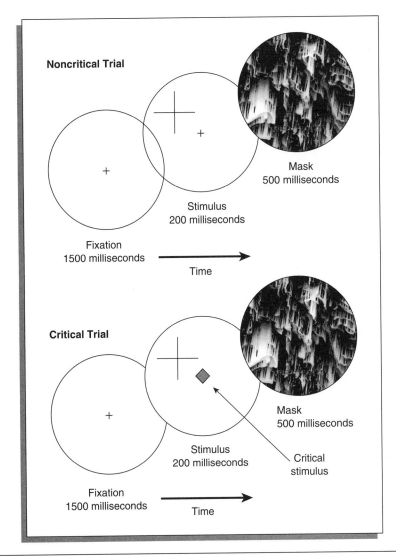

Figure 3.11 Noncritical and critical trials in a task used to study inattentional blindness.

SOURCE: From Mack, A., & Rock, I., *Inattentional blindness.* Copyright © 1998. Reprinted with permission of MIT Press.

The emotional content of the stimuli matters in attentional blink, however. Instead of using letters, Anderson (2005) presented participants with words in rapid succession that were either emotionally arousing or neutral in content. When the second target word was arousing, the size of the

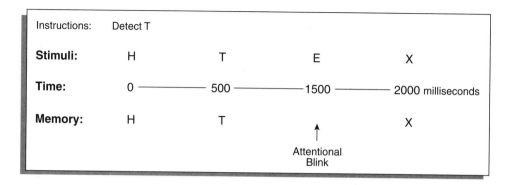

Figure 3.12   A task used to study attentional blink.

SOURCE: From Shapiro, K. L. (1994). The attentional blink: The brain's "eyeblink." *Current Directions in Psychological Science, 3,* 86-89. Reprinted with permission of Blackwell Publishing, Ltd.

attentional blink effect was reduced. In other words, it was easier to detect the words with emotional content. The refractory or blink interval was shorter when a word of emotional significance was there to heed. Anderson's finding indicates that emotional stimuli receive a high priority and are more likely to attain conscious status even when attention is overtaxed

Subliminal Perception

Inattentional blindness and attentional blink both indicate that unattended stimuli are processed to a degree, but not in a manner that allows their conscious perception. The term **subliminal perception** refers to unconscious perception without attention. Based on the facts just reviewed, the term is somewhat misleading. Although unattended stimuli are processed, they are not perceived as whole stimuli and so have little, if any, impact on the ability to recall or recognize the information. By hiding a message in a visual advertisement or by presenting the message for only a few milliseconds in a moving picture, advertisers had hoped to influence future purchasing behavior without the awareness of consumers. Subliminal messages have also been aurally presented and masked by high levels of noise or hidden by being played backward. The latter technique in particular has spurred public outcry, including a rancorous debate in the California legislature over the subliminal influence of rock music on its listeners.

The facts indicate that if a message is not perceived and not remembered, then its impact is unlikely to be significant as compared with one that is both perceived and remembered. Vokey and Read (1985) tested listeners' ability to identify the meanings of backward statements. Each statement fit one of five categories: nursery rhymes, Christian, satanic, pornographic, or advertising. The listeners simply had to identify the correct category, giving them a 20% chance of being correct through random guessing. The listeners performed at about this chance level (19%), indicating that they had not analyzed the meanings of the backward statements. Holender (1986) reviewed many similar negative findings.

Because the subliminal stimuli are not perceived, it is no wonder that they cannot be recalled or recognized. But because their features are processed preattentively, it might also be expected that carefully chosen tests can reveal such processing (Merikle & Reingold, 1992). For example, researchers have found that subliminally presented information slightly alters our future emotional responses to the material even though it cannot be explicitly remembered (Kunst-Wilson & Zajonc, 1980; Seamon, Marsh, & Brody, 1984). People are more inclined to like a stimulus if it has been presented in a subliminal manner previously. Coren (1984) concluded that subliminal advertising operates solely at this level of emotional response. The meaning of the message need not be understood or remembered explicitly for such emotional changes. It appears, then, that the emotional qualities of stimuli are processed automatically and without the need for attention.

More than 200 studies have documented that subliminal repetitions enhance our degree of emotional comfort with the stimulus, but the mechanism responsible for the effect is still uncertain. Monahan, Murphy, and Zajonc (2000) suggested that the mere exposure effect improves one's general mood by reducing alertness and tension. They argued that the effect is not dependent on a sense of familiarity with repeated stimuli and can generalize to both related stimuli and even unrelated novel stimuli. If this explanation proves to be correct, then the emotional changes caused by repeated subliminal exposure are diffuse in their effects.

SUMMARY

1. Attention refers to the selection of certain stimuli for processing to the exclusion of others. It also refers to the concentration of mental resources on a particular process. Two broad classes of theories have developed to explain attention. Filter theories address the selective nature of attention, whereas capacity theories address the allocation of resources to specific mental processes. Filter theories postulate a bottleneck in the flow of information from initial sensory processing to registration in conscious

awareness. Capacity theories recognize that one or more bottlenecks exist but add the assumption that mental processes compete for limited resources as well.

2. Early selection theory places a bottleneck or filter immediately after sensory memory. Pattern recognition of attended material proceeds, while unattended material fades rapidly from sensory memory because it fails to pass the selective filter. Attenuation theory also places the bottleneck after sensory registration, but it assumes that the filter merely lessens or attenuates the signal strength of unattended material. If the threshold for pattern recognition for a given stimulus, such as one's name, is sufficiently low, then even the weak unattended signals might undergo pattern recognition. Late selection theory places the filter after all pattern recognition of attended and unattended stimuli has taken place. This view holds that all stimuli are fully analyzed for their meaning, yet the filter excludes all but the attended stimuli from entering conscious awareness and memory systems.

3. Single capacity theory assumes that mental processes compete for a general pool of attentional resources. Two tasks can also interfere with each other if they both demand a high level of general resources. The general pool is always limited, although the exact amount of available capacity fluctuates with arousal and other factors. The percentage of available capacity used by a process defines the degree of mental effort involved. Multiple capacity theory assumes that pools of resources can be defined in terms of several independent dimensions. Auditory versus visual resources is one such dimension, while verbal versus spatial resources is another. If two tasks both demand, say, verbal capacity, then performance suffers. If one draws on verbal capacity while the other taps spatial capacity, then dual task performance can proceed without interference. Multiple capacity theory, therefore, integrates the insights of filter theories and single capacity theory to provide a comprehensive and detailed description of attention.

4. Automatic processes require little, if any, mental effort. Moreover, they occur without intentional control; even when an individual attempts to stop an automatic process from operation, it unfolds anyway, as demonstrated by the Stroop effect. Finally, automatic processes operate outside the scope of conscious awareness. Processes develop automaticity either through genetic programming or as the result of extensive practice. Learning proficiency at a skill often entails developing automaticity of underlying processes through practice. Controlled processes contrast with automatic processes on each point. They demand extensive mental effort, they require intentional control to operate, and they enter conscious awareness.

5. The processes and neural basis of visual attention is beginning to be understood. The focus of controlled processing in vision can be likened to a spotlight. The beam of spotlight varies in size, being more diffuse when attentional demands are light and contracting to a narrow beam when demands are heavy. Even when no eye movements are involved, it takes as long as 200 milliseconds to turn the beam off in one location and to bring it back to full strength in another location. The pulvinar thalamic nucleus plays a role in filtering irrelevant stimuli. It does so by controlling how sharply tuned a neuron in the neocortex is to a specific stimulus feature and by altering the size of a neuron's receptive field from the receptor cells in the eye. Other neural circuits appear to turn off the attentional spotlight in one location and move it to a new location. Another neural circuit mediates executive attention, which controls thoughts and behaviors by focusing on relevant mental representations and inhibiting irrelevant ones.

6. According to the feature integration theory, attention is necessary for visual pattern recognition. Feature detectors operate preattentively or automatically, allowing the identification of shape, color, and other single properties. The identification of a conjunction of two properties, such as color and shape, requires attention. Therefore, attention is the glue that binds together features into a whole object. Evidence shows that with the absence of attention, conscious perception of an object fails to occur, even when the object is fixated directly by the eyes. Inattentional blindness and attentional blink are examples of this failure to perceive in the absence of attention. Another phenomenon, called blindsight, shows that processing of a visual object in the occipital cortex is necessary for it to enter visual consciousness. Nonetheless, the location of the object can still be guessed correctly despite the individual's "blindness" in the sense of conscious perception.

KEY TERMS

selective attention	priming
divided attention	mental effort
shadowing	Stroop effect
early selection	automatic processes
attenuation	controlled processes

algorithm

spatial neglect

executive attention

anterior cingulate gyrus

feature integration theory

binding problem

inattentional blindness

attentional blink

subliminal perception

CHAPTER 4

MEMORY SYSTEMS

The topic of this chapter has been studied intensely by psychologists since the pioneering work of Hermann Ebbinghaus more than a century ago (Ebbinghaus, 1885/1964). The intense interest in memory is hardly mysterious. The lives of individuals have meaning only because of memory. Our immediate and distant past defines who we are, what we believe, what we can do, and what we feel. Try to imagine what your life would be like if you lost all memory. Imagine no recollection of where you were born, where you grew up, what you did in school, where you work, whom you live with, what you look like, and even what you thought or did just moments ago. The loss of perception or attention would be tragic, but one would still possess a sense of identity so long as memory remained intact. The loss of memory, by contrast, would steal one's very life and personhood.

How is it possible to remember where you lived five years ago, what you were doing five days ago, or what you were thinking five seconds ago? The central story of memory research has been revealing the complexities of these commonplace achievements of recollection. As will be described here, the three-store model of memory asserts that memory must first be divided into sensory, short-term, and long-term (see Figure 4.1). The first level of a hierarchical system of memory comprises these three stores. As will be seen in this chapter and the next, each of these stores includes subcomponents. The short-term store also is linked with attention in a system called *working memory* that will be discussed at the end of this chapter.

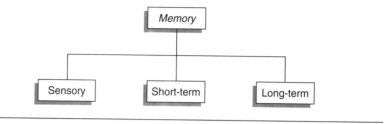

Figure 4.1   A hierarchical memory system: Three basic stores.

Memory involves more than these three separate storage systems. It also involves three basic processes that form mental representations and operate on them. *Encoding* concerns perceiving, recognizing, and further processing an object or event so that it can be remembered later. The way information is encoded into a mental representation makes a substantial difference in how well it is remembered, as will be seen. It is entirely possible that an event, for example, is forgotten because it was not well-encoded in the first place. Encoding must be followed by the successful *storage* of the event's mental representation in long-term memory. An event may be encoded and held for a brief period of time in short-term memory. For it to be remembered over a long period of time, however, it must be stored in long-term memory. The failure to transfer information from short-term memory to permanent storage in long-term memory is another way memory can fail. Finally, *retrieval* concerns searching long-term memory and finding the event that has been encoded and stored. An event may be available if it is encoded properly and stored successfully in long-term memory. Yet if this event cannot be retrieved successfully, then it is inaccessible to consciousness.

Memory fails us in multiple ways. Schacter (2001) described seven common malfunctions of memory, which he referred to as the seven "sins" of memory. *Transience* refers to the rapid loss of memory over short periods of time. In this case, information fails to be transferred into long-term memory. *Absent-mindedness* refers to breakdowns in attention that prevent encoding the event in short-term memory in the first place. *Blocking* refers to an inability to retrieve information from long-term memory. Transience, absent-mindedness, and blocking are all, then, sins of omission, malfunctions that result in a loss of memory for information that we would like to remember.

There are also sins of commission, in which we remember incorrect information or information that we would very much like to forget. For example, *misattribution* of the source of a memory can cause a person to confuse an event that he or she saw in a movie or even dreamed with an event actually experienced. *Suggestibility* refers to our tendency to become confused in our recollections because of comments made by others about what really happened. Eyewitness testimony about a crime can be incorrect because of misattribution and suggestibility, causing miscarriages of justice in our legal system. *Bias* refers to the way in which our current beliefs affect our reconstruction of the past. Retrieval from long-term memory is biased by the way we think and feel now about the event being remembered. The final sin—*persistence*—is not a distortion of memory, but rather an unwelcome imposition of the past in full detail. Repeated retrieval of painful memories that we would much prefer to forget is another sin of commission that we are all familiar with. When a traumatic event persistently intrudes on consciousness, the result can be psychologically debilitating, as happens in post-traumatic stress disorder.

The seven sins of memory documented by Schacter (2001) will be encountered throughout the next three chapters. The sins of omission will be seen in this chapter's presentation of sensory, short-term, and long-term memory and in Chapter 5, where the focus will be on memory encoding processes. In Chapter 6, the focus will be on retrieval processes, and distortions of memory and the persistence of unwanted memories will be discussed.

SENSORY MEMORY

As introduced in Chapter 1, Atkinson and Shiffrin (1968) proposed that human memory is not unitary. According to the three-store model, it is necessary to distinguish among sensory, short-term, and long-term stores that differ in their capacity and duration of storage. Sensory memory refers to the brief persistence of stimuli following transduction. Its function is to permit stimuli to be perceived, recognized, and entered into short-term memory. Without sensory memory, events in the environment would be forgotten as soon as they registered in the nervous system. To date, research has focused on the kinds of sensory memory associated with sight and hearing rather than other sensory modalities such as touch (see Figure 4.2).

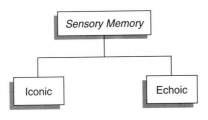

Figure 4.2   A hierarchical memory system: Components of sensory memory.

Iconic Memory

In vision, the brief persistence of sensory memory is called **iconic memory** and was investigated by Sperling (1960). An observer saw an array of nine letters presented for only 50 milliseconds using a device called a tachistoscope. A sample array is shown in Figure 4.3 along with the results of the experiment. When immediately asked to recall as many letters as possible, the typical participant managed to report four or five. Sperling called this the "whole report condition." He suspected, however, that all of the letters persisted briefly in iconic storage. But once the letters were located in space, their shapes were specified, and their names were recognized, some letters were lost. In terms of the three-store model, the letters may have been briefly available in iconic memory, but verbally reporting the letters required their

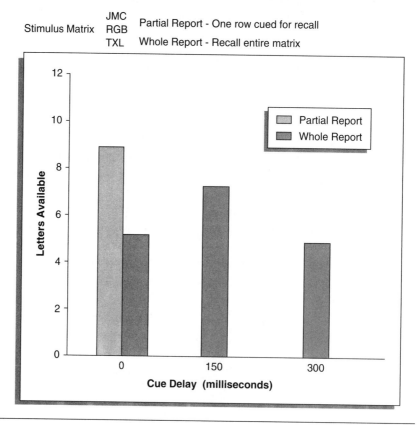

Figure 4.3   Partial report task used to study the capacity and duration of iconic memory.

SOURCE: Adapted from Sperling (1960).

conscious recognition and representation in short-term memory. By the time the observer named four or five, the others had long faded from sensory storage and were no longer available for processing.

To test his hypothesis, Sperling (1960) arranged a partial report condition, in which the observer had to report only the letters from a single row but did not know in advance which row. A high-pitched tone occurred after the 50-millisecond presentation to indicate that only the letters J-M-C needed to be reported. Similarly, a medium-pitched tone cued the middle row, and a low-pitched tone cued the bottom row. Sperling reasoned that if the observer could report all three letters from a single row without knowing in advance which row would be cued, then the true number of letters available in iconic memory equaled three times the number given under partial report. Sperling then delayed the onset of the partial report cue systematically from 0 to 1 seconds, to examine how quickly the iconic storage was lost. As seen in Figure 4.3, with an immediate cue, the observer recalled on average about two and a half letters, implying that nearly all nine letters persisted in iconic storage. But within about 200 to 300 milliseconds, the estimated number of letters available dropped to four or five—no different from the number obtained in the whole report condition.

> Visual sensory memory is called iconic memory; it has a large capacity but a brief duration of about 250 milliseconds.

Sperling's work indicated that iconic memory has a large capacity—greater than what can be reported at once—and a duration of only about 250 milliseconds. Several later experiments by others suggest that the iconic store holds most, if not all, sensations registered by the retina for a brief period of time (e.g., Averbach & Coriell, 1961).

Schacter's (2001) concept of transience as a sin of memory refers to information that fails to be transferred from short-term storage to long-term storage. For most of us, transience in sensory memory is not a problem and persistence is rarely observed. There is, however, a rare exceptional case of eidetic imagery, more commonly known as photographic memory, in which the details do persist for longer durations. Some college students find that they can remember images of textbook pages they have studied intensively, such that on tests they can retrieve seemingly accurate images of particular pages. Neisser (1981) found that such strong visual imagery skills are more common in children and are usually lost by the end of adolescence. However, a stringent test for eidetic imagery requires the ability to superimpose one pictorial image held in sensory memory onto another to form a third novel picture, such that what one perceives reflects both input images.

The only clear case of eidetic imagery ever documented was that of Elizabeth, an artist who used powerful visual imagery skills to imagine vividly a picture of her work in progress on a blank canvas; she used eidetic imagery to hallucinate the painting or drawing. Elizabeth was tested in the laboratory for this ability by viewing two random dot patterns, one presented to each eye (Stromeyer & Psotka, 1970). When viewed separately, the 10,000 dots in a pattern looked random, signifying nothing. When viewed stereoscopically (i.e., with the unique patterns presented to the left and right eye simultaneously), they merged to form a recognizable object such as the letter T. The researchers presented Elizabeth's right eye with a 10,000-dot pattern for 1 minute. Following a 10-second rest, she viewed with her left eye the accompanying 10,000-dot pattern and, when asked to superimpose the two, immediately reported seeing the letter T coming at her. She then looked at both patterns through a stereoscope and confirmed that her eidetic image of the T appeared exactly as it should. Note that this implies the ability to retain in memory the precise location of 10,000 random dots! Further tests showed that she could retain the right eye image for up to 24 hours before superimposing on it the left eye pattern. Thus, in this case one finds a strange persistence of sensory memory that stands as the exception to the transience that is the rule.

Echoic Memory

The auditory system also stores sensations briefly in a component dubbed **echoic memory** by Neisser (1967). Experiments parallel to Sperling's partial report study have been conducted to test the capacity and duration of echoic storage (Darwin, Turvey, & Crowder, 1972; Moray, Bates, & Barnett, 1965). Using stereo headphones, Darwin et al. (1972) presented three separate sequences of letters to an individual: one to the left ear, one to the right ear, and one dichotically (to both ears) that is perceived in the center of the head. Using the same comparison of whole report (report all sequences) versus partial report (report the left, right, or center sequence only), the researchers concluded that more items were stored than could be reported, just as in the case of iconic memory. However, the duration of echoic memory seemed to be much longer, on the order of 2 seconds rather than 250 milliseconds, judging from the effects of delaying the partial report cue.

> Auditory sensory memory is called echoic memory; its duration is brief, but aural stimuli such as speech are also stored for longer periods of time in short-term memory.

Many subsequent studies have addressed this discrepancy. In reviewing this work, Cowan (1988) concluded that the studies on echoic memory have actually tapped into two phases of storage. The first one is clearly sensory in nature and persists for about 250 milliseconds, comparable to the duration of iconic sensory memory (e.g., Massaro, 1970). The second phase lasts much longer, at least three or four seconds (Crowder, 1982). Auditory representations persisting for several seconds have been not only perceived but also recognized and named. Hence, the long phase observed in these studies is actually a result of storage in short-term memory (Penney, 1989).

SHORT-TERM VERSUS LONG-TERM MEMORY

All of us have experienced looking up a novel telephone number in the directory and then repeating it silently until we reach for the telephone and dial the number successfully. Without silent rehearsal, the meaningless sequence of digits is easily lost from memory if we wait too long to dial or are interrupted. Subjectively, the number seems available only temporarily in a short-term store. Our experience is quite different from the automatic, well-learned recall of our own telephone number. Unlike the fragile short-term memory, our own number seems locked permanently in a long-term store from which it can be retrieved with ease. Other numbers less often used, such as that of a friend not called for years, can sometimes also be retrieved from a seemingly permanent form of memory, but only with great effort.

Introspection along these lines has suggested a distinction between short-term and long-term memory from the time of James's *Principles of Psychology* in 1890. James referred to immediate memory of events currently attended to as primary memory and all other memory as secondary. Atkinson and Shiffrin (1968) referred to these as short-term and long-term memory in their three-store model. A classic way to study the distinction between these two kinds of memory stores involves hearing or reading a list of words and then trying to recall them without any restrictions on the order of output. You can try this free recall task by reading aloud each word given in Box 4.1. After doing so, close the book and try to

BOX 4.1

A Demonstration of the Free Recall Method of Verbal Learning and Memory

Read each word aloud at a rate of about one per second. Cover up each word as you read, to avoid rereading any items. Alternatively, you can ask a friend to read these words aloud to you. After reading or hearing the words, close the book and try to recall as many words as you can. Do not be concerned about the order of recall. You can write them down in whatever order you like.

1. brick	9. pencil
2. truck	10. lamp
3. stove	11. goat
4. apple	12. cabbage
5. door	13. baseball
6. book	14. tree
7. ladder	15. window
8. rifle	

write down as many of the words as you can remember in whatever order you like. Next, check how many words you correctly recalled. In particular, make a note of how many of the first five words you recalled. Next, look at the items in the middle of the list, numbered 6 to 10. Finally, how many of items 11 to 15 did you recall?

Serial Position Effects

The typical outcome of this free recall procedure is known as the **serial position effect** and is illustrated in Figure 4.4 with the curve labeled "immediate recall." The initial words on the list are recalled reasonably well, a phenomenon called the **primacy effect.** If you recalled most or all of the initial items on the list, then you showed a primacy effect. The words in the middle of the list are typically forgotten. Finally, the words at the end of the list are also remembered well; in fact, these are the words most likely to be recalled first. Were these the items you tended to write down first? Did you recall most or all of them? The high level of recall and early output is aptly labeled the **recency effect.** These effects have been known for more than a century (Nipher, 1878).

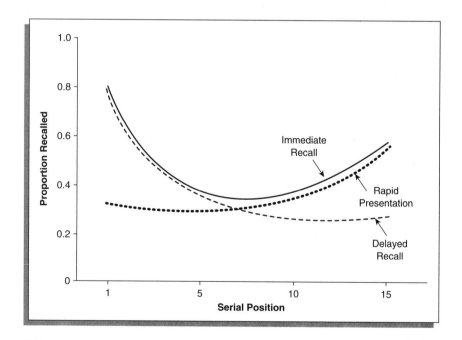

Figure 4.4   Serial position effects and the distinction between short-term and long-term memory.

The serial position effect can readily be accounted for in terms of the Atkinson and Shiffrin model and related mathematical models (Murdock, 1974). Once a word was recognized, it passed from sensory memory to short-term memory. If it remained in short-term memory and was rehearsed, then the word was transferred to the long-term store. Because the short-term store has limited capacity, the initial items on the list remained in the short-term store longer than did the later items. Once the capacity of the store was exceeded, a new word entered only by displacing a previous word. So, the initial list items remained in short-term memory long enough to be transferred via rehearsal to long-term memory. Thus, the primacy effect arises from the retrieval of information from long-term memory. The recency effect, on the other hand, reflects retrieval from the short-term store. The final words on the list still reside in the short-term store and can be retrieved so long as recall is immediate; in other words, they did not need to be rehearsed. Although the serial position effect is open to alternative interpretations (Crowder, 1993; Greene, 1986), it remains a source of support for distinguishing between short-term and long-term stores (Healy & McNamara, 1996).

Also shown in Figure 4.4 are two dissociations that further support the distinction. The recency effect can be eliminated without affecting the primacy effect by delaying recall for 30 seconds (Glanzer & Cunitz, 1966). It is important to prevent participants from rehearsing the list during this delay by giving them an attention-demanding task to perform, namely, counting backward by sevens from a number (e.g., 93, 86, 79, 72, 65, . . .). The delay eliminates the use of short-term memory but leaves intact recall from long-term memory. By contrast, speeding the rate of presenting the items, so that they remain in short-term memory for a shorter amount of time and are less likely to be rehearsed, eliminates the primacy effect while sparing the recency effect (Atkinson & Shiffrin, 1968).

> Free recall of a list of words reveals a serial position effect. The final items in the list are recalled first and well—the recency effect. The initial items in the list are also recalled well—the primacy effect. The three-store model attributes the recency effect to the short-term store and attributes the primacy effect to the long-term store.

The process responsible for the transfer of items from the short-term to the long-term store is presumably rehearsal, for example, repeating the words silently. To establish a direct link between rehearsal and the primacy effect, Rundus (1971) asked people to say aloud any words from the list that they wished during a five-second interval between each word presentation. Rundus found that the initial items on the list received far more rehearsals than did later items. People tended to repeat aloud the first words many times, but then as the short-term store filled to capacity, they had more words competing for rehearsal than could be handled. Thus, Rundus established a compelling explanation of the primacy effect in terms of rehearsal.

Neurological Dissociations

Another reason for distinguishing short-term memory from long-term memory came from the study of amnesia, specifically **anterograde amnesia.** This refers to difficulty in remembering events that occur after the onset of amnesia. **Retrograde amnesia,** on the other hand, refers to the loss of memory of events that occurred prior to the onset of the illness.

Anterograde Amnesia. In a famous case, a patient known by his initials, "H. M.," suffered from untreatable epilepsy. He finally found relief from violent seizures following the bilateral surgical removal of the frontal portions of the medial temporal lobe, including the hippocampus. Illustrated at the left of Figure 4.5 is a normal hippocampus in the left and right medial temporal lobes. At the right of the figure, bilateral lesions of the hippocampus are shown, similar to those produced in the anterior region of H. M.'s medial temporal lobe. Although the operation was a success in treating the epilepsy, H. M. suffered severe anterograde amnesia as a consequence.

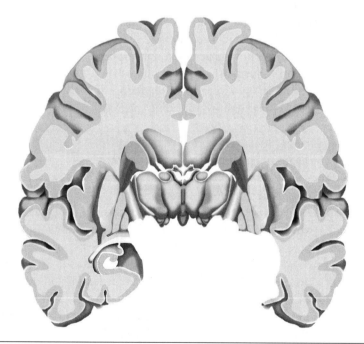

Figure 4.5   The loss of the hippocampus in H. M. is illustrated at the right of the figure. At the left of the figure, the normal position of the hippocampal formation is shown for comparison. In H. M., the loss was bilateral, affecting both the right and left medial temporal lobes.

Milner (1966) described H. M.'s memory loss in the following words:

He could no longer recognize the hospital staff, apart from Dr. Scoville himself, whom he had known for many years; he did not remember and could not relearn the way to the bathroom, and he seemed to retain nothing of the day-to-day happenings in the hospital. . . . A year later, H. M. had not yet learned the new address, nor could he be trusted to find his home. . . . He is unable to learn where objects are usually kept. (p. 113)

Milner (1966) and her colleagues used several tests to document in detail the nature of H. M.'s loss of memory. They found that he showed profound deficits in learning and remembering both verbal material, such as word lists, and nonverbal material, such as faces and sequences of lights. Specifically, Milner concluded that such anterograde amnesia reflected a failure to transfer information from short-term into long-term memory. Other cases of anterograde amnesia confirm this conclusion. Amnesia patients show a strong recency effect in recalling a list of words, much like the normal control participants (Baddeley & Warrington, 1970). Short-term memory per se is fine. However, the patients showed no primacy effect at all, as would be expected if their problem centered on difficulties in transferring new events into long-term memory.

> Anterograde amnesia is forgetting events that occurred after brain trauma. It appears to reflect a disruption in the transfer of events to long-term memory during learning. Retrograde amnesia is forgetting events that preceded the trauma and reflects forgetting from long-term memory.

Besides the evidence from H. M., it is known that bilateral damage from a stroke to the CA1 field of the hippocampus prevents the learning of new event information (Zola-Morgan, Squire, & Amaral, 1986). Additional evidence comes from the magnetic resonance imaging (MRI) data on the living brains of four patients with severe anterograde amnesia that show a smaller than normal hippocampus in all four patients (Squire, Amaral, & Press, 1990). Deficits in new learning are also found when the hippocampal region of monkeys is lesioned experimentally (Mishkin, 1978; Zola & Squire, 2000). Finally, functional MRI (fMRI) studies have shown that the medial temporal lobes, including the hippocampus, are bilaterally activated when normal participants encode novel pictures into long-term memory. This activation is illustrated in Color Plate 5 in the section of color plates, from a study reported by Martin, Wiggs, and Weisberg (1997).

The serial position effect provides another indicator of the role of the hippocampus in the storage of events in long-term memory. When primacy items from early in a list of words were successfully recalled, fMRI images revealed activation of the medial temporal lobe region that contains the hippocampus (Talmi, Grady, Goshen-Gottstein, & Moscovitch, 2005). By contrast, recency items from late in the list were not accompanied by hippocampal activation when they were successfully recalled. This result further reinforces the dual-store interpretation of the serial position curve and supports a role for the hippocampus in long-term memory storage.

Squire (1992) theorized that the hippocampus binds together the various places in the neocortex that process different features of a new event, such as the shape, color, and location of a visual object. In primates, these areas of the neocortex project to the hippocampus. Thus, the hippocampus and related structures in the medial temporal lobe are positioned to integrate the features of an event, each of which is processed and stored in different regions throughout the neocortex. The binding action of the hippocampus is necessary, according to Squire's theory, to remember objects that are no longer in the focus of attention. For example, in perceiving a visual object, shape, color, and location are identified by the object recognition pathway in the temporal lobe and the location pathway in the parietal lobes reviewed earlier. Over a short-term period, the simultaneous and coordinated activity in these neocortical regions suffice to keep the object in mind. But if one's attention shifts from the object to a new visual scene or to an internal train of thought, then the object can be retrieved only because the hippocampus had bound together the right shape, color, and location. A cue, such as the object's shape, could then be processed by the hippocampus to reactivate all of the relevant neocortical sites and retrieve the whole object from memory. As discussed in Chapter 3, attention is necessary to bind together features during perception. The hippocampus provides an index of where in the neocortex one can find all of the features that together compose the memory representation of the object.

> The hippocampus and related structures in the medial temporal lobe bind together the features of an event represented in regions distributed throughout the neocortex. Binding the features in memory is necessary to remember the event when it is no longer the focus of attention.

The process of successfully storing an event in long-term memory is called **consolidation**. Once an event is fully consolidated in long-term memory, then the task of the hippocampus in indexing and binding features is completed. Retrieving the event from long-term memory can then proceed without the involvement of the hippocampus. Activation of the hippocampus would still be found in retrieving a recently learned event that has not yet been fully consolidated in neocortical areas, but not in retrieving an event that has been consolidated (McClelland, McNaughten, & O'Reilly, 1995).

Retrograde Amnesia. Given that the hippocampus is needed to bind together features for storage in long-term memory, one can ask how long the consolidation process takes. Studies of retrograde amnesia in patients with hippocampal damage provide an answer to this question. Not only do hippocampal lesions cause anterograde amnesia that disrupts new learning, but they also cause loss of events that occurred prior to the accidents or strokes that caused the lesions. By studying how far back in the past the patients' retrograde amnesia extends, one can determine the length of time the hippocampus stays involved with the retrieval of learned events. The temporal gradient of amnesia for past events is shown for different groups of participants in Figure 4.6, compiled by Squire, Haist, and Shimamura (1989). They tested patients' recall of public events that had occurred from 1950 to 1985.

As can be seen, amnesic patients recalled just as many public events from the 1950s as did normal controls. However, the amnesic patients did progressively worse than the controls for the events from the 1960s, 1970s, and 1980s that occurred closer to the date they suffered hippocampal lesions. Presumably, the consolidation process had not yet been completed for these events, and so they were lost to retrograde amnesia.

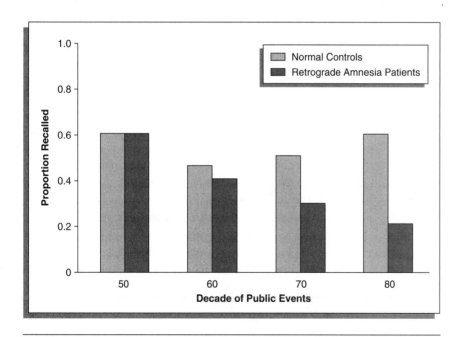

Figure 4.6   Recall of past public events in retrograde amnesic patients.

SOURCE: From Squire, L. R., Haist, F., & Shimamura, A. P. (1989). The neurology of memory: Quantitative assessment of retrograde amnesia in two groups of amnesic men. *Journal of Neuroscience, 9,* 828-839. Reprinted with permission of the Society of Neuroscience.

Impaired Short-Term Memory. So far, the discussion of neuropsychological evidence has focused on problems that arise in storing and consolidating new events in long-term memory. Other evidence on the separation of short-term and long-term memory comes from cases with impaired immediate recall. Warrington and Shallice (1972) first documented what seems to be a defect in short-term memory per se in the patient "K. F." The normal span of short-term memory is about seven items. However, K. F. and others like him show a dramatically smaller short-term memory, particularly when auditory rather than visual presentation is used. K. F. could correctly repeat a single letter even after a 60-second delay. But a mere two letters spoken to him were rapidly forgotten. Three letters showed still greater loss over time, even for those presented visually.

> Evidence from patients suffering from anterograde amnesia, retrograde amnesia, and reduced short-term memory capacity supports the distinction between short-term and long-term memory.

BOX 4.2

A Digit Span Test Demonstrating the Limited Capacity of Short-Term Memory

Cover the digit sets given below with a piece of paper and then uncover one set at a time. Read the set quickly, look away, and then try to recall it correctly by writing the numbers in the correct order on another sheet of paper.

6842

59317

274319

4952876

52968471

629479876

123456789

Capacity

Long-term memory is nothing if not spacious. A lifetime of memories can readily be stored, and there are no known limits to how much one can experience, learn, and remember. By sharp contrast, short-term memory is notorious for its limits in storage capacity (Miller, 1956). This can be easily seen in a test of the span of short-term memory for digits, as illustrated in Box 4.2. How many digits were you able to recall correctly in the right order? For most individuals, five or six items can be recalled fairly easily, but eight or nine digits burden short-term memory. In fact, relatively few people accurately recall a nine-digit series, as required by the next to last digit set. But what about the final set? Although it also contains nine items, all nine are easily remembered.

Miller (1956) recognized that the capacity limitation of short-term memory is a very real biological constraint. However, Miller further recognized that a nonbiological cultural process can overcome this limitation. He called the process **chunking.** It is easy to remember the final set of digits because they compose a single chunk: the ascending order of single-digit numbers. Meaningful patterns of information, often those grounded in the cultural tool of language, allow a person to remember far more than seven individual items. By grouping meaningful information together, we form a coherent chunk of information.

Although the digit span results suggest a capacity limitation of seven chunks, other results place the capacity of short-term memory at only three to five chunks (Broadbent, 1975). The precise capacity of short-term memory varies depending on the task used to make the estimate and the materials used in the task (Cavanagh, 1972). Also, the higher estimates of capacity are distorted by contributions from rehearsal and long-term memory, on the one hand, and sensory memory, on the other (Cowan, 2000). When these factors are controlled effectively, it becomes clear that pure short-term memory capacity is limited to about four chunks.

Duration

As noted earlier, you can retain a telephone number long enough to dial it by rehearsing the number silently. But what if someone interrupts the rehearsal or another task at hand distracts you from dialing? How long will the digits of the telephone number persevere? The answer appears to be about 20 seconds. Depending on the specific task and materials used to assess the duration, estimates range from as brief as 10 seconds to as long as 30 seconds (Cowan, 1988). Here lies the sin of memory called transience (Schacter, 2001).

The classic method for studying the duration of short-term memory is called the Brown-Peterson procedure after the pioneering research by Brown (1958) and Peterson and Peterson (1959). In this task, an individual listens to a series of three random consonants—a trigram—followed by the presentation of a three-digit number. As a distracting activity, the person counts backward by threes, speaking aloud to the pace of a metronome that clicks every half second. The counting continues for various unpredictable intervals ranging from 3 to 18 seconds; immediate recall without the intervening distraction also is tested at times. Forgetting over this brief interval can be closely approximated by a power function (see Figure 4.7) in which the rate of forgetting levels off as time increases. This is the classic forgetting curve that obtains regardless of whether the retention interval is 20 seconds, 20 weeks, or 20 years (Rubin & Wenzel, 1996). Thus, information in short-term memory is forgotten over a relatively brief time interval, even when it consists of only three chunks below the capacity limit.

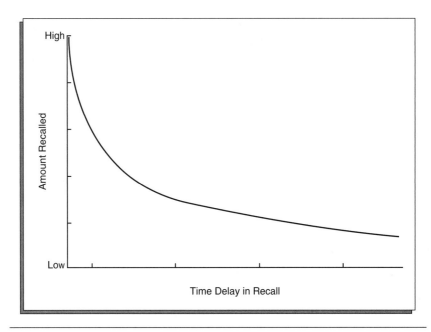

Figure 4.7   The classic forgetting curve showing the loss of information from memory as a function of retention interval.

SOURCE: From Peterson, L. R., & Peterson, M. J., Short-term retention of individual verbal items, in *Journal of Experimental Psychology, 58,* pp. 193-198. Copyright © 1959, American Psychological Association. Reprinted with permission.

The duration of long-term memory must be measured in terms of years, not seconds. Once material is stored in long-term memory, it may well persist for a lifetime. Because of the difficulties in measuring such durations, a precise estimate cannot be given. We do know, from the remarkable studies by Bahrick and his colleagues (Bahrick, 1983, 1984; Bahrick, Bahrick, & Wittlinger, 1975), that the duration of long-term memory is at least 50 years. Memory for information acquired in high school or college was assessed many years after graduation. For example, the names and faces of classmates, foreign language vocabulary, and locations of buildings on a college campus were checked. Although much of the information was forgotten, Bahrick (1983) found clear evidence of apparently permanent storage even 50 years after graduation. For example, after 46 years, students could recall the names of campus buildings and correctly place them on a map of the campus.

Conway, Cohen, and Stanhope (1991) measured what students remembered about their cognitive psychology class over a period of about 10 years.

They tested their participants for the names of researchers and for concepts acquired by the students. Conway et al. controlled for the differences in the degree of original learning of the material by taking into account participants' grades received in the course. Accurate recognition of both names and concepts declined quickly over the first 40 months or so but then stabilized. It remained well above chance even 125 months later. It should not come as a surprise to any student that free recall of the same information showed more forgetting. Recognition is typically easier than recall. Still, even on the recall measure, Conway et al. found retention of about a third of the material after 10 years (see Figure 4.8).

> The capacity of short-term memory is limited to about four chunks of information, and its duration is less than 30 seconds. The capacity limits of long-term memory are unknown, and its duration is measured in decades.

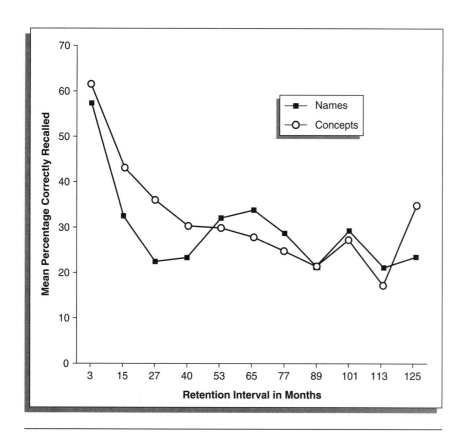

Figure 4.8 Long-term retention of facts about cognitive psychology.

SOURCE: From Conway, M.A., Cohen, G., & Stanhope, N., On the very long-term retention of knowledge acquired through formal education: twelve years of cognitive psychology, in *Journal of Experimental Psychology: General, 120,* 395-409, © 1991 American Psychological Association. Reprinted with permission.

What can you remember about your life when you were a baby? Although long-term memory can retain information for decades, our earliest experiences in life are virtually always forgotten. The inability to recall events from the first two or three years of life is called infantile amnesia (Howe & Courage, 1993; Spear, 1979). The reason for such amnesia is still unclear. One view is that the events of infancy are permanently stored but irretrievable. An alternative view is that these events were never encoded and stored adequately in the first place.

Freud (1900/1953) championed the first view. Repression of early, anxiety-provoking experiences was a defense mechanism to protect the ego in psychoanalytic theory. Freud used free association to unlock early memories. Another technique for doing so is hypnotic age regression, in which an individual presumably assumes the personality held at an earlier age (Nash, 1987). Repression is not the only explanation for retrieval failure, however. Perhaps the events are coded by the infant in a way that is not linked to the retrieval cues used by an adult. For example, an infant would encode the world without using language to label objects and events. An adult's attempts to search memory would commonly be organized around linguistic labels for concepts.

Other theorists question the permanence of early childhood memories (Kail, 1984; Loftus & Loftus, 1980). Maybe we cannot retrieve them simply because they do not exist. One reason for this impermanence is that the attentional and perceptual systems of the infant might not have been sufficiently developed to encode the events properly in the first place. Another possibility is that they were encoded and could be retrieved for a brief period of time, but then the events decayed from memory.

Research on the phenomenon has demonstrated that even two-year-olds can recall events that happened three or even six months in the past (Fivush, Gray, & Fromhoff, 1987). Moreover, Perris, Myers, and Clifton (1990) reported that 2½-year-old children could recall a single experience in a psychology laboratory that occurred when they were 6½ months old! That attests either to the remarkable memory of young children or to the bizarreness of psychology laboratories.

Yet Howe and Courage (1993) pointed out that the nature of these recollections by preschoolers is very fragmentary. These theorists contended that until children develop a concept of the self, which takes place at about the age of 18 months, they cannot possibly organize memories autobiographically. Shortly thereafter, at about the age of 22 months, children acquire the pronouns "I" and "you." Language acquisition provides an enormously powerful tool for organizing memory as an autobiographical narrative (Nelson, 1990). The source of infantile amnesia most likely lies either in the initial absence of a self-concept or in the absence of language needed to support memory for experiences.

Other Distinguishing Criteria

The capacity and duration differences among sensory, short-term, and long-term memory are summarized in Figure 4.9. Besides these basic distinctions among memory stores, efforts were made to identify other differences such as the codes used to store information, the causes of forgetting, and the means of retrieval. As first noted by Craik and Lockhart (1972), these criteria failed to dissociate the three stores. For example, it turned out that short-term and long-term memory rely on visual, acoustic, and semantic codes. Because of such similarities, Craik and Lockhart argued against a structural view of memory and in favor of a process view. Specifically, they suggested that memory representations are linked to the perceptual and higher order cognitive processes that are involved during encoding and storing events. As we will see in Chapter 6, their focus on encoding processes strongly influenced the direction of research over the past 30 years.

Coding. Sperling (1960) proposed that the format of iconic storage was precategorical. That is, only preliminary pattern recognition processes had operated on the information, allowing one to locate items in space but not to name them or identify them as members of a category. Sperling argued this position on the basis of studies that included a matrix with half letters and half numbers. The observer failed to show any advantage with a partial report cue to name, say, only the letters, whereas the location cue of the top, middle, or bottom row resulted in nearly perfect recall. However, Merikle (1980) later showed that the haphazard arrangement of the letters and numbers forced the observer to process them one at a time. By carefully arranging the format and spacing of the display, Merikle demonstrated that categorical distinction between letters and numbers could be used to a degree. Thus, location and other physical features are processed faster than

	Differences in Memory Stores		
	Sensory	*Short Term*	*Long Term*
Duration	250 milliseconds	20 seconds	Years
Capacity	Large	4 chunks	Very large

Figure 4.9 The different characteristics of sensory, short-term, and long-term memory.

the semantic category to which a stimulus belongs, but it is hard to draw a firm line between iconic and short-term memory on the basis of the coding format. A similar difficulty exists for echoic memory (Penney, 1975, 1989).

In fact, even long-term memory uses sensory codes. Paivio (1971, 1983, 1991) marshaled an extensive body of evidence showing that people can verbally encode information into long-term memory using words or visually encode it using images. These representations are derived from and retain the qualities of perceptions received through our sensory modalities. Linguistic stimuli are coded verbally as words as a result of perceiving speech and writing. Nonlinguistic stimuli are coded as images of what one has seen, heard, felt, tasted, or even smelled. **Dual coding theory** holds that information is best remembered when it is stored in long-term memory using both verbal and imaginal codes. As is discussed further in Chapter 5, if you were to learn the list presented in Box 4.1 by both forming an image of each item in your mind's eye and attending to the names, then your overall level of recall would improve.

Initially, short-term memory appeared to be based on a sensory code, specifically the acoustic or articulatory code involved in vocalizing names. Intrusion errors in immediate recall typically reflected confusions in stimuli that sound alike or that are enunciated in similar ways (R. Conrad, 1964). For example, people often incorrectly recalled the letter B in tests of short-term memory when the correct item was V. Confusion based on a visual code of how letters looked—their orthographic similarity—rarely occurred. The letters F and E differ by only a single distinctive feature in visual coding, yet Conrad's participants failed to confuse them. The high rate of intrusion errors in short-term memory for stimuli that are pronounced alike is called the **phonemic similarity effect.** The acoustic alphabet (e.g., "Alpha," "Bravo," "Charlie," "Victor") used by the military and others avoids such acoustic errors by assigning a name for each letter that is unique in terms of the acoustic-articulatory code.

> The phonemic similarity effect refers to the high rate of intrusion errors in short-term memory for stimuli that are pronounced alike.

Thus, when processing verbal material for later recall, people clearly use an acoustic-articulatory code. But it became clear from later research that short-term memory is not limited to this type of sensory code. Visual codes are used in short-term memory when people hold mental images in the mind's eye for several seconds (Brooks, 1968; Penney, 1975, 1989). Semantic codes are also used to store material in short-term memory (Wickens, 1972). To see the logic behind this conclusion, consider an experiment by Wickens, Dalezman, and Eggemeier (1976).

Wickens et al. (1976) presented three words on each trial, followed by backward counting to prevent their rehearsal. Each triad of words came from the same semantic category (types of fruit) on the first three trials. On the fourth trial, the researchers shifted the category in the experimental condition to vegetables, flowers, meats, or professions. The control condition received another triad of fruits. The results are shown in Figure 4.10. Recall decreased systematically on the first three trials as it became more and more difficult to remember which specific fruits had been presented on a particular trial. Then, on the fourth trial, there was an improvement in recall for those receiving a new category. Notice that the degree of semantic similarity between fruits and the new categories accounted for the size of the improvement. This is striking evidence that semantic codes are used in short-term memory. The farther apart the categories are in meaning, the greater the

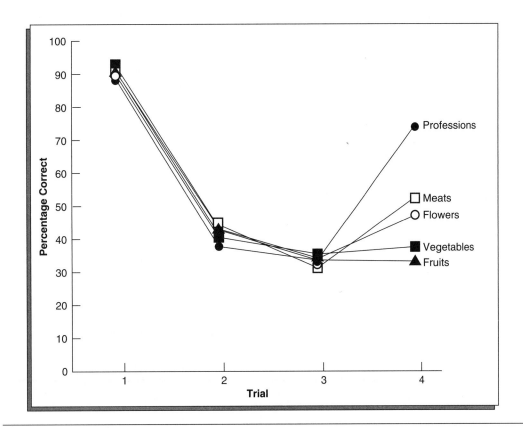

Figure 4.10   Release from proactive interference showing semantic coding in short-term memory.

SOURCE: From Wickens, D. D., Dalezman, R. E., & Eggemeier, F. T. (1976). Multiple encoding of word attributes in memory. *Memory & Cognition, 4*(3), Figure 1, p. 308. Reprinted with permission of the Psychonomic Society.

release. This outcome shows convincingly that the semantic code of each triad is stored in short-term memory. Similar semantic codes show less release from **proactive interference** than do dissimilar codes.

Forgetting. The decrease in correct recall observed on the first three trials in the Wickens et al. (1976) experiment illustrates an important cause of forgetting called *interference.* Proactive interference means that past learning interferes with the ability to learn and remember new information. For example, first learning a list of words (List A) would interfere with learning and recall of a second list (List B). Imagine an experiment in which we first presented List A, then presented List B, and then tested List B. Proactive interference is defined as poorer recall of List B relative to a condition that first rests, then receives List B, and then is tested on List B. The buildup of proactive interference explains why performance declined in the Wickens et al. experiment until release was obtained by shifting to a novel category on the fourth trial. **Retroactive interference** refers to recent learning interfering with the recall of previous learning. Thus, a person who learns List A, List B, and then recalls List A does more poorly than one who learns List A, rests, and then recalls List A. Learning List B interferes with the recall of List A.

So, it appears that interference is one source of forgetting in short-term memory. Waugh and Norman (1965) tested a simple alternative explanation of such forgetting, namely, that the information decays over time and is no longer available for recall. Participants heard a long sequence of digits followed by a probe digit, which prompted them to recall the digit that had followed the probe earlier in the list. The probe occurred after either one digit or several intervening digits. This allowed an assessment of whether recall declined with increases in the amount of retroactive interference. The digits came at a fast rate in one condition and at a slow rate in another; thus, the time that passed before the probe occurred was longer in the slow rate condition. If decay over time is an important source of forgetting, then recall should be poorer in the slow condition than in the fast condition. Waugh and Norman found that recall decreased with the number of digits intervening before the probe occurred. Thus, interference affected forgetting, yet the rate of presentation had no reliable impact on recall. Decay with time did not seem to be a factor.

Interference is not limited to short-term memory, however. It has long been known that interference is a major source of forgetting in long-term memory (McGeoch, 1942). Theorists during the 1940s and 1950s developed detailed models of how forgetting takes place when wrong responses interfere with right ones. At the same time, findings that followed Waugh and Norman's (1965) work showed that decay in fact does play some part in the forgetting found in short-term memory, in addition to interference (Baddeley & Scott,

1971; Reitman, 1974). There is more to forgetting than just decay and interference, as will be seen in Chapter 6, but for now the essential point is that the loss of information from short-term and long-term memory can take place in similar ways.

Consistent with this point, Rubin and Wenzel (1996) examined 210 published data sets that looked at short-term and long-term forgetting with retention intervals of seconds, days, weeks, and months. In all cases, forgetting followed the same function, as illustrated in Figure 4.7. It did not matter whether the time scale was short or long; the course of forgetting looks the same. The only exception was with respect to autobiographical memories—events with personal meaning for the individual—which were retained well even for long periods of time.

Retrieval. Just as short-term and long-term memory are difficult to distinguish on the basis of forgetting, the retrieval processes involved may also overlap. A **serial search** means that the items in memory are somehow ordered and are examined one at a time, starting with the first item and proceeding to the next. A **parallel search,** by contrast, means that all items in memory are examined simultaneously, not serially. Obviously, a parallel search process would result in much more efficient retrieval of information, especially when the amount of information that must be searched is large, as is the case in long-term memory.

If a search is serial, then when does it terminate? A **self-terminating search** is one that stops as soon as the item being sought is found. Thus, in a serial self-terminating search for the letter K among the letters D-B-K-X-M ordered in memory, the search would end after examining the third letter. By contrast, an **exhaustive search** is one that continues to examine the remaining items in memory even after the target item has been found. In our example, a serial exhaustive search would look at all five letters one at a time. It would not stop at the third position even though the target was found.

The classic study of these retrieval processes in short-term memory came from S. Sternberg (1966). On each trial, the participant memorized a short list of letters. The number of letters in the memory set varied from one to six, within the capacity of short-term memory. Next, Sternberg presented a probe letter. In the preceding example, the memory set size was five and the letter K was the probe. The person then pushed a "yes" button or a "no" button as rapidly as possible to indicate whether the probe could be found in the memory set. For example, K brings a yes response, whereas L brings a no response.

If all items in memory are searched in parallel, then the set size should not affect retrieval time. Furthermore, a negative trial in which the probe could not be found would be no slower than a positive trial in which the probe matched one of the items. By contrast, if a serial search is used, then reaction time should increase linearly as a function of set size. Each additional letter should add a constant number of milliseconds to the search time. An exhaustive serial search implies that the negative trials and positive trials should take exactly the same amount of time per item; their slopes should be equal. That is, the search does not stop just because a target is found on the positive trials. By contrast, a self-terminating serial search should reveal an advantage—a less steep slope—for the positive trials because the search stops as soon as the target is found.

Sternberg's (1966) results indicated that retrieval from short-term memory involves a serial exhaustive search (see Figure 4.11). A linear equation is fit to these data with a *y* axis intercept of 397 milliseconds and a slope of 38 milliseconds. The search time increased linearly with set size, and both positive and negative trials showed identical search times per item. This outcome is

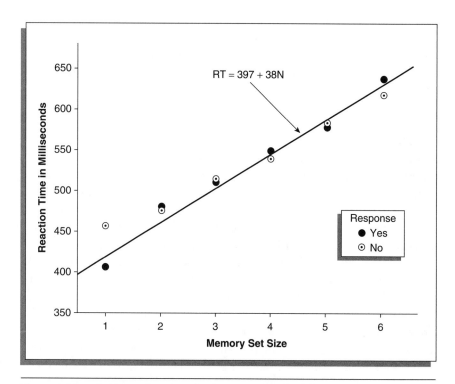

Figure 4.11   Evidence for a serial exhaustive search of short-term memory.

SOURCE: Reprinted with permission from Sternberg, S., High-speed scanning in human memory, in *Science, 153*, 652-654. Copyright © 1966 AAAS.

NOTE: RT = reaction time.

counterintuitive in that a self-terminating search seems more logical. Why bother searching all items in memory even after the target has been found? The answer may be related to the extremely rapid rate at which we search our short-term memory. The slope of the function is only 38 milliseconds, which is the extra time needed to examine each additional letter in the memory set.

The story is not this simple, however. The research spawned by S. Sternberg's (1966) results eventually led to the conclusion that a parallel search probably best characterizes short-term memory (Greene, 1992). Retrieval from long-term memory is also often parallel. It is impossible to explain the rapid speed with which humans are able to retrieve events, facts, and conceptual knowledge if every item in memory is searched in a serial manner. Even a self-terminating search does not help much, given the vast amount of information stored in long-term memory. At the same time, searches in long-term memory may proceed in a serial manner. For example, which letter comes five letters after K in the English alphabet? To arrive at the answer probably involves searching forward from K to L, M, N, and O, not directly retrieving P. Thus, it is not possible to distinguish between short-term and long-term memory on the basis of retrieval processes.

Conclusion

The three-store model has fueled major advances in our understanding of human memory. Despite significant challenges to the model, its core asser-tion that sensory, short-term, and long-term stores can be distinguished in terms of storage capacity and duration still stands and accounts for an impressive range of evidence (Estes, 1988; Healy & McNamara, 1996). Today, the focus of memory scholars is (a) how short-term memory is put to work in learning, comprehending, and other cognitive tasks and (b) how long-term memory is organized into separate systems. The remaining section of the chapter addresses these points in turn.

WORKING MEMORY

The short-term store explained how people are able to retain a list of words, digits, or other simple stimuli over a time span of several seconds. However, this theoretical construct does not seem adequate to explain the kind of retention of information that is needed in more complex cognitive tasks. For example, individual differences in reading ability are not strongly correlated with mea-surements of how many digits an individual can retain (Daneman & Carpenter, 1980). When reading this or any other book, it helps to remember the meaning

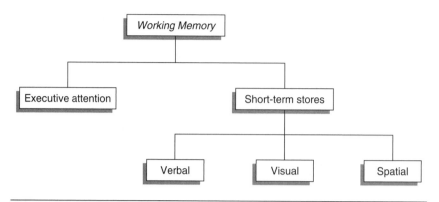

Figure 4.12   A hierarchical memory system: Components of working memory.

of a previous sentence in order to comprehend the meaning of the next sentence. Similarly, when carrying on a conversation, you need to hold in mind the assertions just made by your partner in order to formulate a response. Everyday cognitive tasks, such as reading and conversing, involve processing the information held in short-term memory to create a train of thought.

A system more complex than the short-term store was required to adequately explain performance in tasks that required a sustained train of thought. **Working memory** refers to the system for temporarily maintaining mental representations that are relevant to the performance of a cognitive task in an activated state. It includes short-term stores for mental representations that are coded in specific ways, as shown in Figure 4.12. Although these stores might be separate from long-term memory, another possibility is that working memory is best viewed as the representations that are currently active in long-term memory (Cowan, 1988). Working memory also includes executive attention, to control the mental representations held in short-term or active memory. As noted in Chapter 3, executive attention is a supervisory attentional system that inhibits some mental representations and activates others.

The term *working memory* stresses that the system is needed to accomplish cognitive work. The span of working memory is measured in a dual task situation demanding that attention be paid to more than remembering a list of words. For example, in the reading span test, participants must read and understand a series of sentences in addition to remembering the last word of each sentence (Daneman & Carpenter, 1980). In the operations span test, participants must perform a series of mental arithmetic problems in addition to remembering the words paired with each problem (Engle, Cantor, & Carullo, 1992). Unlike the digit span test, these tests of working memory capacity require actively processing task-relevant information at the same time that material is held in short-term storage. Attention is divided between two task requirements in these tests. Working memory span successfully predicts individual differences in performance in a wide range of complex cognitive tasks, including reading, writing, reasoning, and problem solving (Engle, Tuholski, Laughlin, & Conway, 1999).

Multiple Components

Numerous alternative models of working memory have been proposed, but they typically share the assumption that working memory consists of multiple components (Shah & Miyake, 1999). The earliest and a highly influential multicomponent model was proposed by Baddeley (1986). The model initially posited two short-term stores that specialize in the transient retention of verbal information, on the one hand, and visual or spatial information, on the other. These components were called the *phonological loop* and a *visual-spatial sketch pad,* respectively. The phonological loop is further fractionated into a passive memory store and a rehearsal loop that refreshes the activation of items held in the store. The phonological loop, then, allows one to maintain verbal information over time by repeating it covertly—silently articulating the letters or words. The visual-spatial sketch pad maintains representations used in visual imagery. It permits one to rehearse information by visualizing it or to imagine a problem and then seek a solution to it in the mind's eye (see Figure 4.13).

A third transient storage component was added in a revised version of the model (Baddeley, 2001). This component, called an *episodic buffer,* stores integrated representations that bind visual, spatial, and verbal codes from the other short-term stores together with information held in long-term memory. When features are bound together during perception, an integrated event representation is temporarily held in the episodic buffer and is available to conscious awareness. Complex events or scenes that combine multiple sources of information can thus be held and manipulated in working memory. Our ability to think about the past, plan for the future, and solve problems relies on actively maintaining such episodic representations. The episodic buffer, therefore, links the long-term memory system with a separate short-term memory system. Other alternative models handle the need for this linkage by assuming that working memory consists of the currently active subset of long-term memory representations (Cowan, 1988).

The final component of working memory is the *central executive.* This is the executive attentional component whose function is to control the use of the short-term and long-term memory stores (Baddeley & Logie, 1999).

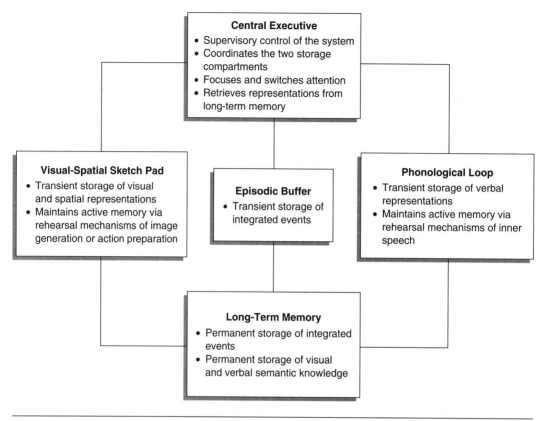

Figure 4.13   A multicomponent model of working memory.

SOURCE: From Baddeley, A. D. Is working memory still working? *American Psychologist, 56,* 849-864. Copyright © 2001, The American Psychological Association. Reprinted with permission.

The supervisory attentional system described in Chapter 3 serves here to control and regulate the memory stores in carrying out complex mental tasks. Both verbal and visual-spatial representations are needed to read, for instance, and the memory stores holding these must be coordinated. In everyday thought tasks and in tasks for measuring working memory capacity, attention must be focused on different stimuli and switched at appropriate moments. Relevant information must also be retrieved from long-term memory and brought into the focus of attention as one reads, writes, or solves problems. The central executive, then, is itself a complex component involving several functions (Baddeley, 1996).

> Working memory refers to the system for temporarily maintaining mental representations that are relevant to the performance of a cognitive task in an activated state.

Supporting Evidence

Here the discussion will focus on the phonological loop and visual-spatial sketchpad because they have been the most thoroughly researched components of Baddeley's model. To begin, the phonemic similarity effect discussed earlier is consistent with the idea that verbal working memory stores phonological representations. Errors are common when similar sounding words or letters are retained over short periods of time (Baddeley, 1986). Furthermore, Martin, Shelton, and Yaffee (1994) reported on two brain-injured patients who had poor memory spans. One failed to remember phonological information, presumably because of damage to the phonological store of verbal working memory, and had trouble repeating sentences. The other failed to remember semantic information and had trouble comprehending sentences. The observed dissociations indicate that there is a semantic as well as a phonological store in working memory.

If the rehearsal component of the phonological loop were damaged, then performance on a short-term memory task ought to suffer as a consequence. It turns out that there are a variety of motor output problems known as apraxia or dyspraxia. One kind of dyspraxia involves an impairment in the capacity to program speech output, including the inner speech needed for silently rehearsing information in the phonological loop. This, indeed, causes errors in verbal memory performance, as predicted by the Baddeley model (Waters, Rochon, & Caplan, 1992). Other studies have identified patients who fail on a test that measures spatial working memory ability but who do fine on a test of visual or object working memory relative to normal controls (Della Sala, Gray, Baddeley, Allamano, & Wilson, 2000). A double dissociation has been demonstrated on these tests. That is, separate patients show the reverse pattern, failing the test of visual working memory and succeeding on the spatial test.

Neuroimaging has recently demonstrated that different regions of the brain are involved in the multiple components of working memory. From a large literature based on animal testing, it is known that the prefrontal cortex is a necessary neural substrate for working memory (Goldman-Rakic, 1995). The neuroimaging findings confirm this point and further show some other regions involved. These studies use the method of subtraction to isolate the processes involved in maintaining different kinds of information in working memory such as verbal, spatial, and visual object representations. For example, in the verbal condition, participants try to retain a set of four letters in memory and are presented with a test probe that either was or was not in the set. Working memory for locations in space and for the shape of objects was also assessed.

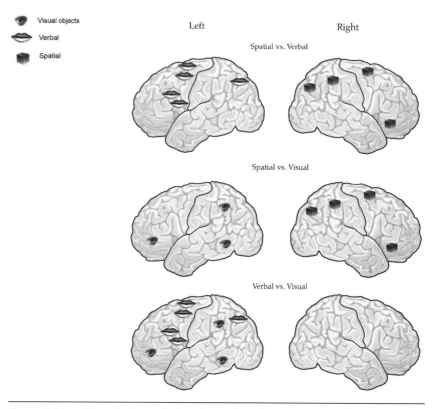

Figure 4.14   Dissociating verbal and spatial working memory with positron emission tomography (PET) data.

SOURCE: From Smith, E. E., & Jonides, J., Working memory: a view from neuroimaging, in *Cognitive Psychology, 33,* copyright © 1997. Reprinted with permission.

> Working memory includes components for transiently storing phonological or verbal features, visual features, spatial locations, and integrated episodes. It also includes an executive attentional component for controlling access to the stores.

The data are summarized in Figure 4.14 by first showing the sites in the left and right hemispheres that showed the greatest PET activation in the spatial versus verbal conditions. The verbal condition activated a region associated with Broca's area and motor areas in the frontal cortex associated with speech production and the covert rehearsal loop. A region in the left posterior parietal lobe was also activated, presumably as a result of storing the phonological representation that was refreshed via rehearsal. By contrast, the spatial condition activated regions in the right parietal and frontal cortex.

As shown in the middle row of Figure 4.14, the results have further shown that maintaining visual objects in working memory activates still different cortical regions in the left hemisphere (Smith & Jonides, 1997). In other words, the visual and spatial components of working memory must also be dissociated. One component stores visual objects and another stores their spatial location, a result that is consistent with the separate "what" versus "where" pathways of perceptual analysis discussed earlier. In fact, it appears that the temporary storage of working memory is mediated by the same brain mechanisms used during perception (Jonides, Lacey, & Evan Nee, 2005). Mental representations that become conscious during perception gradually fade with time and interference unless they are attended to and rehearsed.

Relative to our ability to learn and retrieve events stored in long-term memory years ago, the transient nature of working memory may seem unimpressive. But as Goldman-Rakic (1995) explained, it is no less important than long-term memory:

> The brain's working memory function, i.e., the ability to bring to mind events in the absence of direct stimulation, may be its inherently most flexible mechanism and its evolutionarily most significant achievement. At the most elementary level, our basic conceptual ability to appreciate that an object exists when out of view depends on the capacity to keep events in mind beyond the direct experience of those events. For some organisms, including most humans under certain conditions, "out of sight" is equivalent to "out of mind." However, working memory is generally available to provide the temporal and spatial continuity between our past experience and present actions. Working memory has been invoked in all forms of cognitive and linguistic processing and is fundamental to both the comprehension and construction of sentences. It is essential to the operations of mental arithmetic; to playing chess; to playing the piano, particularly without music; to delivering a speech extemporaneously; and finally, to fantasizing and planning ahead. (p. 483)

SUMMARY

1. The three-store model of memory distinguishes among sensory, short-term, and long-term stores. This highly influential model sought to identify unique characteristics with each store. The efforts proved to be successful with regard to capacity and duration but less so with regard to coding, forgetting, and retrieval. The capacity of short-term memory is limited to about four chunks of information, and its duration is less than 30 seconds. The capacity limits of long-term memory are unknown, and its duration is measured in decades.

2. The hippocampus plays a critical role in storing events in long-term memory. The hippocampus, a structure in the medial temporal lobe of the brain, binds together neural activity from locations distributed across the neocortex during learning. Until an event is consolidated in long-term memory, the hippocampus is needed to index the locations of the distributed memory representation. Damage to the hippocampus causes severe anterograde amnesia, in which recent new events cannot be stored in long-term memory.

3. Free recall of a list of words reveals a serial position effect. The last items in the list are recalled first and well—the recency effect. The initial items in the list are also recalled well—the primacy effect. The three-store model attributes the recency effect to the short-term store and attributes the primacy effect to the long-term store. The model also accounts for evidence from patients suffering from anterograde and retrograde amnesia and from reduced short-term memory capacity.

4. Working memory refers to the system for temporarily maintaining mental representations that are relevant to the performance of a cognitive task in an activated state. It involves short-term memory stores plus attentional control over processing in a cognitive task. Baddeley's model postulates stores for verbal information, called the phonological loop; nonverbal information, called the visual-spatial sketch pad; and integrated event representations, called the episodic buffer. The central executive controls processing in these short-term stores. Neuroimaging research has demonstrated that the phonological store and rehearsal loop are supported by regions of the left hemisphere. Visual or object-based working memory and spatial or location-based working memory are supported by separate regions in the right hemisphere.

KEY TERMS

iconic memory	dual coding theory
echoic memory	phonemic similarity effect
serial position effect	proactive interference
primacy effect	retroactive interference
recency effect	serial search
anterograde amnesia	parallel search
retrograde amnesia	self-terminating search
consolidation	exhaustive search
chunking	working memory

CHAPTER 5

REMEMBERING EVENTS

So far in this book, long-term memory has been described as if it were unitary. In the coming chapters, multiple systems of long-term memory are differentiated and described. Consider, for a moment, everything you need to know to be able to drive a car. You need to know what a car looks like, what a steering wheel does, and what the functions are of the two or three pedals on the floor, among other things. You need to know the rules of the road, the meaning of traffic signs, and the purpose of the solid and dashed lines on the streets. You further need several perceptual, motor, and cognitive skills to start the vehicle, put it in gear, steer, brake, and navigate your way to a destination. How does remembering any of this impressive array of knowledge depend on being able to recall the events that took place around you five minutes ago? It turns out that long-term memory for such knowledge can be preserved even when an individual suffers severe anterograde amnesia and can no longer remember recent events. Long-term memory seems to be partitioned into different systems that can function or fail independently of one another.

The experiments that distinguished short-term from long-term memory were concerned with remembering recent events. This is called **episodic memory** and will be the focus of this chapter once it is differentiated from other kinds of long-term memory. The chapter considers how new events are learned, that is, how they are encoded and stored in episodic memory. Much is known about the operations that support the learning of new events. Next, the processes involved in retrieving or failing to retrieve events from long-term memory are discussed. Finally, the manner in which retrieval cues enable the recollection of past episodes is addressed. Forgetting occurs when the available retrieval cues fail to activate available, but inaccessible, event representations.

TYPES OF LONG-TERM MEMORY

Just as working memory involves more than one component, long-term memory does not appear to be unitary. Scholars disagree about the criteria that must be satisfied to conclude that there are multiple systems of long-term memory. Mathematical models, and related computer simulations, begin with the assumption that the fewer systems of memory, the better. Not only is a single long-term store a more parsimonious explanation of memory phenomena, but it surely is easier to model with the necessary precision of mathematics (Hintzman, 1990). The danger with the mathematical perspective is it overlooks the messy nature of biological organisms in the search for an elegant computer simulation.

From the perspective of evolutionary biology, however, fewer and better need not coincide at all. Different systems evolve precisely because they afford successful adaptations to the challenges posed by the environment. Just as with other characteristics of an organism, a novel system of memory shown by a subpopulation of a species will come to dominate if it aids, in some fashion, survival and reproduction. A separate memory system evolves when the functions of existing systems fail to meet the demands of a new environmental challenge (Sherry & Schacter, 1987). The danger with the biological perspective lies in strewing our theories needlessly with a separate memory system for each seemingly separate memory phenomenon. The evidence favoring multiple systems is presented next, followed by some criticisms of how such evidence has been interpreted.

Declarative Versus Procedural Memory

Philosophers have distinguished between declarative and procedural knowledge—knowing *what* versus knowing *how.* Knowing the rules and traditions of baseball is not the same as being able to play baseball. Knowing how is often tacit or unconscious, whereas knowing what is explicit or conscious. As shown in Figure 5.1, memory theorists have proposed that the

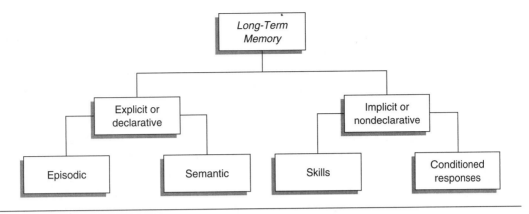

Figure 5.1   Hierarchical memory system: Types of long-term memory.

long-term memory store be divided into two major systems: declarative and procedural (e.g., Tulving, 1985; Zola-Morgan & Squire, 1990).

Declarative memory refers to knowledge of events, facts, and concepts, in short, knowing what the world presents to us. Declarative memory is sometimes referred to as explicit memory because one is consciously aware of the kinds of mental representations involved. It is possible to gain informational access to these representations and, in some cases, report on them verbally. In other cases, they are coded as images that are difficult to verbalize but are consciously accessible nonetheless.

As shown in Figure 5.1, declarative memory, in turn, consists of two components. **Semantic memory** stores knowledge of concepts and facts. Knowing what a baseball is reflects conceptual knowledge. Knowing Mark McGwire often hit baseballs over the outfield fence for a home run when he played for the St. Louis Cardinals is factual knowledge stored in semantic memory. However, a memory of actually witnessing a home run by Mark McGwire during a particular game at a particular place and time is a memory of an event. Remembering an event requires the *episodic* component of declarative memory.

Procedural or **nondeclarative memory** refers to the skills and conditioned responses that reflect knowing how to respond to the world. Procedural memory is sometimes called implicit memory because it uses mental representations that are not accessible to conscious reflection. Motor skills, such as running and typing, are familiar to all. One's body knows how to run or type without the mind being consciously aware of the representations that do the work. In fact, attempting to become consciously aware of the steps involved in a motor skill, such as one's tennis stroke or golf swing, can disrupt procedural memory. Thinking about it only gets in the way.

Not all skills are motor. Perceptual skills such as reading or appreciating the visual arts are also part of procedural memory. So, too, are highly cognitive skills such as writing or problem solving. In fact, procedural memory involves other kinds of behaviors in addition to motor, perceptual, and cognitive skills, such as conditioned responses (see Figure 5.1). A stimulus in the environment triggers a learned response and this, too, is a form of procedural memory. Conditioned responses can be learned through operant conditioning, in which a response is associated with a stimulus by using rewards. A conditioned response can also be stored in procedural memory as a result of classical conditioning, in which a conditioned stimulus is associated with an unconditioned stimulus. For example, a classically conditioned fear response to lightning (conditioned stimulus) might develop because the thunder (unconditioned stimulus) that follows lightning automatically elicits fear (unconditioned response).

It appears that the different kinds of long-term memory are supported by different brain structures (Squire, 1992). For example, it is well-established that the procedural memory pathways needed for classical conditioning of skeletal muscles are found in the cerebellum rather than in the hippocampal system used in the conscious recollection of events from episodic memory (R. F. Thompson, 2000). Furthermore, there is a rapidly growing body of research using positron emission tomography (PET), functional magnetic resonance imaging (fMRI), and lesion studies that isolates different brain regions for different kinds of nondeclarative memory. Learning sensorimotor skills (e.g., tracing a figure viewed in a mirror), perceptual skills (e.g., reading mirror-imaged text), and cognitive skills (e.g., solving problems) each involves a different neural substrate. Furthermore, the brain regions that mediate classical conditioning are different from those involved in operant conditioning.

> Long-term memory is made up of multiple memory systems. A major division in the hierarchy of these systems is the distinction between declarative memory (knowing what) and nondeclarative memory (knowing how).

Types of Tests. Explicit or direct tests require the conscious recollection of information, for example, when a person recognizes or recalls a past event. Implicit or indirect tests require the use of information stored in long-term memory, but not its conscious recollection, to improve performance (Richardson-Klavehn & Bjork, 1988; Schacter, 1987). *Perceptual priming* is a good example of an implicit task that depends on nondeclarative memory. Priming is an increase in the accuracy, probability, or speed of a response to a stimulus as a consequence of prior exposure to the stimulus. In perceptual priming, a prior occurrence of the prime (e.g., the word "chair") improves the chances of later perceiving a very brief exposure to the same word (Jacoby & Dallas, 1981). Repeating the typeface of a visually presented word similarly results in perceptual priming (Schacter & Tulving, 1994). One recognizes the word "table" more quickly if its prior occurrence appeared in lowercase letters (table) than if it appeared in uppercase letters (TABLE). Neuroimaging methods indicate that regions just outside the primary visual cortex in the occipital lobe support this kind of nondeclarative memory (Buckner, Goodman, et al., 1998).

Interpreting Test Dissociations. Tulving and Schacter (1990) argued that dissociations on implicit and explicit tests support the multiple system viewpoint. To illustrate, one variable is the use of normal versus amnesic individuals. Amnesic patients forget recent or past episodic events, yet they still show priming effects right along with normal individuals (Graf, Squire, & Mandler, 1984; Shimamura, 1986). Warrington and Weiskrantz (1970) pioneered the use of a word completion test to reveal normal priming effects in amnesics. They first presented a printed list of words and tested the ability of amnesic and normal individuals to recall and recognize them correctly. They also asked the participants to complete a word fragment (cha___) with the first English word that came to mind. If "chair" appeared on the original study list and the individual completed the fragment as chair, then priming occurred. Although the amnesic patients failed badly at recall and recognition, priming on word completion showed no decrement.

Milner (1965) discovered that "H. M." could learn how to trace the outline of a shape while looking in a mirror rather than at the shape. Such motor skill learning remained intact despite the anterograde amnesia for episodic events caused by H. M.'s brain surgery. Learning perceptual skills also may be preserved in amnesic patients (Moscovitch, 1982), as may learning a classically conditioned response (Weiskrantz & Warrington, 1979). When a flash of light is emitted just prior to the onset of a puff of air to the eye, both normal and amnesic individuals acquire a conditioned eye blink response to the presentation of the light alone. Although the amnesic patients retained the conditioned response on a test 24 hours later, they had no conscious recollection of having gone through the conditioning experiment only 10 minutes after it was completed.

Drug-induced dissociations between implicit and explicit memory tests have also been documented. Drugs such as alcohol and scopolamine can produce amnesia for episodes that occurred during the altered state of consciousness. Despite this amnesia, the drugs leave unimpaired performance on implicit tests of procedural nondeclarative memory (Hashtroudi, Parker, DeLisi, Wyatt, & Mutter, 1984; Nissen, Knopman, & Schacter, 1987). Some controversial evidence even suggests that patients show priming effects for words presented to them while under general anesthesia. The words could not be recalled by the patients after the surgery. But when asked to free associate to a cue word, they responded more often with the words presented during anesthesia than did a control group not given the words (Kihlstrom, Schacter, Cork, Hunt, & Bahr, 1990).

Episodic Versus Semantic Memory

As shown in Figure 5.1, declarative memory consists of two subcomponents: remembering events and knowing facts and concepts (Tulving, 1985). Episodic memory concerns the recollection of events that took place at specific places and times in the past. Semantic memory concerns factual and conceptual knowledge about the world and the words used to symbolize such knowledge. Such memory makes no reference to specific episodes in time and space. Suppose that you spot a bicycle on campus. Recognizing the two-wheeled object as a member of a category illustrates the use of semantic memory; the concept and the word used to refer to the object are activated. If you begin to think about the properties of bicycles in general (e.g., they have two wheels, a seat, and handle bars), then you are still using semantic memory. If, however, you begin to recall the bicycle you received on your sixth birthday, then you are using episodic memory. The specific memories you have of learning to ride it and the accidents you had with it are episodic memories located at places and moments in the past.

> Episodic memory is a specifically dated occurrence of an event in a particular context. Semantic memory refers to factual and conceptual knowledge about the world. They are subsets of declarative memory.

The anterograde amnesia case presented earlier in the chapter shows that episodic and semantic memory can be dissociated. H. M. showed a profound inability to store new episodic memories in long-term memory. However, his general knowledge of the world and his verbal abilities were not at all impaired. Intelligence tests provide a way to assess the factual and conceptual knowledge along with word meanings. H. M. scored very well on an intelligence test, recording an IQ of 112, where 100 is an average score (Milner, 1966).

Unlike H.M., most of us have the ability to store events from our life in episodic memory and to later retrieve those events with reasonable accuracy. However, a highly unusual case of extraordinary episodic memory of autobiographical events was recently discovered (Parker, Cahill, & McGaugh, 2006). For a woman identified as A. J., recollections of the past intrude on her daily existence in an uncontrolled manner. She spends large amounts of time recalling her past in great detail. For example, if given a date from, say, 15 years ago, A. J. can report what she was doing that day and the day of the week on which the date fell. She does this without using mnemonic techniques to improve encoding events into episodic memory (mnemonic techniques will be discussed later in this chapter). She does keep a diary to record her daily activities, but so do many others who do not show such a syndrome of heightened episodic memory.

Another form of evidence in support of the distinction between episodic and semantic forms of declarative memory comes from a dissociation of two kinds of judgments made on a recall test. Participants are asked to make judgments about whether they know an event occurred in the past or whether they remember its occurrence (Rajaram & Roediger, 1997). *Remembering* means having recollections of personal experiences from the past through mental time travel; that is, taking the self back in time to relive specific episodes. Thus, when you recall the day you graduated from high school, you can mentally travel back in time and recollect particular events, people, and interactions involving you personally. *Knowing* refers to being aware of facts and concepts in the absence of personally reliving past experiences. Knowing can take the form of a feeling of familiarity about abstract concepts or of being aware that past events happened without the mental time travel of re-experiencing them. You may, for example, know that a speech was made at commencement exercises, but recollecting the speech, or the face or name of the speaker, might not be possible. Knowing reflects retrieval from semantic memory.

Consider an experiment in which participants are given a list of words and then a recognition test is administered. Half of the items on the test are new and half are old. For each item the participants decide is old, they then introspect about the conscious experience associated with this decision and indicate whether they remember the item or simply know that it was on the list. Tulving (1985) introduced this procedure in an effort to measure episodic memory directly with "remember" judgments and to measure semantic memory with "know" judgments.

It turns out that remembering and knowing judgments are affected differently by variables that influence memory. For example, if an item is repeated in a list several times in succession, then the number of "know" responses is high. However, if the repetitions are spaced out so that several items intervene between each repetition, then the number of "remember" responses is high (Parkin & Russo, 1993). As another example, alcohol (Curran & Hildebrandt, in press) and the antianxiety drugs called benzodiazepines (Bishop & Curran, 1995) reduce the number of "remember" judgments given to old items on a recognition test. But the drugs have no effect on the "know" responses. If one assumes that "remember" judgments reflect episodic memory, whereas "know" judgments reflect semantic memory, then such dissociations strengthen the case for a separation of episodic and semantic memory (Gardiner & Richardson-Klavehn, 2000).

Criticisms of Multiple Systems

Although there is growing evidence in favor of multiple systems of long-term memory, serious challenges have been raised to the hypothesis. Different processes operating on a single declarative memory system can also give rise to dissociations (Hintzman, 1990; Jacoby, 1983; Johnson & Hasher, 1987; Roediger, 1984). For example, Roediger and Blaxton (1987) observed that learners often initiate top-down or conceptually driven processes, such as focusing on ways to organize new information. Bottom-up or data-driven processes are forced by the stimuli or data themselves, such as whether the modality of presentation was auditory or visual. It may be that implicit tests, such as perceptual priming, are more affected by data-driven processes, whereas explicit tests depend more on conceptually driven processes. Thinking about the meaning of stimuli during their encoding, as opposed to their perceptual appearance, could affect only explicit tests because such a difference in the level of encoding influences the functioning of conceptually driven processes but not data-driven processes. Perhaps amnesic patients demonstrate priming effects in a word completion task because such priming reflects data-driven perceptual processes.

Jacoby (1991) further observed that the implicit tests of memory are not pure measures of nondeclarative memory. It is possible that one recollects having seen a prime earlier in the task, and so part of the facilitation could reflect episodic memory. Nor are explicit tests a pure measure of only episodic memory. For example, on a recognition test, one might call an item "old" because it seems vaguely familiar rather than remember it as having actually been on the study list. When an individual intends to recollect an event and experiences a subjective awareness of remembering, consciously controlled processes are at work. Automatic processes of familiarity from past exposure can influence memory without intention or awareness.

To illustrate, Jacoby, Woloshyn, and Kelley (1989) demonstrated that familiarity with a name from a recent past exposure can automatically cause one to categorize the name as famous even though it is unknown. Participants are first read a list of names, either giving it full attention or dividing attention with another task. Next, they are asked to judge whether the names on a second list are famous or not. Some of these names are famous and some are nonfamous. Still others are nonfamous names that were repetitions of names heard in the first part of the experiment. When distracted in the divided attention condition, participants were likely to mistakenly think that repeated nonfamous names were, in fact, famous. One brief and relatively unattended exposure was all it took to trigger an automatic influence on memory.

These are important criticisms of the multiple systems position, and more work is needed on (a) how tasks are affected differently by conceptually driven versus data-driven processes and (b) how a single process such as the unconscious influence of familiarity affects both direct and indirect tests. However, it is unclear whether the processing point of view can accommodate all of the data now available (Gabrieli, 1998; Schacter, Wagner, & Buckner, 2000). Although the debate on this issue continues, the terms *semantic declarative memory* and *episodic declarative memory* are used in the remainder of the book and are contrasted with different kinds of nondeclarative memory for ease of exposition.

ENCODING AND STORING EVENTS

The three-store model assumes that encoding and storing events in long-term memory involves rehearsal. The nature of the rehearsal processes brought into play at encoding is critical, as suggested by Craik and Lockhart (1972). **Maintenance rehearsal** refers to recycling information within short-term or working memory by covertly verbalizing it. **Elaborative rehearsal** refers to linking information in short-term memory with information already stored in long-term memory. Elaborative rehearsal can take many forms. Organizing items into categories, associating items with other known information, and forming visual or auditory images of the items are examples of elaborative rehearsal. For instance, as noted in Chapter 4, it is easier to remember a list of words if one visualizes the object to which each word refers in addition to encoding the sound of the word itself (Paivio, 1971, 1983). Imagery works better for concrete objects that can readily be visualized (e.g., elephant) as compared with abstract concepts (e.g., gravity).

Mnemonic techniques designed to improve memory generally rely on elaborative encoding in the form of visual images (Bower, 1972; McDaniel & Pressley, 1987). Imagery has been recognized as crucial to memory from the time of the ancient Greeks. Cicero recounted a story about the Greek poet Simonides, who delivered a long poem at a Roman banquet. On finishing, Simonides left the building just moments before catastrophe struck. The building collapsed, burying everyone in the rubble. According to the legend,

BOX 5.1

A Demonstration of the Method of Loci

The method of loci is a mnemonic technique that uses familiar locations as an aid to memory. To illustrate, first picture a sequence of 10 locations at home or on campus that you know well. Now, try to form an image with each of the following grocery items, placing one item at each location in order. For example, for the first item, you might imagine a banana peel on the front steps of your home. Try to create a distinctive image for each item and location.

Bananas	Olives
Lettuce	Bread
Crackers	Hamburger
Bacon	Tuna
Milk	Mustard

Now, close the book and try to recall the items by taking a mental walk to each of the 10 locations. Most people find it much easier to remember the 10 items when using this imaginal technique than when trying to simply rehearse the items repetitively using maintenance rehearsal. Recall from Chapter 4 how difficult it was to retain more than seven or so chunks of information. Yet, most people find it easy to recall all 10 items using the method of loci, a type of elaborative rehearsal.

Maintenance rehearsal refers to recycling information within short-term or working memory by covertly verbalizing it. Elaborative rehearsal refers to transferring information to long-term memory by linking it with information already stored there.

Simonides was able to survey the ruins and recall the names of the victims by first imagining where they had been seated.

The mnemonic called the *method of loci* (places) consists of identifying a sequence of familiar locations and then forming an image of each item to be remembered at each of the locations. Once a clear image is formed, the locations provide a plan for retrieving the items. By imagining a walk to each of the locations in the sequence, one can remember the items (Bower, 1970). A demonstration of the method of loci is presented in Box 5.1.

One reason for the superior recall produced by the method of loci and related techniques is that mental images provide a second code, in addition to the word itself, for the memory system (Paivio, 1971, 1983). Without forming a mental image of the words to be remembered, one is left with only a verbal code. Further investigation of imagery and mnemonics suggests that the imagery makes an event in memory more distinctive and, hence, easier to recall (Marschark, Richman, Yuille, & Hunt, 1987; McDaniel & Einstein, 1986). Mnemonics also benefit memory by providing a set of retrieval cues that match the cues encoded with the to-be-remembered material (Bower, 1970). Taking a mental walk with the method of loci is a retrieval plan as well as an encoding plan. Each location visited at the time of retrieval allows one to reconstruct the event originally stored there with relative ease.

Craik and Lockhart (1972) made the strong claim that only elaborative rehearsal results in permanent long-term learning because of the necessity to analyze broadly and deeply the features of the stimulus. Because maintenance rehearsal merely recycles items in working memory, it presumably does not result in improved recall. Although early experiments supported this claim (Craik & Watkins, 1973), it became clear through further research that maintenance rehearsal helps memory some, albeit much less than does elaborative rehearsal (Darley & Glass, 1975; Greene, 1987).

Levels of Processing

In Chapter 2, we examined how sensory and semantic features are analyzed during pattern recognition. Data-driven and conceptually driven processes rapidly and accurately identify the objects, events, and symbols of our environment. These perceptual processes operate automatically when attention is devoted to a stimulus and occur to some degree even when the stimulus is unattended. In memory research, the effect of **levels or depths of processing** refers to a memory superiority for events attentively processed at a semantic level as compared with a sensory level.

The usual procedure directs a person to attend carefully to either sensory-level features (e.g., Is the word in capital letters? Does the word rhyme with "blue"?) or semantic features (e.g., Does the word fit the sentence "He slipped on his _____"?). In answering these orienting questions about the word "shoe," the focus of attention would be visual, acoustic, or semantic features. These three conditions reflect increasing levels or depths of processing. Recognition or recall of the target words is then tested. The results showed that visual and acoustic encoding is inferior to semantic encoding on memory tests (Craik & Lockhart, 1972). Craik and Tulving (1975) interpreted this level of processing difference in terms of elaborative rehearsal. Semantic encoding produced a more elaborate representation of the target words in memory, which supported superior recall and recognition.

Is there an orienting task that produces maximal elaboration and memory? Some research suggests that processing the information in relation to our self-concept is superior, a finding called the **self-reference effect.** Rogers, Kuiper, and Kirker (1977) found that when people asked whether a word applied to themselves (e.g., ambitious), later recall rose above that obtained for even the semantic orienting task. The recall results for physical, acoustic, semantic, and self-reference levels of processing are shown in Figure 5.2. Of interest, the same outcome occurs when people make judgments about consumer products shown in advertisements (D'Ydewalle, Delhaye, & Goessens,

> Levels or depths of processing refer to a memory superiority for events attentively processed at a semantic level as compared with a sensory level. Processing events semantically in reference to one's self-concept results in particularly strong memory.

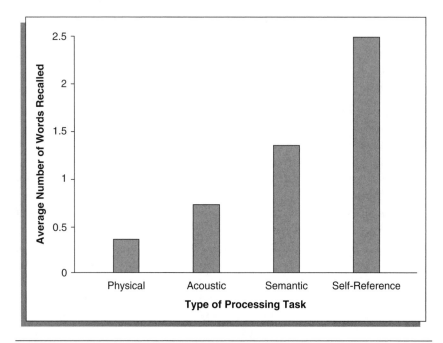

Figure 5.2   Recall as a function of the level of processing.

SOURCE: Adapted from Rogers et al. (1977).

1985). Answering the question "Have you ever used this product?" supported greater recall of brand names than did a semantic orienting task. Other evidence indicates that the key ingredient in this effect involves relating the information to highly developed representations in long-term memory, providing many links with well-ingrained information (Bellezza, 1986).

Transfer-Appropriate Processing

The principle of **transfer-appropriate processing** holds that test performance hinges on engaging in an encoding process that is compatible with the demands of the test. For example, different kinds of studying may be called for depending on the nature of the test. Practice at generating and organizing ideas would be highly appropriate as a way to prepare for an essay test, but such preparation might transfer less well to a multiple choice test.

Morris, Bransford, and Franks (1977) found that the typical levels of processing effect can be reversed by picking a test that is appropriate to visual or acoustic orienting tasks. They showed that the overlap between encoding and retrieval processes mattered more than the nature of encoding per se. For example, in one condition, participants were tested for recognition of words based on whether they rhymed with a word presented earlier, rather than on recognition of the identity of the word, as is typical. The authors found that rhyme encoding supported better rhyme recognition than did semantic encoding. Because rhyme encoding is appropriate for the rhyme retrieval test, it transfers better than semantic encoding. The fact remains, however, that recalling or recognizing an event depends critically on its meaning—its semantic features. Because remembering an event requires the retrieval of semantic information, it is semantic encoding that transfers well to standard recall and recognition tests.

Distinctiveness

Plainly, the extent to which one stores information in an elaborate manner predicts how well it will be remembered. But why should elaboration have this effect? One part of the answer is that elaborative rehearsal results in learning the distinctive features of items (Hunt & Einstein, 1981; Hunt & McDaniel, 1993). **Distinctiveness** refers to how the items to be learned are different from each other and other items already stored in memory. A highly distinctive representation is one that can be discriminated easily at the time of retrieval. The more the item stands out in memory, the easier it is to find.

Suppose that you are asked to memorize a list of nonsense syllables and one odd item: a number. People rarely forget the isolated distinctive number, an effect named after its German discoverer, von Restorff, and described in English by Koffka (1935). The power of distinctiveness can be seen in Eysenck's (1979) variation on the levels of processing effect, in which he compared sensory versus semantic orienting tasks. His sensory task entailed attending to the sounds of words. In a distinctive encoding condition, Eysenck used unusual pronunciations of the words designed to produce a highly distinctive, albeit sensory, level of processing. Because the unique pronunciations stood out in memory, they were remembered just as well as the words processed with a semantic focus. Typically, semantic encoding produces greater elaboration, which in turn increases the likelihood of storing a distinctive code. Eysenck's finding shows that it is distinctiveness per se that ultimately matters.

Picture Memory. It has long been known that people can recognize with a high degree of accuracy a long series of complex pictures that they have viewed for only a few seconds each. People can discriminate old pictures from new ones nearly perfectly when there are hundreds (Shepard, 1967) or even thousands of pictures (Standing, 1973). The reason seems to be that the pictures used in these studies contained many highly distinctive features, allowing observers to discriminate one from another. However, suppose that you must discriminate a picture of a particular $20 bill from a thousand such pictures. When the pictures all relate to the same schema, there is no distinctiveness and so recognition suffers (Mandler & Ritchey, 1977; Nickerson & Adams, 1979). This point is revisited after a discussion of the role of schemas in retrieval.

Flashbulb Memories. An especially intriguing phenomenon may also shed light on the power of distinctiveness. A **flashbulb memory** is a vivid recollection of some autobiographical event that carries with it strong emotional reactions (Brown & Kulik, 1977; Pillemer, 1984). Depending on your age, you might be able to recall clearly exactly what you were doing, seeing, hearing, and feeling on receiving the news that President Kennedy was assassinated in 1963, that an attempt was made on the life of President Reagan in 1981, that the space shuttle *Challenger* exploded in 1986, or that the World Trade Center was destroyed by a terrorist attack in 2001. As Pillemer (1984) noted, "images of only a tiny subset of specific episodes—death of a loved one, landing a first job, getting married, hearing about public tragedies—persist over a lifetime, with little subjectively experienced loss of clarity" (p. 64). One explanation for why flashbulb memories are so well recalled is that they are highly distinctive events in long-term memory (McCloskey, Wible, & Cohen, 1988).

Some researchers have challenged whether so-called flashbulb memories are really more accurate than normal memories. For example, two-and-one-half years after the *Challenger* explosion, participants in one study confidently recalled many details about the incident, but many of these recollections were inaccurate (Neisser & Harsch, 1992). Similarly, memories for the terrorist attack of September 11, 2001 have not proven to be more accurate than memories for nonemotional events occurring about the same time (Talarico & Rubin, 2003). Others, however, have confirmed that flashbulb memories can, indeed, be real for many people so long as the precipitating events had strong personal impacts on them (e.g., Conway et al., 1994).

> Distinctive memory representations can be discriminated from other related memories. Strong recognition of distinctive pictures, and possibly flashbulb memories, illustrates the power of distinctiveness in enhancing memory.

One brain mechanism that facilitates the storage of emotionally charged information resides in the amygdala (Phelps, 2006). Neuroimaging studies have shown that the degree of activation of the amygdala during encoding is predictive of how well emotional stimuli are later remembered. The most likely explanation of this phenomenon is that the emotional arousal causes the amygdala to hasten the process of consolidation in the hippocampus. This is known because of careful studies using animal models that demonstrate how the amygdala modulates processing in the nearby hippocampal region of the limbic system (McGaugh, 2004). Events that have a powerful emotional impact on an individual are usually readily stored in long-term memory and appear to be easily discriminated from other memories.

Synesthesia. A bizarre demonstration of the power of distinctive encoding came from a famous case study. Over a period of 20 years, Luria (1968) studied the memory abilities of an individual referred to as "S." He tested S.'s memory span for a variety of materials and found it remarkable and seemingly without limit. In Luria's words,

> I gave S. a series of words, then numbers, then letters, reading them to him slowly or presenting them in written form. He read or listened attentively and then repeated the material exactly as it had been presented. I increased the number of elements in each series, giving him as many as thirty, fifty, or even seventy words or numbers, but this, too, presented no problem to him.
>
> The experiment indicated that he could reproduce a series in reverse order—from the end to the beginning—just as simply as from start to finish; that he could readily tell me which word followed another in a series, or reproduce the word which happened to precede the one I'd name. He would pause for a minute, as though searching for the word, but immediately after would be able to answer my question and generally made no mistakes. . . . It was of no consequence to him whether the series I gave him contained meaning words or nonsense syllables, numbers or sounds; whether they were presented orally or in writing. . . . As the experimenter, I soon found myself in a state verging on utter confusion. An increase in the length of the series led to no noticeable increase in difficulty for S., and I simply had to admit that the capacity of his memory *had no distinct limits;* that I had been unable to perform what one would think was the simplest task a psychologist can do: measure the capacity of an individual's memory. (pp. 9–11)

Further testing only compounded Luria's (1968) confusion, for it turned out that the duration of S.'s memory, as well as its capacity, seemed to have no limit. Some tests revealed error-free recall of word lists presented 15 years earlier! Moreover, S. could recall the context in which a list had been presented, describing the place in which Luria had read him the words, the chair in which Luria sat, and even the clothes Luria had worn.

From early childhood, S. experienced *synesthesia,* or cross-talk among sensory modalities such that sounds, for example, were experienced visually as well as aurally. Normal individuals experience mild degrees of synesthesia in that colors are reliably associated with specific pitches of sounds (Marks, 1987). The bright colors of yellow and white elicit high pitches, whereas the dark colors of black and brown echo low pitches. But S. experienced an extreme form in which tones and noises would be apprehended as "puffs" and "splashes" of color. He would perceive the "color" of a speaker's voice, and each speech sound assumed a visual "form" with its own "color" and "taste." Plainly, these images added a unique distinctive code to memory.

Relational Processing

Clearly, then, learning how items to be remembered differ from each other is critical for good memory. **Relational processing** refers to how the items to be learned are related to each other and to other items stored in memory (Hunt & Einstein, 1981; Hunt & McDaniel, 1993). Instead of detecting differences, relational processing looks for similarities. It has long been known that well-organized information is better remembered. A learner must discover the relations among items or, when none is apparent, create his or her own subjective relations.

Category Cues. Tulving and Pearlstone (1966) showed the power of organization in their comparison of free and cued recall. The participants studied a list of 48 words that came from several categories, such as tools, fruits, and vehicles. The words occurred in a random order, but the learners noticed the organization of the items nonetheless (see Bousfield, 1953). When asked to recall as many words as possible with no hints or cues (free recall), the participants clustered related items together, for example, apples, oranges, and grapes. More interestingly, if the participants remembered a single item from a category, then they likely remembered most of the others. Conversely, if they forgot an item, such as "truck," then the other examples of vehicles also were forgotten. In other words, the category served to organize their recall.

But only about a third of the words were remembered in free recall. Tulving and Pearlstone (1966) also provided some participants with the category names as retrieval cues. Remarkably, the cues roughly doubled the number of words successfully recalled. This result for cued recall shows the powerful effect of organization as an aid to retrieval. It also shows that events may be available in memory but inaccessible to recollection without the right retrieval cues. More is said about retrieval cues later in the chapter.

Subjective Organization. The tendency to cluster items from the same semantic category is, perhaps, not surprising. Yet organization plays a critical role in recall even when a clear basis for it is lacking. Tulving (1962) presented people with lists of unrelated words and tracked their free recall over a series of trials. Over a series of trials of studying the words and attempting to recall them in whatever order the person wished, each participant adopted a consistent pattern of output. That is, each person imposed a **subjective organization** on the words, recalling clusters of items in the same manner trial after trial, even though the clusters themselves were purely idiosyncratic. The more categories people used in organizing the study items, the better they did on both recall tests and delayed recognition tests (Mandler, Pearlstone, & Koopmans, 1969).

Organization, encoding the relations among events and prior knowledge, benefits both learning and remembering. First, the events may be chunked together during their storage (Mandler, 1979). Just as finding meaningful groupings increases learning on tests of short-term memory, the same effect may be seen in long-term memory. Second, organization provides retrieval cues that are vital to remembering (Tulving & Pearlstone, 1966). The categories imposed by the materials or by the learner serve as highly effective retrieval cues.

> Subjective organization refers to the way individuals impose an idiosyncratic organizational scheme on unrelated items to be remembered.

RETRIEVAL PROCESSES

Forgetting may be caused by an inability to retrieve information that is available in memory. Such forgetting may reflect the temporary or even permanent lack of accessibility of information. This could arise because of interference from similar competing information stored in memory or because of a failure to activate the retrieval cues associated with the forgotten information. Contemporary research has focused on the cue-dependent nature of remembering and forgetting. It has emphasized how the context and knowledge related to material in memory play pivotal roles in successful retrieval.

To illustrate, recalling an event from episodic memory, such as one's 10th birthday party, requires retrieval of the time, the place, and the circumstances of stored information. Retrieval can be an active process of re-imagining the perceptions, the feelings, and possibly the thoughts about the event and its context. Being provided with a cue, such as a photograph taken at the party, can trigger a chain of recollections that at first seemed lost from memory. The cue activates related knowledge in long-term memory that eventually allows one to retrieve, or perhaps reconstruct, the needed information. What one knows about birthday parties in general affects both how one's 10th birthday party was encoded and how it will be later retrieved.

Retrieval Mode

Retrieval involves at least two kinds of subprocesses (Moscovitch, 1992). On the one hand, there are the general operations involved in attempting to remember an event, and these are observable regardless of whether the search is successful. The effort to retrieve has been referred to as **retrieval mode.** On the other hand, there are the operations specifically associated with successful recovery of the event.

Several studies with PET and fMRI have shown that a region in the anterior prefrontal cortex of the right hemisphere is activated when an effort is made to retrieve an event (Buckner, 1996). This is not the only area activated, but it is the best understood to date. For example, as seen in Color Plate 6 in the section of color plates, strong PET activation can be observed in the right hemisphere in temporal regions in addition to prefrontal regions when recollecting a highly emotional episode from more than a year in the past (Fink, Markowitsch, Reinkemeier, Bruckbauer, Kessler, & Heiss, 1996). In contrast to the right prefrontal and other regions activated in episodic retrieval, prefrontal regions in the left hemisphere are highly activated during the encoding of events into episodic memory. These activation sites are summarized in Figure 5.3. Tulving, Kapur, Craik, Moscovitch, and Houle (1994) proposed the hemispheric encoding/retrieval asymmetry (HERA) model to account for the neuroimaging findings.

It has been difficult to say for certain whether the right prefrontal activation genuinely reflects a retrieval mode as opposed to successful recovery because of limitations in the scanning procedures (Schacter et al., 2000). Scans had to be compared between a group of trials in which retrieval was usually successful and a group of trials in which forgetting was likely, and so the data were noisy. However, new fMRI procedures allow comparisons of scans for individual items on a recognition test. By comparing correct hits on old items (retrieval mode plus retrieval success) versus correct rejections of new items (retrieval mode only), the issue can be resolved. The data from such studies show convincingly similar activation levels in the right anterior prefrontal cortex for both hits and correct rejections (Buckner, Koutstaal,

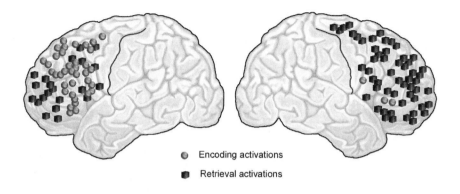

Figure 5.3   Different regions of the left and right prefrontal cortex are involved in episodic encoding and retrieval.

SOURCE: From Nyberg, L., & Cabeza, R. (2000). Brain imaging of memory. In E. Tulving & F.I.M. Craik (Eds.), *The Oxford handbook of memory* (pp. 501–519). Reprinted with permission of Oxford University Press.

Schachter, Dale, Rotte, & Rosen, 1998). Thus, the activation observed there is unrelated to retrieval success.

Neuroimaging evidence has identified numerous regions of the brain that appear to be activated when events are successfully retrieved from long-term memory. Different locations are observed depending on whether the events recollected are verbal or nonverbal in nature (Nyberg & Cabeza, 2000). The wide distribution across all lobes of the cortex in both hemispheres is to be expected, given that the representation of an event is distributed by its features, as discussed in Chapter 4. The hippocampus is also involved in retrieval of recently learned information. The medial temporal lobe initially stores an event prior to its consolidation in distributed areas throughout the neocortex (McClelland et al., 1995). Finally, certain areas of the prefrontal cortex in both the left and right hemispheres are more active when retrieval succeeds than when it fails (Buckner, 1996). Thus, a variety of prefrontal regions are involved both in the effort to search for an event representation and in its actual retrieval.

Behavioral studies also support the idea that intentional efforts to retrieve are different from the processes of successful retrieval. As pointed out earlier in this chapter, encoding processes do not function well at all when attention is not allocated to them. A comparison of the effects of divided attention on encoding and retrieval has revealed a sharp difference (Craik, Govoni, Naveh-Benjamin, & Anderson, 1996). Dividing attention at encoding greatly reduces recall and recognition performance. The time needed to respond on a secondary task provided a measure of the effort devoted to encoding. The data showed that the effort given to encoding was under conscious control and was lessened in the divided attention condition.

By contrast, dividing attention at retrieval had little, if any, impact on success in recalling and recognizing events. But it caused a major increase in the effort devoted to retrieval, particularly in free recall when the retrieval was most intentional and least automatic. Of great interest, the effort measure did not vary at all with the number of items successfully retrieved. Thus, the effort measure apparently reflected retrieval mode, which is under intentional control as one tries to recollect past events. Success in retrieval, on the other hand, appears automatic and undisturbed by divisions of attention. As Craik et al. (1996) pointed out, their data fit well with the neuroimaging results that discriminate the retrieval mode as a control process carried out in the right prefrontal cortex from the process that actually recovers items from memory.

> Retrieval mode refers to the effort to retrieve an event from long-term memory as opposed to its actual retrieval. Activation in the right prefrontal cortex supports retrieval mode, whereas numerous regions are involved in successful retrieval.

Encoding Specificity

Tulving (1983) proposed that remembering depends on activating precisely the same cues at retrieval that were originally encoded with the event in question. Tulving's principle of **encoding specificity** asserts that "specific encoding operations performed on what is perceived determines what retrieval cues are effective in producing access to what is stored" (Tulving & Thomson, 1973, p. 369). The interaction between encoding and retrieval conditions is the key to high levels of recall and recognition.

For instance, Light and Carter-Sobell (1970) presented people with a cue and a target word to study, such as STRAWBERRY-JAM. Later, the participants tried to recognize whether the target word (JAM) had appeared during study. If on the test the cue word was switched (TRAFFIC-JAM), they had a harder time recognizing the target than if the retrieval cue matched the encoding cue. Furthermore, when encodings are highly distinctive and retrieval cues are available that match the encoding cues precisely, recall performance can be dazzlingly accurate. Mantyla (1986) obtained better than 90% accuracy in cued recall for a list of 600 words!

Recall of Unrecognizable Events. If one studies a list of words and later tries to remember them on a recognition test versus a recall test, performance is often better on the recognition test (Kintsch, 1970). A cued recall test generally yields better performance than a free recall test in which no retrieval cues are provided. But cued recall still fails to come close to the accuracy typically observed on a recognition test. This makes sense if you think of the word on the recognition test as the perfect retrieval cue; it is an exact copy. Not only is the word familiar, but it allows one to retrieve the context in which the word was originally seen in the experiment (Mandler, 1980).

Suppose that you see someone at a party who looks familiar. Recognition requires not only a judgment about familiarity but also an identification of the context in which you have encountered the person before ("Oh, yes, she was at the grocery store."). This identification is much easier when looking at the person than when given a weakly related cue ("think of shopping") or given no cues at all.

Tulving and Thomson (1973) arranged a situation in which the encoding specificity principle counterintuitively predicts accurate recall of an unrecognizable word. They presented a list of to-be-remembered target words (e.g., BLACK) along with encoding cues that were weak associates of the targets (e.g., TRAIN). After presentation of the list, the participants were given strong semantic associates of the target words (e.g., WHITE) and were asked to think of related words. Not surprisingly, target items (BLACK) were often generated. Next, the participants were asked to examine all of the words they generated and to indicate which, if any, had originally been presented as targets. Finally, a cued recall test was given in which the encoding context (TRAIN) served as the retrieval cue.

Tulving and Thomson (1973) found that the participants successfully recognized the targets only a quarter of the time. But when given the proper cue (TRAIN), the participants recalled the targets a stunning two-thirds of the time. What is so striking about this is that the retrieval cue is only a weak associate of the target. Yet, because it had been encoded with the word initially, it was the ideal cue for recall. This phenomenon of recall of unrecognizable words strongly supports the principle of encoding specificity.

Tip of the Tongue States. Surely, you have seen a familiar face that you could not quite place, or perhaps you could not retrieve the person's name. People often experience a feeling of knowing or familiarity in which some name, word, date, or other information cannot be retrieved despite a certainty that it is available in memory (see Box 5.2). When such feelings become particularly intense, psychologists refer to the experience as a **tip of the tongue (TOT) state.** Brown and McNeill (1966) studied such TOT states for words by giving people definitions of rare words and asking them to recall the words. Of interest, when people experienced a TOT state, they could correctly identify the number of syllables in the forgotten word more than 60% of the time. Further investigation showed that "TOTs (a) are a nearly universal experience, (b) occur about once a week, (c) increase with age, (d) are frequently elicited by proper names, (e) often enable access to the target word's first letter, (f) are often accompanied by words related to the target, and (g) are resolved during the experience about half of the time" (Brown, 1991, p. 204).

BOX 5.2

A Demonstration of the Tip of the Tongue State

Try to name the capitals of the following states in the United States and countries in the European Union. Is there one (or more) for which you believe you know the answer but cannot retrieve it? Can you guess how many syllables are in the name? Can you guess the initial letter of the name?

State	Country
Maine	Finland
New Hampshire	Belgium
Georgia	Denmark
South Dakota	Italy
Arizona	Germany
Tennessee	United Kingdom
Rhode Island	Luxembourg
Iowa	Portugal
Virginia	Austria
Oregon	Sweden

TOT states suggest that information may be available in memory but inaccessible. The forgetting seems to be clearly caused by a failure to find the right retrieval cue. Sometimes, we can successfully recall the forgotten information by stumbling on a thought or perception that triggers the memory. The principle of encoding specificity explains this as another example of cue-dependent forgetting. Numerous other experiments have documented the principle that the specific cues associated with an event during learning provide the key to later recall (e.g., Begg & White, 1985; Jacoby, 1974).

Environmental Context. The context in which learning is experienced ought to serve as a retrieval cue at the time of test, according to the encoding specificity principle. This has been tested by varying the environmental and psychological context in a large number of experiments. Of interest to students, Smith, Glenberg, and Bjork (1978) had people learn a list of words in a particular room and then later try to recall them in the same room or in one very different in appearance. The environmental context affected recall in the direction one would expect. The same room provided the right retrieval cues and supported superior performance. Although the effect was not large, it might pay off to study for an exam in the same room in which you will be tested.

A more compelling demonstration of the importance of reinstating the encoding context was provided by Godden and Baddeley (1975). Scuba divers learned a list of words underwater or on dry land. They were then tested in one of these two contexts, and the results showed a strong crossover interaction, as shown in Figure 5.4. Recall dropped substantially when learning occurred on dry land but then testing was underwater. However, when learning was underwater, performance improved by going underwater again at test relative to testing on land.

Psychological Context. The emotional state of the individual also may serve as an effective retrieval cue. A **mood congruence effect** may be studied by instructing people to think about positive or negative life events in order to induce a happy mood or an unhappy mood. Bower (1981) found that the best learning occurs when the material being learned fits with the induced

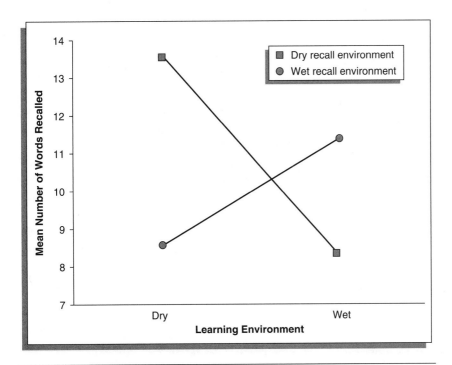

Figure 5.4   Number of words recalled in a dry or wet environment after learning in a dry or wet environment.

SOURCE: From Godden, D. R., & Baddeley, A. D., Context-dependent memory in two natural environments: On land and underwater. *British Journal of Psychology, 66,* 325-331. Copyright © 1975. Reprinted with permission.

mood. Thus, depressing information is best learned when in a sad mood (Blaney, 1986). **State-dependent learning** is sometimes observed when a person's mood or state of consciousness (e.g., sober, intoxicated) is directly manipulated during learning and retrieval. That is, recall performance when one's mood at retrieval matches the mood at the time of learning is not reliably better than when the moods do not match.

Several drugs, on the other hand, have shown state dependency effects when dosages are sufficiently large to produce clear signs of intoxication, such as slurred speech (Eich, 1980, 1989; Overton, 1971). These include commonly used drugs such as alcohol, barbiturates, and marijuana. Information learned in a sober state is better retained when later recalled in a sober state, whereas information learned in an intoxicated state is better retained when tested while intoxicated. As one would expect from what we know about the importance of cognitive effort and elaboration during study, recall is by far the best during sober learning and sober testing.

However, there is a strong asymmetry in the relationship (Eich, 1989). Alcohol and prescription drugs (e.g., benzodiazepines such as Valium and Xanax) reduce the encoding and storage of details about the context of an event (Curran, 2000). As illustrated in Figure 5.5, if one is sober at study, then retrieving the information at the time of test is relatively easy both when one is sober and when one is intoxicated. At times, intoxication at retrieval can, in fact, increase the amount remembered (Curran, 2000). By sharp contrast, when the learner is initially intoxicated at study, there is a consistent decline in performance when the retrieval mode is shifted to sobriety.

It should also be noted that intoxication during encoding greatly impairs the degree of learning in the first place. An alert and sober state of mind is required for successful learning (Curran, 2000). It has been known for centuries that drugs can cause forgetting. Alcohol is by far the most widely used drug with this feature, but millions of people also take antidepressants and antianxiety drugs that can cause some memory problems. The elderly are particularly vulnerable because they may combine medications that have psychoactive properties. For example, 10% to 15% of the population over 65 years of age take sleeping pills that can produce brief memory loss. In extreme cases, older adults can experience confusion and memory loss that resembles dementia. It is important for physicians to distinguish between true organic dementia and dementia that is temporarily induced by prescription medications.

> Tip of the tongue experiences and state-dependent learning show that the right retrieval cues are critical to successful recall, as predicted by the encoding specificity principle.

Application. The encoding specificity principle has important implications for medical, police, and legal professionals who rely on the recollections of

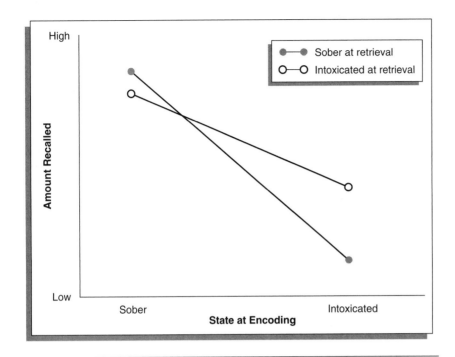

Figure 5.5   Asymmetry in drug-induced state-dependent learning.

an individual to determine the facts of a case. For example, doctors often try to obtain an accurate clinical picture by interviewing a patient about, say, eating habits. An accurate picture is needed to diagnose eating disorders, such as anorexia and obesity, and to understand the causes of diabetes, high blood pressure, heart disease, allergies, and other conditions. Unfortunately, our current eating habits distort recollections of past habits. If our current habits differ in important respects, then the information about the past is inaccurate (Croyle, Loftus, Klinger, & Smith, 1992).

To improve the accuracy of information obtained by medical, police, and legal professionals, Fisher and Geiselman (1992) developed the Cognitive Interview. The method is illustrated in Box 5.3. It entails asking respondents (a) to mentally picture the personal and environmental

---

BOX 5.3

Encoding and Retrieval Procedures Used in the Cognitive Interview Method

Try to form a mental image of all the circumstances surrounding the event.

Report everything you can remember about the event. Report even bits and pieces of information that are incomplete.

Recall the event in several sequences rather than just one.

Recall the event from several perspectives rather than just one.

context of the event to be remembered; (b) to report all recalled information, including partial information; (c) to recall the specific events in not just one order but several; and (d) to recall the specific events from several different perspectives. Notice that the first aspect of the procedure tries to reinstate the encoding context at the time of recall, in keeping with the encoding specificity principle. Partial information might serve as a retrieval cue for additional recovery of information, much as happens in the TOT phenomenon. Trying different orders and perspectives helps to avoid the use of a single schema for guiding the reconstruction of events. The Cognitive Interview improves the quality of information obtained in police questionings of eyewitnesses (Geiselman, Fisher, MacKinnon, & Holland, 1986) and in patients' recollections of food consumption (Croyle et al., 1992).

SUMMARY

1. Long-term memory is not a unitary store, according to the multiple systems hypothesis regarding the structure of long-term memory. There is a fundamental division in long-term memory between declarative (knowledge of what) and nondeclarative (knowledge of how) systems. Declarative memory is further divided into episodic memory (events that are encoded in terms of specific times and places of occurrence) and semantic memory (general knowledge of facts and concepts). Nondeclarative memory includes skill learning, priming, conditioning, and habituation.

2. Encoding and storage of episodic information in long-term memory varies with the kind of rehearsal given to information stored in short-term memory. Simply recycling information through attention and short-term storage, or what is called maintenance rehearsal, is not highly effective. Repeating a list of words illustrates maintenance rehearsal. Elaborative rehearsal is superior and depends on establishing links between the information held in short-term memory and the information already stored in long-term memory, for example, by forming visual images of the objects referred to by the words in a list. Mnemonic techniques, such as the method of loci, are kinds of elaborative rehearsal.

3. The level of processing also affects learning success, with deep semantic processing supporting better memory than shallow sensory processing. This probably reflects the importance of establishing a distinctive memory representation that can be easily retrieved in the future. Finally, the organization of newly learned information is necessary for successful recognition and recall.

4. Encoding processes are important, but they cannot be considered apart from retrieval processes. The encoding specificity principle asserts that events are recognized or recalled only when retrieval cues at the time of test match the encoding cues at the time of learning. The retrieval cues allow one to activate the to-be-remembered episode and its context. From this perspective, forgetting represents a failure to access an episode because the retrieval cues are inadequate.

KEY TERMS

episodic memory

declarative memory

semantic memory

nondeclarative memory

maintenance rehearsal

elaborative rehearsal

levels or depths of processing

self-reference effect

transfer-appropriate processing

distinctiveness

flashbulb memory

relational processing

subjective organization

retrieval mode

encoding specificity

tip of the tongue (TOT) state

mood congruence effect

state-dependent learning

CHAPTER 6

MEMORY DISTORTIONS

Each day, one has countless thoughts, fantasies, and recollections about the events of earlier in the day, last week, or years ago. When we fantasize about events that may happen in the future, there is no confusion about whether the mental experience accurately reflects reality. However, when we think back on events from the past, the possibility of confusing our memory of events with the actual events that transpired is quite real. Where is the line that separates fantasies about the past from accurate recollections? How does one know that an event is not distorted in minor or even major ways? Memory distortion can be more pernicious than forgetting because the rememberer may not be able to tell that the recollection is in error.

As will be seen in this chapter, there are several ways in which encoding, storage, and retrieval processes can lead to inaccurate, distorted episodic memory. This chapter also documents the role of organized sets of concepts or schemas in constructing episodic representations at encoding and in reconstructing them at retrieval. An episodic memory is influenced by the general knowledge of the world stored in semantic memory. The rich warehouse of semantic memory is necessary for the abstract thinking capacities of humans, but it can get in the way of perfectly accurate memories of past events.

RECONSTRUCTIVE RETRIEVAL

Schemas play a critical role in perception by providing expectations, as discussed in Chapter 2. They play a similar crucial role in memory. The schemas of long-term memory represent everything that we know. These schemas are intricately organized in a complex web of relations. The concepts and facts of semantic memory and the specific autobiographical events of episodic memory are linked in countless ways.

Imagine a scenario of a cat prowling for mice. Where might the cat find mice? In a barn on a farm, of course. Immediately, images of farms come to mind. You might recall the farm you grew up on, one you visited as a child, or one you saw in a movie last week. In turn, images of cows, pigs, horses, and other farm animals might then come to mind. The thought of a horse would perhaps bring to mind the time you went horseback riding with friends. More images pop into your mind as you reflect on each of the friends on the trip. The possibilities of such free association are endless because the schemas of long-term memory are massively interconnected. As a result of such organization, virtually any thought, through some chain of associations, can lead to any other thought.

Much, if not all, of what we learn and retrieve from memory passes through the organizational web. The schemas provide expectations that help us to learn but also, at times, to miss events that do not fit with these expectations. The schemas help us to remember but also, at times, to distort memories in order to conform to momentary expectations. The key point here is that schemas enable us to fabricate how past events most likely unfolded. The term **reconstructive retrieval** refers to schema-guided construction of episodic memories that interpret, embellish, integrate, and alter encoded memory representations.

> The term reconstructive retrieval refers to schema-guided construction of episodic memories that interpret, embellish, integrate, and alter encoded memory representations.

Many experiments have documented that recall may, at times, be driven by a schema-based reconstructive process. For instance, Brewer and Treyens (1981) showed how our recollections of places are schema based. After waiting in an experimenter's office for 35 seconds, people were taken to another room and asked to recall the office (see Figure 6.1). Virtually everyone recalled that the office had a chair, a desk, and walls, but only about one of four participants recalled unexpected items such as a skull. Moreover, items that fit preconceptions about a psychologist's office, such as books, were falsely recalled by some participants.

Figure 6.1　　Office scene used in a study of reconstructive retrieval.

SOURCE: From Brewer, W. F., & Treyens, J. C., Role of schemata in memory for places. *Cognitive Psychology, 13,* 207-230, copyright © 1981. Reprinted with permission.

Reconstructing Laboratory Events

The role of schemas in text comprehension and memory is particularly well-researched (Bower, Black, & Turner, 1979; Dooling & Christiansen, 1977; Spiro, 1980). These and numerous related experiments took as their starting point the classic work by Bartlett (1932) on schemas and reconstruction. Particularly well-known are Bartlett's studies in which participants tried to recall a folk tale of North American Indians—the War of the Ghosts. Before discussing the results, try reading the story shown in Box 6.1. Then, after 15 minutes or so, test yourself by trying to write down the story from memory, without going back and rereading it.

BOX 6.1

The "War of the Ghosts" Story Used by Bartlett

One night two young men from Egulac went down to the river to hunt seals, and while they were there it became foggy and calm. Then they heard war cries, and they thought, "Maybe this is a war party." They escaped to the shore and hid behind a log. Now canoes came up, and they heard the noise of paddles and saw one canoe coming up to them. There were five men in the canoe, and they said, "What do you think? We wish to take you along. We are going up the river to make war on the people."

One of the young men said, "I have no arrows."

"Arrows are in the canoe," they said.

"I will not go along. I might be killed. My relatives do not know where I have gone. But you," he said, turning to the other, "may go with them."

So one of the young men went, but the other returned home.

And the warriors went on up the river to a town on the other side of Kalama. The people came down to the water, and they began to fight, and many were killed. But the young man heard one of the warriors say, "Quick, let us go home; that Indian has been hit." Now he thought, "Oh, they are ghosts." He did not feel sick, but they said he had been shot.

So the canoes went back to Egulac, and the young man went ashore to his house and made a fire. And he told everybody and said, "Behold, I accompanied the ghosts, and we went to fight. Many of our fellows were killed, and many of those who attacked us were killed. They said I was hit, and I did not feel sick."

He told it all, and then he became quiet. When the sun rose, he fell down. Something black came out of his mouth. His face became contorted. The people jumped up and cried.

He was dead.

SOURCE: From Bartlett, F. C. (1932). *Remembering: A study in experimental and social psychology.* Reprinted with permission of Cambridge University Press.

Several features of Bartlett's results indicated that recall took place through an attempt to fabricate or reconstruct the original story. Within 15 minutes of reading the story, people recalled an abstracted summarized version. Three kinds of errors occurred through reconstructive retrieval. **Leveling** refers to a loss of details. The story was leveled to a shorter version. In particular, unfamiliar terms and ideas were omitted. For example, the place called "Kalama" might be forgotten in describing the warriors' journey. Or, the number of men in the canoe might be dropped. Or, the term "town" might be remembered as "village" because our knowledge about Indians includes the assumption that they reside in villages.

The reconstruction also resulted in the assimilation of events into a schema. **Assimilation** means that the recollection was rationalized or normalized to fit with preconceived notions. For example, the Indian who had been shot might be described as "hurt" or "wounded" because these terms are more in keeping with our general knowledge. The actual term used (i.e., "sick") might be assimilated to a schema about battles and being shot. Or, one might falsely remember that the two young men were going fishing on the river rather than hunting seals.

Finally, besides losing details and altering them to fit expectations, the participants embellished some facts. **Sharpening** refers to remembering details that were not actually stated but that could be inferred from general knowledge. For example, one might remember that "they told him he was hit by an arrow." The story did not actually say anything about an arrow hitting the Indian, but it could be readily inferred from the facts given in the story and from general knowledge about battles among Indians. Remembering that many were wounded in the battle is another example of drawing inferences from a schema. All that was stated is that many were killed; it was not stated directly that some were injured but not killed. The battle schema might again support an inference that not all of the wounds were fatal.

Thus, reconstructive recall causes the loss of some details and the erroneous inclusion of other details. Inferences were drawn based on general knowledge rather than on what was actually stated in the story. Other facts were assimilated into the schema so that it reflected general knowledge rather than the original story. Over hours, weeks, months, and years, repeated attempts to recall the story magnified all of these distortions. Each retelling of the story provided yet another opportunity for a creative reconstruction of a story that bore less and less resemblance to the original narrative.

For comparison purposes, consider the recall of an individual who lacked normal reconstructive processes. Shown in Panel (a) of Box 6.2 is the story as it was recalled by "S.," who, as you may remember from Chapter 5, recalled events verbatim in remarkably accurate detail. Astonishingly, this recall protocol was collected one year after S. heard the story. In Panel (b) is a typical recall protocol from a college student after a retention interval of only 15 minutes. Examine the story for examples of leveling, assimilation, and sharpening, and notice their conspicuous absence from the recall of S.

Bartlett's pioneering research was strong on theory but weak on methodology. Yet his basic findings stand up under rigorous experimental design and

---

BOX 6.2

a. Recall of the "War of the Ghosts" by a Mnemonist (V.P.) One Year After Hearing the Story

One day two young men from Egliac went down to the river to hunt seals. While there, it suddenly became very foggy and quiet, and they became scared and rowed ashore and hid behind a log. Soon they heard the sound of paddles in the water and canoes approaching. One of the canoes, with five men in it, paddled ashore, and one of the men said, "What do you think? Let us go up-river and make war against the people."

"I cannot go with you," said one of the young men. "My relatives do not know where I have gone. Besides, I might get killed. But he," said he, turning to the other young man, "will go with you." So one of the young men returned to his village, and the other went up-river with the war party.

They went to a point beyond Kalama, and the people came down to the river to fight them, and they fought. Soon the young man heard someone say, "This Indian has been wounded." "Maybe they are ghosts," he thought, because he felt perfectly okay. The war party suggested leaving, and they left, and the young man went back to his village.

There he lit a fire in front of his abode, sat down to await the sunrise, and told his story to the villagers. "I went with a war party to make war with the people. There was fierce fighting, and many were killed, and many were wounded. They said I was wounded, but I did not feel a thing. Maybe they were ghosts."

He had told it all, and when the sun came up, he gave a little cry. Something black came out of his mouth. He fell over. He was dead.

SOURCE: Hunt and Love (1972).

BOX 6.2

**b. Recall by an Undergraduate
Student 15 Minutes After
Hearing the Story**

Two men went down to the water to fish for
seals. It became calm and foggy. They heard
noises, so they went to shore and hid behind a
log. They heard the sound of paddles and saw a
canoe coming closer. The canoe had five men in
it, and they asked the two men to come fight
with them. The man first said he had no arrows,
but the men in the canoe said there were plenty
in the canoe. Next he said he could not go
because his relatives did not know where he
was, but he told the other man he could go. So
the other man went with them to fight, and the
first man went home. When they got to the
village, the people came down to the water to
fight. Then the man heard the Indians say to
hurry up and leave because he had been shot.
He thought they were fighting ghosts, and he
told the village he was in the presence of ghosts
because they had shot him and he did not feel
sick. When he finished his story, he became
silent. The next morning, he fell over. Something
black came out of his mouth. The people
watched him as he died.

---

data analysis procedures (Bergman &
Roediger, 1999). With instructions to
recall the story in a verbatim manner,
participants got less than 20% right after
a delay of only 15 minutes. As shown
in Figure 6.2, the degree of accuracy
dropped by half after a week and by half
again after six months. By contrast, major
distortions in elements of the text propositions held constant over these time
intervals. The latter included normalizing
events to fit a schema (e.g., replacing
"canoe" with "boat," replacing "hunting
seals" with "fishing") or using a schema to
infer a missing detail (e.g., recalling the
Indian was hit by an "arrow" even though
the story fails to specify this detail).

Reconstructing
Autobiographical Events

Much is now also known about the
way we reconstruct autobiographical
memories of personal, as opposed to
public, events (Conway, 1992). The terrorist attack on the World Trade Center
was a public event. You know about the
events in New York City on September
11, 2001 because of news accounts, even if you were not there to experience
them firsthand. The events of your 10th birthday, on the other hand, are
known only by you, your parents, and perhaps a few other people. An autobiographical event is one that you personally experienced.

Conway (1992) found that people remembered autobiographical events
in terms such as "when I lived in X" or "when I worked for Y." Such lifetime
periods as these extended over years or even decades. These periods are the
first level of retrieval cues that serve to orient us in autobiographical time and
trigger more specific recollections. A lifetime period might evoke moods, significant goals, or general themes of the period but not concrete events. A
second level of retrieval cues is general events. These are chronologically
organized personal experiences that cluster about thematically important

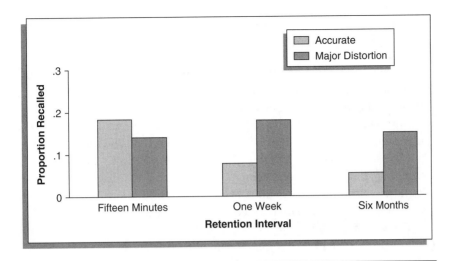

Figure 6.2   Proportions of text propositions recalled of the War of the Ghosts after varying retention intervals.

SOURCE: From Bergman, E. T., & Roediger, H. L., III., Can Bartlett's repeated reproduction experiments be replicated? *Memory & Cognition, 27*(6), 937-947, copyright © 1999. Reprinted with permission of the Psychonomic Society.

landmarks in time. First-time experiences such as falling in love, taking a first job, graduating from high school, and moving away to college serve to remind one of related general events. A third level of retrieval cues consists of concrete images or sensory replays of a specific event. In Conway's view, these detailed recollections are always integrated with schema-based representations of general events. What seems like a discrete recollection is, in fact, tied into higher levels of memory structure.

Recalling one's life inevitably uncovers the significant general events or episodes that define the self. They are recalled not as isolated events but rather as part of a narrative that gives life meaning (Bruner, 1990). Life narratives provide us with a sense of who we are, but that says nothing about their accuracy. In addition to life narratives, people recall flashbulb memories of public events, such as the 1986 *Challenger* explosion, and unique personal experiences (Neisser & Libby, 2000). Personal experiences can be particularly well-remembered. Individuals who experienced the 1989 Loma Prieta earthquake in California provided accounts written a year and a half after the event that were highly similar to those written only a few days after the earthquake (Neisser, Winograd, Bergmand, Schreiber, Palmer, & Weldon, 1996).

Historians are often faced with the task of weighing autobiographical accounts against other known information. For example, John Adams, at 86 years of age, recalled with remarkable clarity his conversation, 50 years earlier, with Thomas Jefferson over the authorship of the U.S. Declaration of Independence. Adams wrote in a letter to Thomas Pickering that Jefferson asked him to draft the declaration and demanded to know why Adams would not do so. "Reasons enough," Adams declared. "Reason first—You are a Virginian, and a Virginian ought to appear at the head of this business. Reason second—I am obnoxious, suspected, and unpopular. You are very much otherwise. Reason third—You can write ten times better than I can." "Well," Jefferson replied, "if you are decided, I will do as well as I can." Jefferson, for his part, denied Adams's story and insisted that a five-member committee of the Second Continental Congress had appointed him to author the most famous document in American history (McGlone, 1998, p. 413).

The verbatim detail of Adams's account is worrisome, suggesting that it might reflect a schema-based sharpening of details that were in error. In fact, McGlone (1998) noted that Adams had recalled the story differently 20 years earlier in another letter to Pickering. Moreover, in working on his autobiography in 1805, Adams could not recall what he had said. What is more, in his earliest account in 1779, Adams explained to a French diplomat that a committee of five members had appointed Jefferson to draft the document. His first account, closest in time to the actual events, accorded with Jefferson's recollection! Thus, Adams's later fabrication about Jefferson offering the authorship to him illustrates how an event representation becomes integrated with schemas representing general autobiographical knowledge (Conway, 1992). Over the years, Adams's story changed as he entered new periods in his life, with some elements dropping out as novel elements were added.

ENCODING DISTORTIONS

In addition to reconstructive retrieval, schemas sometimes constructively distort memory during encoding in multiple ways. The strength and generality of these effects are in dispute (Alba & Hasher, 1983; Mandler, 1984). So, we focus on three that are reasonably well-supported to illustrate constructive effects: **selection**, **interpretation**, and **integration**.

Selection

The selective encoding of information that fits with prior knowledge defines selection. This idea was well-illustrated in an experiment by Bransford and Johnson (1972). They presented people with the following obscure text:

The procedure is actually quite simple. First you arrange items into different groups. Of course one pile may be sufficient depending on how much there is to do. If you have to go somewhere else due to lack of facilities, that is the next step; otherwise, you are pretty well set. It is important not to overdo things. That is, it is better to do too few things at once than too many. In the short run this may not seem important, but complications can easily arise. A mistake can be expensive as well. At first, the whole procedure will seem complicated. Soon, however, it will become just another facet of life. It is difficult to foresee any end to the necessity for this task in the immediate future, but then, one never can tell. After the procedure is completed, one arranges the materials into different groups again. Then they can be put into their appropriate places. Eventually they will be used once more, and the whole cycle will then have to be repeated. However, that is part of life. (p. 722)

In first reading this, you likely felt what Bartlett (1932) called an "effort after meaning" as various schemas actively struggled to shape the sentences into a comprehensible pattern. Without knowing the title or topic of the text in advance it is difficult to select the sentences to fit into a preconceived schema, and therefore comprehension is poor and so is subsequent recall. The data from Bransford and Johnson's (1972) experiment show this plainly in the first column of Figure 6.3. However, when given the topic of "washing clothes" before reading the text, participants' ratings of comprehension and recall scores both improved greatly. Notice that receiving the topic after reading failed to help. The schema must be active to select details at the time of learning.

Interpretation

Inferences and suppositions are made to conform new material to activated schemas; these define interpretation. Prior knowledge provides a basis for interpreting the meaning of events, and these interpretations become part of memory. Johnson, Bransford, and Solomon's (1973) results illustrate interpretation well. Consider these two versions of a brief passage that were presented to different groups of people:

1. John was trying to fix the birdhouse. He was pounding the nail when his father came out to watch him and to help him do the work.

2. John was trying to fix the birdhouse. He was looking for the nail when his father came out to watch him and to help him do the work.

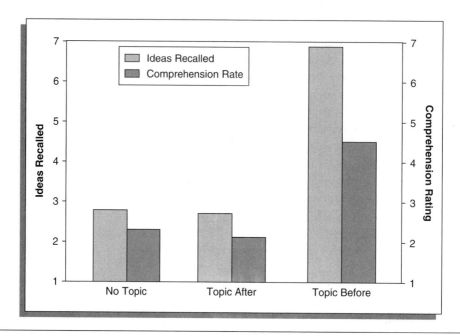

Figure 6.3   Recall and comprehension of the "washing clothes" story.

SOURCE: From Bransford, J. D., & Johnson, M. K., Contextual prerequisites for understanding: Some investigations of comprehension and recall. *Journal of Verbal Learning and Verbal Behavior, 11,* 717-726, copyright © 1972. Reprinted with permission.

The two passages were the same but for a minor change. Johnson et al. (1973) later gave a recognition test that included the following novel sentence:

3. John was using the hammer to fix the birdhouse when his father came out to watch him and to help him do the work.

The researchers found that the group of individuals who had read Passage 1 was much more likely to say that they had previously seen Passage 3 in the experiment. The false recognition of Passage 3 indicates that these individuals inferred that John was using a hammer, an assumption that fits well with the expectations of schemas activated by the passage.

Integration

The third type of encoding distortion, integration, refers to combining features of different events into a unified memory representation. As a result of integration, we remember the main idea or gist of an event rather than the details of its occurrence. Bransford and Franks (1971) investigated integration by presenting people with a long list of sentences. In Figure 6.4, you can read a sample of these sentences. Answer the question after each one to ensure that you comprehended each sentence.

Now take a moment to decide whether the sentences in Figure 6.5 are old sentences that appeared earlier in Figure 6.4 or are new sentences. Check old or new for each one before reading further in the text. After finishing the recognition test, count the number of items that you checked as old sentences.

Typically, people indicate that well more than half of the 30 sentences in Figure 6.5 are old sentences. In fact, none of the test sentences occurred earlier. The test sentences, however, represent plausible sentences based on the schemas that were activated in reading the original sentences. The individual features or ideas of the original sentences become integrated into larger organized ideas. The integration is so compelling that people actually are more confident that they saw a sentence containing all related ideas than they are about having seen sentences containing fewer ideas. This is exactly opposite of what one would expect if we stored the individual sentences in memory verbatim.

> Selection of a subset of event features, interpretation of events to fit preexisting schemas, and integration of features from multiple events are encoding failures that cause memory distortions.

Bransford and Franks's (1971) results are plotted in Figure 6.6. The number of ideas in the test sentence increased from one to four. Noncase sentences were totally novel and unrelated to the schemas activated during reading. They were readily rejected as new sentences. As you can see, the participants falsely recognized new sentences that contained more than one idea, and their confidence increased with each additional idea. The same result occurred for actual old sentences. These results plainly show how integration can distort memory by giving us the gist of the original events.

SOURCE MONITORING

Why is it that our fantasies, conjured during daydreams, are not later routinely confused as memories of real events? The vivid hallucinatory dreams of rapid eye movement (REM) sleep are still more puzzling. Given that they seem so real at the time, why are dreams not later remembered as having really occurred? One reason is that memory involves **source monitoring** processes (Johnson, Hastroudi, & Lindsay, 1993).

> Source monitoring refers to evaluative processes that attribute mental experiences to either external sources (i.e., perceived events) or internal sources (i.e., thoughts, fantasies, and dreams).

Instructions: Read each sentence, count to five, answer the question, and go on to the next sentence.	
Sentence	Question
The girl broke the window on the porch.	Broke what?
The tree in the front yard shaded the man who was smoking his pipe.	Where?
The hill was steep.	What was?
The cat, running from the barking dog, jumped on the table.	From what?
The tree was tall.	Was what?
The old car climbed the hill.	What did?
The cat running from the dog jumped on the table.	Where?
The girl who lives next door broke the window on the porch.	Lives where?
The car pulled the trailer.	Did what?
The scared cat was running from the barking dog.	What was?
The girl lives next door.	Who does?
The tree shaded the man who was smoking his pipe.	What did?
The scared cat jumped on the table.	What did?
The girl who lives next door broke the large window.	Broke what?
The man was smoking his pipe.	Who was?
The old car climbed the steep hill.	The what?
The large window was on the porch.	Where?
The tall tree was in the front yard.	What was?
The car pulling the trailer climbed the steep hill.	Did what?
The cat jumped on the table.	Where?
The tall tree in the front yard shaded the man.	Did what?
The car pulling the trailer climbed the hill.	Which car?
The dog was barking.	Was what?
The window was large.	What was?
STOP. Cover the preceding sentences. Now read each sentence in Figure 6.5 and decide whether it is a sentence from the list given above.	

Figure 6.4   A memory experiment: Part 1.

SOURCE: From Jenkins, J. J. (1974). Remember that old theory of memory? Well, forget it! *American Psychologist, 29,* 785-795, copyright © 1974, The American Psychological Association. Reprinted with permission.

Instructions: Decide whether each sentence is old or new.		
Sentence	*Old*	*New*
1. The car climbed the hill.		
2. The girl who lives next door broke the window.		
3. The old man who was smoking his pipe climbed the steep hill.		
4. The tree was in the front yard.		
5. The scared cat, running from the barking dog, jumped on the table.		
6. The window was on the porch.		
7. The barking dog jumped on the old car in the front yard.		
8. The tree in the front yard shaded the man.		
9. The cat was running from the dog.		
10. The old car pulled the trailer.		
11. The tall tree in the front yard shaded the old car.		
12. The tall tree shaded the man who was smoking his pipe.		
13. The scared cat was running from the dog.		
14. The old car, pulling the trailer, climbed the hill.		
15. The girl who lives next door broke the large window on the porch.		
16. The tall tree shaded the man.		
17. The cat was running from the barking dog.		
18. The car was old.		
19. The girl broke the large window.		
20. The scared cat ran from the barking dog that jumped on the table.		
21. The scared cat, running from the dog, jumped on the table.		
22. The old car pulling the trailer climbed the steep hill.		
23. The girl broke the large window on the porch.		
24. The scared cat which broke the window on the porch climbed the tree.		
25. The tree shaded the man.		
26. The car climbed the steep hill.		
27. The girl broke the window.		
28. The man who lives next door broke the large window on the porch.		
29. The tall tree in the front yard shaded the man who was smoking the pipe.		
30. The cat was scared.		
STOP. Count the number of sentences judged "old."		

Figure 6.5 A memory experiment: Part 2.

SOURCE: From Jenkins, J. J. (1974). Remember that old theory of memory? Well, forget it! *American Psychologist, 29,* 785-795, copyright © 1974, The American Psychological Association. Reprinted with permission.

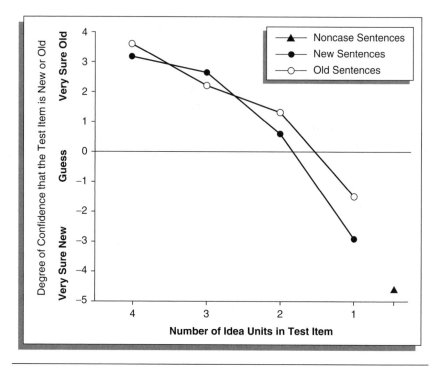

Figure 6.6   Confidence in recognition judgments for both old and new
sentences varies with the number of idea units expressed.

SOURCE: From Bransford, J. D., & Franks, J. J., Abstraction of linguistic ideas. *Cognitive Psychology, 2,* 331-350, copyright © 1971. Reprinted with permission.

Source monitoring refers to evaluative processes that attribute mental experiences to different sources. External sources are perceived events in the
environment, whereas internal sources are thoughts, fantasies, and dreams.

Memory Illusions

Discriminating external from internal sources is essential to avoid falling
victim to false memories of events that never happened. One of the most disturbing kinds of memory distortion is when one has the illusion of remembering an experience that in fact never happened (Roediger, 1996). Before
reading any further, try the demonstration given in Box 6.3. Read the list of
words one at a time at a rate of about one each second. Then look away from
the list and count backward from 60 at a slow and steady pace. Finally, try to
recall as many of the words from the list as you can in any order you like.

Numerous experiments using word lists similar to the one in Box 6.3 have enabled researchers to study an interesting illusion of memory (Deese, 1959; Roediger & McDermott, 1995). Check for yourself the accuracy of your recall. Were you able to recall words from the beginning of the list, showing the classic primacy effect? What about a recency effect? Were the final few items in the list remembered accurately? Typically, the middle items of the list are not particularly well-recalled. Many participants have trouble remembering "sill," "house," "open," "curtain," and "frame" but have no trouble at all remembering "window." The problem is that "window" was not, in fact, an item on the list. Remembering

BOX 6.3
A Memory Demonstration
Read each word in the following list at a rate of about one word per second. Next, count backward from 60 to 0 at a rate of about one number per second. Finally, without looking again at the list, write down as many of the words as you can remember.

door	sill	view
glass	house	breeze
pane	open	sash
shade	curtain	screen
ledge	frame	shutter

"window" is an illusion of memory. It illustrates what is called a **false verbal memory**, created as a result of hearing or reading a list of words that are semantically related to the falsely remembered word. The words actually presented in the list are "window's" top 15 associates in semantic memory—the words that come to mind in free-associating to the target word. People in such experiments may falsely recall the target word as often as half the time, at about the same level of accuracy as they recall words actually presented in the middle of the list.

The nonpresented target word (e.g., window) is activated as a result of seeing or hearing close semantic associates. As we will see in Chapter 7, semantic memory is organized according to similarity. A close associate of "window" is likely to activate the representation of "window" itself. With 15 close associates at work, "window" is strongly active in memory, creating an illusion of its having been actually presented. To avoid false recall, it is necessary to monitor items generated as potential targets and to distinguish between those with sensory plus semantic activation and those with only semantic activation. Thus, effectively monitoring the source of a memory can prevent the illusion. If one remembered "window" and then attributed this experience to an internal source (e.g., thinking about "window" as the other words were read or heard), then the intrusion could be edited from recall. An internal source presumably lacks the sensory features of sound and sight that ought to be available for true memories with external origins.

There is strong evidence that the availability of perceptual details helps people to avoid the illusion. For example, when a picture is presented along with each aurally presented word in the list, false recognition of the critical items is substantially reduced (Schacter, Israel, & Racine, 1999). The visual features of the pictures of actually presented words were distinctively different from internally generated intrusions of critical items, allowing participants to tell the two apart. In addition, Smith and Hunt (1998) found that reading the list of words, as compared with hearing the list, also helps participants to discriminate true memories from false memories of the critical items. As will be discussed in Chapter 8, reading activates representations of both the visual appearance of the words and the sound of words. Thus, participants have two kinds of perceptual details available in memory when reading the list of words. If you failed to experience the memory illusion after reading the list in Box 6.3, then try reading it aloud to a few friends and see whether they experience the illusion as a result of aural presentation.

Despite the strong behavioral evidence that distinctive perceptual details help one to avoid verbal false memories, it has proved difficult to capture these differences in brain activation patterns using neuroimaging methods (Curran, Schacter, Johnson, & Spinks, 2001). Attentional monitoring failures result in exceptionally high levels of false memories in patients with lesions in the prefrontal cortex (Melo, Winocur, & Moscovitch, 1999). Recall that the prefrontal cortex is a necessary region for the executive functions of working memory, such as attending to errors and inhibiting inappropriate responses.

Memory distortions can arise from reconstructive retrieval, flawed encoding, and failures to attribute mental experiences to the proper source. These factors are not unrelated, however. If the binding of features together into a cohesive event during encoding is disrupted, then errors in source memory can become more likely (Kroll, Knight, Metcalfe, Wolf, & Tulving, 1996). When researchers gave participants a list of words to study in which certain syllables could be combined differently to make new words, they sometimes observed binding failures. As shown in Figure 6.7, if the first and second syllables of "fiction" and "buckle" are not bound successfully, then the parts might be recombined into a word not actually presented—"fickle." Such a mistake is called a **conjunction error** because two syllables are incorrectly conjoined during recall and not noticed as a novel word. In this case, the conjunction error arises partly because of a failure (a) to encode the words properly and (b) to realize that "fickle" came from an internal rather than an external source. Kroll et al. (1996) discovered that patients with lesions in the hippocampal regions of the left hemisphere were three to four times as likely to make conjunction errors as were normal controls. Recall that this region is critical in encoding words for long-term storage.

Study	Binding Success	Binding Failure	Recall
decade	decade		decade
fiction		fic____	fickle Conjunction error
island	island		island
meeting	meeting		meeting
buckle		____kle	
police	police		police

Figure 6.7   Conjunction errors of memory.

Confabulation

Because cognition is so actively constructive, it is understandable that people can falsely recognize an event or include false intrusions in their otherwise accurate recollections of past events. However, can the constructive nature of cognition also cause one to generate a false past—an autobiographical history that never happened? Providing a narrative account of autobiographical events that never happened is called **confabulation**.

Serious pathological degrees of confabulating a past that never happened are characteristic of a variety of confusional states, including Korsakoff's syndrome, which is caused by chronic alcoholism (Kopelman, 1999). A key feature of Korsakoff's syndrome is severe anterograde amnesia, and poor memory for recent events usually accompanies this condition. Confabulations appear as spontaneous outpourings of recollections that the patient cannot control and cannot monitor as false. Sometimes, confabulations include bizarre events that could not possibly be true, and yet the patient appears perfectly satisfied that the events really happened.

Confabulation is, at least in part, a breakdown in the ability to attribute fantasies to an internal imagined source and to edit this content to prevent false recollections. The spontaneous confabulation seen in neurological patients is, indeed, associated with prefrontal cortical damage to the executive functions of working memory (Kopelman, 1999). The delusional memories seen in patients suffering from schizophrenia may appear to be similar to confabulations, but they do not arise from lesions in the prefrontal cortex. For example, Kopelman described a garage mechanic who claimed to have been responsible for a well-publicized murder of an aristocrat living in London eight years earlier. Although completely convinced of the truth of this story, the man had no other signs of memory problems and lived a seemingly normal life until he became preoccupied with the delusional "murder." It was his preoccupation with this false memory that led to his hospitalization and eventual diagnosis of schizophrenia.

EYEWITNESS TESTIMONY

Researchers are keenly interested in how constructive processes influence the accuracy of eyewitness testimony. Criminal trials in courts of law often depend on the firsthand testimony of witnesses to crimes. Assuming that a witness is not intentionally lying but rather is trying to provide an accurate account, just how certain can the judge and jury be that the testimony is correct?

Neisser (1981) analyzed the testimony of John Dean regarding meetings Dean had with President Nixon during the Watergate scandal of the early 1970s. Because Nixon had secretly taped conversations with Dean in the Oval Office, there was a transcript (with a few gaps) against which Dean's recollections could be checked. At the time of the congressional hearings at which Dean recounted his conversations with the president, news commentators found Dean's memory quite remarkable, given the many details he confidently offered in his testimony. Yet by comparing Dean's sworn testimony to the tape transcripts that the president eventually was forced to turn over to Congress, Neisser could identify the errors in Dean's testimony.

Reconstructive Retrieval

On the whole, Dean did very well in recalling the gist of what Nixon had said. Dean integrated information about different meetings and conversations into broad themes. Yet he also added faulty details. Regarding the September 15 meeting that had taken place nine months before Dean's testimony, Neisser (1981) observed,

Comparison with the transcript shows that hardly a word of Dean's account is true. Nixon did not say any of the things attributed to him here: He didn't ask Dean to sit down, he didn't say [H. R.] Haldeman had kept him posted, . . . he didn't say anything about [G. Gordon] Liddy or the indictments. Nor had Dean himself said the things he later describes himself as saying. (p. 9)

All of these faulty details were reconstructions of what Dean believed he must have heard, said, and done. Schemas most likely sharpened these details as Dean reconstructed the original events for his testimony.

Attorneys in criminal trials are well aware that the testimony of an eyewitness exerts a powerful influence on jurors. The members of a jury typically believe that eyewitness reports are accurate unless, for some reason, deliberate lying by the witness is suspected. In reality, eyewitnesses can fall victim to distortions of memory because of inaccurate encoding and retrieving of episodes (Loftus, 1979). Errors can and do occur, even when witnesses are confident that their testimony is accurate, leading in turn to wrongful convictions. According to some estimates, roughly 8,500 such miscarriages of justice occur each year in the United States alone, with as many as half attributable to incorrect eyewitness testimony (Loftus, 1986).

Besides focusing on reconstructive retrieval, efforts to explain these inaccuracies have focused on (a) selective encoding by the witness, (b) attempts to mislead the witness through slanted questioning, and (c) implanted memories. Adult eyewitness testimony is given substantial weight in criminal court proceedings despite the laboratory evidence documenting the potential for error (Ross, Read, & Toglia, 1994; Thompson, Hermann, Read, Bruce, Payne, & Toglia, 1998).

Selective Encoding

The scene of a crime might not be plainly visible because of poor lighting and fleeting glimpses of the perpetrator (Buckhout, 1974). Moreover, eyewitnesses to violent crimes, particularly when they are the victims, may experience such a tremendous level of stress that they fail to encode the events adequately. Selective encoding could, theoretically, diminish recall of a crime scene. To illustrate the principle in a less severe situation, the social anxiety of being the next in line to give a public address can lower subsequent recall of the speech given just before one's own speech (Bond & Omar, 1990). Because attention is focused inward on worries about taking the stage next, the previous speech is not encoded very well.

Not all scholars agree that emotional duress while witnessing a crime weakens encoding, however. For example, Christianson (1992) concluded that only the peripheral details of the crime tend to get lost under high levels of stress. The central features or gist of the event are often remembered especially well through effects of selective attention, elaboration, and distinctiveness. At a neurological level, the amygdala is involved in heightening memory for the gist of emotionally negative experiences (Adolphs, Denburg, & Tranel, 2001). Neurologically normal individuals better recall the gist of negative stimuli, accompanied by poorer memory for peripheral details, compared with neutral stimuli. In patients with bilateral damage to the amygdala, this normal pattern is reversed, such that the details of negative stimuli are remembered well but not the gist. It appears that the amygdala assists in selectively encoding the gist as opposed to the details of negative emotional events. Finally, as noted in Chapter 5, whatever information is encoded during emotional duress, it is likely to be consolidated well in long-term memory. Emotional arousal enhances the consolidation process (McGaugh, 2004). Thus, most errors in eyewitness testimony are likely to be caused by factors other than selective encoding.

In particular, memory for facial appearance is often remarkably accurate (Bahrick et al., 1975), possibly because face perception is served by a specialized module, as discussed in Chapter 2. However, a witness may still fail to recognize a stranger who has just committed a crime if the witness attended to, say, the weapon carried by the perpetrator rather than his or her face. The unexpected and rapid occurrence of the events in a crime may cause selective encoding that interferes with accurate identification (Naka, Itsukushima, & Itoh, 1996).

Errors in eyewitness identification are particularly likely when the police lineup is not properly composed (Wells, 1993). "Fillers" are individuals whom the police do not regard as suspects in the crime. If the fillers selected do not match the general description of the suspect given by the eyewitness prior to the lineup, then they do not serve as useful control cases. In the most extreme case, suppose that in a six-person lineup the five fillers look nothing at all like the person described by the witness. If an innocent suspect is the only one in the lineup who fits the description, then chances of misidentification are strong. Experiments using staged crimes have shown that misidentifications can exceed 90% when conditions at the time of the crime plus conditions at the time of the lineup conspire against the eyewitness.

The problem of misidentification in lineups is particularly acute when the witness and suspect are of different racial and ethnic backgrounds (Wells & Olson, 2001). For example, Asians recognize other Asians better than they recognize Caucasians, and the reverse relation also holds for Caucasians. Same-race identification is better than other-race identification. One explanation for this finding is that people attend more to the faces of people of their own race than they do to the faces of people of different races (Anthony, Copper, & Mullen, 1992; Chance & Goldstein, 1981). Recent evidence indicates that the greater familiarity of same-race faces results in a greater degree of holistic processing, which is known to mediate successful face recognition (Michel, Rossion, Han, Chung, & Caldara, 2006).

The Misinformation Effect

Work by Loftus and her colleagues has shown that the questions asked of eyewitnesses after an event can potentially influence their memory. When the questions contain misleading information they may distort memory, a finding called the **misinformation effect**. For example, Loftus and Palmer (1974) presented people with a film of a traffic accident and then questioned them, as might an investigator or an attorney, about what they had witnessed. One of several questions asked was "How fast were the cars going when they hit each other?"

In the various conditions of the experiment, the verb "hit" was replaced by more or less violent words, as shown in Figure 6.8. Later on in the experiment, the participants gave estimates of how fast the cars were traveling when the accident occurred. The results showed that the average speed estimate varied in direct relation to the wording of the question. By using the word "smashed," the interrogator apparently distorted the participants' memory representation of the accident, causing people to give high estimates of vehicle speed.

Moreover, a week later, new questions were posed such as "Did you see broken glass?" In fact, no broken glass appeared in the film, and 80% of the

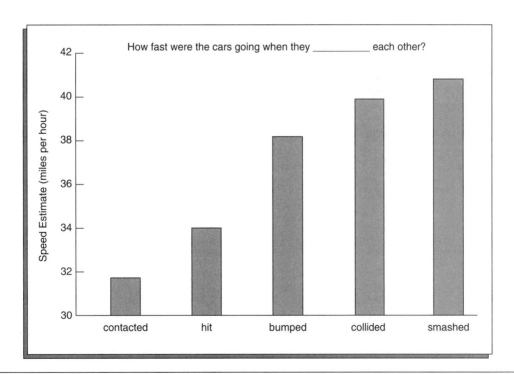

Figure 6.8   Data illustrating the misinformation effect.

SOURCE: From Loftus, E. F., & Palmer, J. C., Reconstruction of automobile destruction: An example of the interaction between language and memory. *Journal of Verbal Learning and Verbal Behavior, 13,* 585-589, copyright © 1974. Reprinted with permission.

participants correctly answered "no" to this question. Yet most of those who answered "yes" were in the condition that had been asked about the cars smashing into each other. As time wore on, the leading question continued to shape the nature of the recollection.

The misinformation effect can be strikingly large. Loftus, Miller, and Burns (1978) showed people a series of slides portraying an accident in which a red car stops at an intersection, turns the corner, and hits a pedestrian. Some participants saw a yield sign at the intersection but were asked either 20 minutes or a week later whether a second car passed the red car "while it was stopped at the stop sign." After providing the misleading information, Loftus et al. administered a recognition test that required participants to say which of a pair of slides had been part of the accident series. The key pair showed the red car at either a stop sign or a yield sign. When the misinformation occurred 20 minutes after the accident, the participants incorrectly picked the stop sign about 60% of the time. This rose to 80% when the misleading question was asked after a week.

When misleading information is given long after the witnessing of the event, it is likely to be more highly accessible and easy to retrieve at the time of test. The ease of retrieving the misinformation thus effectively blocks the retrieval of the original correct information (Eakin, Schreiber, & Sergent-Marshall, 2003). Besides misleading questions from a police interrogator, there is other misinformation to which eyewitnesses are susceptible, according to Eakin et al. For example, if the witness does not report the event right away and then discusses it with other witnesses, misinformation might come from the reports of those other witnesses. Misinformation might also come from news reports about the incident on television, for example.

> The misinformation effect refers to distortions in memory created by misleading information introduced through the questions used by an interrogator of a witness.

Implanted Memories

During criminal investigations, it is not uncommon for authorities to state repeatedly that a suspect was involved in a crime. *Memory implantation* refers to an individual creating a false memory in the mind of another person by means of suggestions and questions about the imagined event. Is it possible to implant false memories in an eyewitness to the crime by suggesting a suspect's guilt?

By intermixing true and false information, Loftus and Pickrell (1995) discovered that memory implantation is, in fact, theoretically possible. Adults were told by a close family member about three true events from their past plus one false event that they supposedly had experienced when they were between four and six years of age (e.g., getting lost in a shopping mall). The researchers found that some of the participants began to recall, from the suggestion alone, that they had been lost in a mall. Indeed, a few provided explicit accounts of how terrifying they had found the experience to be. The false recollections, in some cases, grew more detailed over time. Zaragoza and Mitchell (1996) found that repetitions of the suggestion increased the chances of participants' consciously recollecting the false event as actually having occurred. Thus, it is indeed possible to implant a memory, at least in laboratory circumstances, and the effects of repeated exposure to suggestions can be consistent across individuals and persistent over time.

Because of their suggestibility, children may be the most vulnerable to memory implantation when they are eyewitnesses to a crime (Ceci & Bruck, 1993, 1995). Laboratory research indicates that preschool-aged children are especially vulnerable to suggestion as compared with older children and adults. But clinical psychologists who specialize in working with abused children contend that such findings do not apply to important actions, particularly those involving a personal bodily experience. It is common for experts in clinical psychology, social work, and psychiatry to testify in court that children do not lie about events as traumatic as physical abuse and could not be falsely led through suggestion to believe abuse occurred. Although young children may be highly suggestible regarding unimportant peripheral events, there is reason to doubt that they are equally suggestible when it comes to sexual abuse.

Ceci, Leichtman, Putnick, and Nightingale (1993), however, reported that a false memory of having been kissed during a bath can indeed be planted in the mind of a young child. In an anatomical doll study, nearly a quarter to a third of 3-year-olds inaccurately answered abuse questions such as "Did he touch your private parts?" and "How many times did he spank you?" (Goodman & Aman, 1990). Such findings may imply that suggestion has led to a false memory, but Ceci and Bruck (1993, 1995) noted that children might also lie for social reasons (e.g., avoiding punishment, game playing, personal gain). Ceci, Crossman, Gilstrap, and Scullin (1998) reported seven experiments showing that the suggestibility of young children is not constricted to a single domain of unimportant peripheral events. They demonstrated children's suggestibility about embarrassing genital touching and painful events during checkups at a pediatrician's office. Ceci et al. concluded that "there is no event domain that is impervious to the deleterious effects of suggestions, especially when they are repeatedly delivered over long retention intervals" (p. 29).

Thus, memory implantation in eyewitnesses to a crime is a possibility, particularly for young eyewitnesses. Is it also possible to implant false memories in the mind of a confused, tired, and fearful suspect? Kassin and Gudjonsson (2004) explained that an interrogation of a person is undertaken only after an information-gathering interview has taken place to ascertain whether the person committed the crime. Once the person is identified as a suspect, the next step of interrogation is undertaken with the purpose of obtaining a confession. The methods used can be highly confrontational and accusatory. Repeated suggestions that the suspect committed the crime are a routine part of the interrogation procedure. It is not uncommon for the interrogator to claim he or she has evidence of the suspect's involvement and knowledge of the suspect's past. Through the process of social influence, it is theoretically possible that an innocent suspect may not only make a false confession, but also come to believe or internalize his or her guilt in committing the crime. A few murder cases have been identified as examples of such internalized false confessions, according to Kassin and Gudjonsson. Other exonerating evidence later came to light in the investigations that showed the suspect could not have committed the crime and proved the falsehood of the confession believed even by the suspect.

Recovered Memories

The tabloid press frequently reports cases of seemingly sane individuals who recall being abducted by aliens and taken aboard unidentified flying objects (UFOs), living past lives as other persons, being sexually abused during satanic rituals, or witnessing cannibalism of children (Loftus & Ketcham, 1994). From a scientific viewpoint, such reports are difficult to accept as anything other than false because they are so bizarre and implausible. How, then, might they be understood? One reasonable explanation is that such recollections are delusional false memories instilled through sociocultural mechanisms (Spanos, 1996). A **delusional false memory** is a false memory of an event experienced by an individual who has strong beliefs that a bizarre event could actually occur. It is not well-understood how a delusional belief originates, but the culture and social circles of the individual play a role, according to Spanos (1996). The delusional memory is implanted by suggestions coming from the sensational stories covered in tabloids; bizarre stories reported on television; and statements made by friends, family, and oneself, much as occurs under the effects of hypnosis.

Consider stories about encounters with a UFO, for example. Betty Hill was an avid believer in UFOs before the night that she and her husband, Barney, claimed to have seen a strange light following their car (Klass, 1989). Betty's sister suggested that she and her husband may have been "irradiated" by the light, and soon Betty began to have nightmares in which she and Barney were abducted by aliens who took them on board a UFO, communicated with them telepathically, performed medical tests, and showed Betty a star map. A psychotherapist who treated Betty for her nightmares used hypnosis to elicit detailed reports of these events from both her and Barney, who had heard these accounts from his wife numerous times. The psychotherapist concluded that the reports were delusional false memories shared by the couple. Such false memories, then, are likely similar to confabulations but differ in that the individuals do not suffer from lesions in prefrontal cortical regions. The power of their belief system constructs the delusional memories (Kopelman, 1999).

Repression. During the 1990s, numerous allegations of child abuse were reported by the victims as adults, years after the incidents had taken place. These forgotten memories of abuse sometimes surfaced while an adult was in therapy for severe emotional distress and an inability to cope with daily life (Olio, 1989). A famous case involved Eileen Franklin's recovered memory that her father, George, not only sexually abused her and her sisters but also abused and murdered her best friend 20 years earlier (MacLean, 1993). A clinician testified that Eileen had recovered a repressed memory of the murder. The trauma of the murder had caused Eileen to repress the memory throughout her childhood, according to the testimony in the trial. The defense cited the laboratory evidence that misleading questions and other factors can cause distortions in memory. The jury convicted George Franklin of murder. He served five years behind bars before his conviction was reviewed by an appeals court and overturned on the grounds that Eileen's recollections were probably false memories.

Therapists working with individuals who experience recovered memories typically have attributed these individuals' forgetting to **repression**. Repression generally refers to an inhibitory process of excluding events from retrieval. Although today repression is usually thought to occur unconsciously, in Freud's original conception of this process the term also referred to the conscious suppression of unwanted material (Erdelyi, 2001). According to classical Freudian theory, repression is a defense mechanism that protects the ego from anxiety by preventing unpleasant memories from entering consciousness. One can readily see why a person would be motivated to repress traumatic experiences and exclude them from consciousness to avoid the anxiety that traumatic memories provoke.

Another possibility suggested by memory researchers—and, interestingly, by Freud himself—is that supposedly lost and then recovered memories of sexual and other abuse are false memories. They may reflect the reconstructive processes of schemas, leading one to recall vividly events that never transpired. We have seen that strong laboratory evidence shows that false memories are possible. Do such findings have **ecological validity?** Do they generalize to actual real-world events? People can have false memories about a wide variety of everyday events that they hear or read about as well as those they personally experience (Neisser & Libby, 2000). It is unclear whether events as traumatic as child abuse can be falsely remembered, but it is certainly possible that suggestions from therapists and others may prompt the reconstruction of false memories.

> Recovered memories may reflect either the retrieval of a previously repressed event or an inaccurately reconstructed false memory.

A vocal debate over these issues has divided the therapeutic community and the academic research community (Lindsay & Read, 1994). Therapists, for their part, have generally maintained that the trauma of rape or other forms of child abuse can, indeed, produce amnesia for the events. Through the course of psychotherapy, the victim recovers these forgotten events as part of the healing process. Academic researchers, on the other hand, have generally argued that trauma-induced amnesia is rarely, if ever, the correct explanation. The recollections brought to consciousness are far more likely to be false memories inadvertently induced by the suggestions and practices of the therapist. The therapeutic techniques used to help an individual often include memory work; the individual regresses to an earlier age under hypnosis, receives sexually suggestive questions or dream interpretations from the therapist, or tries to remember childhood events while drugged with sodium amytal. The therapist tries to break through the defense mechanism of repression with these techniques. The client is not consciously trying to suppress thinking about the traumatic event. Rather, the client has no recollection of the event even occurring, although the trauma may be causing him or her anxiety or depression or may be responsible for an eating disorder, a sleep disorder, alcohol or drug abuse, or other significant difficulties. Abuse as a child is horribly traumatic, and so repression as well as conscious efforts to forget about the event are anticipated by the therapist (Olio, 1989).

The problem is that there is little sound empirical evidence that adults can forget traumatic events for years and then recover them accurately (Loftus, 1993; Spanos, 1996). Traumatic memories are notoriously difficult to suppress consciously and are a defining feature of posttraumatic stress syndrome. Victims recall trauma all too easily and frequently, possibly as a way of coping with what has happened to them. In some cases, traumatic memories are stored in a fragmented form that is susceptible to being forgotten (Shimamura, 1997). However, in these circumstances the memory fragments are highly susceptible to distortions and inaccuracies if they are reconstructed later. Thus, the repression and subsequent accurate recovery of sexual abuse memories is unlikely. This does not mean, however, that it is impossible. Some cases have been substantiated in which prior abuse was apparently forgotten and later recovered (Schooler, Bendiksen, & Ambadar, 1997).

Hypnosis and other techniques of recovered memory therapy have the strong potential of convincingly suggesting events that might never have taken place (Spanos, 1996). Normally, adults can monitor reality in order to draw a clear line between events stemming from memory and those generated in fantasy (Johnson, 1988), but this line can be tragically erased in so-called recovered memory cases by the methods of the therapy itself (Loftus, 1993). In some cases, the clients later came to realize that the recollections of sexual abuse uncovered through the practices of therapy were, in fact, false memories. The lives of everyone involved were shattered by the false accusations.

Trauma-Induced Amnesia. Recovered memory is not the only possible response to a real traumatic experience. According to Yuille and Daylen (1998), the impact of trauma on memory may well be complex, affecting different individuals in different ways. In some extreme cases, there may be a dissociation of consciousness, producing **trauma-induced amnesia**. This could cause the victim to experience the trauma as if it were happening to someone else or to travel mentally to a different place and time to psychologically avoid the trauma altogether. Dissociation may also affect the storage and retrieval phase by causing amnesia for events that were at one time remembered. Trauma-induced amnesia is rare, but cases have been documented (Schacter & Kihlstrom, 1989).

> Trauma-induced amnesia is a rare kind of dissociated consciousness. The victim experiences the trauma as if it were happening to someone else or psychologically avoids the trauma by mentally traveling to a different place and time.

Conclusions. As illustrated in Figure 6.9, there are several possible causes of recovered memories and different possible responses to traumatic events. As noted in Path A, one may remember the trauma all along or possibly repress the memory for a period of time before it is recovered (Path B). Another possible response to trauma is to forget the event altogether as a result of a dissociation of consciousness at the time of encoding (Path C). As shown in Path D, a recovered memory might also be false, the result of a belief that an event occurred (dotted line) rather than a perception of the event (solid line). Confabulation, misinformation, and memory implantation are possible sources of such false beliefs.

There are two important conclusions to draw from the controversy surrounding recovered memories. First, therapies used in clinical practice must

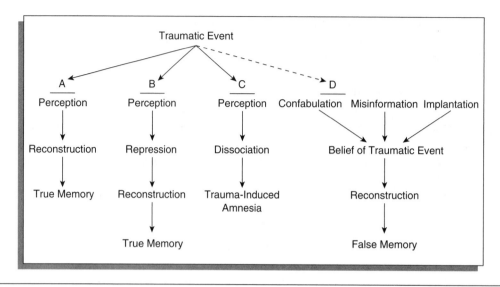

Figure 6.9   Four possible scenarios for the recollection of a traumatic event.

be critically examined to make certain that they do no harm. A technique may promise benefits, but these must always be weighed against its costs. Second, the ecological validity of laboratory studies on false memory must also be critically examined when drawing conclusions. The laboratory research demonstrates that false memories are real and helps to explain the experiences of patients in therapy. But this does not mean that trauma-induced amnesia never occurs or that forgotten trauma never resurfaces in or out of therapy. It is difficult, if not impossible, to examine in the laboratory the effects of severe physical or psychological trauma on human memory. For ethical reasons, the experiences of individuals who have been raped, beaten, shot at, or otherwise traumatized in real life can never, in principle, be evaluated in laboratory settings. Field and case studies of assault victims, combat veterans, and concentration camp survivors may offer insights into such effects, but they are never as definitive as well-controlled laboratory experiments.

SUMMARY

1. Schemas shape how events are retrieved from long-term memory. A schema is a set of organized concepts that provides expectations about the world. Just as schemas guide human pattern recognition from the top down, conceptually driven processes also guide the reconstruction of events from

memory. As a result, details of an event may be dropped from recollection, a process called leveling. Details may also be assimilated or normalized in order to fit the expectations provided by the schema. Finally, a schema-based reconstruction of an event may also sharpen details, elaborating a point by using general knowledge about the world rather than information actually encoded and stored.

2. Schemas also influence what is encoded and stored in episodic memory in the first place, causing memory distortions. They establish expectations that result in selection of the features of events that are encoded in the first place. Schemas also constructively guide the encoding of events through a process of interpretation. Inferences are drawn at the time of encoding as well as during reconstructive retrieval. Finally, schemas influence encoding through integration, which means that features of different events are combined into a unified memory representation. As a result of integration, we remember the main idea or gist of events rather than the details of their occurrence.

3. Source monitoring refers to evaluative processes that attribute mental experiences to different sources. External sources are perceived events in the environment, whereas internal sources are thoughts, fantasies, and dreams. A laboratory demonstration of a memory illusion shows that after a list of words closely associated with a target word is viewed, the target itself is falsely remembered as being on the list. In the illusion, the target word is activated internally but is incorrectly attributed to an external source. Normally, source monitoring processes enable us to easily differentiate between a fantasy and a real memory. These processes break down in Korsakoff's syndrome, which is associated with chronic alcoholism. The patient makes up false memories out of thin air. Confabulations appear as spontaneous outpourings of recollections that the patient cannot control and cannot monitor as false.

4. The constructive and reconstructive properties of human memory have important implications for our legal system. The reliability of eyewitness testimony has been studied extensively. Selective encoding, misleading questions used by interrogators, and the implantation of memories through hypnosis and therapy have been shown to distort recall in laboratory settings. The ecological validity of this research has been challenged. In particular, there is still considerable controversy over whether traumatic events, such as sexual abuse, can produce amnesia for an event that is later recovered. The suggestibility and credibility of young children as witnesses, or of adults who have recovered supposedly repressed memories of sexual abuse, are at the center of this debate.

KEY TERMS

reconstructive retrieval

leveling

assimilation

sharpening

selection

interpretation

integration

source monitoring

false verbal memory

conjunction error

confabulation

misinformation effect

delusional false memory

repression

ecological validity

trauma-induced amnesia

CHAPTER 7

KNOWLEDGE REPRESENTATION

Factual and conceptual knowledge constitute key ingredients in speaking and listening, in reading and writing, and in problem solving and thinking. Without an ability to acquire, represent, and use knowledge about the world and its meaningful symbols, high-level forms of human cognition would not be possible. It is through semantic memory that we categorize the world, allowing us to ignore the details and to see a specific object as a general kind. Lakoff (1987) aptly underscored the importance of categorization as follows:

> There is nothing more basic than categorization to our thought, perception, action, and speech. Every time we see something as a *kind* of thing, for example, a tree, we are categorizing. Whenever we reason about *kinds* of things—chairs, nations, illnesses, emotions, any kind of thing at all—we are employing categories. Whenever we intentionally perform any *kind* of action, say something as mundane as writing with a pencil, hammering with a hammer, or ironing clothes, we are using categories. The particular action we perform on that occasion is a *kind* of motor activity. . . . They are never done in exactly the same way . . . , yet . . . we know how to make movements of that kind. Any time we either produce or understand any

utterance of any reasonable length, we are employing dozens if not hundreds of categories: categories of speech sounds, of words, or phrases and clauses, as well as conceptual categories. Without the ability to categorize, we could not function at all, whether in the physical world or in our social and intellectual lives. (pp. 5–6)

In this chapter, the fundamental questions about the representation of knowledge in semantic memory are examined. First, the nature of concepts and how they are mentally represented is considered. Second, the question of whether concrete images are represented differently from abstract conceptual knowledge is weighed. Third, some models of how people use semantic memory to answer simple factual questions are presented.

REPRESENTING CONCEPTS

Concepts are the general ideas that enable the categorization of unique stimuli as related to one another. The concept of a tree, for example, allows for considerable variations in the individual examples of trees that fit the general idea. A tree concept includes a set of variable dimensions, such as the types of roots, trunks, branches, and leaves, that may be instantiated in a large number of ways. Many unique trees all fit the general concept. The stimuli categorized may be concrete objects or abstract ideas. Mathematical (e.g., imaginary numbers), philosophical (e.g., free will), and psychological (e.g., depression) concepts are among those that group together highly abstract entities.

Rule-Governed Concepts

The classical approach to categorization assumed that concepts are defined by a set of singly necessary and jointly sufficient features. In other words, the defining features of a concept were governed by a conjunctive rule stating that each and every feature must be present for an object to fit the concept. For example, the concept of a cow could be understood in terms of the features animate, four-legged, hoofed, female, adult, and other distinctive features that set the object apart from, say, a buffalo. **Rule-governed concepts** specify the features and relations that define membership in the class on an all-or-none basis (Bourne, 1970; Bruner, Goodnow, & Austin, 1956). The classical view of categorization regarded all concepts as rule-governed.

Some abstract concepts can be viewed as rule-governed. The definitions of real numbers, gravity, grand larceny, and a touchdown in American football can be specified by mathematicians, physicists, lawyers, or referees, for example. When a football is carried by the runner so that it crosses the vertical plane above the goal line of the opponent without being dropped, a touchdown is scored. This is not to say that reasonable people cannot argue whether a particular play in question resulted in a touchdown, but rules of football spell out the concept unambiguously. Fans may disagree about the features of the play, but not about the concept itself.

Not all abstract concepts fit the classical view very well, however (Lakoff & Johnson, 1980). For example, what are the defining features of truth or justice? Moreover, the objects encountered every day in the environment do not belong to rule-governed concepts (Rosch & Mervis, 1975; Smith & Medin, 1981)

Object Concepts

Object concepts refer to natural kinds (biological objects) and artifacts (human-made objects). They are often organized hierarchically in subordinate, basic, and superordinate categories. An example of a hierarchy of natural kinds would be *robin* (subordinate), *bird* (basic), and *animal* (superordinate) (Rosch, Mervis, Gray, Johnson, & Boyes-Braem, 1976). Similarly, *claw-hammer, hammer,* and *tool* illustrate a hierarchy of artifacts.

In contrast to rule-governed concepts, there did not appear to be any set of defining features for object concepts. The philosopher Ludwig Wittgenstein was the first to articulate that some linguistic categories seemed to defy the classical description by lacking defining features. For instance, take the concept of a "game." As Lakoff (1987) observed,

> Some games involve mere amusement, like ring-around-the-rosy. Here there is no competition—no winning or losing—though in other games there is. Some games involve luck, like board games where a throw of the dice determines each move. Others, like chess, involve skill. Still others, like gin rummy, involve both. (p. 16)

Games do have a "family resemblance" to one another. Each member shares some features in common with other members, but no set of defining features is common to all. Rather, what makes games a category is that the examples show similarities to one another in a wide variety of ways. Object concepts are ill-defined in that it is difficult to decide whether or not a particular poor example falls within the legitimate range of membership.

The fuzzy boundary of class membership can be readily seen from the results of Labov (1973), who presented people with the cup-like objects seen in Figure 7.1. Exactly at what point does an object cease to be a cup and become a bowl, a glass, or a mug? For instance, the first four items varied in terms of the ratio of the width of the cup to its depth. Labov's results showed

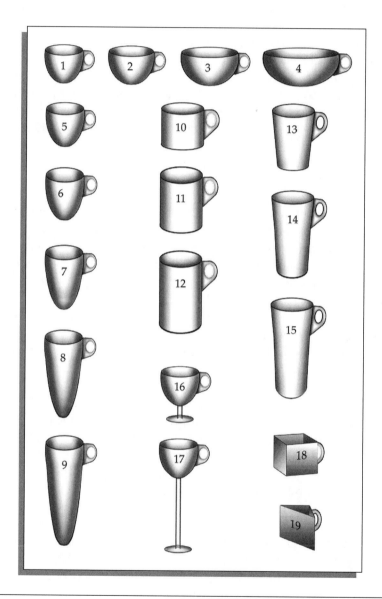

Figure 7.1   The boundary of the object concept of cup is fuzzy.

SOURCE: From Labov, W., The boundaries of words and their meanings, in C. J. N. Bailey & R. W. Shuy (Eds.), *New Ways of Analyzing Variations in English,* copyright © 1973. Reprinted with permission of Georgetown University Press.

that when participants were thinking about food, the probability of their calling the object a bowl increased gradually—not abruptly—as this ratio increased. Similarly, the probability of their calling the object a cup decreased gradually, but for middle ratios, both responses often occurred, reflecting the fuzzy boundary of membership. In a neutral context, the cup response became less likely, but people were more reluctant to call Item 3 or 4 a bowl. This difference in judgment with context shows the flexible boundary of object concepts; it shifts depending on which other concepts are active in memory.

Prototypes. An object differs from other members of a concept in terms of its features and the frequency of occurrence of these features in the category (Attneave, 1957). For example, birds differ from one another in terms of size, color, and shape of wings. The range and frequency of occurrence of these features is also represented; one easily understands that a turkey has rare features whereas a sparrow has more common features. The **prototype** is the best or most typical member of a category and serves as an important mental representation of the concept. Moving away from the prototype, there is a gradient of membership. At least for residents of North America, the robin assumes the role of prototype for the bird concept (see Figure 7.2). The turkey lies far out on the gradient from the prototype, whereas the blue jay and sparrow lie closer. The crow or the eagle falls in between these extreme cases.

Rosch and Mervis (1975) asked people to rapidly list all the features they could think of for a variety of common objects. The objects fit the

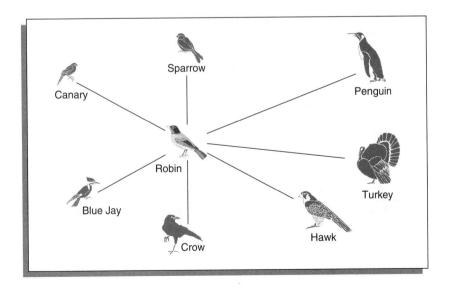

Figure 7.2   Typicality of members in a basic-level category.

Table 7.1   Typicality of Members in Superordinate-Level Categories

Item	Furniture	Vehicle	Fruit	Weapon	Vegetable	Clothing
1	Chair	Car	Orange	Gun	Peas	Pants
2	Sofa	Truck	Apple	Knife	Carrots	Shirt
3	Table	Bus	Banana	Sword	String beans	Dress
4	Dresser	Motorcycle	Peach	Bomb	Spinach	Skirt
5	Desk	Train	Pear	Hand grenade	Broccoli	Jacket
6	Bed	Trolley car	Apricot	Spear	Asparagus	Coat
7	Bookcase	Bicycle	Plum	Cannon	Corn	Sweater
8	Footstool	Airplane	Grape	Bow and arrow	Cauliflower	Underpants
9	Lamp	Boat	Strawberry	Club	Brussels sprouts	Socks
10	Piano	Tractor	Grapefruit	Tank	Lettuce	Pajamas
11	Cushion	Cart	Pineapple	Tear gas	Beets	Bathing suit
12	Mirror	Wheelchair	Blueberry	Whip	Tomato	Shoes
13	Rug	Tank	Lemon	Ice pick	Lima beans	Vest
14	Radio	Raft	Watermelon	Fists	Eggplant	Tie
15	Stove	Sled	Honeydew	Rocket	Onion	Mittens
16	Clock	Horse	Pomegranate	Poison	Potato	Hat
17	Picture	Blimp	Date	Scissors	Yam	Apron
18	Closet	Skates	Coconut	Words	Mushroom	Purse
19	Vase	Wheelbarrow	Tomato	Foot	Pumpkin	Wristwatch
20	Telephone	Elevator	Olive	Screwdriver	Rice	Necklace

SOURCE: From Rosch, E. H., & Mervis, C. B., Family resemblances: Studies in the internal structure of categories. *Cognitive Psychology, 7*, 573-605, copyright © 1975. Reprinted with permission.

superordinate categories of furniture (e.g., chair, piano, telephone), vehicle (e.g., car, tractor, elevator), fruit (e.g., orange, grapefruit, olive), weapon (e.g., gun, tank, screwdriver), vegetable (e.g., peas, lettuce, rice), or clothing (e.g., pants, pajamas, necklace). A total of 20 objects per category were used, and they clearly varied in typicality, as can be seen from the examples (see Table 7.1).

The key outcome was that few features applied to all 20 objects. Those few that were common to all failed to distinguish the category from numerous other natural categories (e.g., "You eat it" was listed for all fruits, yet this applies to all foodstuffs). What defined the category was not a small set of defining features but rather a large number of features that applied to some, but not all, instances. Rosch and Mervis (1975) referred to this as the **family resemblance structure** of object concepts. The researchers computed a family resemblance score that reflected the sum of the frequency with which features applied to all instances of the category. They found that this family resemblance score correlated strongly with ratings of typicality. Thus, "orange" and "apple" achieve high typicality ratings in the "fruit" category because they exhibit features that occur frequently among all members of the category. "Tomato" and "olive" are given low typicality ratings because their features are not characteristic of most fruits.

The speed with which people categorize an example varies with how close it is to, or how far it is from, the prototype. One can correctly categorize a robin as a bird faster than one can a crow, which in turn can be categorized faster than can a turkey (Rosch, 1975). The order in which children learn the members of a category also depends on their typicality. Highly typical instances are acquired sooner than are atypical instances (Rosch, 1973). The **typicality effect** refers to the gradient of category membership, or differences in how well specific instances represent a concept.

> Object concepts have fuzzy boundaries and a gradient of category membership, with some instances more typical than others.

Concepts as Theories. Object concepts are also coherent in that they are integrated with other concepts through theories about how the world is structured. Put differently, a concept is embedded in and consistent with people's background knowledge and **folk theories** (Keil, 1989; Medin & Ortony, 1989; Murphy & Medin, 1985). For example, a person's knowledge and intuitions about biology dovetail with the concept of a bird. If a person believes that birds breathe, eat, and reproduce, then these abstract theoretical constraints would lead one to reject a robotic manufactured robin as not really being a robin. It may look and act exactly like a robin, but if the person knows it is not an animate object, then it fails to fit the concept.

A concept can be coherent even when there are no obvious perceptual or functional similarities among its instances. For example, what are the similarities that put children, money, photo albums, and pets in the same category? Without considering how the concept is embedded in a person's knowledge about the world, this makes no sense at all. However, in the context of "things to take out of the house in case of a fire," individuals are able to list these and other examples without difficulty (Barsalou, 1983). In this case, then, the concept is coherent only by considering, in relation to the nature of fires, the importance of personal property and related world knowledge.

Similarity to perceptual and functional features, then, provides only part of the story of how human categorization works. Deeper, less accessible, theory-based features about the internal structure of natural kinds of objects (e.g., the genetic structure of a dog) constrain our categorizations as well as surface features (Gelman, 1988; Keil, 1989). The representation of a dog in semantic memory includes a theory about the internal structure of the organism. It is this internal structure that really makes a dog a dog. The functional uses of a dog (e.g., hunting) are less relevant to its classification, but functional uses are absolutely critical for artifacts such as a cup (e.g., drinking). Barton and Komatsu (1989) gave participants descriptions of objects that were either natural kinds or artifacts. The researchers changed either the internal molecular structure (e.g., a goat with altered chromosomes, a tire not made of rubber) or the functional features (e.g., a female goat not giving milk, a tire that cannot roll) of the examples to see how these different types of features affected categorizations. They discovered that changes in molecular structure were most important for natural kinds (e.g., a goat with altered chromosomes is not really a goat), whereas the opposite was true for artifacts (e.g., a tire that cannot roll is not really a tire).

Artifacts and natural kinds may be differentiated at a neural level of representation. Patients with associative agnosia can have highly specific losses in their ability to make semantic categorizations. For example, one patient, "J.B.R.," lost the ability to identify the names of objects of living things, such as dogs and horses, but had little trouble with inanimate objects, such as umbrellas and chairs (Warrington & Shallice, 1984). Recall from Chapter 2 that the temporal lobe serves as the termination point for the lateral "what" pathway involved in object recognition. Patients with lesions in different regions of the temporal lobe experience deficits in naming particular categories of objects (Damasio, Grabowski, Tranel, Hichwa, & Damasio, 1996). As shown in Figure 7.3, damage to the anterior region of the temporal cortex causes problems in naming the faces of famous people. Damage to the inferotemporal cortex, along the lower region, is associated with problems in naming animals. Lastly, naming tools was problematic for patients with lesions near the intersection of the temporal, occipital, and parietal lobes.

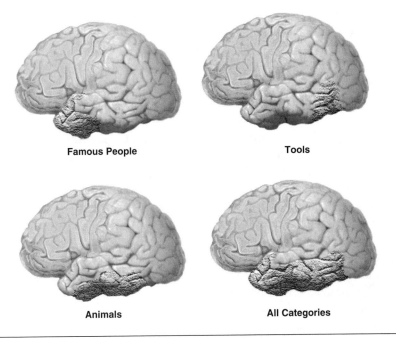

Famous People

Tools

Animals

All Categories

Figure 7.3   Regions in the temporal lobe are associated with representations of specific semantic categories.

Schemas

As discussed in earlier chapters, a schema is a cognitive structure that organizes related concepts and integrates past events. We saw that schemas are important in understanding the constructive aspects of perception and memory. Researchers have delineated specific kinds of schemas in developing theories of knowledge representation. For example, **frames** are schemas that represent the physical structure of the environment. Minsky (1977) proposed the term in his theoretical analysis of the perception of a complex visual scene such as a room or the office considered in Chapter 6. Frames are also used in generating mental maps of the environment and in other forms of remembering and imagining. The essence of a frame is a detailed structural description that specifies the concepts and the relations among concepts that define a given physical environment.

Scripts are schemas that represent routine activities (Abelson, 1981; J. M. Mandler, 1984). They are usually sequential in nature and often involve social interactions. Schank and Abelson (1977) described the restaurant script to illustrate this schema. Each script specifies a theme (eating in a restaurant), typical roles (customer and waiter), entry conditions (hungry customer), and a sequence of scenes and actions within scenes (ordering, which involves getting a menu, reading a menu, etc.). Cantor, Mischel, and Schwartz (1982) studied common social situations and found that they are organized in a stereotypical manner. People can readily describe a prototypical blind date or job interview, for instance.

> Frames and scripts organize conceptual knowledge about the physical environment and routine activities, respectively.

The sequential nature of many scripts affects their use in perception and memory. Barsalou and Sewell (1985) asked people to recall scenes from a script or examples from an object concept in order of typicality, from the most representative to the least representative. In the case of a script (how to write a letter), recall proceeded at a steady rate, as if the people searched memory in an orderly sequential fashion. By contrast, in the case of an object concept (tool), recall started at a rapid rate, as people quickly retrieved prototypical examples and then slowed progressively.

Meta-representations

So far, semantic memory has been discussed as a system for faithfully representing reality through object representations. However, it is known that during the second year of life, an infant learns to pretend by deliberately distorting reality in play situations. Given that the semantic memory system is just beginning its development at this young age, why does the ability to distort reality in mental representations not stand in the way of development? It seems odd from an evolutionary standpoint, if the sole goal in cognitive development were to represent reality as accurately as possible. However, another goal appears to be laying the foundation for creative thought, which requires the flexibility to distort reality to see the world in different ways. But how is all of this accomplished?

Leslie (1987) discovered that the development of meta-representations underlie the ability to pretend. A **meta-representation** is a mental representation of another mental representation. Through a meta-representation, one can think about another thought. Primary representations of objects and events in the real world must be accurate and literally correct. Otherwise, primary representations would not help individuals to adapt to their environment. When a toddler pretends that a banana is a telephone, for example, he or she must have a meta-representation that links or equates the primary representations of the two objects. Otherwise, the child's primary representations of a banana and a telephone would be distorted right at the time when the child is coming to learn about different objects and their names in the world. By using a meta-representation, the meanings of banana and telephone are not changed, but the child can still pretend that they are the same object for a period of time. Meta-representations are adaptive because they add a high degree of flexibility and creativity to cognition.

At about the same age, children figure out when others are pretending as well. For example, if a child sees his or her mother pretending that a banana is a telephone, then the child's learning to represent the concept of a telephone could go seriously astray. Unless the child can represent that the mother is using a meta-representation that temporarily links banana and telephone, the child might well come to think of bananas and telephones as literally the same. Instead, the child is learning to mentally represent the mental states of other humans. The child realizes that the mother is only pretending. Understanding that other humans possess mental states is yet another adaptive function.

Premack and Woodruff (1978) coined the term "theory of mind" to refer to the human ability to infer that others, like ourselves, have mental states. Pretending appears to be critical in the development of meta-representations and a theory of mind. Even though a theory of mind is beginning to develop at two years of age, it requires more pretend play and the development of reasoning ability for it to fully emerge (Leslie, 1987). But by four years of age, children can do complex reasoning using meta-representations. They can, for example, predict the consequences of another person having a false belief. Suppose that Mary hides some candy in a box and then leaves the room (see Figure 7.4). Barbara then moves the candy to a basket without Mary seeing this. Now, where will Mary look for the candy?

Baron-Cohen, Leslie, and Frith (1985) found that young toddlers mistakenly think that Mary, the hider, will know that the candy had been moved from the box to the basket. By four years of age, however, the child can appreciate that Mary has a false mental representation of the situation and will look in the box where she left the candy.

These developments in meta-representations may reflect the maturation of an innate theory of mind module (Baron-Cohen, 1995). Failure to develop this module leads to a condition called **mindblindness,** which refers to an inability to understand that other people possess mental representations. Mindblindness is a feature of autism, a kind of pervasive developmental disorder characterized by repetitive behaviors and deficits in social interaction and communication. Autistic children have trouble understanding the role that mental states play in predicting another person's behavior and in recognizing the mental states of others. Many avoid eye contact and interactions with others. Failures in social communication are a major feature of autism, and they seem to arise because of mindblindness.

PROPOSITIONS AND IMAGES

So far, we have discussed mental representations without concern for their nature. Exactly how is declarative knowledge coded in the mind? What is its

Mary hides the candy in a box.

Mary goes away.

Barbara moves the candy to the basket.

Where will Mary look for her candy?

Figure 7.4   A task for studying the development of meta-representations and a theory of mind.

SOURCE: Baron-Cohen, Leslie, and Frith (1985).

format? One possibility is a perceptual format. An **imaginal code** is a concrete means of mental representation that directly conveys perceptual qualities. For example, if an object is perceived through the visual sensory modality, it is then possible to form a mental image of the object that seems like the original perception. A **propositional code** is an abstract means of mental representation that is not linked to any sensory modality. A propositional code instead represents the features of an object and its relationships to other objects without forming an image. To illustrate, consider the concept of a bird. Shown in Panel (a) of Figure 7.5 is an imaginal representation of a robin, the prototype of the category. The prototype can also be represented as a propositional code, as illustrated in Panel (b). Note that propositional codes are similar to the verbal codes hypothesized in dual coding theory:

> The format of knowledge representations may be a concrete, perceptual-like imaginal code or an abstract, verbal-like propositional code.

both assume that the name of an object is stored in long-term memory (see Chapter 4). They differ, however, in that verbal codes are associated with the perceptual qualities of speech and writing, whereas propositional codes are purely abstract (Paivio, 1986).

Identifying precisely how visual, auditory, and other kinds of images are mentally represented and neurally coded by the brain, however, has been an ongoing and difficult challenge (Kolers, 1983). Some have argued that images are actually based in propositional representations to which one does not have conscious access (Pylyshyn, 1981). On the other hand, some evidence clearly suggests that visual images behave like perceptions, not propositions. The key distinction is that visual images possess a spatial or analog quality that cannot, in principle, be explained in terms of an abstract, propositional, or verbal representation.

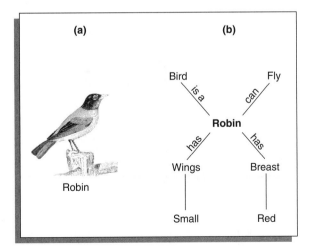

Figure 7.5   An imaginal and a propositional code for the concept of a robin.

The Nature of Images

Shepard and his colleagues pioneered the study of visual images with an extensive series of experiments on mental rotation (Metzler & Shepard, 1974; Shepard & Cooper, 1983; Shepard & Metzler, 1971). The researchers presented people with pictures of three-dimensional objects such as those shown in Figure 7.6. They presented a pair of objects and asked the viewers to decide whether the objects were identical except for their orientation.

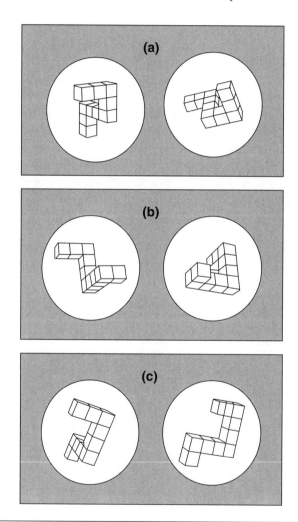

Figure 7.6 Try to mentally rotate the left object of each pair so that it matches the right object.

SOURCE: Reprinted with permission from Shepard, R. N., & Metzler, J. Mental rotation of three-dimensional objects. *Science, 171*, 701-703. Copyright © 1971 AAAS.

For example, compare the two objects in Panel (a). Are they the same or different? By mentally rotating the object on the left, you can verify that it, in fact, matches the object on the right. In Panel (b), the same response is again called for after rotating the figure. However, in Panel (c), the left object can be rotated 360 degrees and it will still not match the right object. Thus, this trial calls for a different response.

Shepard and his colleagues systematically varied the angle of rotation required to determine that the pair of objects is the same. They reasoned that if mental images are like real objects in the mind's eye, then the time required to make a same/different decision ought to increase as a linear function of the angle of rotation. If instead the decision is based on a propositional representation of the objects, then a rotation of 180 degrees should be no slower than one of 90 or 45 degrees. In each case, the degrees of rotation would simply be a variable in one of the propositional arguments (e.g., left object, clockwise rotation, picture plane, 180 degrees). Their results are illustrated in Figure 7.7 (Shepard & Metzler, 1971). Decision times increased as a linear function of the angle of rotation. Thus, there is a striking resemblance between rotating a real object and rotating a mental representation of that object. The images behave in a manner analogous to the real objects.

Analog Properties. Kosslyn (1980, 1981) and his colleagues explored the analog aspect of mental imagery in detail. For example, Kosslyn (1975) showed that the time to scan a mental image depended on "how far" one must scan. Participants memorized a picture of an object, such as a boat, as shown in Figure 7.8. They were then instructed to visualize the object and to scan the mental image to find a feature from a particular starting point. They pressed a button as soon as they "found it" in the image. The results showed that when scanning an image of the boat from the left, participants took longer to find the anchor than they did to find the porthole. Just as the time to scan the picture would take longer with the greater real distance, the same result applied to the mental scan time as well.

Similarly, small images are harder to scan to find features than are large images. Kosslyn (1975) instructed people to imagine a target animal, such as a rabbit, next to a small animal (a fly) or a large animal (an elephant). Try this yourself. Most people report visualizing a very small image of a rabbit next to an elephant and a much larger image of a rabbit next to a fly. When then asked to search for a property of the target (the rabbit's ears), people take about 200 milliseconds longer when "looking" at the small image than when "looking" at the large image. Because the image is an analog of the real rabbit, a small image is harder to visualize clearly.

Finally, Kosslyn, Ball, and Reiser (1978) asked participants to memorize several locations on a map. Next, participants were asked to form a mental

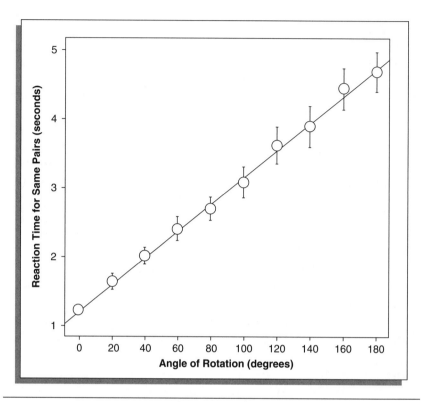

Figure 7.7   Mental rotation time increases with the degrees of rotation required to judge the objects as the same.

SOURCE: Reprinted with permission from Shepard, R. N., & Metzler, J. Mental rotation of three-dimensional objects. *Science, 171,* 701-703. Copyright © 1971 AAAS.

image of the map and focus attention on a specific starting location. The experimenters then named a second location and asked the participants to mentally find their way, in a straight-line path, to the new location. The results showed that the time needed to perform this mental scan increased proportionally to the real distances on the map. If the new location was close to the starting location, then the scan time was brief. If it was far away, then more time was needed.

Imagery Versus Perception. All of these studies suggest that visual imagery is functionally the same as visual perception. The **functional equivalence hypothesis** states that visual imagery, while not identical to perception, is mentally represented and functions the same as perception (Finke, 1989). For example, close your eyes and imagine in your mind's eye the room in which

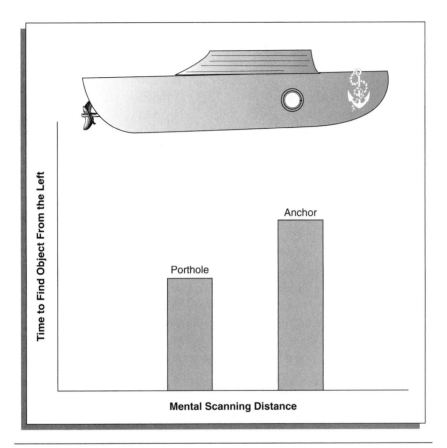

Figure 7.8   A study of scanning mental images.

SOURCE: From Kosslyn, S. M. (1973). Scanning visual images: Some structural implications. *Perception and Psychophysics, 14*(1), 90-94. Reprinted with permission of the Psychonomic Society.

you are now seated. Once you have an image of the room, imagine that a close friend enters the room and walks toward you. Your experience is likely to be similar, although not identical, to actually perceiving the room and the movement of your friend walking toward you. The objects and spatial relations among them seem to be represented much the same way as they are in viewing reality. According to this hypothesis, experiencing a change in a mental image ought to be analogous to experiencing a

> The functional equivalence hypothesis claims that visual imagery uses the same mental representations, processes, and neural structures as does visual perception.

change in perception. The spatial relations of a visual image ought be analogous to the spatial relations of a real environment.

Recent neuroimaging studies further support the view that imagery uses the same neural machinery as does perception. Positron emission tomography (PET), functional magnetic resonance imaging (fMRI), and event-related potential (ERP) studies indicate that brain activity during imagery is localized in the areas known to be used in vision. For example, when a person is reading a list of concrete nouns (e.g., cat) and forming an image of each object, greater ERP recordings are obtained from the primary visual cortex in the occipital lobe than when the person is just reading the nouns and not forming an image of each object (Farah, Peronnet, Gonon, & Girard, 1988). Lesions in the visual areas not only disrupt sight but also disrupt imagery (Farah, 1988). A patient with bilateral lesions in the ventral occipitotemporal areas known to be involved in face perception had trouble imagining faces well-known to him. For example, when asked to imagine the face of Abraham Lincoln, it appeared to him as a short round face. Finally, Kreiman, Koch, and Fried (2000) directly recorded the activity of single neurons in medial temporal lobes of patients undergoing surgery to correct epilepsy that failed to respond to drug treatments. They identified neurons that showed selective changes in firing rates while viewing a particular object (e.g., a face, a baseball) and again when imagining the same object. The activity recorded from the regions of the brain known to be involved in declarative memory might have reflected either the retrieval of the object from long-term memory or the maintenance of the image in working memory.

There is an important difference between perception and imagery, however. Images must be maintained in working memory, whereas perceptions are continuously available without relying on memory. Finding a hidden part of an object is much easier when one can perceive the object than when it is mentally imagined (Reed, 1974). Study the object shown in Figure 7.9. Now, form a mental image of the object and, without looking back at the book, try to find a rectangle in the image. Could you find one? What about a parallelogram? Participants in Reed's study correctly identified the hidden parallelogram only 14% of the time when they had to rely on a mental image held in working memory. Reed concluded that the object was verbally labeled as the Star of David and stored propositionally in working memory (Star, David) rather than as an image that might be manipulated and searched.

Mental Maps. One common use of imagery is to construct spatial mental models. As Tversky (1991) explained,

There are many simple, everyday tasks, such as following road directions, using instructions to assemble a bicycle, reading a novel, or helping to

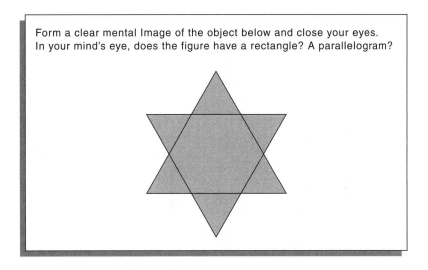

Form a clear mental Image of the object below and close your eyes. In your mind's eye, does the figure have a rectangle? A parallelogram?

Figure 7.9   The Star of David demonstration of the limitations of visual imagery.

solve your child's geometry homework, that seem to entail constructing a spatial mental model from a description. In order to comprehend *Go straight till the first light, then turn left, go down about three blocks to Oak, and make a right,* it is useful to have a spatial representation. (p. 109)

Mental maps reveal one's beliefs about the environment. Which city is farther west—San Diego, California, or Reno, Nevada? The mental map that most people generate places San Diego farther west (Stevens & Coupe, 1978). After all, California is west of Nevada, so surely San Diego must be farther west (see Figure 7.10). It turns out not to be the case. Similarly, most people regard Philadelphia, Pennsylvania, as farther north than Rome, Italy, but this is incorrect as well (Tversky, 1981). Rome is associated with a warm Mediterranean climate and so is assumed to be farther south than it really is.

The distortions in our mental maps reflect our beliefs about how the world is organized. Tversky (1981) argued that these beliefs and associated images are simplified by using two heuristics or rules of thumb. One is the alignment heuristic. The odd shapes of the United States and Europe are difficult to imagine exactly, so people tend to align their shapes at the same latitude. Doing so would definitely place Rome at a southern location relative to Philadelphia. But in reality, Europe lies at a more northern latitude relative to the United States.

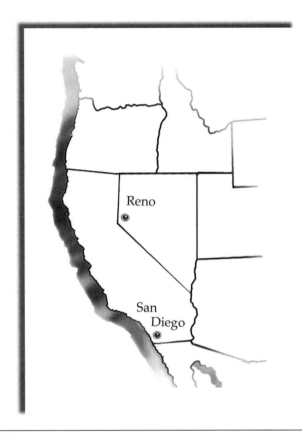

Figure 7.10   Mental maps of the United States versus real maps.

People also use a rotation heuristic, according to Tversky (1981). This suggests that states or countries that are tilted in reality are visualized as more vertical than they really are. They are rotated to the perpendicular, in other words. This explains the San Diego/Reno confusion. California is imagined in the mind's eye as more or less vertical, forming the western boundary of much of the United States. In fact, California is rotated such that San Diego lies much farther east than most people realize. Reno, sitting on the border of California and Nevada, actually lies slightly west of San Diego. Because of the rotation heuristic, the mental map constructed is at odds with reality.

The Nature of Propositions

Knowledge can be coded in terms of abstract representations called propositions instead of as images. In logic, a proposition refers to the smallest unit of knowledge that one can sensibly judge to be true or false. "Fred is tall" is a proposition; "tall" or "is tall" is not. A proposition is an assertion that may be understood and evaluated. It is an abstract representation of the meaning conveyed by language—by all words, phrases, sentences, paragraphs, and whole speeches and documents.

One way to show the elements of a proposition is in a list format (Kintsch, 1974). The list begins with a relation followed by a set of arguments. Verbs, adjectives, and other phrases that convey a relationship are listed first. The arguments follow in a specified order; they define the agent of an action (e.g., who does X?), the object of the action (e.g., does X to what?), the time of the action, and other elements of a meaningful assertion.

> A proposition is coded as a relation and a set of arguments specifying an assertion that may be true or false.

The propositional code, then, breaks down knowledge into individual factual components and represents how they all are related to each other. Consider a few of the sentences that Bransford and Franks (1971) presented to participants in their experiment concerned with integration in memory encoding. As shown in Figure 7.11, each sentence can be represented by a set of abstract propositions in which each is expressed as a relation and a set of arguments.

Propositions provide an abstract and elemental representation of the meaning of verbal information. They provide the mental code for language. The outcome of Bransford and Franks's (1971) study illustrates this point well. Recall from Chapter 6 that they tested recognition memory for sentences of the type illustrated in Figure 7.11. People recognized sentences as old if they

---

1. The jelly was sweet.
    (Sweet, Jelly, Past)

2. The ants in the kitchen ate the jelly.
    (Eat, Ants, Jelly, Past)
    (In, Ants, Kitchen, Past)

3. The ants ate the sweet jelly that was on the table.
    (Sweet, Jelly, Past)
    (East, Ants, Jelly, Past)
    (In, Ants, Kitchen, Past)
    (On, Jelly, Table, Past)

Figure 7.11   Propositional representations of the sentences used in an experiment on integration in memory encoding.

contained a large number of propositions expressed in the study sentences, even though the specific sentences presented on the test were, in fact, new. For example, this new sentence, "The ants in the kitchen ate the sweet jelly which was on the table," was falsely recognized by nearly all of the participants. It represented the prototype sentence that captured the propositions that occurred frequently in the study sentences.

Latent semantic analysis (**LSA**) is a mathematical procedure for automatically extracting and representing the meanings of propositions expressed in a text. It allows one to compare the similarity of the propositions in two texts without going through the tedious task of manually determining the propositions of each sentence (Kintsch, 1998). It can, for example, represent the propositions of an entire encyclopedia in a computer database. The procedure works by representing the co-occurrence of words and their contexts (Landauer & Dumais, 1997). For example, the word "model" occurs in numerous contexts in this book. LSA represents the associations between this word and its contexts in order to provide a usage-based meaning of "model." It does this for every word it encounters in the text. Words that occur infrequently in the same contexts (e.g., model) are well-defined by their usage, whereas words that occur frequently in many contexts are less so (e.g., the). The net result allows one to compute the similarity in meaning between two words, between a word and a paragraph, or between two paragraphs.

Once LSA has extracted and represented the meaning of a text, it can use this representation to answer questions about it. For example, the mathematical procedure used in LSA was applied to the 4.6 million words that compose Grolier's *Academic American Encyclopedia.* These words came from 30,473 articles written at a level appropriate for young students. The model's knowledge of word meanings was then tested using the Test of English as a Foreign Language (TOEFL). Each item presents a test word along with four alternatives that are more or less close in meaning. The task is to select the word closest in meaning to the test word. Because LSA can compute the similarity in meaning of two words, it is well-suited for taking this test once it has been trained by "reading" an encyclopedia. In fact, LSA was about as well-prepared as typical applicants to U.S. colleges from non-English-speaking countries who score an average of 64.5% correct on the TOEFL. When LSA was tested, it picked the correct choices 64.4% of the time. By learning the similarity of word meanings from where and how often they occur in an encyclopedia, LSA behaves as if it knows English vocabulary.

> LSA is a mathematical procedure for extracting and representing the propositions expressed in a text. It allows one to compare two texts in terms of the similarity of their propositional content and to answer questions about a text.

USING SEMANTIC MEMORY

How do people use semantic memory to answer simple questions? Is a dog a kind of animal? Is a hammer? How do you retrieve information about these object concepts to give the right answer? Models of the retrieval process have been proposed and tested by manipulating the specific kinds of questions asked and observing how the time to respond correctly was affected. In this final section of the chapter, these models are presented to show how the process of answering even simple questions is difficult to unveil.

Semantic Network Models

The subordinate, basic, and superordinate levels of concepts and their associated features can be organized into a hierarchical structure called a **semantic network model.** Figure 7.12 illustrates a small portion of what

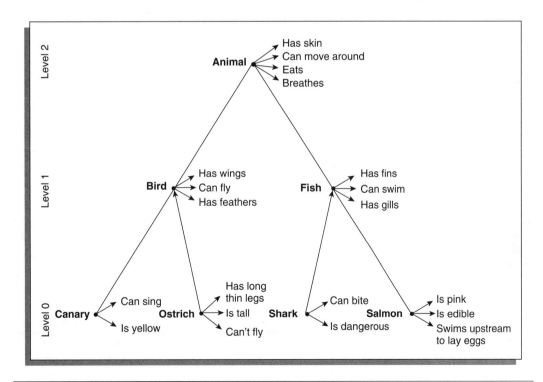

Figure 7.12   A hierarchical network representation of concepts.

SOURCE: From Collins, A. M., & Quillian, M. R., Retrieval time from semantic memory. *Journal of Verbal Learning and Verbal Behavior, 8,* 240-247, copyright © 1969. Reprinted with permission.

you know about the object concept of animals, with Level 0 representing the subordinate level, Level 1 the basic level, and Level 2 the superordinate level. Collins and Quillian (1969) proposed that retrieving information from this network involves working through the various levels as demanded by the task. For example, verifying that a canary can sing involves entering the network at Level 0 and searching the propositions attached to the canary node. But verifying that a canary can fly requires moving through the network to Level 1. Still more mental travel time is required to answer that a canary has skin, for this feature applies to all animals; it is a superordinate or Level 2 feature.

Notice that this hierarchical representation of features saves space in long-term memory. It is not necessary, theoretically, to store that a canary can fly and has skin because these facts can be deduced from the hierarchical structure of memory. The **cognitive economy assumption** claims that the features of a concept are represented only once at either the subordinate, basic, or superordinate level of the hierarchy. Although it may take more time to use semantic memory organized in this manner, less storage space is required than if properties were stored redundantly at all levels of the network.

Collins and Quillian (1969) examined how quickly people verified both conceptual feature questions and category questions (see Figure 7.13). Notice that, as predicted, the time needed to answer feature questions increased as a function of feature level. In addition, verifying that a canary is a canary (an identity judgment) is faster than verifying that a canary is a bird (a basic-level categorization). The most time was needed to verify membership in a superordinate category—that a canary is an animal. Note that nearly one-tenth of a second is needed to move from one level to another in answering the category questions. Also note that searching the features associated with a particular level of category requires about 200 milliseconds more.

> *WordNet* uses a semantic network to represent the meanings of 122,000 English words. Each noun, verb, adverb, and adjective in *WordNet* is defined by a synset or the set of all synonymous words.

Collins and Quillian's (1969) proposal that concepts, or the words that name them, can be represented by a massive semantic network has proved to be very useful in designing a novel kind of dictionary. Instead of listing the words alphabetically, *WordNet* represents the semantic relations among words (Miller, 1999). A noun, verb, adjective, and adverb in the language is represented by a **synset,** a set of synonyms for each noun, verb, adjective, or adverb in the language. If a word has more than one meaning, then it appears in more than one synset. *WordNet* contains 122,000 words in 100,000 synsets. The synsets, in turn, are organized in the network by 139,000 pointers representing semantic relations. *WordNet* easily retrieves synonyms and antonyms for a given term. This can be very useful in information retrieval systems because it expands the number of possible

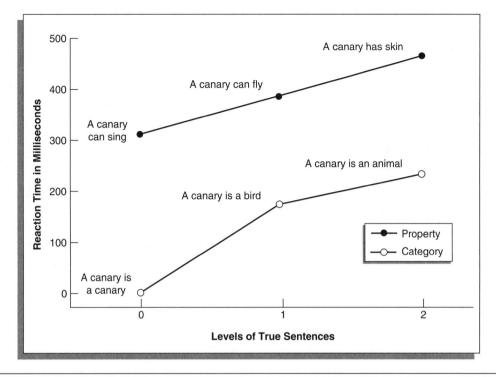

Figure 7.13   Time required to categorize a noun and to verify its properties.

SOURCE: From Collins, A. M., & Quillian, M. R., Retrieval time from semantic memory. *Journal of Verbal Learning and Verbal Behavior, 8,* 240-247, copyright © 1969. Reprinted with permission.

items to search in a database. Furthermore, the different meanings of a word in different contexts are recognized by *WordNet.* Thus, the term "board" will not be misunderstood when one is intending to search for a "surfboard" versus a "bulletin board."

Subsequent research on Collins and Quillian's (1969) model muddied the waters, however. To begin, Rips, Shoben, and Smith (1973) reported that the hierarchical structure of the network was not consistent. If it were, then one should verify that "A collie is a mammal" faster than "A collie is an animal." The class of mammals is a subset of all animals; therefore, strictly speaking, it ought to be searched faster than the superordinate class. The results did not show this, suggesting that people did not clearly represent a strict hierarchy of class relations.

Furthermore, the assumption of cognitive economy also encountered problems. The associative strength or frequency with which a property occurred proved to be more important than the level of hierarchy. Conrad (1972) reported that strong associations (e.g., an orange is edible) can be quickly answered even though the property of edible ought to require moving to a higher level in the network. Moreover, Conrad failed to find differences where Collins and Quillian (1969) expected them. For instance, the verification time remained the same for these types of statements: "A shark can move," "A fish can move," and "An animal can move." In other words, if one selects a high-level property, theoretically it should take more time to move back down the network to the fish and animal levels (the reverse direction of the Collins and Quillian experiment). The results indicated no difference.

> Typicality effects and violations of the cognitive economy assumption led to the rejection of Collins and Quillian's model of semantic memory.

Finally, the typicality effect discussed earlier finds no place in a network model. Why should it be faster to verify that a robin is a bird than to verify that a canary is a bird? Obviously, the specific network model proposed by Collins and Quillian (1969) failed to capture the necessary phenomena. Later attempts came closer (Collins & Loftus, 1975), but at the cost of a lack of precision in their predictions (Chang, 1986).

The Feature Comparison Model

Other researchers took a different tack from network models to account for the typicality effect observed with simple inquiries to semantic memory. Smith, Shoben, and Rips (1974) assumed that people first tried to retrieve the typical or characteristic features of a concept in order to answer a question such as "Is a robin a bird?" Such a list of features works best for the prototype, robin, and is satisfactory for other examples related to the prototype (e.g., canary). However, for cases that are very different from the prototype (e.g., penguin), the overall similarity is not satisfactory. Instead, a second stage is needed in which the defining features of the concept, which go beyond obvious perceptual similarities, must be retrieved. Thus, the sentence "A robin is a bird" will yield a high degree of similarity between the example and the characteristic features and can be answered without further search. By contrast, "A penguin is a bird" requires a two-stage analysis to yield the correct answer. The **feature comparison model,** then, assumes that, first, characteristic and defining features are assessed in answer to simple categorization questions and, second (if necessary), defining features are retrieved.

Besides providing an explanation of the typicality effect, the feature comparison model also nicely accounts for another consistent result in the literature, the **category size effect.** D. E. Meyer (1970) reported that deciding whether a relation applies for a small category (e.g., all robins are gems) is faster than deciding whether it applies for a large category (e.g., all robins are stones). To respond "false" to these statements, one must search the categories of gems and stones in long-term memory. Meyer reasoned that the larger the category that must be searched, the more time is needed to disconfirm the statement. The same result occurred for true categorical statements (e.g., all collies are dogs vs. all collies are animals). Of course, we saw this same outcome in the category-level effect reported by Collins and Quillian (1969).

The feature comparison model explains the category size effect by noting that Stage 2 processing would be needed only for large categories. For instance, to decide that a robin is a bird, one's initial comparison of all features would yield a high degree of similarity. An immediate "true" response would be possible. Yet to decide that a robin is an animal would demand the extra step of comparing defining features alone. Perhaps the unusual violation of the category size effect noted earlier might stem from featural similarity. Recall that people can judge "A dog is an animal" faster than "A dog is a mammal." The overall similarity of dog and animal might be quite high, leading to an immediate response after Stage 1 processing. Because the term "mammal" is less familiar to most people than "animal," a second stage of processing the defining features may be needed.

> The feature comparison model accounts for typicality effects and the category size effect by postulating a two-stage process of checking first, defining and characteristic features and second, defining features only.

In sum, the feature comparison model accounts for most of the major results in the literature on semantic memory. However, it too has problems (Chang, 1986). One empirical problem is that false statements involving concepts that are highly similar ought to require Stage 2 processing, and thus take extra time to answer. For example, "All dogs are cats" should take more time to disconfirm than "All animals are birds." The latter statement should be disconfirmed after Stage 1 only. Yet Glass and Holyoak (1975) found that highly similar concepts, such as dogs and cats, are disconfirmed the fastest. Thus, even relatively simple uses of semantic memory are complex to model.

Nevertheless, feature overlap is clearly a central quality of how questions are answered using semantic memory. The category-based induction task illustrates this point as well as does the task presented earlier. This task can be illustrated by the following statements: "Robins have wings," "Bluebirds have wings," and "How likely is it that all birds have wings?" Osherson, Smith, Wilkie, Lopez, and Shafir (1990) found that this inductive argument is much stronger than one that lessens the degree of feature overlap in the premises, such as the following: "Robins have wings," "Ostriches have wings," and "How likely is it that all birds have wings?" The overall similarity of features is one important determinant of how people reason with the concepts of semantic memory.

SUMMARY

1. Object concepts refer to natural kinds (biological objects) and artifacts (human-made objects). An object concept categorizes objects and events of significance in the real world. As with any concept, an object concept treats objects that differ as the same if they fall within its defining boundary. With object concepts, this membership boundary is fuzzy or flexible. Concepts are often organized hierarchically. The hierarchy of subordinate (robin), basic (bird), and superordinate (animal) concepts illustrates this point. Rule-governed concepts, by contrast, are defined by logical relations among a set of defining features. Their membership boundaries are clear-cut and inflexible. For example, the abstract mathematical concept of an integer is well-defined.

2. All concepts specify the dimensions along which members differ from one another and order the members in terms of a gradient of membership or typicality. The prototype represents the best example of a given concept. Concepts may also be coherent, in the sense that they relate in a deep theoretical manner to other concepts or other representations of world knowledge. Concepts may also be organized hierarchically, with the basic level of categorization providing the optimal amount of information about its members. Schemas organize related concepts in meaningful ways. For example, a restaurant script, a kind of schema, organizes everything we know about the routine activities of entering a restaurant, ordering food, paying for the food, and so on.

3. Semantic memory contains factual and conceptual knowledge represented by means of imaginal and propositional codes. Imaginal codes are concrete and perceptual-like, whereas propositional codes are abstract and verbal-like. Each proposition codes for a single limited assertion about the world that can be judged as true or false. Propositional codes, then, break down knowledge into individual factual components and represent how they all are related to each other. An image behaves in much the same manner as the object it represents. Imagery and perception are functionally equivalent. For example, the time needed to rotate a mental image increases linearly with the angle of rotation, much like the time needed to rotate the object itself. Behavioral and neuroimaging evidence indicates that a dual coding system is used in human semantic memory.

4. Two of the major models of how we retrieve information from semantic memory were presented. Network theory assumes that knowledge is represented hierarchically and that features connected at a superordinate level

are not redundantly represented at lower levels. Retrieving a fact involves working through the various levels of the network and searching the relevant nodes for feature information. Feature comparison theory assumes that each concept includes a list of characteristic and defining features. Retrieving a fact first involves a comparison of overall similarity based on both feature types. If similarity is low, then a second stage of comparison is needed based on defining features only. The feature comparison model handles experimental results best, although it, too, has difficulties in accounting for some findings.

KEY TERMS

rule-governed concepts

object concepts

prototype

family resemblance structure

typicality effect

folk theories

frames

scripts

meta-representation

mindblindness

imaginal code

propositional code

functional equivalence hypothesis

latent semantic analysis (LSA)

semantic network model

cognitive economy assumption

synset

feature comparison model

category size effect

CHAPTER 8

LANGUAGE

DEFINING LANGUAGE

Language is a system of symbols that are used to communicate ideas among two or more individuals. Language uses both mental and external representations. An author communicates with a reader using the symbols of letters and words to get across ideas. In conversation, the speaker and listener exchange mental representations using spoken rather than written symbols. Languages share four rudimentary properties (Clark & Clark, 1977). A language must be learnable by children, it must be able to be spoken and understood readily by adults, it must capture the ideas that people normally communicate, and it must enable communication among groups of people in a social and cultural context.

Language can be used to communicate factual information, but this is not its sole function (Atchison, 1996). Venting emotions, joke telling, and social greeting all are common uses of language that are not aiming to articulate facts. Moreover, some factual knowledge is very difficult to convey with language. For example, try to describe to a friend what a spiral is without resorting to gestures or drawing a diagram. Or, try instructing someone, in words alone, how to tie a square knot. Such visual-spatial knowledge is not easily captured in words.

At the heart of language is the use of symbols to convey meaning. Humans use words, or patterns of sound, to refer to objects, events, beliefs, desires, feelings, and intentions. The words carry meanings. If your friend says he is happy, then you interpret this to mean something about his emotional state. If, instead of speaking, your friend whistles a tune, then his behavior may say something about his emotional state, but it is less meaningful. Your friend might whistle by habit or whistle when he is angry, sad, or happy. Unlike speech, whistling is not specialized to convey a clear meaning. Once humans learn a word, they can retrieve its mental representation, hold it in working memory, and use it in thought. The word itself is represented separately from the object or event to which it refers.

The words used by humans typically are arbitrary; they lack any connection between the symbols and the meanings they carry and so differ across languages. "Uno," "ein," and "one" are arbitrary sounds referring to the same numerical concept. A single scratch in the dirt or mark on a clay tablet would be a nonarbitrary way of referring to the number one. Ten such marks would nonarbitrarily refer to ten. But the use of nonarbitrary symbols can get very cumbersome. The invention of Arabic numerals for representing numerical quantities vastly simplified the task of representing, say, 432 jars of olive oil or wine.

By putting together strings of words in different orders, one can express a very large number of different meanings. Consider, for example, a six-word sentence. Suppose that one selected 1 of 10 possible words for the first word of the sentence, 1 of another set of 10 possible words for the second word, and so on. The number of unique sentences that could be generated following this procedure would equal 10^6 or 1,000,000 sentences. Because you are not limited to only six-word sentences or to 10 possible choices, the number of unique sentences that you might utter is infinite.

Origins of Language

How did language begin? The answer is unknown and perhaps unknowable, but the question is too tantalizing to ignore. Linguists have reconstructed what they believe early languages were like up to about 10,000 years ago by studying the relationships among the written records of ancient languages, dating back about 5,000 years (Atchison, 1996). However, scholars believe that the origins of language lie much farther back in human evolutionary history. Casts made from the skulls of *Homo habilis*, our early ancestor from more than two million years ago, reveal what could have been Broca's speech area (Tobias, 1987). However, the unusual shape of the human vocal tract, a necessary requirement for speech, emerged later, perhaps 150,000 to 200,000 years ago, in *Homo sapiens sapiens* (Corballis, 1989; Lieberman, 1984).

A long-debated idea on the origin of language claims that it developed from gestures. However, it appears that language and gestures may well have evolved together (Atchison, 1996). When our ancestors first began to communicate their thoughts to other individuals, they needed a way to refer to specific objects and to relate those objects. It is known that gestures are often synchronized in time with oral statements to convey meaning (Goldin-Meadow, McNeill, & Singleton, 1996). Spoken and gestural outputs are synchronized even in congenitally blind individuals who have never seen anyone gesturing. It could be that gestural and spoken output developed in tandem, with each specialized to communicate particular kinds of information.

Another idea is that language evolved as a consequence of the large brain of humans (Gould & Lewontin, 1979). Language might be an example of taking an existing biological structure and adapting it for a new function. The problem with this view is that language is a very complex function. Adapting an existing structure to handle such a complex new function would seem to be unprecedented. As Atchison (1996) noted, "A type of wading bird uses its wings as a sunshade: there is no evidence of any bird using what was originally a sunshade as wings" (p. 75).

A plausible alternative is that language and a large brain emerged more or less simultaneously (Deacon, 1997). As our hominid ancestors lived together in increasingly larger groups, the degree of social interaction increased. Deception possibly became more important, in order to gain an advantage in getting the food, water, and shelter needed for survival. These kinds of social forces may have selected for a slightly larger brain but at the same time selected for means of communication. Thus, language and brain size may have fed off each other in evolution. Increasingly sophisticated means of communication demanded increasingly complex brain structures.

Meaning, Structure, and Use

Semantics. **Semantics** is the study of meaning. A theory of semantics must explain how people mentally represent the meanings of words and sentences. The expression of one's thoughts and their comprehension by listeners or readers obviously depend on these mental representations. As discussed in Chapter 7, sentence meanings can be represented in the form of propositions, that is, abstract codes for the concepts and schemas referred to in a sentence. For example, "The professor praised the industrious student" can be analyzed into two propositions. Each involves a list that starts with a relation followed by one or more arguments:

(praise, professor, student, past)

(industrious, student)

The sounds that we generate when saying a sentence must code meaning in a consistent manner so that listeners can understand our utterances (see Figure 8.1). The coding begins with the phonemes or phonological segments that distinguish one meaningful word from another. As introduced in Chapter 2, *pill* and *kill* convey different meanings because they differ in their initial phoneme. Each phoneme is produced by the vocal apparatus in a unique manner. The /p/ of *praised* and the /b/ of *braised* are pronounced nearly identically; they differ only in that the vocal cords vibrate for /b/ but not for /p/. This difference, called voicing, is also seen between /s/ and /z/. Say each aloud, and you can feel with your fingers on your Adam's apple the vibration with /z/.

The phonemes of a language are the building blocks of meaningful units, the morphemes. A **morpheme** is a minimal unit of speech used repeatedly in a language to code a specific meaning. A word, such as *pill,* is a morpheme, but so, too, are prefixes and suffixes, such as *pre-* and *-es.* Each morpheme signals a distinct meaning. The suffix *-ed* tells us that the action took place in the past.

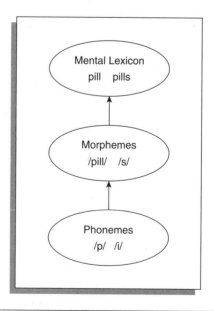

Figure 8.1   Meaningful units of language.

So, the word *killed* is composed of two morphemes, each of which conveys a specific meaning.

All the morphemes in a language, taken together, make up a **mental lexicon** or the dictionary of long-term memory that humans rely on in speaking and listening and in reading and writing. Each morpheme is a lexical entry in this dictionary in the mind. In particular, one is concerned in semantics with content words, that is, the verbs and especially the nouns that refer to natural (e.g., chair) or formal (e.g., the legal definition of marriage) concepts. Function words, such as articles (e.g., the) and prepositions (e.g., by), often serve a grammatical rather than a semantic role. For example, the "by" in "Jill bought groceries by the week" plays the grammatical role of starting a prepositional phrase; the entire phrase could easily be replaced by the adverb "weekly" without a change in meaning. The content words, on the other hand, all contribute to the unique meaning of the sentence.

> A morpheme is a minimal unit of speech used repeatedly in a language to code a specific meaning. The word *killed* is composed of two morphemes: kill and -ed.

Syntax. Another landmark of language is its structure. The grammatical rules that specify how words and other morphemes are arranged to yield acceptable sentences are called **syntax.** Technically, syntax is only part of the study of grammar, the complete set of rules by which people speak and write correctly (including, e.g., punctuation). Here, however, grammar is seen as an abstract set of syntactic rules that describe how the morphemes of a language are sequenced to generate an acceptable sentence. Syntactic rules ensure that speakers and listeners, as well as writers and readers, all are playing the same structural game with language. Because language must follow a linear order—one word after another—either in time (as occurs in speech) or in space (as occurs with text), some convention is needed to order the words and the parts of words (e.g., past tense suffixes).

In English, for instance, a declaration consists of a subject (S) followed by a verb (V) followed by an object (O). Some languages, such as German, follow an S-O-V pattern instead. The grammar of a language specifies the rules that enable one to generate all acceptable sentences; at the same time, these rules do not allow the generation of ungrammatical sentences. Non-sentences in the language fail to meet one or more of these rules. If you can speak and understand a language, then you have learned and can use its grammar even if what you know is implicit and not available for conscious articulation. In learning a second language, students sometimes discover, at a conscious level of analysis, grammatical distinctions in their native tongue (e.g., the pluperfect tense).

> Syntax refers to the rules that specify how words and other morphemes are arranged to yield grammatically acceptable sentences.

An implicit knowledge of grammar provides one with linguistic intuitions (Chomsky, 1965). Being able to identify the parts of speech in a sentence—knowing what is the subject as opposed to, say, the verb—is one such intuition. Another is recognizing that two different sentence structures mean the same thing (e.g., "The student passed the exam" and "The exam was passed by the student"). Recognizing syntactic ambiguity, in which multiple structures are possible, is yet another linguistic intuition (e.g., "Visiting relatives can be a pain"). A very basic intuition is recognizing whether a string of words is a grammatical sentence.

To illustrate further the concepts of semantics and syntax and the idea of linguistic intuitions, consider the three assertions shown in Box 8.1. The first assertion is an English sentence, for it conveys meaning and is syntactically correct. The second assertion is not a sentence because it violates syntactic rules. All of the elements of meaning are there, but they are in the wrong order. The third assertion violates no syntactic rules, yet it fails to make any sense. Your mental representation of the noun "ideas" does not allow them to sleep in any fashion, let alone to dream about a psychologist.

Experiments on comprehension also reveal our sensitivity to grammar. A classic study by Garrett, Bever, and Fodor (1966) illustrates this point. These authors presented listeners with a series of sentences through earphones; they superimposed on the tape-recording of each sentence the sound of a click. The click occurred at various locations relative to the boundaries among the phrases in a given sentence. The listener's task was to identify the location at which he or she heard the click. It turned out that the sound of the click tended to be heard between two syntactic phrases in a sentence even when its actual location occurred earlier or later. Two of the sentences used by Garrett et al. are shown in Figure 8.2. The final words in each sentence ("influence the company was given an award") were tape-recorded once and inserted into the sentences. Thus, the listener heard precisely the same words and pauses, and the click occurred during the first syllable of the word "company." Yet in Sentence A, the word "influence" ends a prepositional phrase and "the" starts the main clause of the sentence. In Sentence B, the word "company" ends a subordinate clause, with "was" being the verb of the main clause. Listeners given Sentence A heard the click occur earlier than

---

BOX 8.1

Syntax and Semantics: A Demonstration

Which of these sentences is grammatical? Which is meaningful?

1. The psychologist slept fitfully, dreaming new ideas.

2. Fitfully the slept new, ideas dreaming psychologist.

3. The new ideas slept fitfully, dreaming a psychologist.

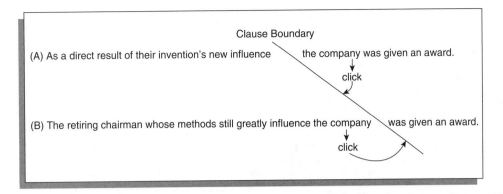

Figure 8.2 The grammatical structure of a sentence influences the perception of a click embedded in the first syllable of the word "company."

did those given Sentence B. Perception of the click "migrated" toward an important syntactic boundary used in comprehending the sentence. This boundary occurred earlier than the click in Sentence A and later than the click in Sentence B.

Pragmatics. The third landmark is the uses or functions of language in social intercourse. Humans may speak or write with themselves as their only audience. But more commonly, the utterances made and texts composed are embedded in a discourse community. Language is intended for and shaped by those who collectively listen, read, comprehend, interpret, and respond to our uses of language. For example, consider the difference in the following two utterances:

It is hot in this room.

Open the window!

The first sentence informs others about how one feels about the room temperature. The second sentence commands someone to let some cool air into the room. But note that in a specific setting, the first sentence might be used to achieve the goal of the second in a polite way. Instead of commanding directly, one can achieve the same effect by merely informing someone standing next to the window.

Pragmatics refers to the manner in which speakers communicate their intentions depending on the social context. A **speech act** is a sentence uttered to express a speaker's intention in a way that the listener will recognize (Grice, 1975). There are distinct kinds of speech acts. We inform, command, question, warn, thank, dare, request, and so on. A direct speech act assumes a grammatical form tailored to a particular function. For example, "Open the window" directly commands. An indirect speech act achieves a function by assuming the guise of another type of speech act. For example, one might question ("Can you open the window?"), warn ("If you don't open the window, we'll all pass out"), threaten ("If you don't open the window, I'll shoot!"), declare ("The window really should be open"), inform ("It really is hot in here"), or even thank in a sarcastic tone ("Thanks a lot for opening the window").

> Pragmatics addresses the various ways in which speakers communicate their intentions depending on the social context. Speech acts serve to inform, command, question, warn, and so on but may do so indirectly rather than directly.

Grice (1975) proposed that when two people enter into a conversation, they, in essence, enter into an implicit contractual agreement called the **cooperative principle.** It means that the participants agree to say things that are appropriate to the conversation and to end the conversation at a mutually agreeable point. One way to understand this contractual agreement is to recall times when people have violated it. Have you ever heard someone say something that makes no sense whatsoever in the context of the ongoing conversation or seen someone walk off abruptly to end a conversation without warning? The cooperative principle dictates otherwise. We agree to speak audibly, to use languages that listeners understand, and to follow the rules of those languages.

For example, participants try to be informative by saying what others need to know to understand and by not providing unnecessary details, as shown in the following exchange:

Steven: Wilfred is meeting a woman for dinner tonight.

Susan: Does his wife know about it?

Steven: Of course she does. The woman he is meeting is his wife. (Clark & Clark, 1977, p. 122)

Steven misled Susan here by failing to provide enough information in his use of the term "a woman." Susan inferred that the woman in question was someone other than Wilfred's wife.

Contrasts to Animal Communication

Humans are not unique in using communication or the exchange of information between a sender and a receiver coded in the form of signals understood by both. Pioneering work on communication in the animal kingdom was conducted by von Frisch (1950). The waggle dance of the honeybee directs other members of the hive to distant sources of nectar. The precise nature of the dance communicates the direction and distance from the hive of a source discovered by the dancing bee. Since 1950, an extensive array of communication systems have been documented, including the antennae and head gestures of weaver ants, the alarm calls of vervet monkeys, and the complex signaling of dolphins and whales (Griffin, 1984).

One difference between animal communication and human language is the failure of animals to use symbols to represent objects. The dance of the honeybee, for example, conveys information about the environment after the bee comes from a source of nectar. The honeybee dance is not symbolic because it is tied directly to the situation. It is not a separate entity that the bee uses to communicate at a later time when not just returning from or preparing to go to a food source. In human beings, words are detached from their referents, and we use them to recall events from the past or to imagine events that have never even happened. Also, as noted earlier, human beings use purely arbitrary symbols that have no relation to the concept being communicated.

Another fundamental difference is that most animal communication does not involve a theory of mind (Seyfarth & Cheney, 2003). When a human being speaks, the listener learns about the mind of the speaker—his or her attitudes and dispositions to think or behave in particular ways (Pinker, 1994). Tests for most animals have failed to show that they make any attributions about the mental state of others. The exception to this generalization is the chimpanzee, where the tests of theory of mind have been mixed. Thus, at least for most animals, communication signals are not modified by the sender to tailor the message to the mental state of the listener. A vervet monkey's leopard call is not vocalized in different ways depending on whether the listener believes a leopard might be in the area or has no clue. Human beings, on the other hand, routinely make an attribution about the state of mind of the listener and frame the communication accordingly.

Attempts have been made to teach American Sign Language (ASL) and specially designed languages to chimpanzees, orangutans, and gorillas. Gardner and Gardner (1969, 1975), for example, raised a chimpanzee named Washoe in an environment comparable to one suitable for a human baby. Those who raised Washoe "spoke" to the chimp using ASL. They trained Washoe to use sign language to ask for what she wanted. Washoe learned more than 130 signs. When shown the picture of an object, she could make the appropriate sign. More important, Washoe occasionally improvised signs or combined them in novel ways. For example, on first seeing a swan, Washoe gave the sign for "water" and the sign for "bird."

Terrace, Petitto, Sanders, and Bever (1979), however, doubted that what Washoe and other apes learned was really language. In particular, they doubted that the apes showed the generative capacity or **productivity** of human language. Productivity refers to the ability to create novel sentences that can be understood by other speakers of the language. Terrace and his colleagues raised Nim Chimsky, a young male chimpanzee. Like Washoe, Nim learned about 130 signs and could use these to request objects or actions that he wanted at the moment. Terrace, however, concluded from careful review of videotapes that Nim's signs were often repetitions of what his human caretaker had just signed. Terrace found little evidence that Nim could combine signs according to syntactic rules. Nim could not generate a simple sentence, in other words.

Other researchers question Terrace's strongly negative conclusion regarding primates' lack of capacity to learn human language. For example, Savage-Rumbaugh, McDonal, Sevcik, Hopkins, & Rupert (1986) reported excellent success in teaching chimpanzees to communicate using a set of shapes as symbols—called lexigrams—on a computer keyboard, instead of ASL. A chimp named Kanzi learned the associations between an object in the world, the sound of the English words spoken by a caretaker, and the visual lexigram. Caretakers talked to him about daily routines, such as taking baths, games of tickle, trips to visit other primates, watching TV shows, and many other events. He learned the words and lexigrams for orange, peanut, banana, apple, bedroom, and chase first, because these most interested him. By the age of six, Kanzi could identify 150 lexigram symbols when he heard the spoken words. He could also perform correctly 70%–80% of the time in comprehending and responding to sentences, such as "Put the rubber band on your ball" or "Bite the stick." Of interest, this level of performance was just as good, if not slightly better, than that observed in a two-year-old child who was also given the same experiences with lexigrams and listening to her mother speak to her (Savage-Rumbaugh & Rumbaugh, 1993).

Even so, no one disagrees that young children with small vocabularies greatly exceed trained apes in their linguistic abilities. A six-year-old child has a vocabulary on the order of 16,000 words (Carey, 1978). By adulthood, vocabulary is measured in the tens of thousands of words. Humans can express more ideas than animals for another reason in addition to vocabulary size. As seen earlier, grammar provides a means for producing novel expressions that have never been spoken before. For example, "My dog ordered caviar at the ball game, surprising even the shortstop." It is highly unlikely you have ever heard someone say this sentence. Although

> Language uses symbols that refer to events displaced in time and space. The mental lexicon and grammar of a language are productive, allowing one to generate an infinite number of novel sentences.

some sentences are used repetitively to the point of annoyance (e.g., "Have a nice day"), it is not difficult at all to generate utterly novel sentences.

REPRESENTATIONS OF LANGUAGE

How are the rules of grammar, the mental lexicon, and other constituents of language represented in the mind? Which regions of the brain support these mental representations? Are linguistic representations to some extent pre-wired through genetic predispositions, or are they entirely learned? To what extent are the cognitive processes that manipulate linguistic representations specific to language, and to what extent are they general processes that operate throughout perception, attention, memory, and thinking? In this section, some preliminary answers to these root questions about the mental representation of language are provided.

Universal Grammar

The language or languages that you heard and learned to speak as a young child shaped many aspects of your knowledge about language. For example, the word in your mental lexicon that you use to refer to the family pet is *dog, chien,* or *hund,* depending on whether you acquired English, French, or German. However, other aspects of language are culturally invariant. Linguistic universals are properties that are shared by all natural languages found and learned in diverse cultures around the world. For example, at about three or four months of age, babies all over the planet start babbling, producing sounds that are similar to adult speech but quite meaningless. The babbling peaks before a child's first birthday, when often the first understandable word will be uttered (de Villiers & de Villiers, 1978). The first words are invariably composed of a single syllable made up of a consonant and vowel (CV) or two syllables that repeat the same two sounds (CVCV), as in "mama" or "dada," the words all parents want to hear.

Universal grammar refers to the genetically determined knowledge of human language that allows children in all cultures to rapidly acquire the language to which they are exposed. Many aspects of semantics and pragmatics vary across languages and are not universal. However, the syntactic structure of languages may, at least in part, reflect an innate universal grammar. A language acquisition device (LAD) is the innate mechanism that presumably analyzes the linguistic inputs to which we are exposed and adjusts its parameters to fit that language. Universal grammar and the LAD are thought to reflect an innate cognitive module that is independent of other cognitive systems (Chomsky, 1986; Fodor, 1983). According to this theory, the universal grammar allows certain parameters of variation among languages, and these parameters are set during the acquisition process.

Parameter Setting. For example, during parameter setting, a child exposed to Italian would learn to put a positive setting on the pronoun omission parameter. In Italian, in contrast to English, it is permissible to omit the pronoun before a verb because the inflection on the verb conveys the necessary information about the subject of the sentence. For example, "I love" can be expressed as "Amo." The child exposed to English instead of Italian would learn a negative setting for the parameter of pronoun omission.

To take a different illustration, consider the syntactic order of subject (S), verb (V), and object (O) introduced earlier. A word order parameter in the universal grammar would allow certain combinations and not others. Greenberg (1966) concluded from his examination of natural languages that only four of the six possible orders are used and that one of these (VOS) is quite rare. The common orders are SOV, SVO, and VSO. In theory, the developing infant would come equipped at birth with the implicit knowledge that natural languages never follow the OVS and OSV orders. Children the world over would come prepared to examine whether the language (or languages) to which they are exposed conform to one of the four possible word orders.

Languages also differ in the degree of word order variation allowed. Russian, for example, tolerates more variation in the order of words in a sentence than does English. Pinker (1990) hypothesized that children are programmed to assume that the grammar of their native language demands a fixed order of words. The evidence suggests that early utterances indeed follow a strict ordering, regardless of the language being learned. In the case of English, these early utterances approximate the grammatically correct order. For Russian children, however, their utterances initially fail to show the full scope of possible word orders. It appears that an innate language acquisition device guides children to try out a fixed order first.

Absence of Input. Two kinds of arguments have been advanced in favor of universal grammar from atypical cases in which infants fail to receive language input. First, congenitally deaf children have never heard spoken language; some are not taught standard sign language either. Despite the absence of speech or sign input, such children invent their own gestural language that reflects properties of speech acquired by children with normal hearing (Goldin-Meadow & Mylander, 1990). For example, one-word utterances by normal children occur at about 18 months of age, and these are later followed by two- and three-word utterances. The deaf children similarly invent one-sign gestures at 18 months, followed later by two- and three-sign gestures. Presumably, an innate language acquisition device dictates this common pattern of development.

Second, there may be a critical period during which the LAD is open to input (Lenneberg, 1967). Feral children have been found living with animals, without any contact with a community of speaking humans. If found after five years of age, such children are typically unable to learn the phonology of human speech. Without exposure to the phonemes of a particular language, the representations that start out as babbling and eventually develop into speech seem to be lost and unrecoverable after the early years of life. Although less severe, there may be a critical period for learning a second language as well. If you have not learned the phonology of a second language by the time of puberty, then native speakers can detect your foreign accent with ease (Nespor, 1999).

During the 1970s, a child named Genie, who suffered from severe neglect comparable to any "wolf child," was found in Los Angeles (Curtiss, 1977). From about 20 months of age until she was discovered at 13 years of age, her parents isolated her in a small closed and curtained room. Her mother visited her only a few minutes each day to feed her. The child had no exposure to radio or television. Her father beat her for making noise and, along with her brother, barked at her like a dog rather than speaking to her. They believed that she was severely retarded. After her rescue, she was tested for language comprehension, and she had no knowledge of grammar. Because she was past puberty, the critical period hypothesis predicts that Genie should have failed to learn once put in a language-rich environment. However, the results were mixed. Genie began producing single words five months after her rescue and two-word utterances at eight months. Her learning of phonology looked very much like normal language acquisition. She started with consonant-vowel monosyllables, for example, and worked up to longer words. Her grammatical development was poor, by contrast. Genie never did master syntax. The small number of feral children and the possibility of mental retardation not specific to language prevent drawing strong conclusions (McDonald, 1997).

> Universal grammar refers to the genetically determined knowledge of human language that allows children in all cultures to rapidly acquire the language to which they are exposed. It is unclear whether language is innate.

Neural Systems

The localization of language was proposed very early in the scientific study of the brain. In 1861, Broca reported on a patient who had lost his ability to produce meaningful speech but who retained his ability to hear and comprehend speech (McCarthy & Warrington, 1990). The patient received the nickname "Tan" because he uttered only this sound. Broca observed that the muscles of the vocal apparatus were not at fault, for Tan could eat and drink without difficulty. Broca speculated that Tan suffered from damage to a specific area in his brain that controlled speech, located in the third convolution of the frontal lobe in the left hemisphere. As it turned out, Tan suffered brain damage in many areas, but we still refer to this part of the brain as Broca's area, in honor of his early investigations (see Figure 8.3). **Broca's aphasia** refers to an inability to speak fluently without effort and with correct grammar. Speech is halting and often consists of short sequences of nouns so that the grammatical structure of a sentence is broken. Dronkers, Redfern, and Knight (2000) provided this example of the speech of a Broca's patient in a picture description task:

> O, yeah. Det's a boy an' a girl . . . an' . . . a . . . car . . . house . . . light po' (pole). Dog an' a . . . boat'N det's a . . . mm . . . a . . . coffee, an' reading. (p. 951)

The patient with Broca's aphasia can comprehend single words and short grammatical sentences, however.

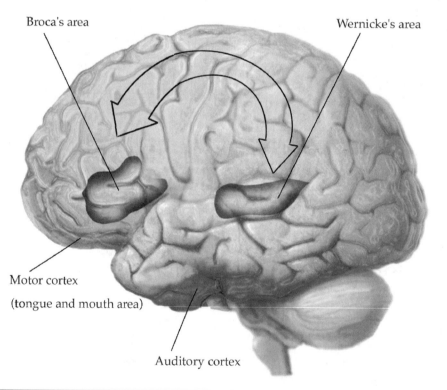

Figure 8.3 Broca's area and Wernicke's area in the left hemisphere.

SOURCE: Adapted from Goodglass (1993).

In 1874, Wernicke reported on patients who could speak easily (albeit unintelligibly) but who failed to comprehend speech (McCarthy & Warrington, 1990). They tended to pronounce phonemes in a jumble, sometimes uttering novel words or neologisms. Postmortem examination of one such patient revealed a lesion in the area just behind or posterior to Broca's area. **Wernicke's aphasia** refers to a comprehension dysfunction. Speech is fluent and effortless, although often semantically meaningless. Dronkers et al. (2000) provided the following example of the Wernicke's patient:

> Ah, yes, it's, ah . . . several things. It's a girl . . . uncurl . . . on a boat. A dog . . . 'S is another dog . . . uh-oh . . . long's . . . on a boat. The lady, it's a young lady. An' a man. They eatin'. 'S be place there. This . . . a tree! A boat. No, this is a . . . It's a house. Over in here . . . a cake. An it's, it's a lot of water. Ah, all right. I think I mentioned about that boat. (p. 951)

Although Broca's area is specialized for the production of speech sounds, it, too, plays a role in the perception and comprehension of speech. As the speech sounds or phonemes are taken in by the auditory processing regions of the temporal lobe, they activate regions in the inferior frontal lobe of the brain. Broca's area is included among these regions, most likely as a way to maintain the phonological codes of the incoming speech (Gernsbacher & Kaschak, 2003). These are the same codes used to prepare for the articulation of speech, either aloud or silently in the form of inner speech. The motor regions of speech production in Broca's area are thus recruited as part of the speech perception process (see Chapter 2). Recent research has shown that this perceptual-motor link is not present in newborn infants but begins to emerge by the age of six months (Imada, Zhang, Cheour, Taulu, Ahonen, & Kuhl, 2006). The neural linkage between speech sound processing in the temporal lobe and Broca's area is significantly strengthened by the time the infant is one year of age, as the infant learns the ability to comprehend and produce phonemes and first words.

Laterality. Hemispheric dominance or **brain lateralization** in humans means that one hemisphere controls key motor and cognitive functions. Approximately 90% of people reveal a left dominant hemisphere, meaning that they are right-handed. Recall that the brain shows contralateral control, such that the motor and sensory nerves of the right side of the body are controlled by the left hemisphere of the brain. Right-handedness is found universally across diverse cultures (Corballis, 1989). Moreover, language is localized in the left hemisphere of virtually all right-handed individuals. When right-handed people suffer damage to their left hemisphere, the frequency of aphasia is high (McCarthy & Warrington, 1990). Only rarely does a right-handed individual lose language function from damage to the right hemisphere.

Researchers investigated the localization of language in a remarkable series of studies involving split-brain patients (Gazzaniga, 1970, 1995; Gazzaniga, Bogen, & Sperry, 1965). These individuals suffered horrendous seizures from epilepsy that could not be controlled by the usual therapies. During the 1950s, physicians treating such severe cases successfully controlled the seizures by cutting the connective tissue between hemispheres, called the **corpus callosum**. An epileptic seizure could be likened to an electrical storm; by severing the hemispheric bridge, the surgeons isolated the storm to one hemisphere, lessening its devastation. After recovering from the surgery, these patients behaved quite normally and revealed no cognitive deficits to casual observers. Yet careful testing revealed highly selective deficits.

If a right-handed, split-brain patient was given a common object such as a coin, then the patient's ability to verbalize the name of the object depended on which hand he or she used. If the coin was placed in the patient's right hand, then all information about it would be processed by the left hemisphere. This was because of contralateral control, whereby the left hemisphere controlled the right side of the body and the right hemisphere controlled the left side. Because of the language centers in the left hemisphere, the patient could readily name the object as a coin. But if the coin was placed in the patient's left hand, thereby sending the information to the right hemisphere, then the patient was unable to name the object. When pressed to point to the object just placed in the left hand, the patient could do so— but only by pointing with his or her left hand. This astonishing outcome showed that the right hemisphere indeed knew what the object was but could not name it because language use depended on involving the left hemisphere.

Further experiments verified these observations by taking advantage of the fact that the objects in the left visual field project only to the right visual hemisphere, as discussed in Chapter 2. The split-brain patient sat in front of a display screen and fixated on a central point. A stimulus was flashed briefly (100–200 milliseconds) in the left visual field so that it was received and processed only by the right hemisphere. The patient was unable to name the object, suggesting that language requires processing in the left hemisphere. If asked to pick up the object with the left hand from among some alternatives behind a screen, the patient was usually successful because the right hemisphere successfully recognized the object.

Thus, in right-handed individuals, language critically depends on processing in the dominant left hemisphere. The situation for left-handed individuals is much more complicated, by the way. It appears, from the various tests just noted, that most left-handed individuals show speech functions in both hemispheres. Some left-handers show speech localized in the left hemisphere, and few, if any, reveal localization in the right hemisphere (McCarthy & Warrington, 1990).

Of great interest, activation is observed in the left hemisphere, including Broca's area, when deaf individuals who learned ASL as their first language observe someone making signs (Neville & Bavelier, 2000). As shown in Color Plate 7 in the section of color plates, the pattern is very similar to that observed in the left hemisphere when hearing individuals read English. Although ASL does not involve speech, it has a complex grammar expressed through hand motions and spatial locations (Poizner, Bellugi, & Klima, 1990). Thus, the fMRI results imply that there is a strong biological predisposition for the grammar of a language—whether it involves sounds or visual signs—to be represented in the left hemisphere. The native users of ASL learned English as a second language late in life, after the critical period for grammar acquisition. As can be seen in Color Plate 7, reading English resulted primarily in right rather than left hemisphere activation. This result suggests that the bias for left hemisphere language representation is not expressed when learned after a critical period of development.

Although Broca's and Wernicke's areas in the left hemisphere are rightfully viewed as necessary for language in most humans, it is incorrect to think of language as localized. Many other cortical and subcortical regions are also necessary for comprehension and expression of language, particularly when the reading and writing of visible language is considered in addition to spoken language (Goodglass, 1993). The language zone is pictured in Figure 8.4 from a lateral view of the left hemisphere. It extends beyond Broca's and

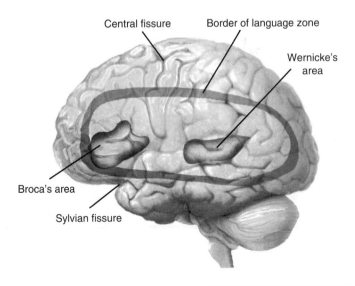

Figure 8.4   The language zone in the left hemisphere.

SOURCE: From Goodglass, H., *Understanding Aphasia,* copyright © 1993. Reprinted with permission from Academic Press.

Wernicke's areas anteriorly into the frontal lobe and posteriorly into the parietal lobe. It includes regions that are both superior and inferior to the Broca's and Wernicke's areas in terms of their vertical location in the left hemisphere. Neuroimaging of sentence comprehension has revealed that besides Wernicke's area (word/phonological processing) and Broca's area (production/syntactic processing), there are temporal and frontal regions involved in phonological and lexical-semantic processing (Gernsbacher & Kaschak, 2003). Parallel regions in the right hemisphere are also active, particularly in the comprehension of multiple sentences linked together in discourse. Thus, language is a prime example of how a complex cognitive function involves multiple distributed regions of the brain.

COMPREHENSION OF LANGUAGE

Recognizing the words of a sentence is necessary for comprehension, but it is only a beginning. One must also recognize the syntactic relations among the words to build a mental structure of the sentence's meaning. Similarly, to grasp the relation between one sentence and the next, it is necessary to build mental structures that represent meaning. The structures built by a listener or reader start at the local level of words and sentences and proceed to the global units found in extended discourse. In building these structures, one must "read between the lines" or infer meanings that are not explicitly stated. One must also identify the intended meaning of a sentence when words with more than one literal meaning are used or when words are used in non-literal ways, such as in metaphors.

As in building any structure, the laying of a foundation is critical (Gernsbacher, 1990). The time and effort needed to develop mental structures that incorporate the meaning of the text provide useful information about the process. For example, the first sentence of a paragraph takes longer to read than do later sentences because the reader uses it to lay the foundation for a mental structure (Cirilo, 1981; Cirilo & Foss, 1980). This result occurs even when the topic sentence comes later in the paragraph (Kieras, 1978). So, the extra time reflects foundation building, not just the time needed to process the most important or informative sentence.

Word Recognition

The problem of speech recognition was treated in Chapter 2 as a perceptual problem of identifying words that are run together in spoken sentences and phonemes that are coarticulated. However, there is also a memory retrieval problem that must be addressed. Assuming that people know anywhere from 30,000 to 80,000 words, how is it that they retrieve the right representation so quickly?

Data-driven processes work to recognize visual patterns from the bottom up. In the case of words, there are three distinct domains of features that must be identified (e.g., Graesser, Hoffman, & Clark, 1980; Perfetti, 1985; Stanovich, Cunningham, & Feeman, 1984). For example, consider the features associated with the word "bird." When one hears a spoken word, the sounds are identified as phonological features. These are the phonemes used by the speaker to pronounce "bird." Orthographic features refer to the letters used to a spell a word in a visual format. When one reads a word, the individual letters and the visual shape of the word as a whole are processed as orthographic features. The **graphemes** used to represent visually the phonemes of a language must be identified. As shown in Figure 8.5, the identification of graphemes can also activate phonological features. This can happen not only when reading a word aloud but also when reading it silently. The identification of the phonological and/or orthographic features drives the bottom-up identification of the lexical-semantic features—the meaning of the word. Words or morphemes are verbal labels for underlying concepts. Morphemes and the concepts to which they refer constitute the lexical-semantic domain.

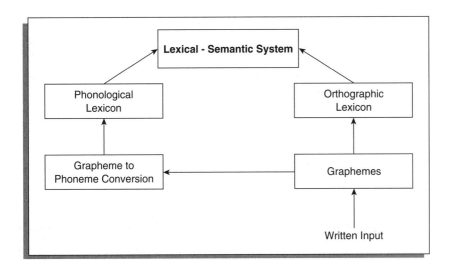

Figure 8.5   Domains of features activated in the comprehension of spoken and written words.

SOURCE: Adapted from Caramazza (1991).

A PET study has shown that specialized areas in the left hemisphere respond to words and pseudowords, both of which look like words in that they follow the orthographic rules of English (Petersen, Fox, Snyder, & Raichle, 1990). As shown in Color Plate 8 in the section of colored plates and the associated table, false fonts and letter strings activate the visual cortex just as do words and pseudowords. All four kinds of stimuli involve a low-level analysis of visual features taken on by the visual cortex at the rear of the brain in both hemispheres. But only the words and pseudowords prompt an analysis by a specialized system in the left hemisphere that analyzes the visual form of words as such. Reading well demands that one handle words effectively and efficiently.

Equally convincing evidence has stressed the role of top-down or conceptually driven processes, as seen in the word superiority effect and other findings discussed in Chapter 2. By using world knowledge and the context in which a word is encountered, it is possible to form hypotheses and make good guesses regarding its identity (Palmer, MacLeod, Hunt, & Davidson, 1985; Thorndike, 1973–1974). In fact, context enables one to identify words even when the critical data are missing, as seen in the following sentence: Rexmaxkaxly xt ix poxsixle xo rxplxce xvexy txirx lextex of x sextexce xitx an x, anx yox stxll xan xanxge xo rxad xt—wixh sxme xifxicxltx (Anderson, 1990; Lindsay & Norman, 1977).

When words do not fit the expectations of conceptually driven processes, there is extra effort required in analyzing the data from the bottom up. This added effort can be detected by monitoring brain waves during sentence comprehension in an event-related potential (ERP) that occurs as a negative voltage change that reaches its peak amplitude 400 milliseconds after the unexpected word appears (Kutas & Hillyard, 1980, 1984). The ERP is labeled an N400. Kutas and Hillyard (1980) presented readers with a set of mundane sentences that occasionally included an anomalous or low-probability word. For example, compare these two sentences:

He likes ice cream and sugar in his *socks*.

He likes ice cream and sugar in his *tea*.

Recording from a region in the parietal lobe, Kutas and Hillyard (1980) observed a significant negative component voltage 400 milliseconds after the last word of the first sentence but not the second sentence. In the context of these sentences, the word "socks" is semantically anomalous, whereas "tea" is predictable from conceptually driven processes.

In addition, a large N400 component occurs following the first word of the sentence (He), and smaller ones occur after each succeeding word

(Kutas, Van Petten, & Besson, 1988). Notice that the first word of a sentence, as well as the unexpected final word of "socks," must be processed from the bottom up and fit into a mental structure for the sentence. The N400, then, is sensitive to the meaning of the word and is triggered when its meaning is unpredictable. The largest N400 is obtained for a semantically unpredictable word, regardless of whether it comes in the middle or at the end of the sentence.

Sentence Comprehension

Complex sentences are harder to comprehend than simple sentences. For example, a sentence that negates an assertion is harder to comprehend than one that simply asserts a proposition. This occurs because the listener or reader must first presuppose a positive proposition and then deny it. Clark and Chase (1972) presented readers with a picture like that shown in Figure 8.6 and one of four sentences:

The star is above the plus. (true affirmative)

The plus is above the star. (false affirmative)

The plus is not above the star. (true negative)

The star is not above the plus. (false negative)

As you can see from Figure 8.6, Sentences 1 and 3 are true statements, whereas Sentences 2 and 4 are false statements. Clark and Chase (1972) argued that the negative sentences (Sentences 3 and 4) required the reader to engage in more processing than did the affirmative assertions of Sentences 1 and 2. Specifically, they argued that the negatives entail both the supposition that the star is above the plus and the assertion that this supposition is false. To expose the additional effort required by the reader, Clark and Chase measured the time required to verify each type of sentence.

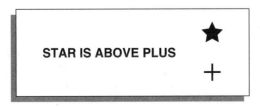

STAR IS ABOVE PLUS

Figure 8.6   A sentence comprehension task.

SOURCE: From Clark, H. H., & Chase, W. G., On the process of comparing sentences against pictures. *Cognitive Psychology, 3,* 472-517, copyright © 1972. Reprinted with permission.

If the negative sentences require the reader to presuppose the positive assertion, then the time needed to comprehend this assertion must be factored into total verification time. From the observed times for each of the four sentences, Clark and Chase (1972) estimated that comprehension of the simple assertion (the star is above the plus) takes slightly more than 1,450 milliseconds. All four sentences required this amount of time. The researchers further estimated that the time needed to deny the assertion adds roughly another 300 milliseconds. Only Sentences 3 and 4 needed this extra time.

Another dimension of complexity is voice, with active voice easier to comprehend than passive voice. Still another is the use of simple sentences with one independent clause versus a sentence with a dependent clause in addition to an independent clause. Just, Carpenter, Keller, Eddy, and Thulborn (1996) presented people with sentences of different complexities and recorded brain activation using fMRI. The simplest sentence to comprehend was written in active voice and conjoined two clauses without embedding a relative clause. An example of an active conjoined sentence is "The reporter attacked the senator and admitted the error." A somewhat more complex sentence can be constructed from these same words by embedding a relative clause after the subject of the sentence, which interrupts the main clause. An example of a subject relative clause sentence is "The reporter who attacked the senator admitted the error." Finally, in the most complex sentence, the first noun serves as both the subject of the sentence and the object of the relative clause. An example of an object relative clause sentence is "The reporter who the senator attacked admitted the error." Although this type is grammatical, it is very complex in structure. After reading each sentence, the participants answered a question to measure whether comprehension was successful (e.g., "The reporter attacked the senator, true or false?").

The results of the Just et al. (1996) study showed that as the sentences increased in grammatical complexity, there was an increase in processing time and in the probability of incorrectly answering the comprehension question. In addition, activation levels in Wernicke's area in the left hemisphere showed a systematic increase across the three kinds of sentences. Of interest, the activation levels were substantially lower in this same brain region in the opposite right hemisphere, but even there a reliable increase was obtained as the sentences became more difficult to understand. Furthermore, a similar pattern of results was found for Broca's region. Just et al. noted that the role of Broca's area in comprehension is unknown but that it may generate articulatory codes for the words of the sentence or may assist with syntactic processing.

Bridging Inferences. **Anaphora** is the use of a word to substitute for a preceding word or phrase. The idea may be illustrated with these sentences (adapted from Gernsbacher, 1990, pp. 108–109):

1. *William* went for a walk in Verona, frustrated with his play about star-crossed lovers. *William* meandered through Dante's square, when the balcony scene came to him suddenly.

2. *William* went for a walk in Verona, frustrated with his play about star-crossed lovers. *The bard* meandered through Dante's square, when the balcony scene came to him suddenly.

3. *William* went for a walk in Verona, frustrated with his play about star-crossed lovers. *He* meandered through Dante's square, when the balcony scene came to him suddenly.

Writers frequently use anaphora to establish referential coherence, especially anaphoric pronouns, as illustrated by Example 3. Of the 50 most common words that appear in print in the English language, nearly one-third are pronouns (Kucera & Francis, 1967).

Given-New Strategy. Clark (1977) theorized that readers (and listeners) employ the **given-new strategy** to assist them in making the correct inferences. This strategy is based on the assumption that writers cooperate with readers to help make their meanings understood, just as speakers do in conversations. Specifically, writers clearly mark information that the readers already understand, that is, the given information that provides a shared basis for communication between writers and readers. Writers also mark what they are now making an assertion about, that is, the new information that they want readers to grasp.

On coming to the second sentence in Example 1, the reader determines what is being asserted as new information (someone is having trouble in generating examples) and what is old information (the person in question is William). The reader next identifies a unique antecedent for the given information in working memory. The new information can then be fit into a new structure that links the predicates of both sentences to the same person.

Haviland and Clark (1974) found that the time needed to read and comprehend a sentence varied with the explicitness of the anaphora. This would be expected if readers used the given-new strategy and experienced more or less difficulty in identifying a unique antecedent for the given information. The

> The given-new strategy in reading assumes that writers mark information already understood and information meant to be a new assertion.

term "The bard" identifies the antecedent only by applying one's knowledge of English literature and the writings of William Shakespeare. The pronoun "He" could, in a longer text, match more than one antecedent, so the reference in Example 3 is the least explicit. Thus, in Example 1, a unique referent is specified by repeating the name verbatim. In Examples 2 and 3, the reader must infer a link that is not explicitly given. Haviland and Clark aptly called these **bridging inferences** because the reader must build a bridge between two ideas to grasp their relation.

Polysemy. So far, comprehension has been discussed as if each word in a sentence could mean only one thing. **Polysemy** is the property of language that a single word can have more than one meaning. When a reader encounters words with more than one interpretation, how do cognitive processes arrive at the right meanings? Homonyms and metaphors illustrate the problem that polysemy poses for comprehension.

Suppose that the reader comes across a homonym, such as *bug* or *watch*, that can be interpreted in different ways. The preceding words might bias the interpretation (e.g., spiders, roaches), or the syntax might accomplish the same purpose (e.g., "I like the watch" vs. "I like to watch"). But what becomes of the other meaning? One possibility is that it simply decays with time (Anderson, 1983). However, the findings of Gernsbacher and Faust (1991) indicate unintended meaning is actively suppressed and lost sooner than would be expected by decay alone. When only one meaning of a homophone was supported by the context (e.g., Pam was diagnosed by a quack), the inappropriate meaning (i.e., the sound of a duck) was no longer active after 350 milliseconds. But when the context failed to bias a specific meaning (e.g., Pam was annoyed by the quack), both meanings remained activated for up to 850 milliseconds. Thus, it is likely that an active suppression of the inappropriate meanings takes place when the context steers the interpretation process away from those meanings.

Similarly, to comprehend a metaphor (e.g., time flies), one must ignore or suppress the literal meaning of words in order to grasp the intended meaning. It is possible that readers first try a literal interpretation and then look for nonliteral meanings. Alternatively, they may use the context of the metaphor wisely and immediately capture the nonliteral interpretation. Experiments have shown that with the proper context, the nonliteral meaning of a metaphor is grasped without first trying the literal interpretation (Glucksberg, Gildea, & Bookin, 1982; Inhoff, Lima, & Carroll, 1984). For example, Inhoff et al. (1984) measured how long readers spent looking at and trying to comprehend a sentence with a metaphorical interpretation such as the meaning of "choked" in the following sentence:

1. The directors mercifully choked smaller companies.

For some readers, this sentence was preceded by an appropriate metaphoric context such as the following:

2. The company used murderous tactics.

For others, the sentence was preceded by a context designed to encourage a literal reading of the term "choked" such as the following:

> Words in a text must be actively interpreted because they can have more than one meaning. In comprehending metaphors, for example, the nonliteral meaning—not the literal meaning—must be activated.

3. The company used competitive tactics.

Inhoff et al. (1984) found that readers spent less time in comprehending the metaphoric Sentence 1 when it was preceded by Sentence 2 than when it was preceded by Sentence 3. The metaphoric context of Sentence 2 primed activation of a nonliteral interpretation of "choked."

Discourse Comprehension

Structures develop at multiple levels—words, sentences, and discourse (Foss, 1988). Numerous models have been proposed regarding the high level of global structures that characterize discourse as a whole (Kintsch & van Dijk, 1978; Meyer, 1975; Thorndyke, 1977). To begin, just what is meant by the term "discourse"? When does a collection of sentences constitute true discourse versus just a bunch of sentences? The answer, according to Johnson-Laird (1983), is when the references in each sentence are locally coherent with one another and when the sentences can be fit into a global framework of causes and effects. We first consider the issue of referential coherence and then examine Kintsch and van Dijk's model of the global structure of discourse.

Referential Coherence. When the words and phrases of one sentence in a paragraph refer unambiguously to those of other sentences in the paragraph, the sentences possess **referential coherence.** Johnson-Laird (1983) offered the following three collections of sentences to illustrate this property of true discourse:

> (1) It was the Christmas party at Heighton that was one of the turning-points in Perkins' life. The duchess had sent him a three-page wire in the hyperbolical style of her class, conveying a vague impression that she and the Duke had arranged to commit suicide together if Perkins didn't "chuck" any previous engagement he had made. And Perkins had felt in a slipshod sort of way—for at least at that period he was incapable of ordered thought—he might as well be at Heighton as anywhere. (from *Perkins and Mankind* by Max Beerbohm)

(2) Scripps O'Neil had two wives. To tip or not to tip? Dawn crept over the Downs like a sinister white animal, followed by the snarling cries of a wind eating its way between the black boughs of the thorns. When I had reached my eighteenth year I was recalled by my parents to my paternal roof in Wales.

(3) The field buys a tiny rain. The rain hops. It burns the noisy sky in some throbbing belt. It buries some yellow wind under it. The throbbing belt freezes some person on it. The belt dies of it. It freezes the ridiculous field. (pp. 356–357)

Which do you judge to be true discourse? Which is the least qualified for the title?

> A paragraph is referentially coherent when the words and phrases of one sentence refer unambiguously to those of the other sentences.

The difference between Examples (1) and (2) is easy to detect. The sentences in Example (1) hang together, whereas those in Example (2) plainly do not. But what about the sentences in Example (3), which Johnson-Laird generated using a computer program? Although each sentence is nonsensical, the paragraph seems structured. The pronouns of one sentence seem to refer to a previous sentence. Nouns are repeated from one sentence to the next. Words related in meaning—here, words describing weather—are laced throughout. These are among the cohesive ties that a writer uses in creating true discourse (Halliday & Hasan, 1976).

Global Frameworks. The nonsensical sentences generated using the computer in Example (3) illustrate that there is more to referential coherence than local cohesion between one word and the next within and between adjacent sentences. An organizing topic, theme, or global structure is also needed. Theme is absent in the following paragraph from Johnson-Laird (1983), even though each sentence makes sense on its own and the local links between sentences are interpretable:

My daughter works in a library in London. London is the home of a good museum of natural history. The museum is organized on the basis of cladistic theory. This theory concerns the classification of living things. Living things evolved from inanimate matter. (p. 379)

Kintsch and van Dijk (1978) suggested that schemas for different types of discourse guide the construction of a global framework. The individual propositions expressed by the sentences of a text were described by Kintsch and van Dijk as **micropropositions.** The more densely a text is packed with micropropositions, and the more often it demands bridging inferences among these propositions, the harder it is to read (Kintsch, 1974; Miller & Kintsch, 1980). Moreover, the longer a proposition is held active in working memory while establishing referential coherence during comprehension, the more likely it will be encoded successfully into long-term memory and recalled later on (Kintsch & Keenan, 1973).

Kintsch and van Dijk (1978) also contrasted micropropositions with **macropropositions,** defined as the schema-based generalizations that summarize the main ideas or gist of the story. Telling a story, arguing a case, or recalling an episode from memory would each, presumably, invoke a different schema. The pertinent schema would establish certain goals for the reader and sort through which micropropositions are relevant to those goals. The schema would also generalize the form of the relevant propositions in order to make it useful as a summary of the main ideas or gist of the text. The net result is a summary of the text—a macrostructure—that guides comprehension and memory. As shown in Figure 8.7, reading, then, involves more

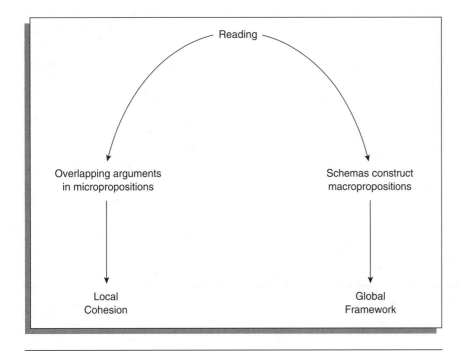

Figure 8.7   Reading requires establishing local cohesion and a global framework.

than establishing cohesion at a local level of the text by finding overlapping arguments in micropropositions. It also involves constructing macropropositions that provide a global framework for understanding the text.

Eye Movements and Comprehension

The interaction of perceptual processes and working memory as reading unfolds in real time has been investigated (Just & Carpenter, 1980, 1992). Each fixation of the eyes on a word or on part of a word provides a discrete input to the visual system. The duration of most fixations ranges from 200 to 350 milliseconds, with great variability (Pollatsek & Rayner, 1989). A rapid eye movement called a *saccade* jumps the focus of foveal vision to a new point in between these fixations. When one reads a book, a saccadic eye movement typically would advance (or at times regress) foveal vision about 5 to 9 character spaces within 15 to 40 milliseconds. The reader, in essence, gains a series of snapshots of information about the text as the eyes jump across and down the page. The span of each snapshot appears to be biased to the right of the fixation point. The reader extracts information from 4 characters to the left of the fixation point and up to 15 characters to the right (McConkie & Rayner, 1975). Although the reader gains no information during a saccade, he or she is unaware of the movement itself.

Reading typically involves fixating about 80% of the content words (nouns, verbs, and modifiers) and 20% of the function words. High-frequency words are fixated in less time than are low-frequency words, indicating that the lexical or semantic properties of the language control eye movements. High-frequency words are often only a few letters in length, but even with word length held constant, the greater the frequency, the shorter the fixation required. Words that are frequent, short, and predictable in the context of the text are often skipped over altogether. Also, the processing of words begins prior to fixating on them. This is possible by previewing a word in parafoveal or peripheral vision. In some cases, the fixation on the word serves primarily to complete processing that had already begun in the periphery of an earlier fixation (Reichle, Pollatsek, Fisher, & Rayner, 1998). Taking into account the time needed to fixate on the input characters, to recognize each word, and to build the necessary mental structures in working memory, it is not surprising that most people read at a rate of about 250 to 300 words per minute. The rate might be much slower with especially challenging text.

> Reading speed is normally about 250 to 300 words per minute. This rate is constrained by perceptual factors in fixating on text and by cognitive factors in building mental structures.

Just and Carpenter (1980) made two key assumptions in linking eye fixations to comprehension. First, the **immediacy assumption** holds that the reader assigns an interpretation to each word as it is fixated. The reader sometimes needs to revise his or her interpretation based on a subsequent fixation. For example, in the sentence "Mary loves Jonathan . . . ," the reader might initially assign one meaning and then repair it when the final word is encountered: "apples."

Second, the **eye-mind assumption** holds that the duration of fixation varies with the amount of information that must be processed in working memory at that instant. In other words, the work of comprehension takes place during the fixation; the next saccadic eye movement is suppressed until the reader is ready to move forward. At times, regressive eye movements are needed so that the reader can go back and reprocess information that was misinterpreted initially. Such a regressive movement would probably take place in reading "Mary loves Jonathan apples." But the reader does not take in several snapshots of data, hold them in memory, and then pause for an extended period of time to comprehend the data.

Just and Carpenter (1980, 1992) found that the more difficult a section of the text is to read, the longer individuals fixate. Good readers with large working memory capacities take extra time to resolve ambiguities of interpretation. The authors' model and findings are consistent with the idea that reading is a time-consuming, high-level cognitive skill. If that is so, then how is speed reading possible? Many programs have claimed that you can learn to read as fast as 1,000 or more words per minute without loss of comprehension. To achieve this would mean holding comprehension steady while reading four times as fast as normal.

One trick taught in speed reading courses is to start fixations slightly to the right of the first word of each line and to take the last fixation to the left of the final word of each line. In other words, one should reduce fixations to a minimum by picking up characters to the left and right of the fixation point as much as possible. Efficiency is further increased by focusing fixations on content words rather than on function words and by drawing inferences to fill in the gaps. So long as the key lexical (e.g., he, walk, dog, friend) and syntactic (e.g., -ed) information is fixated, the other function words of the following sentence can be inferred without fixating on them: He walked the dog of a friend. Finally, in speed reading, one should avoid regressive eye movements that go backward in the text. The speed reader tries to force fixations forward at a rapid rate. Clearly, this is a problem if the material is not immediately understood.

Unfamiliar words, words with multiple meanings, and words that must be linked by means of suppositions or inferences all are going to be misrepresented if the reader blazes ahead without adequate time and effort to build the proper mental structures. The same problem arises in integrating larger units such as paragraphs. Like so many other claims that sound too good to be true, speed reading is not really reading (Masson, 1983). That is, reading at 1,000 or 2,000 words per minute produces a loss of comprehension and memory for the text. When comprehension and memory are assessed carefully in the laboratory using well-designed recognition tests (i.e., where the correct answer cannot be readily guessed without full comprehension) or recall tests, increasing reading rate invariably causes a loss in comprehension. This is especially easy to detect when the text is unfamiliar and difficult to read. Nonetheless, speed reading skills have their place in allowing one to scan familiar texts to get their gist, if not their details, or to search for a specific piece of information. Instead of calling it speed reading, however, a more accurate name would be trained skimming.

SUMMARY

1. Language is a system of symbols that are used to communicate ideas among two or more individuals. It uses both mental and external representations such as printed text. Language uses arbitrary symbols that refer to events displaced in time and space. The mental lexicon and grammar of a language are productive, allowing one to generate an infinite number of novel sentences. A language must be learnable by children, it must be able to be spoken and understood readily by adults, it must capture the ideas that people normally communicate, and it must enable communication among groups of people in a social and cultural context. All human languages make use of 50 or so speech sounds or phonological segments produced by our vocal apparatus. Each such utterance is a phoneme, defined as a basic speech sound that makes a difference in meaning. A morpheme is a minimal unit of speech used repeatedly in a language to code a specific meaning; it is made up of two or more phonemes, such as a word or a suffix.

2. Languages differ in terms of their semantics, syntax, and pragmatics. Semantics concerns the use of symbols to refer to objects, events, and ideas in the world. The words used in language make up the lexicon that must be represented mentally in fluent speakers. Syntax concerns the grammatical rules for ordering words to construct meaningful and acceptable sentences in a language. Pragmatics concerns the use of language within social contexts. People command, inform, warn, and otherwise communicate their

intentions as direct speech acts (e.g., "Open the window") or as indirect speech acts (e.g., "Dreadfully hot in here, don't you think?"). An implicit agreement, called the cooperative principle, governs conversations to ensure that participants say appropriate things and end the conversation at a mutually agreeable point.

3. Universal grammar refers to the genetically determined knowledge of human language that allows children in all cultures to rapidly acquire the language to which they are exposed. Whether language is innate is another hotly debated question that remains unresolved. Language is localized in the left hemisphere of virtually all right-handed individuals. Damage to Broca's area in the left hemisphere causes a language disorder or aphasia. Broca's aphasia refers to an inability to speak fluently without effort and with correct grammar. By contrast, damage to Wernicke's area disrupts language comprehension. Speech is fluent and effortless in Wernicke's aphasia, although it is often semantically meaningless.

4. Text comprehension—reading—has been investigated much more extensively than has writing. The theme of cognition as active construction is well-illustrated by the processes of reading. The reader builds mental structures at the local level of micropropositions expressed in words and sentences as well as at the global or macropropositional level of paragraphs and discourse. Sentences possess referential coherence when the words and phrases of one sentence refer unambiguously to those of other sentences in the same paragraph. In building mental structures, the reader uses more than the literal words on the page. For example, the reader uses his or her knowledge about the world to make plausible bridging inferences during comprehension.

5. Normal reading speed is about 250 to 300 words per minute. This rate is constrained by the perceptual factors in fixating on text and the cognitive factors in building mental structures. The reader appears to assign an interpretation to words, including ambiguous ones, as soon as they are encountered. The amount of time spent fixating on a word corresponds with the difficulty encountered in processing and assigning an interpretation.

KEY TERMS

semantics

morpheme

mental lexicon

syntax

pragmatics

speech act

cooperative principle

productivity

universal grammar

Broca's aphasia

Wernicke's aphasia

brain lateralization

corpus callosum

graphemes

anaphora

given-new strategy

bridging inferences

polysemy

referential coherence

micropropositions

macropropositions

immediacy assumption

eye-mind assumption

CHAPTER 9

PROBLEM SOLVING

E very day, you are faced with problems to solve, from the moment you wake up until the moment you fall asleep. How will you get up in time for class or work? How will you get where you need to go? What will you eat? Finding food may be a minor or major problem depending on where in the world you live, whether you are gainfully employed, whether you have a place to stay where cooking is possible, and so on. To obtain, say, dinner tonight, you must come up with a plan for action. When planning, you might imagine a map of a city or town with grocery stores, fast-food chains, and restaurants with various price ranges. Planning stipulates the goal (e.g., eat a grilled steak) and examines the numerous paths that might be taken to reach the goal (e.g., grill at home, find a steakhouse, "borrow" a steak off the neighbor's grill).

Each path includes numerous steps along the way, some of which fit together to achieve a specific subgoal. For example, a subgoal for grilling at home might be to fire up some charcoal, assuming that local air quality laws allow it. This would involve several steps: going to the garage, finding the charcoal, putting the charcoal in the grill, applying lighter fluid, lighting the coals, waiting five minutes until the coals get cold, reapplying fluid and relighting, and so on. Any one of these steps might send you off on another side path to achieve a new subgoal. For example, it may be necessary to go buy charcoal, to search the house desperately for matches, or to put out a fire on the patio started by all that lighter fluid.

Each day, then, poses new problems to think through. Because of its centrality, problem solving has been studied extensively by psychologists interested in the nature of thinking in general. Problems vary in their demands and elicit different types of thinking. After introducing some different kinds of thinking, this chapter considers the components of representing problems and searching for solutions by means of algorithms and heuristics. Attempts have been made to identify general-purpose representation and search procedures that can be used to solve any kind of problem. As will be seen, human problem solving relies on more than these general problem-solving methods. Some of the common obstacles to successful problem solving are then considered before the chapter closes with a discussion of creativity—its definition, sources, and stages.

TYPES OF THINKING

The dinner problem depicted earlier illustrates what is called **directed thinking**; it is goal oriented and rational (Gilhooly, 1982). Such thinking requires a clear, well-defined goal. One must then find a path that leads to the goal, with the aim of doing so as directly as possible. The costs of each path are certainly taken into account (e.g., it may be easier to find a steakhouse but much more affordable to grill at home). In general, directed thinking avoids wandering aimlessly, exploring odd options, and looking for creative solutions. Just such aimless meandering might be necessary to arrive at highly novel solutions (e.g., "borrowing" the neighbor's steak is creative and highly affordable, albeit unscrupulous and possibly dangerous).

Wandering thought is called **undirected thinking**. Such thought meanders and is anything but rational and goal oriented (Berlyne, 1965). Dreaming and daydreaming were identified early on by Freud (1900/1953) as forms of undirected thought that are not bound by the ordinary constraints of reality. Undirected thinking takes us to destinations that are sometimes murky and sometimes insightful. It can play a role in creativity and in the solutions to problems that are poorly defined.

Well-Defined and Ill-Defined Problems

Directed thinking begins with the assumption that the problem at hand is a **well-defined problem**. In technical terms, such a problem is said to have a definable **initial state** (e.g., need for dinner), **goal state** (e.g., steak dinner), and one or more paths to obtaining the goal. Each path can be specified as a series of intermediate states, some of which are critical **subgoals** (e.g., burning coals). The way in which one moves from one state to the next is defined by a set of rules. Each legal move from the initial state to intermediate states to the final goal state is specifically defined by an **operator**. In solving the problem of having a steak dinner, there are many such operators. If theft is not among them, then the creative solution of snatching the neighbor's steak is never even considered. All of the states and operators taken together define what is called a **problem space**.

At this point, it might help to consider some games and puzzles studied by psychologists in the field of problem solving. Chess is one such game. The initial state is defined by the players lined up on the board for the opening move. The goal state is defined as checkmate. The operators are the legal moves of each game piece (e.g., the bishop may move or attack the opponent's pieces as many spaces as desired, but only along its assigned diagonal on the chessboard). The 64 squares of the chessboard and the six kinds of pieces yield an immense problem space, one so large that even a supercomputer could not possibly check all possible states before deciding on a move in a game (Simon, 1990).

Part of the problem space of a much simpler puzzle that may be familiar to you is shown in Figure 9.1. It is called the Tower of Hanoi problem. The initial state, at the top of the figures, stacks three disks of different sizes on

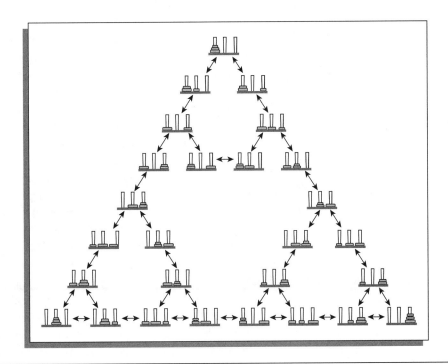

Figure 9.1   Problem space for the Tower of Hanoi. The goal state is shown in the lower right corner.

SOURCE: Kotovsky and Fallside (1989). Copyright © 1989 by Lawrence Erlbaum Associates. Reprinted by permission.

the first of three pegs, as shown. The problem is to move the disks to the third peg so that they are stacked as shown in the goal state in the lower right corner of the figure. The only operator here is to move the top disk from one peg onto another peg, with the restriction that it not cover a smaller disk.

Each drawing in Figure 9.1 represents a state of the problem space, a legally possible state that might be reached by applying the operator. From State 1, one can move the smallest disk either to Peg 2 or to Peg 3, as shown. Moving it to Peg 2 allows only one possible next move, namely, putting the middle-sized disk on Peg 3. From there, as you can see, two possible moves can be made. To solve the Tower of Hanoi problem, one must find a path through the problem space to progress from the initial state to the goal state. The paths on the left of the figure lead to states removed from the goal. Directed thinking, when applied flawlessly to the problem, would result in the path on the far right, a stepwise progression through seven moves.

It should be noted that the problem space that exists for a given person may well include errors or omissions. If an operator is misunderstood, such as the rule for moving a knight in chess, then a flawed problem space would be generated. Similarly, an inexperienced chess player who simply never moved the knights would be working within an incomplete problem space.

> A well-defined problem can be described clearly in terms of an initial state, a goal state, and subgoals. These states, plus all states into which one can move using specified operators, together compose the problem space.

Of course, many problems encountered in daily life seem quite remote from the problems of having dinner, playing chess, and solving the tower puzzle. Finding a career and succeeding at it is an important problem facing most students reading this book. Although the beginning state of such a problem may be clear enough, the goal state certainly is not. The goal of a successful career could be defined in an infinite variety of ways. One can attempt to structure the problems by deciding in advance exactly what defines success (e.g., becoming the head of General Motors or president of the United States). But a truly well-defined problem specifies all of the legal transition states and the operators that generate them. The operators that take one to the head of General Motors or the presidency are difficult, if not impossible, to enumerate, and the ways to get there are many.

Ill-defined problems are those in which the goal state, the initial state, and/or the operators are not clearly defined. Writing an essay, painting a picture, and creating a garden are ill-defined problems. That is, their solution cannot be specified in advance, let alone the path for arriving at the eventual solution. The nine-dot problem illustrates an ill-defined problem, as shown in Figure 9.2. Try to solve this problem before reading the section on creativity later in the chapter.

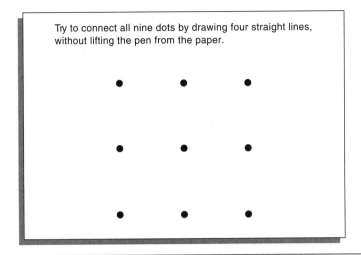

Try to connect all nine dots by drawing four straight lines, without lifting the pen from the paper.

Figure 9.2   The nine-dot problem.

Productive and Reproductive Problem Solving

The Gestalt psychologists of Germany during the early twentieth century distinguished between reproductive and **productive thinking** (Wertheimer, 1959). **Reproductive thinking** entails the application of tried-and-true paths to a solution. The thinker reproduces a series of steps that are known to yield a workable answer by using rote memory. Productive thinking, on the other hand, requires insight and creativity. In the view of the Gestalt psychologists, the thinker must see a new way of organizing the problem, that is, a new way of structuring the elements of thought and perception.

Köhler (1925), another Gestalt theorist, distinguished between problem solving based on insight and trial and error. Trial and error can be regarded as one form of reproductive thinking. The reader may recall that trial-and-error behavior allowed the cats in E. L. Thorndike's (1898) famous puzzle box to discover an escape route. On being placed in the box, a cat pawed randomly about the box, obviously irritated by the confinement. Once it discovered the escape lever, the cat learned to associate the lever with a way to escape.

Köhler (1925) spent seven years studying the problem solving of chimpanzees while stranded on Tenerife, an island in the Atlantic Ocean, during World War I. He designed problems such as the following. A chimpanzee is in a large cage along with several crates. Hanging from the top of the cage, out of reach, is a banana. Köhler reported that in this setting, the chimpanzee would appear to be lost in thought, and then suddenly the proverbial light bulb of insight would flash. The animal would then move the crates under the banana, stacking them to form a ladder to reach the food. In another problem, a chimpanzee insightfully learned to join together two sticks in order to reach a banana lying outside the cage. Such productive or insightful problem solving differed from the trial-and-error learning of Thorndike's cats.

Relations Among Terms

Ill-defined problems often demand productive thinking. Undirected thought, as we will see later in the chapter, is certainly one means for achieving insights. By the same token, well-defined problems often call for reproductive problem solving and directed thought. But it is a mistake to equate the concepts. For instance, in Köhler's experiments, the goal state of reaching a banana was well-defined even if the operators for doing so were unclear. The mutilated checkerboard (MC) problem shown in Figure 9.3 also has elements of both a well-defined puzzle and an ill-defined problem calling for insight (Kaplan & Simon, 1990; Wickelgren, 1974).

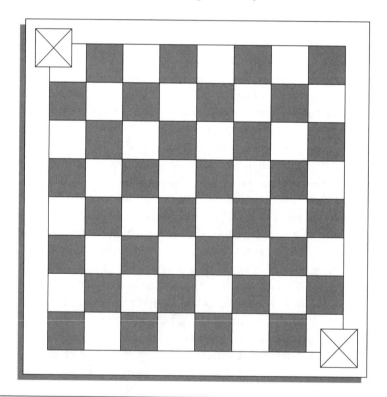

Figure 9.3   The mutilated checkerboard problem.

SOURCE: From Kaplan, G. A., & Simon, H. A., In search of insight. *Cognitive Psychology, 22,* 374-419, copyright © 1990. Reprinted with permission.

In the MC problem, two opposite corners of a standard 8 × 8 checkerboard are removed, as shown. The 62 remaining squares are to be covered by 31 dominos. Each domino is large enough to cover exactly two squares, either in a horizontal direction or in a vertical direction. Placing a domino diagonally on adjacent squares is not allowed. The problem is to show how to cover all of the remaining squares with 31 dominos or to prove logically that it cannot be done. We will return to this problem later (with the solution), so you might give it a try yourself at this point. For now, take note—or better yet, take warning—that the problem seems to be well-defined in that the initial and goal states are stated clearly and the rules for placing the dominos are given. Yet as Kaplan and Simon (1990) observed, "The initial representation that problem solvers almost always form fails to solve the problem. . . . Subjects need to change their representation in a nonobvious way" (p. 378).

It is also misleading to assume that the solution to any given problem stems solely from reproduction or recall versus production or insight. Remembering and creating cannot be so neatly severed. In earlier chapters, we saw how recall from long-term memory always involves an element of imagination or creativity. Reconstructive recall taps the creative elements of human thinking in much the same way that problem solving does. Indeed, it is quite appropriate to view the task of trying to remember an event from, say, five years ago as a problem to be solved. Both directed and undirected thinking, as well as both reproductive and productive thinking, enter into the solution of a recall problem as one constructs a mental model, uses retrieval cues, and so on.

Similarly, insightful problem solving depends on recollecting past experience and knowledge as well as creativity. Without drawing on past knowledge and relating new ideas to old ideas, productive thinking cannot take place. The great creative ideas of Shakespeare, Bach, Picasso, and Einstein were not given birth in a vacuum or created ex nihilo, out of nothing (Boden, 1992). Rather, their creations played off the accumulated knowledge of others whom they had diligently studied. In a much less significant example in Western civilization, the chimpanzees studied by Köhler (1925) needed past experiences with using poles and moving crates before they showed any insights at all in reaching bananas.

> Well-defined problems often require directed and reproductive thinking. Ill-defined problems often require undirected and productive thinking.

A GENERAL MODEL OF PROBLEM SOLVING

Ernst and Newell (1969) developed a computer simulation called General Problem Solver (GPS) as a model for exploring the nature of human problem solving. Their intent was to show that an artificial intelligence (AI) program based on certain general methods could, in fact, solve a wide range of problems. Psychological research has tested whether GPS provides a good simulation of human problem solving.

GPS first translates the description of a problem into an internal representation or model of a problem description. The translator interprets each sentence and attempts to identify the initial state, the goal state, and the operators. The representation of the problem, then, is the problem space that must be searched using methods or techniques of problem solving. A path must be found that takes GPS from the initial state to the goal state. A representation of this solution path is then generated in the final stage.

It is fruitful to think of human problem solving as proceeding in the same manner as GPS. The two essential components are representing the problem and searching the problem space for a solution. We examine more about the specifics of GPS and other AI simulations as we look at the research concerning representation and search.

Representing Problems

UNDERSTAND. Coming up with the right way to represent a problem is a crucial step in solving the problem. Another AI program, UNDERSTAND, addressed this issue (Simon & Hayes, 1976). UNDERSTAND used a reading comprehension system to extract the meaning of the sentences and then constructed a global description of the problem from these parts. Reading comprehension depended on the interaction of working memory and long-term memory. As each sentence of the problem was fed to UNDERSTAND, semantic and syntactic processes in long-term memory derived its meaning. Construction rules stored in long-term memory then operated on these meanings to build the goal state, initial state, and operators of the problem space in working memory. The resulting problem space was then searched using the procedures of GPS that we will come to shortly.

Let us first see how UNDERSTAND operated by looking at the problem reproduced in Figure 9.4 from Simon and Hayes (1976). The construction rules looked for sentences that expressed relations among objects and their features. It especially sought expressions describing the initial state of the problem and the operators that could be used to modify this state. UNDERSTAND assumed that such operators took a primitive form of stating how objects and features should be altered (e.g., "Transfer A from X to Y," "Exchange X with Y," "Insert A at X").

The Monster Problem

S1. Three five-handed extraterrestrial monsters were holding three crystal globes.

S2. Because of the quantum-mechanical peculiarities of their neighborhood, both monsters and globes come in exactly three sizes—small, medium, and large—with no others permitted.

S3. The medium-sized monster was holding the small globe, the small monster was holding the large globe, and the large monster was holding the medium-sized globe.

S4. Because this situation offended their keenly developed sense of symmetry, they proceeded to transfer globes from one monster to another so that each monster would have a globe proportionate to his own size.

S5. Monster etiquette complicated the solution of the problem because it requires:

S6. (1) that only one globe be transferred at a time;

S7. (2) that if a monster is holding two globes, only the larger of the two may be transferred; and

S8. (3) that a globe may not be transferred to a monster who is holding a larger globe.

S9. By what sequence of transfers could the monsters have solved this problem?

Figure 9.4   The monster problem.

SOURCE: From Simon, H. A., & Hayes, J. R., The understanding process: Problem isomorphs. *Cognitive Psychology, 8,* 165-190, copyright © 1976. Reprinted with permission.

Consequently, the meanings of the sentences S1 and S2 in Figure 9.4 were ignored by UNDERSTAND. It used S3 to establish the problem representation. It then used S4 plus the three conditions of S6, S7, and S8 to establish the operators. UNDERSTAND interpreted the new information in the context of given information; it knew how to interpret the operators in light of the problem representation already constructed.

Simon and Hayes (1976) claimed that human problem solving crucially depends on the representation constructed. To test this, they developed a problem that differed only in its descriptive language from the one shown in

Figure 9.4. The two are said to be **isomorphic problems** because of this similarity in their fundamental representation. Specifically, the second problem differed from the first in only two sentences:

S4 Since . . . they proceeded to shrink and expand themselves.

S7 that if two monsters are of the size, only the monster holding the larger globe can change.

Although its language is now couched as a change problem rather than a transfer problem, the underlying structure is still the same. Instead of transferring globes from one fixed monster to another, the globes stayed fixed and the monsters changed in size. The initial state and goal states remained the same.

UNDERSTAND handled the monster isomorphs very much as humans did in Simon and Hayes's (1976) experiments, as revealed by comparisons between simulations and verbal protocol analysis. First, UNDERSTAND constructed a representation of the problem before attempting to solve it. The 14 college students who tried to solve these problems reread the crucial sentences of S3, S4, and S6 to S8 a total of 64 times before making a single move. Most also asked the experimenter questions before beginning to solve the problems. Second, UNDERSTAND constructed a representation for the transfer version of the monster problem in a way that was relatively simple to check for the legality of making a move. By contrast, the change version representation was much more involved and required more time to run the simulation. The students also had a harder time with the change version. More students successfully solved the transfer version and took an average of 11 minutes less time to do so (17 vs. 28 minutes).

> A critical step in finding the solution to a problem is to first find a good way to represent the problem.

Thus, the language used to describe a problem powerfully determines how it is represented mentally. If this were not so, then the students in Simon and Hayes's (1976) experiments (as well as UNDERSTAND) could have painlessly converted the change version of the problem into a transfer problem. Remember that the problems are isomorphic, yet the students failed to convert to a transfer problem even though the change representation is much harder to manage. It appears that human perception and comprehension of a problem strongly influences the ease with which problems are solved.

The MC Problem. Take the MC problem shown earlier (Figure 9.3). How did you represent that problem? Kaplan and Simon (1990) found that most people think in terms of the numbers of squares and dominos and their geometrical arrangement. Perception and comprehension of the problem picture and description would certainly drive one to form exactly such a mental representation. The trouble with this approach is that there is a very large number of possible ways to geometrically arrange the dominos. A computer program tried to prove that 31 dominos could not cover all of the squares by exhaustively trying out alternative placements; it took 758,148 domino placements to succeed. A graduate student in chemical engineering "spent 18 hours and filled 61 pages of a lab notebook with notes, yet still did not solve the problem" (p. 379). Besides drawings of boards and domino placements, the notebook contained many mathematical equations and analyses. Most of us would probably perceive and comprehend the problem in a very similar fashion—to no avail.

The solution to the problem is remarkably simple, assuming that one constructs a manageable representation of the problem. This happens only after an insightful "AHA!" experience. To help attain this, Kaplan and Simon (1990) recommended the following: "If at first you do not succeed, search for a different problem space" (p. 381). The problem space that allows one to solve the MC problem is based on parity, in this case the fixed pattern of alternating black and white squares. Here is the solution:

> Since each of the 31 dominos covers two squares, a covering initially seems possible. To see why a complete covering is actually impossible, observe that a domino must always cover a black and a white square. But removing two squares of the same color (the diagonal corners) from the 8 × 8 board has left an imbalance between the number of black and white squares that remain. After covering 30 black-white pairs with 30 dominos, the problem solver is always left in the impossible situation of having to cover two same-colored squares with the single remaining domino. (pp. 378–379)

Kaplan and Simon (1990) tried to make the parity issue more salient to people by presenting the checkerboard as shown in Figure 9.5. They hypothesized that the bread and butter labels would prompt college students to think about opposites that go together. Kaplan and Simon predicted that the bread and butter labels would yield faster solutions than does giving a standard red/black checkerboard, and their results supported this.

Searching the Problem Space

Two kinds of problem-solving methods must be distinguished: algorithms and heuristics. An **algorithm** is a rule that correctly generates the

butter	bread	butter	bread	butter	bread	butter	bread
bread	butter	bread	butter	bread	butter	bread	butter
butter	bread	butter	bread	butter	bread	butter	bread
bread	butter	bread	butter	bread	butter	bread	butter
butter	bread	butter	bread	butter	bread	butter	bread
bread	butter	bread	butter	bread	butter	bread	butter
butter	bread	butter	bread	butter	bread	butter	bread
bread	butter	bread	butter	bread	butter	bread	butter

Figure 9.5   A checkerboard representation that emphasizes parity.

SOURCE: From Kaplan, G. A., & Simon, H. A., In search of insight. *Cognitive Psychology, 22,* 374-419, copyright © 1990. Reprinted with permission.

solution to a problem given that one can devote sufficient time and effort to applying the rule. For example, an algorithm for solving anagrams is to try every possible letter in every possible position until the word solution appears. This works well for the anagram "atc" but quickly grows tiresome for the anagram "npisatmisaelndsoi." The costs of using the algorithm are just too great despite the fact that it always generates the correct solution. Recall from Chapter 1 the important point that cognition is always limited by the costs of computation. A computer could be programmed to play a perfect game of chess using the game-theoretic "minimaxing" algorithm. The trouble lies in the number of chess positions it would have to examine—a number that exceeds estimates of the known molecules in the universe!

The second type of search method is called a **heuristic,** which refers to a rule of thumb or general strategy that may lead to a solution reasonably quickly with less computational cost. The drawback is that a heuristic, unlike an algorithm, might also fail. One heuristic for solving anagrams is to look for sequences of letters that occur frequently in English (e.g., -tion, dis-, -ism). Another is to eliminate combinations that rarely, if ever, occur (e.g., np, ii). Still another is to draw on knowledge of how words are put together, for example, that a syllable often consists of a consonant, a vowel, and a consonant (e.g., pen). Have you solved this one yet: npisatmisaelndsoi? The solution is "dispensationalism." The next problem—defining it—is left to you and your dictionary.

> An algorithm is a rule for solving a problem that always succeeds given enough time and effort. A heuristic is a rule of thumb that may lead to solution with less computational cost.

Two general algorithms for searching a problem space are trial and error (or random search) and systematic search. For example, trying every letter in every position in an anagram is a type of systematic search. E. L. Thorndike's (1898) cats seemed to use a trial-and-error algorithm in trying to find the escape lever in his puzzle box. There are also many general-purpose heuristics for problem solving. Here, let us consider three of these.

Working Backward. Sometimes, it is useful to start at the goal state of a problem and attempt to work backward to the initial state. It may be easier to see the correct path in a paper-and-pencil maze by starting at the end. The reason why working backward sometimes helps is found in the subgoals that one begins to see by starting with the final goal. Once the problem solver can envision a string of subgoals projecting backward from the goal state, solving the subgoals in a forward direction can be readily accomplished.

Working backward is viable only when the goal state is uniquely well-defined (Wickelgren, 1974). For example, in geometry proof problems, the goal state is precisely stated. It may well help to prune the possible paths of the problem space by starting from the expression to be proved and working backward. Other mathematical problems can be approached in this manner, as students have discovered when solving practice problems in, say, algebra or calculus, where the answer is provided at the end of the text. By contrast, chess illustrates a problem with a well-defined goal that is not uniquely specified. The goal is to checkmate the opponent's king, so that all legal countermoves result in the king still being threatened. However, the precise board positions of the pieces, or even which pieces still remain in the game, are uncertain. Without a specific goal, one can hardly work backward from it.

Analogies. An analogy heuristic looks for similarities between a current problem and one solved in the past. Surely, every student has tried this heuristic in geometry, algebra, or calculus courses. Indeed, the noted mathematician Polya (1957) recommended it highly. Science and engineering courses similarly lend themselves well to this strategy. One looks for a problem worked out in the text that is analogous to the one assigned for homework. The same approach is repeated at test time, although now the student must rely on memory for finding a good analogy.

Gick and Holyoak (1980) studied the use of analogy with the problem given in Figure 9.6. The Gestalt psychologist Duncker (1945) created this problem to investigate the importance of insight and reorganization of problem elements. Gick and Holyoak replicated Duncker's findings that few people are able to have an "Aha!" experience and derive an acceptable solution. The problem is nontrivial. Moreover, it is related to a major problem still facing AIDS researchers today. Thomas (1992) explained in his book, *The Fragile Species,* that researchers must somehow design a virus that will kill the retrovirus that causes AIDS without also killing the body cells that contain it. Try Duncker's radiation problem yourself before reading further.

Gick and Holyoak (1980) reasoned that people need to reorganize the problem by drawing an analogy to another situation. To help this occur, they first presented participants with the attack-dispersion problem of Figure 9.6. They also gave them an explicit hint that the solution to the attack-dispersion problem might be helpful with the radiation problem. Read the attack-dispersion problem and try Duncker's radiation problem once more before reading the solutions to each given in Figure 9.7. Gick and Holyoak found that only 8% of the participants solved the radiation problem when presented in isolation. This figure jumped to 92% when the hint was given. Clearly, the attack-dispersion problem was used as an analogy, allowing virtually all participants to see a solution.

It is important to note that Gick and Holyoak's (1980) participants failed to see the relevance of the attack-dispersion story in the absence of an explicit hint. Just reading the attack-dispersion story and then tackling the radiation problem led to a poor rate of success. People simply do not readily grasp abstract analogies well, despite their value in helping with the solutions to difficult problems.

People do readily see superficial analogies among problems, but these might not be helpful. To illustrate, Ross (1987) taught participants how to solve statistics problems by using a particular principle, such as the algorithm for computing conditional probabilities. The examples used to teach a principle were set in a specific context, such as weather forecasting. When

The Radiation Problem and a Solution Aid

Suppose that you are a doctor faced with a patient who has a malignant tumor in his stomach. It is impossible to operate on the patient, but unless the tumor is destroyed, the patient will die. There is a kind of ray that can be used to destroy the tumor. If the rays reach the tumor all at once at a sufficiently high intensity, the tumor will be destroyed. Unfortunately, at this intensity, the healthy tissue that the rays pass through on the way to the tumor will also be destroyed. At lower intensities, the rays are harmless to healthy tissue, but they will not affect the tumor either. What type of procedure might be used to destroy the tumor with the rays and, at the same time, avoid destroying the healthy tissue?

Attack-Dispersion Story

A small country was controlled by a dictator. The dictator ruled the country from a strong fortress. The fortress was situated in the middle of the country, surrounded by farms and villages. Many roads radiated outward from the fortress like spokes on a wheel. A general arose who raised a large army and vowed to capture the fortress and free the country of the dictator. The general knew that if his entire army could attack the fortress at once, the fortress could be captured. The general's troops were gathered at the head of one of the roads leading to the fortress, ready to attack. However, a spy brought the general a disturbing report. The ruthless dictator had planted mines on each of the roads. The mines were set so that small bodies of men could pass over them safely because the dictator needed to be able to move troops and workers to and from the fortress. However, any large force would detonate the mines. Not only would this blow up the road and render it impassable, but the dictator would then destroy many villages in retaliation. It therefore seemed impossible to mount a full-scale direct attack on the fortress.

Figure 9.6 The radiation problem and a solution aid.

SOURCE: From Gick, M. L., & Holyoak, K. J., Analogical problem solving. *Cognitive Psychology, 12,* 306-355, copyright © 1980. Reprinted with permission.

then given a novel problem involving weather forecasting—one that used a different abstract principle of statistics—they mistakenly drew an analogy to the previous examples. They failed to apply the correct principle because of a superficial similarity to examples of the wrong principle. Thus, drawing the right analogy is a useful heuristic, but one that people do not readily adopt.

Problem Solutions

Solution to the Radiation Problem

The ray may be divided into several low-intensity rays, no one of which will destroy the healthy tissue. By positioning these several rays at different locations around the body, and focusing them all on the tumor, their effect will combine, thus being strong enough to destroy the tumor.

Solution to the Attack-Dispersion Story

The general, however, knew just what to do. He divided his army up into small groups and dispatched each group to the head of a different road. When all was ready, he gave the signal, and each group marched down a different road. Each group continued down its road to the fortress, so that the entire army finally arrived together at the fortress at the same time. In this way, the general was able to capture the fortress and thus overthrow the dictator.

Figure 9.7   Solutions to the radiation problem and attack-dispersion story.

SOURCE: From Gick, M. L., & Holyoak, K. J., Analogical problem solving. *Cognitive Psychology, 12,* 306-355, copyright © 1980. Reprinted with permission.

Means-End Analysis. The means-end heuristic is widely applicable and readily programmable in an AI simulation. This is the search method used by GPS, the simulation discussed earlier. GPS can solve not only the Tower of Hanoi problem but also problems in logic, algebra, and calculus (Ernst & Newell, 1969; Newell & Simon, 1972). Means-end analysis refers to comparing one's current state to the goal state and then finding a means or an operator to reduce the difference. If the analysis turns up that an operator cannot be applied, then the process repeats itself. That is, the heuristic may find that it needs to apply Operator 2 to bring it to a state that allows the application of Operator 1, the thing it set out to do in the first place. The process is therefore recursive. That is, it repeatedly compares states and seeks operators, establishing subgoals and finding ways to reach the subgoals, all on the way to finding a path to the final goal.

Newell and Simon (1972) described the heuristic used by GPS as follows:

1. If an object is given that is not the desired one, differences will be detected between the available object and the desired object.

2. Operators affect some features of their operants and leave others unchanged. Hence operators can be characterized by the changes they produce and can be used to try to eliminate differences between the objects to which they are applied and desired objects.

3. If a desired operator is not applicable, it may be profitable to modify its inputs so that it becomes applicable.

4. Some differences will prove more difficult to affect than others. It is profitable, therefore, to try to eliminate "difficult" differences, even at the cost of introducing new differences of lesser difficulty. This process can be repeated as long as progress is being made toward eliminating the more difficult differences. (p. 416)

To see means-end in action, consider the classic water jar problem first investigated by Luchins (1942). Suppose that you have three jars that are different in capacity as follows:

Jar A: 8 quarts

Jar B: 5 quarts

Jar C: 3 quarts

Assuming that Jar A is full of water, how can you pour out water using the jars to arrive at four quarts in Jar A and four quarts in Jar B? There are no graduated lines on the jars, so you must pour until you either drain the jar or fill up the receiving jar entirely.

GPS approaches this problem by comparing the amounts in Jars A and B to the amounts that they are supposed to contain in the end (see Figure 9.8). It then seeks an operator to reduce the difference between the initial state and the goal state. Consider its opening move, for instance. Two operators are possible. GPS could pour Jar A into Jar B until it fills up. This would result in Jar A with 3 quarts and Jar B with 5 quarts. The total difference after such a transfer would equal 2 quarts. In other words, GPS would still be 1 quart short of the goal for Jar A and 1 quart in excess of the goal for Jar B.

Alternatively, the other legal operator for GPS would be to pour Jar A into Jar C. This would leave 5 quarts in Jar A and fill Jar C with 3 quarts. It would, of course, leave Jar B empty. The total difference after this transfer, therefore, would be 5 quarts, with Jar A in excess by 1 quart and Jar B short by 4 quarts. Which move would you make? Because this transfer produces a difference that is further from the goal than the first possible transfer, the means-end heuristic dictates pouring Jar A into Jar B as an opening move.

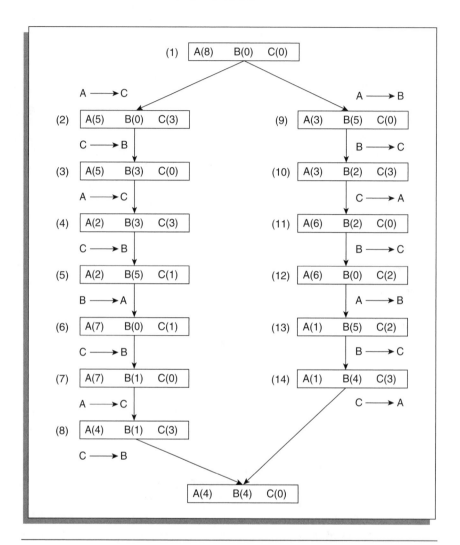

Figure 9.8   Alternative paths to the goal in a water jar problem. Each state shows the contents of Jars A, B, and C. Between each state, the direction of pouring from one jar to another is shown.

SOURCE: From Atwood, M. E., & Polson, P. G., A process model for water jar problems. *Cognitive Psychology, 8,* 191-216. Copyright © 1976, with permission from Elsevier.

Atwood and Polson (1976) investigated this question and found that college students prefer to pour Jar A into Jar B rather than Jar C by a margin of two to one. People overwhelmingly select the same move dictated by means-end analysis, providing evidence that GPS simulates human behavior, at least to a degree. Another powerful source of evidence that people rely, unconsciously perhaps, on the means-end heuristic came from a later state in the problem.

One solution path for the problem is shown on the right in Figure 9.8. At State 11, one must pour Jar B into Jar C. This move takes the problem solver away from the goal of having 4 quarts in Jar B, violating the dictates of means-end analysis. Atwood and Polson (1976) found that more than half of the time, participants stumbled here and tried first to pour Jar A into Jar C as means-end would have it.

> Some general-purpose heuristics for problem solving include working backward from the goal state, finding an analogous problem with a known solution, and means-end analysis or finding a means to move the direction of the goal.

Domain-Specific Knowledge and Metacognition

The general model of problem solving considered thus far has attempted to rely exclusively on all-purpose search heuristics and procedures for representing problems. Because people have evolved by solving problems from a broad range of specific domains, it is reasonable to assume that general-purpose heuristics characterize human problem solving. If a general-purpose cognitive system can handle food gathering, war planning, shelter building, art making, and so on, then it would not be necessary to devise specific procedures for each domain. It also certainly makes sense to hope that an AI model, such as GPS, would prove to be extremely useful in solving real-world technical problems in computer science, robotics, and engineering. Why build models that can solve only the problems of, say, a robot navigating a natural environment when a general-purpose program can do the job?

Knowledge and Power. Research over multiple decades has shown that more is needed than a generalist view of human and artificial intelligence, however (Glaser, 1984). First, knowledge about a specific domain must always supplement general procedures. Knowing how to represent a problem and search the problem space is aided by domain-specific knowledge. For example, having solved domain problems in the past provides an expert with many possible specific instances to use as analogies. As another example, memory for chess positions is far superior for a master player than for a novice (Chase & Simon, 1973). The expert player has no general memory strategy that gives this edge. Rather, it is detailed knowledge of the game itself that allows the expert to encode chunks of information in a superior manner.

This was demonstrated dramatically in Chi's (1978) study of 10-year-old children who played tournament chess and adults who played little chess. In a test of digit span, the adults performed much better than the children.

But a test of chess positions yielded precisely the opposite outcome; now, the children appeared to be the memory experts solely because of their domain-specific knowledge. Many other studies have further shown that knowledge is power when it comes to thinking and problem solving (e.g., Glaser, 1984; Larkin, McDermott, Simon, & Simon, 1980). Second, with maturation and learning, children begin to acquire more than general heuristics and more than domain-specific knowledge. They also learn to monitor what they are doing as they think and to reflect on what they know. The monitoring of cognitive processes and states of knowledge is called **metacognition** because it involves cognition about cognition, or thinking about thinking. Metacognitive skills are especially helpful for monitoring progress while problem solving. Abandoning an unproductive way of representing or searching a problem space and looking for alternatives requires an awareness that things are not going well. Good thinkers are able to evaluate problem-solving efforts as they are under way and to "consolidate gains" at the end of each problem-solving experience (Hayes, 1989). Poor thinkers lack these metacognitive skills.

The Case of Physics. To illustrate, consider the studies done on how experts and novices solve physics problems. Problems are chosen that are within the range of skill of novices, defined as undergraduates with only a background in high school physics and a semester or so of college-level physics. One such problem is finding the velocity of an object sliding down an inclined plane at the point when it reaches the bottom. Often, story problems are presented that require one to read a paragraph and identify the given information and the information that must be calculated. Verbal protocols are collected as novices and experts work through problems of this sort. Experts are defined as those with doctorates in physics who solve physics problems regularly as part of their research and teaching professions. Analyses of the protocols reveal differences in both domain-specific knowledge and metacognition.

First, an expert thinks through the problem before putting down a single formula (Glaser & Chi, 1988). The expert prefers to study the problem and ponder alternatives, undoubtedly in part because his or her knowledge representations are so much richer and offer so many more possible approaches relative to those of the novice. The delay reflects more than greater knowledge, however. It reflects the greater degree of metacognitive control that the expert brings to the task. One interesting illustration is the tendency for the expert to produce a simple qualitative diagram, involving no mathematics, after reflecting on the problem initially. The expert consciously selects a strategy of simplifying the problem to the barest qualitative elements. In that way, alternative approaches can be monitored before investing time and effort in calculations.

Second, the expert has mnemonically encoded theories, formulas, facts, and principles and has developed appropriate strategies for structuring them when required. The knowledge schemas of the expert are naturally both richer and better organized than those of the novice. One consequence of this better organization is that the expert perceives the problem differently than does the novice (Chi, Feltovich, & Glaser, 1981). When reading a problem description, the expert, but not the novice, very quickly triggers the appropriate schema for a solution.

Chi et al. (1981) asked experts and novices to categorize physics problems in order to study the role of knowledge organization. When novices are asked to categorize problems, they group them on the basis of their physical features, such as problems involving inclined planes versus springs versus objects in free-fall. The novice perceives the problem at a relatively superficial or shallow level of analysis. To illustrate, the diagrams of two problems grouped together by novices in a study by Chi et al. are shown in Figure 9.9. As you can see, the problems certainly appear to be related in that both

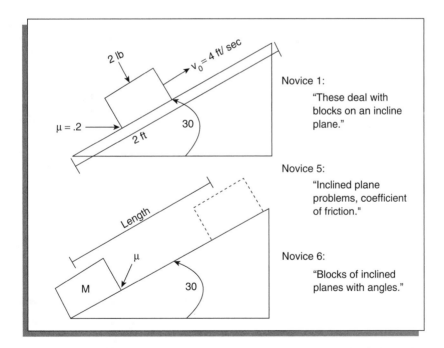

Figure 9.9   Diagrams of two problems grouped together by novices in physics, along with sample explanations.

SOURCE: Chi et al. (1981). Reprinted with permission of Lawrence Erlbaum Associates, Inc.

involve an inclined plane. But in fact, the similarity lies in appearances only; the procedures needed to solve the two problems are quite different.

Experts, on the other hand, perceive the problems at a deeper theoretical level, characterized by principles and laws. For example, each of Newton's three laws of motion encompasses a class of problems whose members appear quite different on the surface. As another example, consider the two problems shown in Figure 9.10, which can be solved by applying the law of conservation of energy. Chi et al. (1981) found that experts readily categorized these problems as related, despite the fact that one involved an inclined plane and the other involved a spring. What mattered to the experts was theoretical principle, not superficial appearance.

Another consequence of highly organized schemas is that experts adopt a different reasoning strategy from that of novices (Larkin et al., 1980). Novices are likely to begin with the unknown quantity in the problem, such as the velocity of the block at the bottom of the inclined plane. From that

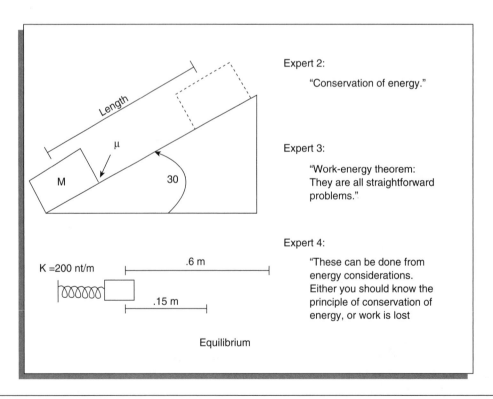

Figure 9.10   Diagrams of two problems grouped together by experts in physics, along with sample explanations.

SOURCE: Chi et al. (1981). Reprinted with permission of Lawrence Erlbaum Associates, Inc.

unknown, they attempt to work backward to the quantities that are given in the problem. They seek an equation that contains the unknown. If that equation also contains another unknown, then they look for yet another equation that will bridge the gap. This procedure, called **backward chaining**, continues until they find an equation with the given information in the problem.

Experts proceed in a forward direction. After having reflected on the problem and perhaps drawn a qualitative diagram, experts select an equation that immediately uses the given information. The result of the first calculation, then, becomes a given piece of information for entry into the next formula. Such **forward chaining** advances until the unknown velocity is calculated and the problem is solved. Experts use the forward chaining procedure whenever the problem strikes them as readily solvable. They are much more efficient as a result, solving the problems in less than a quarter of the time required by novices.

> Expertise in a specific domain aids problem solving in two ways. First, domain-specific knowledge supplements general procedures for representing and solving problems. Second, expertise provides metacognitive control over the processes of problem solving.

CREATIVITY

What can be said about productive thinking or creativity from the perspective of cognitive psychology? Potentially, much can be said, but creativity has not yet been studied extensively in the laboratory as much as have other kinds of thinking tasks. Writing, musical composition, architectural design, computer programming, engineering design, painting, and sculpting are just a few examples of tasks that call for creativity. We have barely begun to study and understand many of these, but creativity has recently started to receive the attention it deserves by researchers in cognitive psychology (Runco, 2004).

An important point needs to be made at the outset. Both the left and the right hemisphere of the brain are required for creative thinking. It is a common misconception that creativity is mediated by the right hemisphere. The entire notion of right brain versus left brain thinking is based on a misunderstanding of contemporary cognitive psychology and neuroscience. The misunderstanding arose from the fact that the right hemisphere is biased toward the processing of visual-spatial information, which is important in art, whereas the left hemisphere is biased toward the processing of language (Ornstein, 1997). In fact, the demands of productive thinking are a perfect example of how the entire brain's activity must be taken into account. Both the left and the right hemisphere are active and must be integrated for creative activity (Katz, 1997). Creative thinking is far too complex to be localized to just one hemisphere.

Historical Versus Process Creativity

We begin by defining **historical creativity** as acts of genius that are widely acclaimed by society as meritorious. Historical creativity refers to ideas that are novel within the context of the whole of human history (Boden, 1992). The creator produces a product—some visible symbol that embodies his or her idea—that may be judged by others (Sternberg, 1988). Consider works of art or equations of physical theory. The Sistine Chapel, the Mona Lisa, the laws of thermodynamics, and the general and special theories of relativity are products that are plainly creative in the historical or product sense.

Hayes (1989) argued that three criteria must be met before a product of the human mind ought to be regarded as creative. First, it must be novel or unique. Certainly, this is implicit in our everyday discussions of creative acts as well as in the distinction we encountered earlier between reproductive thinking, on the one hand, and productive, insightful creative thinking, on the other. Second, a product must be judged as useful in some context. Here, many artists, inventors, scientists, and philosophers have lost in their bids for fame. Their creations may have been novel but were utterly useless. Only when a product somehow connects with the past or finds its niche in a cultural context does it stand a chance of being regarded as creative. This may take time—more time than the creators have. Some have been acclaimed as creative in the historical sense only after their deaths. Third, the products must have demanded some special ability or talent on the part of their creators. Hayes's criteria of novelty, usefulness, and talent give very different answers to the question of what is creative, depending on one's cultural point of view.

> Humans generally have the potential to engage in a creative process in solving everyday problems. However, only rarely are problems large enough and the solutions creative enough to merit recognition in society as historically creative acts.

Boden (1992) and Sternberg (1988) dealt with these difficulties by noting that the process of creativity is every bit as important as the product. So long as the process yields a novel idea, it is important to model how the mind achieved its insight. Whether others judge the idea to be useful or a reflection of genius matters not at all for process creativity. In fact, it makes no difference whether the idea is even novel as far as society is concerned. Suppose that two scientists discover a cure for cancer without any contact with each other. Both were creative in the sense of process, yet perhaps only one will enter the history books as creative.

Stages of Creativity

The process of creativity moves through four stages that have been known for some time (Wallas, 1926). The first stage is **preparation**, which involves studying, learning, formulating solutions, and striving to create. For example, how many different attempts did you make in trying to solve the nine-dot problem from Figure 9.2? It is unlikely that you will solve it without a period of engaging the problem actively and preparing yourself for the next stage. Creating a product that merits the acclaim of society takes years of education and deliberate practice with the intent to excel in performance. A decade of such preparation appears to be necessary regardless of the domain. Preparation is no less important in everyday acts of creativity—figuring out what to write for a term paper assignment, seeing the answer to a personal problem, or coming up with a new arrangement for the annual vegetable garden. But in these cases, the entire process of creativity, including the preparation stage, is briefer.

Because of the extensive preparation required in the case of major creative production, individuals need the support and encouragement of family, friends, teachers, and peers (MacKinnon, 1978; Simonton, 1988). Social, economic, and cultural supports play a role in this cultivation (Hayes, 1989; Ochse, 1990). Without the financial and social supports needed for both formal and informal education, and without a cultural setting that values creative work, creative potential languishes. Because creative potential may be the most critical resource of any nation, it is foolhardy to not adopt policies that nurture the potential of all (Mumford & Gustafson, 1988; Taylor & Sacks, 1981).

Incubation is the second step of the creative process and refers to putting the problem aside and doing other things. The incubation phase can vary widely in duration and form. When working on a major creative project, one may incubate by taking a vacation. When puzzling over a particularly difficult problem in, say, a statistics class, one may incubate by taking a shower, jogging, or going out for pizza. In all cases, incubation entails thinking about something—anything—other than the problem or project that has been the focus of the preparation stage.

The third stage is **illumination**, when the crucial insight seizes consciousness. It is the "Aha!" experience that very quickly suggests the solution to the problem at hand. Have you given up on the nine-dot problem? Or, did you experience the illumination stage and discover the solution shown in Figure 9.11? Illumination can reflect the breaking of a mental set that had led the problem solver in the wrong direction. Illumination or insight is a fleeting sketchy experience, not a protracted, fully detailed solution. It must be followed by the fourth stage of **verification**, when the outlines of the solution must be filled in and checked carefully. It may turn out that illumination failed to generate an acceptable solution to the problem. Creativity is complete only after verification of the insight through painstaking efforts at writing, calculating, sculpting, painting, drawing, designing, building, and so on.

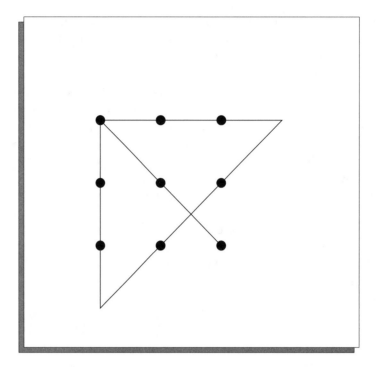

Figure 9.11   The solution to the nine-dot problem.

Creativity Blocks

The perceptual organization of the nine-dot problem leads one to make an important assumption about the solution. When one looks at the square defined by the nine dots, the obvious structure or representation of the problem that comes to mind is that the four lines lie within the square. Although the problem statement says nothing about whether the lines can extend beyond the confines of the square, the perception of the problem strongly suggests exactly that. This illustrates how imposing unnecessary constraints can block creative thought. The flash of insight requires discarding the unnecessary assumption that the lines must fall within the implicit boundaries.

Weisberg and Alba (1981) tested college students' ability to solve the nine-dot problem. In the control group, the students made 20 attempts at a solution. As expected, not a single participant hit on the correct solution. In three experimental groups, the researchers allowed the participants 10 attempts before introducing hints designed to generate insight into the problem. One group of students was told to "go outside the square." A second group was told the same and also was shown the initial diagonal line leading from the lower right-hand dot to the upper left-hand dot. A third group was also told to "go outside the square" and was shown the initial line plus the second vertical line extending down the left side of the square and past the lower left dot. In other words, the groups were given more and more explicit direction to the solution.

Only 20% of the participants solved the problem with the hint to "go outside the square." This is an improvement but is not as dramatic as one might expect if the only difficulty facing the students were the unwarranted assumption about the lines fitting within the square. Weisberg and Alba (1981) contended that another difficulty faced the students, namely, that the problem space is too large; there are too many possible arrangements of lines. By giving one or two of the lines, the researchers expected to reduce the size of the problem space, making the solution more apparent. They succeeded in doing so. With the hint to "go outside the square" and one line, about 60% of the students solved the problem. With two lines given, all of the students solved it.

Fixation. One way in which unnecessary constraints are often imposed is by fixating on a single approach to solving a problem. Typically, it is an approach that proved to be useful in similar past situations, but for the problem at hand it is counterproductive. Suppose that you are asked to measure out a desired quantity of water using three jars with different capacities. You have access to a water tap and can fill any jar as often as you like, but you must fill each jar to the top (there are no gradations for measurement). For instance, suppose that the desired quantity was 5 cups and that Jar A held 10 cups, Jar B held 4 cups, and Jar C held 1 cup. The solution would be to fill Jar A first. Next, pour from Jar A into Jar B once, and then pour from Jar B into Jar C once (i.e., A–B–C). Now, try all six problems in Figure 9.12 before proceeding.

Luchins (1942) found that people fixate on a single set way to solve the water jar problems after discovering that the first two or three can be solved with B–A–2C. Take a look at Problem 6 again. Although B–A–2C works fine, it entails much more effort than does the solution of A–C often overlooked by people. **Fixation** refers to the blocking of solution paths to a problem that is caused by past experiences related to the problem.

Smith, Ward, and Schumacher (1993) examined fixation in a design task. Participants tried to design as many new ideas as possible for a toy creature from an inhabited planet similar to Earth. The ideas had to be entirely novel, unlike any existing objects. One condition was primed for fixation by briefly showing the participants three examples of novel toys or creatures prior to the design task. The control condition saw no examples. After seeing examples, the participants typically fixated on specific features such as designing a creature that had four

	Jar Size			
	A	B	C	Goal
Problem 1	21	127	3	100
Problem 2	14	163	25	99
Problem 3	18	43	10	5
Problem 4	9	42	6	21
Problem 5	20	59	4	31
Problem 6	23	49	3	20

Figure 9.12   A demonstration of fixation in problem solving.

SOURCE: Adapted from Luchins, A. S. (1942). Mechanization in problem solving. *Psychological Monographs, 54*(Whole No. 248).

legs, an antenna, and/or a tail. Despite the fact that they were told to create new ideas that would be as different as possible from the examples, simply seeing prior examples limited their creative vision.

Langer (1989) saw that fixation effects are one type of mindlessness that often characterizes human behavior, particularly in our dealings with other people. All too often, we act from a single perspective or rule that has worked in the past. Instead of exploring our environment carefully to seek out alternative courses of action, we sample just enough features to recognize that our set approach seems to be on track. For example, consider the last time you exchanged greetings, experienced anger over what another person said or did to you, or tried to tackle a common problem as a member of a group. In each case, you may well have acted mindlessly and fixated on a path previously taken rather than explored entirely new options.

Fixation also constrains how we represent problems as well as search for solutions. A mathematics professor was given the following problem by his students (Rubinstein, 1986): Find the next element of the sequence 32, 38, 44, 48, 56, 60. As a hint, the students mentioned that the sequence was familiar to the professor and that the solution was simple. As mathematicians are apt to do, the professor launched into the problem space of polynomial equations and managed to generate a complex solution, not a simple

> Fixation refers to the blocking of solution paths to a problem that is caused by past experiences related to the problem.

one. On his giving up, the students informed him that the answer was "Meadowlark." To see the solution, the professor needed to drop one set and adopt another. Every day he rode the subway, and every day he passed stops at 56th Street, 60th Street, and then Meadowlark.

Functional Fixedness. A special kind of fixation occurs when the problem solver thinks about the normal functional uses of an object (Duncker, 1945). **Functional fixedness** refers to the tendency to see objects as having only a single typical use. A hammer is for pounding nails, for instance. We categorize objects based on their functional features as well as on their perceptual features, and the prototypical function dominates the way we think. Duncker led an individual into a room with a table covered with several small objects. The objects were three cardboard boxes filled with candles, tacks, and matches, respectively; an ashtray; paper; paper clips; string; pencils; and tinfoil. The individual was instructed to mount the candles at eye level on the wall, ostensibly to prepare the room for a vision experiment. Can you think of a way to put the candles on the wall using these materials?

Duncker (1945) found that only 43% of the participants could develop a solution to the problem. He hypothesized that they fixated on the common function of a box, namely to serve as a container. To help break their functional fixedness, he repeated the experiment but this time emptied the candles, tacks, and matches on the table, leaving the three boxes empty. Under these circumstances, all participants solved the problem by first mounting the boxes on the wall using the tacks, so that the boxes served as platforms for the candles.

You have undoubtedly enjoyed the "Aha!" experience during some incubation activity. To the extent that all cognition demands at least minor forms of creativity, insights occur monthly, weekly, or even daily. Boden (1992) recounted some famous flashes of illumination:

Archimedes leapt from his bath in joy and ran through the streets of Syracuse, crying "Eureka!" as he went. He had solved the problem that had been worrying him for days: how to measure the volume of an irregularly shaped object, such as a golden (or not-so-golden) crown.—Friedrich von Kekulé, dozing by the fire, had a dream suggesting that the structure of the troublesome benzene molecule might be ring. A whole new branch of science (aromatic chemistry) was founded as a result.—The mathematician Jacques Hadamard, more than once, found a long-sought solution "at the very moment of sudden awakening."—And Henri Poincaré, as he was boarding a bus to set out on a geological expedition, suddenly glimpsed a fundamental

> The four stages of creative problem solving are preparation, incubation, illumination, and verification.

mathematical property of a class of functions he had recently discovered and which had preoccupied him for days. (p. 15)

Unconscious problem solving offers one explanation of the incubation effect (Baars, 1988). Because incubation involves thinking about something other than the problem, it seems quite natural to assume that processes are underway at an unconscious level that suddenly—without warning—thrust the solution into consciousness. While one is eating, bathing, exercising, or sleeping, one's mind may be thinking about many things consciously, but it still carries on the serious work of problem solving outside of awareness. However, there are two alternatives that are difficult to disentangle empirically from unconscious problem solving. First, the preparation period may result in a buildup of proactive interference for the correct solution. That is, as the individual tries numerous solution attempts and fails to succeed, memory fills up with these wrong approaches and they interfere with retrieval of the right approach. Resting may allow the problem solver to forget these dead-end approaches. Another possibility is that preparation causes fatigue that is alleviated by the incubation phase. By restoring mental energy, the problem solver quickly finds the solution to the problem once he or she begins to search for the answer again.

Sources of Creativity

Although few humans are creative in the historical sense, all of us are creative in the process sense. Indeed, all mental acts can be viewed as creative if one begins with the observation that a person never perceives, recalls, or imagines in precisely the same way twice (Weisberg, 1986). In the immortal words of Hericlitus of ancient Greece, we never enter the same stream twice. The demands of the current situation never exactly match past learning. Schemas are flexible and dynamic in order to deal with the need for novel responding and adaptation.

That creativity is fundamental in human nature opposes the ancient view that the gods, muses, or inexplicable intuition are somehow responsible for acts of genius. Boden (1992) reviewed this romantic explanation and joined Weisberg in rejecting it:

Plato put it like this: "A poet is holy and never able to compose until he has become inspired, and is beside himself and reason is no longer in him . . . for not by art does he utter these, but by power divine." . . .

Over twenty centuries later, the play Amadeus drew a similar contrast between Mozart and his contemporary, Salieri. Mozart was shown as coarse, vulgar, lazy, and undisciplined in every aspect of his life, but apparently informed by a divine spark when composing. The London critic Bernard Levin, in his column in *The Times,* explicitly drew the conclusion that Mozart (like all other great artists) was, literally, divinely inspired. (p. 5)

As Boden (1992) went on to argue, the romantic view fails to even try to explain creativity. It merely sweeps it away under the rug of intuition or into the attic of the muses. As a scientific explanation, it gets us nowhere.

The alternative view assumes that the work on problem solving discussed earlier can tell us much about the process of creativity. It assumes that the problem representations, search heuristics, and diverse forms of knowledge that creators bring to their tasks all are vitally important. Regardless of whether the problem is ill-defined or well-defined, the processes discussed throughout this chapter shed light on creativity (Boden, 1992; Weisberg, 1986). Waiting for one's muse is no longer the heuristic of choice.

Creative Production

Thomas Edison still holds the record for the most patents awarded to a single person by the U.S. Patent Office: 1,093. As Simonton (1997) pointed out, not all of these patents turned out to be useful, and Edison experienced many costly mistakes. In fact, the developmental costs of one of his useless devices exceeded Edison's profits for the electric light bulb. However, like other recognized historical geniuses such as Albert Einstein, Charles Darwin, Sigmund Freud, Pablo Picasso, and Johann Sebastian Bach, Edison turned out massive volumes of work. Picasso, for instance, created more than 20,000 paintings, drawings, and pieces of sculpture in his lifetime. Thus, creative people create a lot—not a particularly surprising outcome, but one that must be taken into account by theories of creativity.

Simonton (1997) suggested that creative production is Darwinian in nature. First, ideas are conceptually combined to generate a large number of variations. Second, there is a variation-selection process in which most ideas are winnowed out as uninteresting. The high productivity rates of historical geniuses, then, are part of the secret of their success. If their rates of conceptualizing new variations of ideas had been any lower, the winnowing process would have eliminated too many ideas. Thus, a Darwinian view of creativity necessarily assumes that the one or two good ideas a person might have cannot be identified without first generating a large number of bad ideas.

The variation-selection process can be viewed as purely random. A creative problem solver in a given field undoubtedly uses heuristics for identifying problems, representing the problem space, and searching the problem space. However, for historically important creative acts, the problem solver's past experience may well no longer provide any useful guidance. Thus, a nondirected random search of the problem space becomes the only workable option, according to this model.

The variation-selection process operates on both an individual and a social level. For example, the problem solver first selects the ideas that must undergo the verification step of demonstrating that an insight is, in fact, a solution. Proven solutions must then be selected for further development, whether they involve publication, seeking a patent, or putting a product into production. Selection at a social level then takes over the work of the creator. Some articles submitted to journals are accepted for publication through a peer review process, whereas others are rejected. Some patents are developed by industry into marketable products, whereas others are left on the shelf. The marketplace further selects those products that it is willing to buy and those that it tosses aside as uninteresting or at least not commercially viable. Because the selection process operates at so many levels, it is difficult for the creator to foresee which solutions will prove to be successful and which will be a waste of time.

SUMMARY

1. People think by manipulating mental representations of the world. Through the use of such representations, people can plan courses of action and simulate their effects prior to taking action. The study of problem solving has shed light on how people go about this. Often in solving a problem, one builds a model of the environment with a clear, well-defined goal in mind. One then tries to find a path that leads straight to the goal with little diversion. Such problem solving illustrates directed thinking. Undirected thinking refers to dreaming, daydreaming, and other forms of thought that meander without concern for attaining a goal. Undirected thinking is neither rational nor goal oriented.

2. A well-defined problem is characterized by an initial state, a goal state, and a set of operators. Each legal move from the initial state to intermediate states to the goal state is defined by an operator. All of the states and operators taken together define the problem space. To solve a well-defined problem, one must select a sequence of operators that

follow a path through the problem space to the goal. An ill-defined problem is missing a clear initial state, goal state, and/or known operators. An ill-defined problem often calls for insight and creativity, what the Gestalt psychologists called productive thinking. Yet even some well-defined problems demand creative insights for solutions.

3. A general model of problem solving entails first representing the problem and then searching the problem space for a path to the goal. Finding a good representation of the problem space is critical and often demands as much insight as does the search process itself. Algorithms are rules for searching the problem space that are guaranteed to succeed, although often at prohibitive costs in time and effort. Heuristics are rules of thumb that may or may not lead to success, but they carry less costs than do algorithms. The General Problem Solver is one of several artificial intelligence programs that simulate aspects of human problem solving. It is based on the premise that a general search heuristic called means-end analysis is powerful enough to solve a wide range of problems. Today, it is recognized that an adequate simulation of human problem solving must address the effects of domain-specific knowledge and metacognition as well as general heuristics.

4. Gestalt psychologists recognized that both perception and problem solving require the proper organization of elements. They identified two common obstacles to successful problem solving. Fixation refers to the tendency to set the mind into a routine approach to problem solving. Thinkers who adopt an automatic or mindless approach to problems often overlook ways of representing and searching the problem space that are ideal. Functional fixedness refers to the tendency to see objects as having only a single typical use. Thinkers prematurely categorize the elements of a problem in accordance with their typical use, thus overlooking novel and useful alternatives.

5. Historical creativity refers to ideas that are novel within the context of cultural history. Few people are recognized as historically creative, yet all of us engage in cognitive processes that are creative, even if our creative products are not judged as novel, useful, or extraordinary. The stages of creativity begin with preparation or working with a problem for an extended period of time. Incubation, or putting the problem aside, is the next stage. The third stage is illumination or coming up with a crucial insight that leads to the solution of the problem. The fourth stage is verification, when the insight is implemented and tested. Creativity appears to follow a Darwinian process. First,

ideas are conceptually combined to generate a large number of variations. Second, there is a variation-selection process in which most ideas are winnowed out as uninteresting. The high productivity rates of historical geniuses, then, are part of the secret of their success. They had good ideas as a consequence of having many ideas in the first place.

KEY TERMS

directed thinking

undirected thinking

well-defined problem

initial state

goal state

subgoals

operator

problem space

ill-defined problems

productive thinking

reproductive thinking

isomorphic problems

algorithm

heuristic

metacognition

backward chaining

forward chaining

historical creativity

preparation

incubation

illumination

verification

fixation

functional fixedness

CHAPTER **10**

REASONING AND DECISION MAKING

T he ability to reason is a hallmark of the human mind. Both ancient and modern philosophers have identified reasoning and language as the pedestals that lift our species above all others. To some scholars, the studies of primates who appeared to learn some aspects of language shook the language pedestal. The pedestal of reasoning and its partner, decision making, are studied here. First, reasoning as it has been defined by philosophers is presented. The surprising news is not that other species are just as capable of reasoning as are humans. Rather, the evidence suggests that people themselves are poor at reasoning, at least when the task is defined in its classical sense. The same can be said about human decision-making abilities when judged against the decision theories of mathematicians. These findings, too, have generated shock waves, transforming the modern view of human thinking.

A description of the **syllogistic reasoning** task comes first in the chapter. *All men are mortal. Socrates was a man. Therefore, Socrates was mortal.* From a major and minor premise, the reasoner must evaluate the conclusion. The rules for doing so correctly are defined by the formal system called the predicate or functional calculus. This comes from a branch of philosophy called symbolic logic. Perhaps you have received instruction in a logic course on the proper way to evaluate syllogisms. The aim here is to consider some psychological reasons such material may have been a real challenge to learn. Next, conditional reasoning is considered. *If P, then Q. P is true. Therefore, Q must also be true.* The conditional rule is its own quagmire, as far as human cognition is concerned. It turns out that people have a very difficult time determining how to deduce the proper conclusions. Finally, decision making is considered in light of the normative models of mathematics, on the one hand, and the realities of human cognition, on the other. As with reasoning, it is seen that people make decisions in ways that do not fit with the optimal ways prescribed by mathematics.

SYLLOGISTIC REASONING

Syllogistic reasoning involves evaluating whether a conclusion necessarily follows deductively from two premises that are assumed to be true. The two premises are referred to as the major premise and the minor premise. Their truth is taken as certain, regardless of whether the statements make any sense in the real world. For example, consider these three syllogisms:

Syllogism 1:

    Major premise: All men are animals.

    Minor premise: Some animals are aggressive.

    Conclusion: Some men are aggressive.

Syllogism 2:

    Major premise: All men are animals.

    Minor premise: Some animals are female.

    Conclusion: Some men are female.

Syllogism 3:

    Major premise: All A are B.

    Minor premise: Some B are C.

    Conclusion: Some A are C.

Do you accept the conclusion of Syllogism 1 as valid? Most readers would. After all, it is not difficult to think of at least a few men who certainly appear to be aggressive. The syllogism does not even require that you conclude that all men are aggressive, a conclusion that more than a few readers might also happily accept.

But then, what to do with Syllogism 2? At least if one puts aside sex change operations, the conclusion does not ring true. The semantics of the conclusion are all wrong. Yet if you examine the first pair of syllogisms, you will see that their form is identical. This point can be driven home by Syllogism 3. Do you accept the conclusion as more valid in this case than in Syllogism 2? Syllogism 1?

The task that philosophers set before us is to ignore the semantics or the meaning of the premises altogether. The premises are simply assumed to be true for the sake of the argument. The preceding examples, then, are really the same syllogism. Because their syntax or structure is identical, their conclusions must be evaluated identically. Either the conclusion is valid in all three, or it is invalid in all three.

The meaningfulness of the premises matters not a wit. One could just as well have said the following. *All men are elephants. Some elephants are plants. Therefore, some men are plants.* The only matter at hand is whether the conclusion must logically follow from the premises. A **valid deductive conclusion** is a conclusion that is necessarily true given that the premises are true. Before reading further, arrive at your evaluation of the validity of our example syllogism(s).

> A valid deductive conclusion necessarily follows from the major and minor premises of a syllogism.

Syllogistic Forms

Presented in Table 10.1 are some of the common syllogistic forms along with the valid conclusions, if any, that follow from the major and minor premises. The conclusion of "Can't say" indicates an invalid syllogism; no conclusion *necessarily* follows from the premises. The first on the list corresponds to the famous "All men are mortal" routine, and as you can see, it is correct to conclude that Socrates was indeed a man. That is, the conclusion must be true given the premises. The next on the list corresponds to our example, and it might surprise you to learn that no valid conclusion follows from these premises. If you missed this, then you are in good company. Only about 10% of college students who have not been trained in logic correctly identify valid and invalid conclusions without error (Dominowski, 1977).

In Figure 10.1, the four types of premises encountered in deductive reasoning are shown. The Euler circles provide a convenient representation of their meanings based on class or set relationships. The universal affirmative—"All

Table 10.1   Examples of Valid and Invalid Syllogisms

Premises	Conclusion
1. All A are B All B are C	All A are C
2. All A are B Some B are C	Can't say
3. No A are B All C are B	No A are C
4. Some B are not A All B are C	Can't say
5. All A are B No C are B	No A are C
6. No B are A Some B are not C	Can't say
7. Some A are B All B are C	Some A are C
8. All B are A All C are B	Some A are C
9. No A are B No B are C	Can't say
10. Some A are B Some B are C	Can't say
11. Some A are not B All B are C	Can't say
12. Some B are A No B are C	Some A are not C
13. All B are A All B are C	Some A are C
14. Some A are not B Some B are not C	Can't say
15. Some B are A Some C are not B	Can't say
16. All A are B All C are B	Can't say
17. No B are A Some B are C	Can't say
18. Some B are not A Some C are B	Can't say
19. All B are A No B are C	Some A are not C
20. All A are B No B are C	No A are C

SOURCE: From Loftus, E. F., Bourne, L. E., Dominowski, R. L., Healy, A. F., *Cognitive Processes, 2nd Edition,* copyright © 1985. Reprinted by permission of Pearson Education, Inc., Upper Saddle River, NJ.

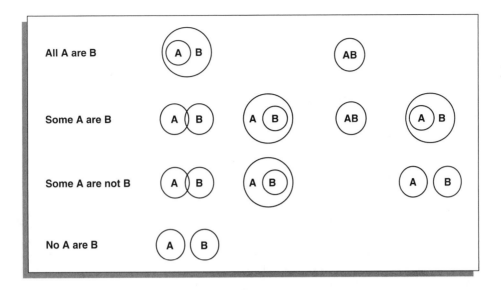

Figure 10.1   Euler circles represent the premises of a categorical syllogism in terms of set relations.

A are B"—has two possible interpretations, as shown. Either the reference classes or sets of A and B are identical or A refers to a subset of B. The universal negative—no A are B—is the only premise that affords a single interpretation! Study the particular affirmative (some A are B) and the particular negative (some A are not B) premises for a moment to understand why they allow each of the meanings shown.

Evaluating the conclusion according to the predicate calculus requires three steps. First, one must accurately consider all possible interpretations of the premises and the conclusion. Second, one must consider all possible combinations of meanings of the major and minor premises. That is, one must consider all pairs of meanings that are allowed by the first step. Third, one must determine whether all possible meanings of the conclusion are consistent with all possible combinations of the premises. If a single interpretation of the conclusion does not follow from a single possible combination of meanings, then no valid conclusion may be drawn. To put this in the form of a question, Is it possible to find one combination of premises that does not fit with one interpretation of the conclusion? If that is so, then the conclusion is invalid. These steps are illustrated in Figure 10.2 for the example syllogism used earlier.

As you can see in Figure 10.2, there are two possible meanings of "All A are B" and four possible meanings of "Some B are C," giving several possible combinations. Consider two of these combinations by combining the first meaning of the major premise with the first two meanings of the minor premise. Combination 1 joins Meaning 1 for the major premise ("All A are B")

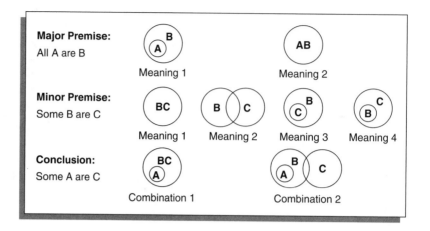

Figure 10.2   All possible meanings of the major and minor premises, followed by two of the eight possible combinations of meanings of these premises. Combination 2 is at odds with the conclusion "Some A are C."

and Meaning 1 for the minor premise ("Some B are C"). Combination 2 joins Meaning 1 for the major premise and Meaning 2 for the minor premise. Note how the relation between B and C expressed in the minor premise is substituted for the set labeled B in the major premise.

For Combination 1, note that this conclusion follows: *The set labeled A falls within the set labeled BC.* For Combination 2, however, the conclusion is at odds with the diagram: *The set labeled A fails to intersect with the set labeled C.* There is, then, at least one interpretation of the conclusion at odds with at least one combination of the premises. The conclusion is invalid as a consequence. Try working out the other six combinations of the meanings of the major and minor premises and see how many support the conclusion "Some A are C."

Common Errors

Ceraso and Provitera (1971) found that people correctly identify a valid conclusion (e.g., Cases 1, 3, 5, 7, and 8 in Table 10.1) about three quarters of the time. Bear in mind that there are a total of 64 different syllogisms obtained by varying the type of premises and the order in which the premises are given. Only a sample of these are shown in Table 10.1. Of the total 64, only 19 allow a valid conclusion to be drawn.

People do much worse for the 45 invalid syllogisms, those for which no valid conclusion follows. People often agree that a conclusion is valid when one really cannot say for certain. For instance, Syllogism 3 in our example often elicited a response of "valid." Ceraso and Provitera (1971) used letters in their syllogisms to remove the possibility that people would evaluate the meaningfulness of the conclusion. Even so, the participants correctly identified invalid conclusions only about a third of the time.

Not only do people perform poorly overall on the invalid syllogisms, but the pattern of errors obtained is quite consistent (Dickstein, 1978). When the major premise contains a universal affirmative (all) statement and the minor premise is a particular affirmative (some) statement, people overwhelmingly regard a conclusion containing the word "some" as valid. They do the same thing if the major premise is also a particular affirmative (some) statement. By contrast, when the major and minor premises both are universal negative statements, people often accept a conclusion that contains the word "no." As you can see from Case 9 in Table 10.1, this is an error.

Cognitive Constraints

An explanation proposed early on by Woodworth and Sells (1935), the **atmosphere hypothesis,** presumed that people do not even attempt to evaluate the conclusion logically. The atmosphere hypothesis was restated by Begg and Denny (1969) in this way. First, if one or more of the premises is negative (either universal or particular), then the conclusion is generally accepted as negative. Second, if one or more of the premises is a particular or "some" statement, then a particular or "some" conclusion is accepted. Although this explanation accounts for part of the errors, it misses the mark on others. Moreover, the hypothesis provides no account of why intelligent college students would blindly follow these heuristics instead of trying to reason correctly (Dickstein, 1978).

Working Memory. One reason may be the limitations of working memory. College students, like the rest of the population, may forget or fail to represent in the first place some possible combinations of premises. Johnson-Laird and Steedman (1978) reported that reasoners try to simplify the combinations of premises by avoiding those that call for class inclusion or subset relations. Go back to Figure 10.2 and note that some premise meanings involve a class inclusion relation (e.g., A is a subset of B). These often will be overlooked in generating combinations of meanings of the major and minor premises. By contrast, simple combinations of meanings (e.g., A, B, and C all referring to the same class) are picked up readily. Similarly, people consider only some of the premise combinations when evaluating the conclusion. If a conclusion fits some but not all of the combinations, then it may well be accepted as valid (Dickstein, 1978).

Illicit Conversion. Another cognitive constraint is the misinterpretation of premises. **Illicit conversion** refers to people converting "All A are B" into "All B are A," taking the converse of the premise as true in addition to the premise itself. So, in the case of "Some A are B," people illicitly convert it into "Some A are not B" (Ceraso & Provitera, 1971; Revlis, 1975). Unlike the atmosphere hypothesis, this hypothesis gives people credit for trying to reason correctly but faults them for starting off on the wrong foot by misinterpreting the premises. Ceraso and Provitera (1971) showed the importance of illicit conversions with their findings that errors decrease when efforts are made to stop such conversions. The researchers expanded the premises to prevent misinterpretations ("All A are B, but there are some B that are not A").

> Incorrect interpretations of premises, such as illicit conversion, and failures to consider all possible combinations of premises explain many of the errors that people make in identifying valid conclusions.

Meaning and Knowledge. Because meaning is so critical for memory and thought, people try to make abstract reasoning problems concrete and easier to manipulate in working memory (Gentner & Stevens, 1983; Johnson-Laird, 1983; Johnson-Laird & Bara, 1984). It is possible to eliminate illicit conversions by stating the premises in meaningful ways, for example (Revlis, 1975). When told that all men are animals, you would not likely infer that all animals are men. Yet exactly this happens when the meaning is stripped from the premise by saying "All A are B." Euler circles and Venn diagrams, taught in logic classes, are examples of external representations that concretize the problem, helping one to see the solution. The format of the external representation makes a difference, however, and some do not especially help (Lee & Oakhill, 1984).

Belief bias refers to people accepting any and all conclusions that happen to fit with their system of beliefs (Henle, 1962). Beliefs and meaning, and not the predicate calculus and other abstract systems invented by philosophers, lie at the core of human thinking. College students in North America reject valid conclusions if they do not correspond to what the students know to be true about the world. The supremacy of meaningful beliefs appears to be universal. In fact, non-Western cultures not exposed to formal schooling find the concept of validity hard to grasp (Cole & Scribner, 1974; Luria, 1976).

Luria (1976) asked illiterate farmers from Central Asia to reason deductively, giving them syllogisms of the following sort: "In the Far North, where there is snow, all bears are white. Novaga Zemlya is in the Far North. What color are the bears there?" The responses were of this sort: "I don't know; I've seen a black bear, I've never seen any others. . . . Each locality has its own animals; if it's white, they will be white; if it's yellow, they will be yellow"; or "How should I know?" (pp. 109–110).

Luria (1976) found that the farmers simply ignored or forgot premises that contradicted their own knowledge and failed to interpret universal statements (e.g., "In the Far North, . . . all bears are white") as really universal. They regarded such statements as the view of a particular person. In short, they regarded the reasoning task not as an abstract game but rather as a question rooted in their own or someone else's real-life experience.

Cole and Scribner (1974) found much the same in their work with the Kpelle tribes of Liberia. These people reasoned from their own personal knowledge. They refused to draw conclusions based on hypothetical premises provided by an experimenter. If pressured by the experimenter to state a conclusion, they justified their answers from personal knowledge, not from drawing valid conclusions from the premises. This may be seen in the following exchange:

Experimenter (local Kpelle man):	At one time spider went to a feast. He was told to answer this question before he could eat any of the food. The question is: Spider and black deer always eat together. Spider is eating. Is black deer eating?
Subject (village elder):	Were they in the bush together?
Experimenter:	Yes.
Subject:	Were they eating together?
Experimenter:	Spider and black deer always eat together. Spider is eating. Is black deer eating?
Subject:	But I was not there. How can I answer such a question?
Experimenter:	Can't you answer it? Even if you were not there, you can answer it. [*Repeats question*]
Subject:	Oh, oh, black deer is eating.
Experimenter:	What is your reason for saying that black deer is eating?
Subject:	The reason is that black deer always walks about all day eating green leaves in the bush. Then he rests for a while and gets up again to eat. (p. 162)

Belief bias is especially powerful when reasoners ignore the premises altogether and focus on the conclusion (Evans, Barston, & Pollard, 1983). In this case, they accept a believable conclusion (e.g., "Some good ice skaters are not professional hockey players") and reject an unbelievable one ("Some professional hockey players are not good ice skaters"). Using verbal protocols, Evans et al. (1983) found that some individuals study the premises and try to reason from them. For these individuals, a serious conflict arises when the conclusion is valid but unbelievable.

> Belief bias causes errors in deductive reasoning. Any conclusion consistent with personal belief is incorrectly assumed to be valid.

Politicians put belief bias to good use. If a politician can stand for a position that most people believe in, then the premises and logic leading to supporting the position receive less scrutiny.

CONDITIONAL REASONING

As noted in discussing concept identification, the conditional rule is expressed as an if-then statement. Conditional reasoning refers to the type of deductive reasoning seen in the following examples:

Deduction 1:

> If the barometer falls today, then it will storm.
>
> The barometer is falling.
>
> Therefore, it will storm.

Deduction 2:

> If P, then Q.
>
> P is true.
>
> Therefore, Q is true.

As in the earlier example of syllogistic deduction, these two deductions convey the same form of conditional reasoning. Given that the first part of the conditional rule is true, then the conclusion reached in each case must be true. It follows as a valid deduction. The abstract form of Deduction 2 removes the meaning from the task and disrupts the typical approach of building a model from concrete experience.

Valid and Invalid Conditional Reasoning

Logicians allow two ways to deduce a valid conclusion from the conditional rule. The first is called modus ponens or **affirming the antecedent**. Deductions 1 and 2 illustrate affirming the antecedent. P is called the antecedent, and Q is called the consequent. Affirming the antecedent means that the second premise asserts that P is true. Given that P is true, then Q must also be true. According to the rule as stated, it can never happen that Q is false if P is true. But what if the premise asserts that the consequent Q is not true? Suppose that you walk outside and see that the weather is balmy. Armed with this knowledge, you could apply the second valid form of conditional reasoning called modus tollens or **denying the consequent.** Given that Q is false (it is not storming), then P must also be false. According to the conditional rule, it can never happen that P is true if Q is false.

A moment's reflection on the conditional rule may reveal the other two types of reasoning that might be tried. Logicians recognize that these can lead to faulty conclusions. The first is **denying the antecedent.** Suppose that you check your barometer and see that it is rising. Your evidence effectively denies the antecedent (not P). Does it follow from this that it will not storm (not Q)? Well, maybe, but not with any certainty, according to the rules of logic. A meteorologist might reach a different conclusion by reasoning inductively from past experience with barometers and the weather. But here, we are concerned with the conditional form of deductive reasoning, that is to say, what must be true according to the rules of logic.

Does not P instead imply that it will storm (Q)? Again, one cannot tell. The if-then rule describes what we must find to be true *given* that the antecedent is confirmed as true. If the antecedent should turn out to be false, then all bets are off. According to the conditional rule as stated, whether it will storm or not can be deduced only *if* the antecedent is true.

The other faulty form of reasoning is **affirming the consequent.** Suppose that you venture outside and find a major storm brewing. Does this tell you with certainty that the barometer is falling? Such a conclusion is certainly possible. But once again, the conditional rule allows us to make statements with certainty only when it is *given* that the barometer is falling. It does *not* make a statement about the barometer *given* that it is storming. In other words, the conditional rule does not claim that it will storm *if and only if* the barometer is falling (although meteorologists would undoubtedly prefer this wording, based on the predictions they have reached by inductive reasoning from past observations of barometers and the weather).

Common Errors

People commit systematic errors in conditional reasoning tasks just as they do in syllogistic reasoning (Rips & Marcus, 1977; Marcus & Rips, 1979). The eight possible forms of the conditional syllogism are shown in Table 10.2. College students were asked whether the conclusion followed from the premises *always, sometimes,* or *never.* The correct responses are marked with an asterisk. Note that the *always* and *never* responses are appropriate when one can affirm the antecedent or deny the consequent, the two valid forms of reasoning. The *sometimes* response is called for in all other cases.

People perform perfectly in applying modus ponens or affirmation of the antecedent (the first two cases in Table 10.2). But errors occur in all other cases. Most striking about these results is the high proportion of errors connected with modus tollens or denial of the consequent. As the last two cases in the table show, about a fourth to a third of the time, people incorrectly give the *sometimes* response. They seem to be unaware that denying the consequent is just as valid as affirming the antecedent.

> Affirming the antecedent and denying the consequent are valid forms of conditional reasoning. Denying the antecedent and affirming the consequent are not.

Failure to deny the consequent is a persistent error in human reasoning. Even after taking a college-level course in logic that covered the issue, students' performance remained abysmal. In fact, students who had taken the course did no better in applying the logic of denying the consequent to this task than did students who had no formal training (Cheng, Holyoak, Nisbett, & Oliver, 1986).

Cognitive Constraints

Wason and Johnson-Laird (1972) undertook a series of experiments to understand further the errors made in conditional reasoning. They provided participants with four cards, as shown in Figure 10.3. Each card had a letter on one side and a number on the other side. They further gave participants this conditional statement:

If a card has a vowel on one side, then it has an even number on the other side.

The participants' task was to decide which card or cards had to be turned over to prove that the conditional rule was true. They were to avoid turning over cards unnecessarily.

Table 10.2 Percentages of *Always, Sometimes,* and *Never* Evaluations of the Eight Forms of the Conditional Syllogism ("If P, then Q")

Minor Premise and Conclusion	Evaluation Response		
	Always	Sometimes	Never
1. P is true Therefore, Q	100*	0	0
2. P is true Therefore, not Q	0	0	100*
3. P is false Therefore, Q	5	79*	16
4. P is false Therefore, not Q	21	77*	2
5. Q is true Therefore, P	23	77*	0
6. Q is true Therefore, not P	4	82*	14
7. Q is false Therefore, P	0	23	77*
8. Q is false Therefore, not P	57*	39	4

SOURCE: From Rubinstein, M. F., *Patterns of problem solving,* copyright © 1975. Reprinted with permission from Prentice Hall.

NOTE: The correct response is indicated by an asterisk (*).

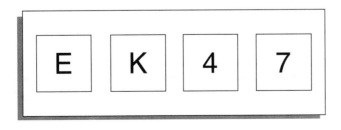

Figure 10.3 The four-card selection task of conditional reasoning.

The results of such experiments showed that nearly half of the time, participants decided to turn over both E and 4. According to the use of modus ponens or affirming the antecedent, the E card had to be turned over. But the 4 card was an error. Affirming the consequent does not allow one to say for certain whether there will be a vowel or a consonant on the reverse side. By sharp contrast, a mere 4% of the participants decided to turn over E and 7. The 7 card denies the consequent. By applying modus tollens, they could disprove the rule by discovering a vowel on the reverse side. Yet hardly anyone thought to do so in this task.

Meaning and Knowledge. One possibility is that people misrepresent the task as a biconditional rule rather than a conditional rule. They may interpret the statement "If P, then Q" to mean "If and only if P, then Q" (Taplin & Staudenmeyer, 1973). This could explain why they so frequently select the 4 card along with the E card in the four-card problem, because in a biconditional rule one would find an even number if and only if the reverse side contained a vowel. It makes perfect sense, therefore, to turn over the 4. Our everyday experience and meaningful uses of language lead us to make such interpretations. Suppose that I say, "If you mow the lawn, then I will give you $10." This promise strongly suggests that if you do not mow the lawn, then I am not about to part with my $10 (Geis & Zwicky, 1971).

On the surface, the failure to apply modus tollens can be taken as evidence that human behavior is not rational. But in the real world, people must take their relevant beliefs and infer something that helps them to achieve a specific goal. For example, if it looks cloudy and also looks like rain outside, then people have no trouble inferring that they should grab an umbrella. Evans and Over (1996) pointed out that violating modus tollens says more about the arbitrary premises of a task lacking ecological validity than it does about irrationality. There is no personal belief at stake in deciding whether a card with a vowel on one side must have an even number on the other side.

In fact, if prior beliefs of personal relevance are brought into the laboratory task, then the outcome changes. If a task activates a schema or model rooted in practical experience, then modus tollens is easy to apply (Cheng & Holyoak, 1985). For instance, suppose that you again have four cards and that each card has the age of a person on one side (16 or 22 years of age) and the person's drink on the other side (soft drink or beer). How would you test the following rule?

If the person is drinking beer, then he or she is over 21 years of age.

As in the other card task, you should turn over as many cards as are necessary to determine whether the conditional syllogism applies. In this situation, you could perhaps draw an analogy to a specific situation encountered in the past. Griggs and Cox (1982) found that college students correctly selected the "drinking beer" and "16 years of age" cards three-fourths of the time. That is about 18 times the correct response rate found in the Wason and Johnson-Laird (1972) experiments with the vowel and digit rule!

> In abstract conditional reasoning problems unrelated to everyday experience, people fail to use denial of the consequent effectively and incorrectly use affirming the consequent. Reasoning about a concrete lifelike situation reduces these errors.

The beer-drinking problem may be familiar and meaningful because humans are genetically prepared to check for social cheaters who do not follow the rules (Cosmides & Tooby, 1992). When the four-card problem is recast as a problem of catching cheaters, it becomes trivial. Implicit social contracts state that one should not receive benefits (beer, in this case) if one does not meet the criteria (being 21 years of age). Cosmides and Tooby (1992) suggested that a heuristic for cheater detection may have evolved because it enables individuals in a group to reciprocate benefits. Our ancestors were good at helping those whom they expected would help them in return. Detecting those who wanted something for nothing was adaptive, and the genes underlying this cognitive mechanism may have become part of the human genome.

Perhaps, but the central point to stress is that knowing the task domain well enough to retrieve the meaning of the concepts involved is critical to effective reasoning. The same point can be made with analogical reasoning rather than conditional reasoning. Suppose that you are given the following test:

A cloud is like a sponge because

    a. both can hold water,

    b. both can give off water,

    c. both are soft,

    d. both are fluffy.

The answers given in Responses a and b reflect a relational focus. If you gave one of these answers, then you mapped some relationship between the functional meaning of cloud and sponge. To do that, you needed to see how what you know about the domain of clouds can be mapped onto the domain of sponges. Gentner and Stevens (1983) found that adults given this kind of test provided a relational response nearly every time (89%). However, children ages four or five years and seven or eight years provide relational responses only 61% and 69% of the time, respectively. Notice that Responses c and d merely describe perceptual features of the object and overlook their meaningful functions. Because adults know enough about clouds and sponges, they can go beyond mere appearances in their reasoning.

Confirmation Bias. Another factor in the failure to apply modus tollens is the tendency to seek confirming evidence. Evidence that disconfirms our beliefs may well be actively avoided. Confirmation bias can be seen in the card problem and many other tasks (Klayman & Ha, 1987; Krauth, 1982). For example, in attitude change experiments, people pay more attention to evidence that confirms their beliefs than to evidence that undermines them (Petty & Cacioppo, 1981). Humans are, it seems, less a thinking species than a believing one.

A striking example of confirmation bias was studied by Wason (1968) in an inductive reasoning task. Unlike the deductive tasks of syllogistic and conditional reasoning, induction requires going beyond the premises to form a general rule. It is useful to think of an inductive conclusion as a belief that one has about the world. The subjective probability or strength of this belief changes as new evidence is accumulated (Rips, 1990). In some cases, new evidence causes one to doubt a belief formed earlier, whereas in other cases the belief becomes further entrenched as fact. The belief may be wrong, but this will be discovered only by seeking and finding disconfirming evidence.

Wason (1968) studied inductive reasoning by first telling participants that they were to discover a general rule that predicts the elements of a sequence. Furthermore, participants learned that 2, 4, and 6 fit the rule. To discover the rule, the participants proposed additional elements, and the experimenter would tell them whether their series fit the rule also. An obvious hypothesis, and one often adopted immediately by the participants, was the rule that the numbers must increase in magnitude by two. Armed with such a hypothesis, people set out to test it by suggesting numerous series of numbers that increase by two. For example, they might offer 8, 10, 12, 14, and 16, and the experimenter informed them that it fit the rule. Next, they might offer 5, 7, 9, 11, 13, 15, and 17, and again the experimenter confirmed their hypothesis. With each confirmation, the participants gained greater confidence that the rule was correct and promptly generated another confirming sequence. Some participants became visibly upset when they vocalized their rules and the experimenter told them that they were wrong!

The rule that Wason had in mind was any series of numbers that increased in magnitude. Thus, 1, 2, and 3 would also have received a nod from the experimenter. The interesting result of Wason's experiment is how few participants thought to propose a series that falsified their hypotheses. Typically, all they sought was confirming evidence.

> Humans often seek evidence that confirms their hypotheses and beliefs. This confirmation bias can lead to false conclusions.

DECISION MAKING

In fields of human endeavor such as economics, politics, law, science, and medicine, people make decisions. Decision theory is the branch of mathematics concerned with how to go about the process optimally (Hastie, 2001). All decision makers are faced with alternative courses of action. Depending on the states of the environment in which these actions are carried out, there may be several outcomes. *Utilities* are the values or gains that the decision maker gets with each outcome. Generally, we assume that the objective is to maximize the utilities that are expected.

Shown in Table 10.3 are the courses of action, states of nature, and outcomes for a farmer who must decide what to plant. Rubinstein (1975) explained the model developed by the farmer this way:

> The states of nature (such as rainfall, levels of temperature, winds, etc.) which are relevant to the success of his crops could be described to various degrees of detail. The simplification to three states—Perfect, Fair, and Bad—constitutes a high level of abstraction. . . . The array of numbers . . . is called a payoff matrix and represents the degree of satisfaction or utility that the farmer believes he will derive. For example, he derives 4 units of utility when he plants crop B and the state of nature is Fair, and he derives no utility when the state of nature is Bad. . . . Normally, you would think of money (say, profit in dollars) as the measure of success in such an enterprise. (pp. 312–313)

Types of Decisions

Some decisions are made under conditions of certainty. That is, we know that particular courses of action will result in particular outcomes for **decisions under certainty.** If the farmer knew for certain that the weather this year was going to be bad, then he would know exactly how to proceed to maximize his

Table 10.3   A Decision Payoff Matrix

Course of Action	State of Nature		
	Perfect	Fair	Bad
Plant Crop A	10	1	−2
Plant Crop B	8	4	0
Plant Crop C	3	3	3

profits. **Decisions under risk** refer to cases in which each state of nature is likely to occur with a known probability (e.g., 10% chance of Perfect, 80% chance of Fair, and 10% chance of Bad). **Decisions under uncertainty** refer to cases in which the probabilities of states of nature are unknown.

Decision making under uncertainty is the most complicated and realistic situation. To proceed effectively, the farmer must arrive at a subjective probability of the various states of nature. Based on past experience, advice from meteorologists, and perhaps a glance at the *Farmer's Almanac,* the farmer assigns probabilities and then determines the best course of action. Suppose that the farmer reasoned that the chances of Perfect, Fair, and Bad weather were 15%, 60%, and 25%, respectively. He could then compute the expected value of utility for each course of action as follows:

> Decisions under uncertainty are difficult because one must estimate the probability that a particular situation will occur.

Crop A: .15(10) + .60(1) + .25(−2) = 1.6

Crop B: .15(8) + .60(4) + .25(0) = 3.6

Crop C: .15(3) + .60(3) + .25(3) = 3.0

If the farmer is accurate in his probability estimates, then Crop B should go in the ground to maximize profits.

Subjective Utility

Do people behave in accordance with expected utility theory? If not, what are the mental processes that lead them to deviate from the normative model? Let us take a simpler example than the crop case and see how people behave relative to expected utility theory. Suppose that you are given a choice between two different bets. You can gamble that you will win $8 with a probability of 1/3 or gamble that you will win $3 with a probability of 5/6. Which bet do you prefer to take?

From a normative point of view, the expected utility of the first choice is $8 × 1/3 = $2.67. The situation is slightly worse for the second choice: $3 × 5/6 = $2.50. So, expected utility theory predicts that most people will choose the first bet, but in fact they do exactly the opposite (Kahneman & Tversky, 1984). Their behavior results from their calculations of subjective utility, which turns out not to be related in a linear way to the actual value of money. Shown in Figure 10.4 is the curvilinear relationship between subjective utility and the magnitude of money lost and money gained.

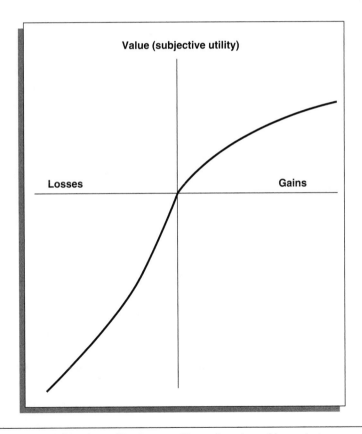

Figure 10.4   Subjective utility is a curvilinear function of losses/gains.

SOURCE: Kahneman, D., & Tversky, A. (1984). Choices, values, and frames. *American Psychologist, 39*, 341–350. Reprinted with permission.

Notice that the function is concave in the region of gains, meaning that further increases in gains do not result in a linear increase in subjective utility. There is a point of diminishing returns in the subjective utility one gains from further gains in money. On the loss side, the function is convex, meaning that further increases in losses do not result in linear decreases in subjective utility. Put simply, after losing a great deal of money, the loss in subjective utility levels off. Good thing, or else we would feel the sting of loss past the point of being bearable! Finally, notice that the curve is slightly steeper in the loss region than in the gain region. This results in people being risk averse. They really hate to lose because subjective utility drops faster with losses than it rises with gains in money.

In the gambling example, the subjective utility of an $8 gain is not more than twice as great as a $3 gain. If one assumes that the subjective utility of a $3 gain is U, then the utility of an $8 gain might only be $2U$. The expected value of the first gamble, then, is $1/3 \times 2U = .67U$ as compared with $5/6 \times U = .83U$. Because now the expected utility is greater for the second gamble, it is not surprising that most people prefer it.

The utility curve shown in Figure 10.4 can cause people to make decisions that are hard to see as rational. A **framing effect** refers to making a different decision depending on where people perceive themselves to be in relation to the curvilinear subjective utility function. To illustrate, Kahneman and Tversky (1984) compared two hypothetical shopping situations. Suppose that you are looking for a $15 item at one store and learn that another store is selling the same item for $10? Do you take the time and effort to save $5? Most people will because the loss side of the utility curve is steep, so it matters subjectively whether one loses $15 rather than only $10. But now suppose that the item you seek costs $125. Would you go to another store to buy it for $120? Fewer people would, even though in both situations the loss is exactly $5. Because the subjective utility curve is convex in the loss region, your subjective sense of loss is scarcely different for $125 as compared with $120.

> Subjective utility shows a curvilinear relation to losses and gains. It is convex in the region of losses and concave in the region of gains. People are risk averse because subjective utility drops faster with losses than it rises with gains in money.

Gambling and investing require individuals to consider the subjective utility curve. Odean (1998) studied the behavior of investors on Wall Street and discovered that they tend to shift their point of reference shortly after buying a stock. The subjective utility curve has a zero point—the point of reference from which gains or losses are judged. Where they set this point of reference is critical in deciding whether they regard a stock as too risky to hold or too risky to sell. In particular, after buying the stock, shifting expectations about future returns in a downward direction cause investors to sell their winning stocks too soon and to hold their losing stocks too long.

For example, investors must decide whether the market price for a stock is too high. If an investor believes that the stock will rise in value, then the market price he or she paid is worth the risk. If the stock, in fact, grows in value and the investor uses the purchase price as the point of reference, then the stock price will be on the concave gains side of the utility curve. However, if after buying the stock the investor lowers his or her expectations of future growth, then the purchase price will fall on the loss side. Even though the stock rose in value, it would now fall on the steep risk-averse portion of the utility curve. As a consequence, even a winning stock will look too risky, and the investors will sell it off too soon.

What if the stock decreased in value instead of gained? The shift downward in expectations insidiously makes the investor too complacent. Instead of the loss falling on the steep slope of the loss side of the function, it places the loss farther out on the convex part of the curve. It is here that the investor becomes less worried about losing money and more willing to accept risks to win money. Ironically, then, the investor is far too willing to hang onto a stock that is already costing him or her money. Based on an analysis of 10,000 accounts at a large brokerage house, Odean (1998) discovered that investors tend to hold losing investments too long and to sell winning investments too soon. A shift in their reference point to lower expectations for the stocks after they were purchased seemed to best account for their behavior.

Emotion and Thinking

Emotions are traditionally not regarded as part of rational thought, but research has clearly demonstrated that they influence human judgment and decisions in important ways (Shafir & LeBoeuf, 2002). An emotional state can shift one away from a decision that might ordinarily be made. For example, when people are in a good mood, they try to maintain the positive emotional state by avoiding negative thoughts. This kind of mood maintenance can impact risk aversion. A loss is to be especially avoided when one is in a positive mood and trying to maintain it. Thus, risk aversion is heightened (Isen, Nygren, & Ashby, 1988). Fear can also affect our judgments by heightening risk aversion. Fischhoff, Slovic, Lichenstein, Reid, and Combs (1978) studied attitudes held about the risks and benefits of different technologies in society. It turned out that judgments about the safety of a technology were affected by emotional factors. For example, nuclear power is feared by people in part because the radioactive waste from the technology must be stored for thousands of years in a safe way that prevents contamination of our water and air. It is also feared because the technology can be used to build nuclear weapons with devastating power. The dread that people feel about nuclear technology causes them to be much more risk aversive than the actual probability of a nuclear accident would warrant.

These kinds of emotional influence led Damasio (1994) to propose the somatic marker hypothesis. This holds that we experience bodily, visceral feelings that guide our decisions based on the anticipated pain or pleasure of the outcomes. According to Damasio, somatic markers reduce the number of options that are considered in working memory by anticipating the emotional consequences of various courses of action. Given the limitations of working memory, the involvement of emotion in the decision-making process is adaptive by constraining the number of choices that need to be weighed and judged. In terms of brain structure, Damasio notes the linkage between what are called the ventromedial regions of the frontal cortex and the emotional centers in the limbic system. The somatic markers of a course of action are normally brought into working memory via these pathways. Lesions in the ventromedial frontal lobe, however, result in the loss of the somatic markers, so that choices are weighed without the benefit of their emotional baggage.

Probability Heuristics

Reasoning under uncertainty requires an assessment of probability, so decisions are necessarily affected by how well people judge subjective probability. Are people good or poor intuitive statisticians? An extensive literature exists on this issue. The research aimed at these questions has told us a great deal about the nature of human thinking. But the answers are still not entirely clear. For example, one can marshal evidence that people are good intuitive statisticians (Peterson & Beach, 1967) and other evidence that they are poor at judging probabilities (Kahneman & Tversky, 1982a). Let us turn to some of the key findings and controversies.

To begin, it is well-established that people can keep track of the relative frequency of events. As discussed previously, frequency of occurrence is automatically compiled when events are encoded into long-term memory. So, it is not surprising that when people are asked to estimate the probability of a particular event, they come reasonably close. It turns out that subjective probability deviates from actual probability in a highly systematic way. High-probability events tend to be underestimated, whereas low-probability

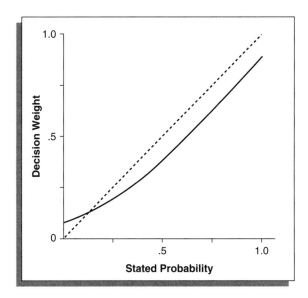

Figure 10.5   Subjective probability systematically deviates from actual probability.

SOURCE: From Kahneman, D., & Tversky, A., On the study of statistical intuitions. *Cognition, 11,* 123-141. Copyright © 1982, with permission of Elsevier.

events are overestimated (Kahneman & Tversky, 1984). Notice that very low-probability events are seen as subjectively more likely than they actually are and receive greater weight in decisions than they deserve (Figure 10.5). This is why the insurance industry can charge the premiums it does. The chances of an earthquake destroying your home are low (depending, of course, on exactly where your home is located). But the subjective probability assigned by the homeowner is often higher than the actual probability, which justifies paying a premium for the protection.

During the 1970s and 1980s, a wide range of cognitive biases and normative fallacies were discovered in tasks calling for decisions under uncertainty. Just as studies of deductive reasoning used a formal normative system to judge how well people performed, human judgments under uncertainty were contrasted with those predicted by statistical theories. Kahneman and Tversky (1973) pioneered these investigations and arrived at the following conclusion in an influential review of the early literature:

> In making predictions and judgments under uncertainty, people do not appear to follow the calculus of chance or the statistical theory of

prediction. Instead, they rely on a limited number of heuristics which sometimes yield reasonable judgments and sometimes lead to severe and systematic errors. (p. 237)

Representativeness. To illustrate the first important heuristic, consider these two alternative outcomes of tossing a coin six times. Imagine an outcome in which heads turns up the first three times, followed by three tails (HHHTTT). An alternative outcome might be HTTHTH. Is the probability of one of these sequences higher than that of the other? Kahneman and Tversky (1972) found that in this and many related tasks, people generally say that the second, random-appearing outcome is more likely.

For those who have had some training in statistics (and can remember and use it effectively), the correct answer is apparent. Both outcomes are equally likely. Each toss of the coin is independent of the others. On any given toss, heads or tails has an equal chance of occurring. The total number of possible sequences is 2^6 or 64. The probability of all heads is 1/64, just as is the probability of any other possible sequence.

Kahneman and Tversky explained that people use a **representativeness heuristic.** This means that events that are representative or typical of a class are assigned a high probability of occurrence. If an event is highly similar to most of the others in a population or class of events, then it is considered representative. Because most of the 64 sequences of coin tosses will necessarily have several alternations of heads and tails, the HHHTTT outcome strikes us as highly unrepresentative and therefore highly unlikely. Also, if an event is highly similar to the process that generates it, then it is considered representative. When tossing a coin is a random process, we expect random-looking outcomes, not "rigged" ones. Never mind that the probability of all heads is just as likely as any other particular outcome.

Over a large sample of, say, 1,000 coin tosses, the likelihood of heads is .50, the same as that of tails. But for a small sample, such as six tosses, a sequence of even six heads in a row does not imply that a rigged or biased coin is being used. Yet sample size is not heeded (Bar-Hillel, 1980; Kahneman & Tversky, 1972). According to the **law of small numbers,** people mistakenly expect even small samples to look random and to mirror the probabilities obtained with large samples (Tversky & Kahneman, 1971).

> The gambler's fallacy results from the mistaken belief that small sample sizes mirror the probabilities obtained with large sample sizes.

Gamblers fall prey to this use of the representativeness heuristic. The **gambler's fallacy** refers to the mistaken belief that future tosses of a coin, drops of the ball in roulette, or rolls of the dice in craps are not independent of past events. If you see seven rolled on the dice five times in a row, then you are likely to bet against another seven coming up again on the next roll. People expect events to even out in the short run because they know that events even out in the long run.

Take another quite different illustration of the representativeness heuristic. Kahneman and Tversky (1982a) asked college students to read character sketches and then to make judgments about them such as the one shown in Box 10.1.

Given the description, would you say it is more likely that Linda is a bank teller or that she is a bank teller and a feminist? Overwhelmingly, the students selected the latter description, a finding that has been replicated many times. However, because bank tellers include both feminists and nonfeminists, it must be the case that the bank teller statement is more likely. The conjunctive rule of probability theory informs us that the probability of a conjunction of two events (A and B) cannot be greater than the probability of A or the probability of B. The tendency to judge the conjunction as more likely is called the **conjunctive fallacy.** Of course, the character description sounds more representative of feminists than of bank tellers, leading us into the snare of the conjunctive fallacy.

BOX 10.1

The Bank Teller Problem

Linda is 31 years old, single, outspoken, and very bright. She majored in philosophy. As a student, she was deeply concerned with issues of discrimination and social justice, and she also participated in antinuclear demonstrations. Now, rank order these assertions from the most probable to the least probable:

a. Linda is a teacher in an elementary school.

b. Linda works in a bookstore and takes yoga classes.

c. Linda is active in the feminist movement.

d. Linda is a psychiatric social worker.

e. Linda is a member of the League of Women Voters.

f. Linda is a bank teller.

g. Linda is an insurance salesperson.

h. Linda is a bank teller and is active in the feminist movement.

SOURCE: Kahneman and Tversky (1982a).

Availability. The second heuristic used to estimate probabilities is based on the ease with which relevant examples come to mind. When deciding whether to buy the stock of a company, you might recall what you heard on television in a business newscast. If a stock shows a major run-up in price or the company attracts positive attention from the media for reasons other than the stock, then it will be featured on talk shows about the market and written about in the financial news. As a consequence, the stock's availability in the minds of investors takes a major hike upward. It will command attention and channel investors to do more research on it rather than on other equally good opportunities that fail to capture media attention (Odean,

1998). The **availability heuristic** suggests that if relevant examples can readily be retrieved from memory, then the class of events must occur with a high probability.

What proportion of nurses are men? What proportion of car mechanics are women? Unless you happened to know several male nurses or female mechanics, both questions would generate low-probability estimates. Tversky and Kahneman (1973) experimentally examined how the ease of recall influences our beliefs about the world. They composed four lists of people, with each list consisting of 19 names of women and 20 names of men. For half of the lists, only the men's names were famous (e.g., Richard Nixon), and for the other half, only the women's names were famous in the 1970s (e.g., Elizabeth Taylor). The researchers studied two conditions: recall and estimate. After hearing the lists read to them, the college students in the recall condition wrote down as many names as they could remember. In the estimate condition, they judged whether the lists contained more names of men or of women.

The results, not surprisingly, showed that the famous names were easier to recall than the other names on the lists. The key result, however, was that the ease of recalling the names had a direct impact on the probability estimates. Specifically, for the lists that included famous females, the students judged that the lists contained more female names. The opposite pattern occurred for the lists with the famous males.

The availability heuristic can distort our understanding of real health risks because of the bombardment of health information from printed news, the Internet, radio, and television. If a story receives heavy coverage by the media, then it is likely to be available for later recall. The degree of risk publicized may be minuscule when compared with the major hazards we face—hazards that receive far less attention and therefore are less available. Because of the availability heuristic, our perceptions of risk may be in error. People may well worry themselves sick over the wrong risks.

Slovic, Fischhoff, and Lichtenstein (1982) reported on their research in the area of risk perception. People estimate that accidents cause as many deaths as do diseases. In fact, diseases, many of which receive little publicity, cause 16 times as many deaths as do accidents. People also judge death by homicide to be as frequent as death by stroke when, in fact, the latter is 11 times more frequent. Frequencies of death from botulism and tornadoes are wildly overestimated. The most underestimated causes of death are smallpox vaccinations, diabetes, and stomach cancer, according to Slovic et al.

In one study, the researchers examined newspaper accounts of death over a period of several months to see whether the availability heuristic could account for the observed distortions in risk assessment. As expected, they found that relatively common causes of death, such as diabetes, emphysema, and various types of cancer, were hardly ever reported by the press. By stark contrast, homicides, car accidents, tornadoes, fires, drownings, and other violent causes of death were reported often. Homicides, in particular, received the heaviest coverage relative to their actual frequency of occurrence. Such findings pose serious challenges to public safety and health programs. People must first know what the real risks are if they are to take sensible steps to avoid them.

Simulation. The problem provided in Box 10.2 illustrates a third heuristic for making probability judgments (Kahneman & Tversky, 1982b). Before reading further, read Box 10.2 and choose which individual ought to be most upset. The investigators noted that both gentlemen are in the same trouble: Both suffered through a traffic jam and both missed their flights. Objectively, both should be equally upset. By chance, then, half of the time people ought to say Mr. Tees, and the other half ought to say Mr. Crane. In contrast to this objective prediction, virtually all of the individuals to whom Kahneman and Tversky (1982b) posed this question responded "Mr. Tees." Why pity Mr. Tees more?

Kahneman and Tversky (1982b) proposed that people call on their knowledge representations or scripts for traveling to the airport. They then simulate the trip themselves and readily imagine alternative scenarios in which Mr. Tees could have made his flight. If only the driver had gone a bit faster, if only Mr. Tees had left five minutes earlier, if only . . . then things would have worked out differently. But only for Mr. Tees. Mr. Crane missed his flight—plain and simple.

The **simulation heuristic** involves the construction of a mental model of a situation and then "running the model" to predict the course of events. Whereas ease of recall underlies the availability heuristic, ease of construction or imagination underlies the simulation heuristic. As our farmer plans what to plant, he may well imagine possible scenarios and try to assess which is the best course. If it is too difficult to imagine perfect weather, then the farmer could well assign a distorted low estimate of probability for this state of nature. Research has revealed two important features of these simulations

---

BOX 10.2

The Airport Drive Problem

Mr. Crane and Mr. Tees were scheduled to leave the airport on different flights at the same time. They traveled from town in the same limousine, were caught in a traffic jam, and arrived at the airport 30 minutes after the scheduled departure time of their flights. Mr. Crane is told that his flight left on time. Mr. Tees is told that his flight was delayed and just left five minutes ago. Who is more upset, Mr. Crane or Mr. Tees?

SOURCE: From Kahneman, D., Slovic, P., & Tversky, A., *Judgment Under Uncertainty,* copyright © 1982. Reprinted with permission of Cambridge University Press.

(Markman & Gentner, 2001). First, they are qualitative in nature and do not require the computational resources needed to carry out detailed quantitative simulations. Second, they often involve the use of visual imagery.

The availability and simulation heuristics help us to understand a common phenomenon both in everyday life and in the psychology laboratory (e.g., Fischhoff, 1975, 1977; Hell, Gigerenzer, Gauggel, Mall, & Muller, 1988; Hoch & Lowenstein, 1989). Namely, once Event X happens, it is easy to believe that Event X was inevitably going to happen. **Hindsight bias** refers to the fact that people confidently judge that they knew an event would occur after it occurs. Before an event took place, a person might not be able to arrive at a solid prediction. But once history runs its course, the person is highly likely to say, "I knew it all along."

For instance, Fischhoff (1975) presented people with historical information about a battle between two armies. Based on this pre-battle information, the participants gave before-the-fact judgments about whether one of the armies would win or whether there would be a stalemate. For example, they assigned a 25% probability that Army A would win. After-the-fact judgments came from participants who were given the same pre-battle information but who then had also been told how the battle really turned out. Now that they knew Army A actually won, they thought that the pre-battle information warranted a more confident prediction, say, 50%. On average, participants gave the highest probability estimates of a particular army winning based on the pre-battle information when making after-the-fact judgments. The same information warranted stronger predictions given the clear vision of hindsight.

> Representativeness, availability, and simulation are powerful heuristics that affect our ability to make decisions in fully rational ways.

Hindsight effects are to be expected if people rely on ease of recall (the availability heuristic) and ease of imagining (the simulation heuristic). Once the critical information about the outcome is known, people cannot put it aside. Indeed, it dominates our recollections and imaginations about the situation at hand, distorting our confidence in our judgments.

Probability or Frequency. A root question in thinking about why we use such heuristics is whether our ability to represent probabilities is deficient. It could be that we process the absolute frequency of events instead of probabilities, which require a representation of relative frequencies. Probability ranges from 0 to 1 and is calculated by knowing the absolute frequency of an event and then dividing it by the maximum number that could have been obtained. In sorting through a deck of cards, you will encounter 13 spades. The probability of picking a spade is 13/52 or .25. So, which number is processed and stored in human information processing: absolute frequency (13) or relative frequency (.25)?

Estes (1976) examined whether absolute or relative frequency prevails using tasks such as the one shown in Box 10.3. The test pits absolute frequency against probability or relative frequency. Candidate B has won more polls than Candidate A in terms of absolute frequency—9 versus 5. But the probability of Candidate A winning a poll is .83 (5/6), whereas for Candidate B the probability is only .50 (9/18). Estes reported that participants generally selected the candidate with the highest absolute frequency of wins, not the candidate with the highest probability. People apparently can make decisions on the basis of probability only when there are about the same number of opportunities for both events. In other words, if both candidates had appeared in 18 polls, then participants would select Candidate B, not Candidate A. Of course, in this case the use of frequency information would make it appear that people could use probabilities effectively.

Numerous other lines of investigation point to the conclusion that people process the frequency with which events occur in the environment. Estes's (1976) polling results are by no means the only task that favors frequency over probability. The evidence from a wide range of tests confirms the view that frequencies of occurrence, and not probabilities, are represented in working and long-term memory (Gigerenzer, Hoffrage, & Kleinbölting, 1991).

> **BOX 10.3**
>
> **The Political Poll Problem**
>
> Here are the results of two opinion polls that compared the popularity of two political candidates. Candidate A had appeared in 6 polls and won 5 of them. Candidate B, on the other hand, had appeared in 18 polls and won 9 of them. Now, for the first time, Candidates A and B will be tested against each other in the same poll. Which candidate do you expect to win?
>
> SOURCE: From Estes, W. K. (1976). The cognitive side of probability learning. *Psychological Review, 83,* 37-64. Reprinted with permission.

> People process and use absolute frequency information, rather than probability or relative frequency information, to make decisions.

Dual Process Theories

Various dual process accounts have been proposed to deal with our capacity to think rationally upon reflection, in accordance with normative models, and our proclivity to ignore rationality and make hastier judgments (e.g., Evans & Over, 1996; Sloman, 1996). Stanovich (1999) summarized these theories by contrasting automatic versus controlled processes. System 1 reasoning is automatic, effortless, and unconscious and arrives at decisions based on associations and immediate emotional responses. System 2 reasoning is controlled, effortful, and conscious and uses rule-based thinking and cool reflection to arrive at decisions. System 2 provides us with the capacity to think in accordance with expected utility theory and other normative models of rationality. However, the heuristic processes discussed in this chapter illustrate the workings of System 1. Such heuristics are presumably ancient human traits that proved adaptive in our evolutionary history. According to evolutionary theory, any genetic code associated with an adaptive physical or cognitive characteristic that confers a reproductive advantage will be selected for over generations and become prevalent in a population.

The bank teller (Linda) problem discussed earlier illustrates the conflict between System 1, automatic processes and System 2, controlled processes. The representative heuristic is expressed when the automatic is not over-ruled by the controlled. The associative system operates on similarity and temporal contiguity. Because the description of Linda is highly similar to one's prototype of a feminist, this conclusion is compelling regardless of what one knows about probability and conjunctive fallacies. On this view, the conjunctive fallacy will be observed when the controlled process of reason fails to intervene in deciding on a response. Whether dual process theory can fully explain the regularities and oddities of human reasoning requires further research, but it offers an interesting application of the distinction between automatic and controlled processes.

SUMMARY

1. Syllogistic reasoning involves evaluating whether a conclusion necessarily follows from two premises that are assumed to be true. A valid deductive conclusion is *necessarily* true given that the two premises are true. People identify valid conclusions about three-quarters of the time. But they perform much worse with invalid conclusions, recognizing them as invalid only about a third of the time. The pattern of errors is very consistent. When the major premise contains the word "all" and the minor premise contains the word "some," people regard a conclusion with the word "some" as valid. When both the major and minor premises contain the word "no," people regard a conclusion with the word "no" as valid.

2. One reason for our poor categorical reasoning performance is illicit conversion. People improperly assume that "If all A are B, then all B are A." Another reason is that considering all possible combinations of what the premises mean places enormous demands on working memory. Not

surprisingly, people simplify the task by considering only a few combinations and by considering only the combinations that are easily interpreted. In general, people reason in ways that are meaningful by constructing mental models. These models need not mirror the formal systems of logicians. One compelling example is the phenomenon of belief bias, whereby people accept a conclusion as valid if it fits their system of beliefs, regardless of the given premises.

3. Conditional reasoning involves deducing a valid conclusion from a rule in the form of "If P, then Q." One way to draw a valid conclusion is affirming the antecedent. By showing that P is true, it follows that Q is also true according to the conditional rule. The second valid form of reasoning is denying the consequent. By showing that Q is false, it follows that P is also false. People reason virtually flawlessly when affirming the consequent. There is a strong tendency toward confirmation bias or seeking evidence that confirms a conclusion. However, people rarely seek evidence that disconfirms the conclusion—denial of the consequent. Furthermore, people do not understand that this is a valid form of reasoning.

4. Making decisions under uncertainty implies that the probabilities of various scenarios must be estimated subjectively. One does not know for certain what the utility will be for a particular course of action, or even what to expect, by an objective calculation. When reasoning under uncertainty, people rely on a variety of heuristics for making predictions and judgments. The representativeness heuristic assigns a high probability of occurrence to events that are judged typical of a class. According to the availability heuristic, an event is likely to occur if specific examples of the event can be easily recalled. Similarly, the simulation heuristic assigns a high probability to events that can be easily imagined to occur because they fit the sequence of a routine script. Finally, it appears that people encode the frequencies of events, not their relative frequencies or probabilities.

KEY TERMS

syllogistic reasoning	affirming the antecedent
valid deductive conclusion	denying the consequent
atmosphere hypothesis	denying the antecedent
illicit conversion	affirming the consequent
belief bias	decisions under certainty

decisions under risk

decisions under uncertainty

framing effect

representativeness heuristic

law of small numbers

gambler's fallacy

conjunctive fallacy

availability heuristic

simulation heuristic

hindsight bias

GLOSSARY

Affirming the antecedent   A valid means of conditional reasoning (If P, then Q; P is true).

Affirming the consequent   An invalid means of conditional reasoning (If P, then Q; Q is true).

Algorithm   A rule that correctly generates the solution to a problem given that one can devote sufficient time and effort to applying the rule.

Analytic processing   Perceiving the features that compose the whole stimulus; contrasts with holistic processing.

Anaphora   The use of a word to substitute for a preceding word or phrase.

Anterograde amnesia   A cognitive disorder characterized by an inability to remember events that occur after the onset of the disorder.

Anterior cingulate gyrus   Brain region involved in the supervisory attentional system, inhibiting automatic responses and selecting the correct response.

Apperceptive agnosia   A type of object recognition failure in which the difficulty lies in identifying the features of a perceptual category; contrasts with associative agnosia.

Assimilation   A distortion of memory caused by reconstructive retrieval processes in which a recollection is rationalized or normalized to fit with schema-based expectations.

Associative agnosia   A type of object recognition failure in which the difficulty lies in identifying the semantic function of an object despite intact perceptual ability; contrasts with apperceptive agnosia.

Atmosphere hypothesis   Presumes that people compare the similarity of the conclusion to the premises in a deductive reasoning task rather than evaluate the conclusion according to the rules of logic.

Attentional blink   The interval of time after the target is presented when other stimuli in the series are not perceived.

Attenuation   Refers to an attentional filter that lowers the strength of the sensory signal on the unattended channel.

Automatic processes   A kind of cognitive process that is unintentional, unconscious, and effortless; contrasts with controlled processes.

Availability heuristic   A decision heuristic suggesting that if relevant examples can readily be retrieved from memory, then the class of events must occur with a high probability.

Backward chaining   A problem-solving heuristic in which an unknown quantity in a problem is identified, and from that unknown an attempt is made to work backward toward the quantities given in the problem.

Belief bias   Refers to people accepting any and all conclusions that happen to fit with their system of beliefs.

Binding problem   Refers to how the features that are distributed in multiple brain regions are integrated to result in the perception of a single object.

Blindsight   Vision that allows the identification of object locations despite the absence of conscious awareness of the objects, as a result of lesions in the occipital cortex.

Brain lateralization   Refers to the degree to which the left or right hemisphere of the brain is specialized for particular cognitive functions.

Brainstem   A structure of the brain consisting of the hindbrain—the medulla and pons—and the midbrain.

Bridging inferences   Inferences required to comprehend anaphoric references in which one word (e.g., a pronoun) is substituted for a preceding word (e.g., a noun).

Broca's aphasia   A disorder of language characterized by a lack of fluency and correct grammar in speech.

Categorical perception   The categorization of speech input at the phonemic level.

Category size effect   In answering simple questions using semantic memory, more time is needed to respond when the semantic category is large (e.g., Is a collie an animal?) than when it is small (e.g., Is a collie a dog?).

Change blindness   Refers to the phenomenon that people fail to notice large changes in visual scenes.

Cerebellum   A structure of the brain that lies over the brainstem at the rear of the head.

Chunking   Relating separate items in a meaningful way so as to form an integrated representation in short-term memory.

Coarticulation   In uttering a word, each time segment of the acoustic signal provides information about the identity of more than one phoneme; phonemes are partly articulated in parallel as well as in series.

Cognitive architecture   The design or organization of the mind's information processing, components, and systems.

Cognitive economy assumption   Claims that the features of a concept are represented only once at either the subordinate, basic, or superordinate level of the hierarchy.

Cognitive science   The study of the relationships among and integration of cognitive psychology, biology, anthropology, computer science, linguistics, and philosophy.

Conceptually driven processes   Expectations derived from schemas in long-term memory that guide pattern recognition and memory encoding; also called top-down processes; contrasts with data-driven processes.

Confabulation   A memory distortion in which one provides a detailed narrative account of events that never happened.

Conjunction error   A kind of verbal false memory in which a word is falsely remembered because its syllables were encountered in two different words studied earlier.

Conjunctive fallacy   In decision making, the error of judging a conjunction of two events as more likely than the probability of either event alone.

Connectionist models   A class of cognitive architecture based on the assumption that the mind is built like the brain with distributed mental representations, massively interconnected neuron-like units, and parallel processing; contrasts with symbolic models.

Consolidation   Refers to the process of successfully storing an event in long-term memory.

Controlled processes   A kind of cognitive process that is intentional, conscious, and demanding of mental effort; contrasts with automatic processes.

Cooperative principle   An implicit contractual agreement among the participants in a conversation to cooperate with one another in conveying meaning.

Corpus callosum   The large band of fibers that connects the right and left cerebral hemispheres together deep in the brain.

Data-driven processes   Analysis of incoming data (e.g., edges, lines) held in sensory memory during pattern recognition and memory encoding; also called bottom-up processes; contrasts with conceptually driven processes.

Decisions under certainty   Decisions made in which the states of nature that determine the outcome of actions are known with certainty.

Decisions under risk   Decisions made in which the states of nature that determine the outcomes of actions occur with known probabilities.

Decisions under uncertainty   Decisions made in which the probabilities of the states of nature that determine the outcomes of actions are unknown.

Declarative memory   Refers to knowledge of events, facts, and concepts.

Delusional false memory   An illusion of memory in which an individual with strong beliefs that a bizarre event can occur comes to actually experience a memory of the event.

Denying the antecedent   An invalid means of conditional reasoning (If P, then Q; P is false).

Denying the consequent   A valid means of conditional reasoning (If P, then Q; Q is false).

Directed thinking   Goal-directed, methodical thinking used in solving problems; contrasts with undirected thinking.

Distinctive features   Perceptual features that discriminate one stimulus from similar stimuli.

Distinctiveness   Refers to how the items to be learned are different from each other and other items already stored in memory; contrasts with relational processing.

Divided attention   The ability to split limited attentional resources among two or more stimuli rather than focusing on a single stimulus; contrasts with selective attention.

Double dissociation   Refers to situations in which an independent variable affects Task A but not Task B and in which a different variable affects Task B but not Task A.

Dual coding theory   Holds that information is best remembered when it is stored in long-term memory using both verbal and imaginal codes.

Early selection Refers to an attentional filter that operates after sensory processing but prior to meaningful semantic processing.

Echoic memory A component in the auditory system that stores sounds for a brief duration.

Ecological validity The similarity of a laboratory task to real-world tasks, allowing valid generalization from the laboratory finding.

Elaborative rehearsal Linking information in short-term memory with information already stored in long-term memory.

Encoding specificity The specific encoding operations performed on what is perceived determines what retrieval cues are effective in gaining access to the stored representation.

Episodic memory The recollection of events that took place at specific places and times in the past.

Event-related potential (ERP) An electroencephalogram (EEG) signal that reflects the brain's response to the onset of a specific stimulus.

Executive attention Supervisory attentional system that inhibits inappropriate mental representations or responses and activates appropriate ones.

Exhaustive search A search of memory that continues to examine the remaining items in memory even after the target item has been found.

Eye-mind assumption Holds that the duration of fixation varies with the amount of information that must be processed in working memory at that instant.

False verbal memory An illusion of memory in which a target word is falsely remembered following the study of a list of words highly related to the target.

Family resemblance structure A characteristic of natural object concepts that are defined by a large number of features that apply to some, but not all, category members; contrasts with rule-governed concepts.

Feature comparison model Assumes that semantic memory includes characteristic and defining features of concepts.

Feature integration theory Posits that automatic preattentive processing of features must be followed by controlled attentional processing to bind the features into a whole object.

Fixation Refers to the blocking of solution paths to a problem that is caused by past experiences related to the problem.

Flashbulb memory   A vivid recollection of some autobiographical event that carries with it strong emotional reactions.

Folk theories   Naive commonsense explanations of scientific phenomena as opposed to theories based on scientific facts.

Formants   Bands of sound energy at particular frequencies in a speech signal.

Forward chaining   A problem-solving heuristic in which the known quantities in the problem are first identified, and then an attempt is made to work forward toward the unknown quantity.

Frames   Schemas that represent the physical structure of the environment.

Framing effect   In decision making, it refers to making a different decision depending on where people perceive themselves to be in relation to the curvilinear subjective utility function.

Frontal lobe   A region of cortex that extends from the anterior of the brain back to the central sulcus and the temporal lobes.

Functional equivalence hypothesis   States that visual imagery, while not identical to perception, is mentally represented and functions the same as perception.

Functional fixedness   An impediment to problem solving, it refers to the tendency to see objects as having only a single typical use.

Functional magnetic resonance imaging (fMRI)   A method of neuroimaging that uses a powerful magnetic field to reveal detailed images of neuronal tissue and the metabolic changes associated with activated regions.

Gambler's fallacy   Refers to the mistaken belief that future tosses of a coin, drops of the ball in roulette, or rolls of the dice in craps are not independent of past events.

Given-new strategy   A comprehension strategy to first identify the old information known already and then to seek the novel information in a sentence.

Goal state   The solution to a problem, it is the final end state of the problem space and the opposite of the initial state.

Grapheme   The minimal unit that carries meaning in written language.

Heuristic   A rule of thumb or general strategy that may lead to a solution reasonably quickly with less computational cost.

Hindsight bias   Refers to the fact that people confidently judge that they knew an event would occur after it had occurred.

Hippocampus A structure of the limbic system located in the medial temporal lobe that is involved in the learning and storage of new events in long-term memory.

Historical creativity Acts of genius that are widely acclaimed by society as meritorious and novel within the context of human history.

Holistic processing Perceiving the whole object; contrasts with analytic processing.

Iconic memory A component that stores visual features for a brief period of time.

Ill-defined problem A problem in which the goal state, the initial state, or the operators are not clearly defined; contrasts with well-defined problems.

Illicit conversion Refers to people converting "All A are B" into "All B are A," taking the converse of the premise as true in addition to the premise itself.

Illumination The third stage of creativity in which insight into the problem solution is obtained.

Imaginal code A concrete means of mental representation that directly conveys perceptual qualities.

Immediacy assumption Holds that readers assign an interpretation to each word as it is fixated.

Inattentional blindness Failure to perceive an unattended object because its features were not bound by attention.

Incubation The second stage of creativity that refers to putting the problem aside and doing other things.

Informational access The capacity to become aware of and able to report on mental representations and the processes that operate on them.

Initial state The beginning of a problem, it is the first state of the problem space and the opposite of the goal state.

Integration Refers to combining features of different events into a unified memory representation.

Interpretation Inferences and suppositions made during memory encoding based on activated schemas in long-term memory.

Isomorphic problems Problems that appear different on the surface in wording, for example, but share the same problem space at a deep level of analysis.

Latent semantic analysis (LSA)   A mathematical procedure for automatically extracting and representing the meanings of propositions expressed in a text.

Law of small numbers   People mistakenly expect even small samples to look random and to mirror the probabilities obtained with large samples.

Leveling   A distortion of memory caused by reconstructive retrieval processes in which details are lost in recollecting an event.

Levels or depths of processing   A memory superiority for events attentively processed at a semantic level as compared to a sensory level.

Limbic system   A functional unit of the brain comprised of the cingulate gyrus, fornix, hippocampus, and other related structures.

Macropropositions   The assertions that represent the gist or a summary of the meaning of a text.

Maintenance rehearsal   Recycling information within short-term or working memory by covertly verbalizing it.

Mental effort   The proportion of available attentional capacity that is momentarily allocated to a cognitive process.

Mental lexicon   A dictionary of long-term memory that stores the morphemes used in speaking, listening, reading, and writing.

Mental representation   An unobservable internal code for information.

Metacognition   Thinking about another thought process in which the object of a mental representation is another mental representation.

Meta-representation   A mental representation whose object is another mental representation.

Method of subtraction   Used by cognitive psychologists to isolate the properties of a single stage of processing by comparing two tasks that differ only in terms of the stage of interest.

Micropropositions   The individual assertions that represent the meaning of a single sentence.

Mindblindness   Refers to an inability to understand that other people possess mental representations.

Misinformation effect   A distortion of memory caused by asking misleading questions about an event encoded in long-term memory.

Module   A set of processes that are automatic, fast, encapsulated apart from other cognitive systems, and instantiated in a localized area of the brain.

Mood congruence effect   Events encoded during one mood are easiest to retrieve during the same mood; for example, positive life events are easiest to remember when in a happy mood.

Morpheme   A minimal unit of speech used repeatedly in a language to code a specific meaning (e.g., words, suffixes, prefixes).

Neocortex   The most recently evolved parts of the cerebral cortex, which is well-developed only in mammals.

Nondeclarative memory   Refers to skills and related procedural knowledge.

Object concepts   Refer to natural kinds or biological objects and artifacts or human-made objects.

Occipital lobe   A region of cortex that lies at the rear base of the brain, just above the cerebellum.

Operator   A legal move in solving a problem; it results in a transition from one state to another within a problem space.

Parallel processing   Refers to cases in which cognitive operations occur simultaneously in parallel.

Parallel search   Means that all items in memory are examined simultaneously, not serially.

Parietal lobe   A region of the cortex that extends toward the rear and sides of the brain beginning at the central sulcus and ending at the occipital lobe and temporal lobe.

Pattern recognition   The step between the transduction and perception of a stimulus in the environment and its categorization as a meaningful object.

Phoneme   Speech sound or phonological segment that makes a difference in meaning.

Phonemic similarity effect   The high rate of intrusion errors in short-term memory for stimuli that are pronounced alike.

Polysemy   The property of language that a single word can have more than one meaning.

Positron emission tomography (PET)   A method of neuroimaging that uses radioactively labeled water (hydrogen and oxygen 15) to detect areas of high metabolic activity in the brain.

Pragmatics   Refers to the manner in which speakers communicate their intentions depending on the social context.

Preparation   The first stage of creativity concerned with studying, learning, formulating solutions, and striving to create.

Primacy effect   Accurate recall of the initial items studied in a list of items in a memory experiment.

Priming   Refers to the presentation of a stimulus biasing how a subsequent stimulus is processed.

Proactive interference   Means that past learning interferes with the ability to learn and remember new information.

Problem space   The initial state, goal state, and all possible states in between that may be reached by applying the operators or legal moves in a problem.

Productive thinking   Entails insight and creativity in the seeking the solution to a problem; contrasts with reproductive thinking.

Productivity   Refers to the ability to create novel sentences that can be understood by other speakers of the language.

Proportion of errors   A measure of errors made in a cognitive task.

Propositional code   An abstract means of mental representation that is schematic and verbal rather than perceptual.

Prosopagnosia   A cognitive disorder characterized by a selective inability to recognize faces.

Prototype   The best or most typical member of a category that serves as a summary representation of a concept.

Reaction time   The number of milliseconds to perform a task; it is used to measure the duration of cognitive processes.

Recency effect   Accurate recall of the last items presented in a list in a memory experiment.

Reconstructive retrieval   Refers to schema-guided construction of episodic memories that interpret, embellish, integrate, and alter encoded memory representations.

Referential coherence When the words and phrases of one sentence in a paragraph refer unambiguously to those of other sentences in the paragraph.

Relational processing Refers to how the items to be learned are related to each other and to other items stored in memory; contrasts with distinctiveness.

Representativeness heuristic A decision heuristic suggesting that if examples are typical of a class, then they occur with a high probability.

Repression A defense mechanism that, in psychoanalytic theory, protects the ego from anxiety by preventing unpleasant memories from entering consciousness.

Reproductive thinking Entails the application of tried-and-true paths to the solution of a problem; contrasts with productive thinking.

Retrieval mode The initial stage of retrieval in which an effortful search is made of long-term memory for the representation of a past event.

Retroactive interference Refers to recent learning interfering with the recall of previous learning.

Retrograde amnesia A cognitive disorder characterized by an inability to remember events that occurred prior to the onset of the disorder.

Rule-governed concepts Specify the features and relations that define membership in the class on an all-or-none basis; contrasts with family resemblance structure.

Schema A mental representation that organizes knowledge about related concepts.

Scripts Schemas that represent routine activities.

Selection The selective encoding of information that fits with prior knowledge.

Selective attention The ability to perceive and attend to a particular stimulus of interest while ignoring numerous other stimuli; contrasts with divided attention.

Self-knowledge Awareness of the self as an entity.

Self-reference effect A level of processing effect whereby encoding processes that relate an item to be learned to self-concepts produces superior memory.

Self-terminating search   Refers to a search that stops as soon as the item being sought is found.

Semantic memory   Factual and conceptual knowledge about the world and the words used to symbolize such knowledge.

Semantic network model   Hierarchical model of semantic memory in which concepts are organized according to subordinate, basic, and superordinate levels and their features.

Semantics   The study of meaning.

Sentience   The basic capacity for raw sensations, feelings, and subjective experience of any kind.

Serial position effect   The outcome when people are asked to recall items presented earlier in a list in any order; the initial and final items of the list are best recalled.

Serial processing   Cases in which cognitive operations occur one at a time in a series.

Serial search   Means that the items in memory are somehow ordered and are examined one at a time, starting with the first item and proceeding to the next.

Shadowing   The participant repeats aloud the stimuli presented to the attended channel and ignores those in the unattended ignored channel.

Sharpening   A distortion of memory caused by reconstructive retrieval processes in which details are added during the recollection of an event by drawing inferences from general knowledge.

Simulation heuristic   A decision heuristic that involves constructing a mental model of a situation and then "running the model" so as to predict the course of events.

Source monitoring   Refers to evaluative processes that attribute mental experiences to different sources.

Spatial neglect   A cognitive disorder of attention in which a portion of the visual field is selectively ignored on a consistent basis despite normal visual abilities.

Speech act   Refers to a sentence uttered to express the speaker's intention in a way that the listener will recognize.

Speech spectrogram   The physical acoustic energy of an utterance by plotting frequency in hertz or cycles per second on the y axis and time in milliseconds on the x axis.

Stages of processing   The steps required to form, modify, and use mental representations in a cognitive task.

State-dependent learning   Sometimes observed when a person's mood or state of consciousness (e.g., sober, intoxicated) is directly manipulated during learning and retrieval, with matches yielding better recall than mismatches.

Stroop effect   Has challenged theorists to account for the detailed patterns of errors and delays observed in experiments.

Subgoals   In a problem space, important intermediate states that must be reached between the initial state and the goal state.

Subjective organization   A consistent organizational pattern for recalling unrelated items from long-term memory that is unique to each individual.

Subliminal perception   Refers to the unsupported claim that unattended stimuli are perceived as whole objects, although certain features may be processed.

Syllogistic reasoning   Involves evaluating whether a conclusion necessarily follows deductively from two premises that are assumed to be true.

Symbolic models   A class of cognitive architecture based on the assumption that the mind is built like a digital computer in which mental representations are symbols stored in memory and manipulated according to rules; contrasts with connectionist models.

Synset   A set of synonyms for the each noun, verb, adjective, or adverb in the language.

Syntax   The grammatical rules that specify how words and other morphemes are arranged so as to yield acceptable sentences.

Temporal lobe   A region of cortex that lies on the side of the brain, beginning below the lateral fissure; it is bordered by the frontal, parietal, and occipital lobes.

Tip of the tongue (TOT) state   A feeling of knowing or familiarity in which some name, word, date, or other information cannot be retrieved despite a certainty that it is available in memory.

Transfer-appropriate processing   Holds that test performance depends on the degree to which the processes engaged at encoding are compatible with the demands of the memory test.

Trauma-induced amnesia   Loss of memory for a traumatic event involving a dissociation of consciousness.

Typicality effect   Refers to the gradient of category membership or differences in how well specific instances represent a concept.

Undirected thinking   Wandering thought, as in daydreams, that may prompt a creative solution to a problem; contrasts with directed thinking.

Universal grammar   Refers to the genetically determined knowledge of human language that allows children in all cultures to rapidly acquire the language to which they are exposed.

Valid deductive conclusion   A conclusion that is necessarily true given that the premises are true in syllogistic reasoning.

Verbal protocols   Tape-recordings of people thinking aloud while they carry out a task provide a rich record of conscious processing.

Verification   The fourth stage of creativity when the solution achieved as an insight must be fleshed out and checked carefully.

Well-defined problem   A problem in which the initial state, goal state, and operators can be stated clearly; contrasts with ill-defined problems.

Wernicke's aphasia   A disorder of language in which speech comprehension is severely impaired and production is fluent but often meaningless.

Word superiority effect   The counterintuitive finding that a letter is recognized more rapidly when presented in the context of a whole word than when presented as an isolated feature.

Working memory   Refers to the system for temporarily maintaining mental representations that are relevant to the performance of a cognitive task in an activated state.

REFERENCES

Abelson, R. P. (1981). Psychological status of the script concept. *American Psychologist, 36,* 715–729.

Adolphs, R., Denburg, N. L., & Tranel, D. (2001). The amygdala's role in long-term declarative memory for gist and detail. *Behavioral Neuroscience, 115,* 983–992.

Alba, J. W., & Hasher, L. (1983). Is memory schematic? *Psychological Bulletin, 93,* 203–231.

Allport, D. A., Antonis, B., & Reynolds, P. (1972). On the division of attention: A disproof of the single channel hypothesis. *Quarterly Journal of Experimental Psychology, 24,* 225–235.

Anderson, A. K. (2005). Affective influences on the attentional dynamics supporting awareness. *Journal of Experimental Psychology: General, 134,* 258–281.

Anderson, J. R. (1983). *The architecture of cognition.* Cambridge, MA: Harvard University Press.

Anderson, J. R. (1990). *Cognitive psychology and its implications* (3rd ed.). New York: Freeman.

Anthony, T., Copper, C., & Mullen, B. (1992). Cross-racial facial identification: A social cognitive integration. *Personality and Social Psychology Bulletin, 18,* 296–301.

Antrobus, J. (1991). Dreaming: Cognitive processes during cortical activation and high afferent thresholds. *Psychological Review, 98,* 96–121.

Atchison, J. (1996). *The seeds of speech: Language origin and evolution.* Cambridge, UK: Cambridge University Press.

Atkinson, R. C., & Shiffrin, R. M. (1968). Human memory: A proposed system and its control processes. In K. W. Spence & J. T. Spence (Eds.), *The psychology of learning and motivation* (Vol. 2, pp. 89–195). Orlando, FL: Academic Press.

Atkinson, R. C., & Shiffrin, R. M. (1971). The control of short-term memory. *Scientific American, 225,* 82–90.

Attneave, F. (1957). Transfer of experience with a class schema to identification of patterns and shapes. *Journal of Experimental Psychology, 54,* 81–88.

Atwood, M. E., & Polson, P. G. (1976). A process model for water jar problems. *Cognitive Psychology, 8,* 191–216.

Averbach, E., & Coriell, A. S. (1961). Short-term memory in vision. *Bell System Technical Journal, 40,* 309–328.

Baars, B. J. (1988). *A cognitive theory of consciousness.* Cambridge, UK: Cambridge University Press.

Baddeley, A. D. (1986). *Working memory.* New York: Oxford University Press.

Baddeley, A. D. (1996). Exploring the central executive. *Quarterly Journal of Experimental Psychology, 49A,* 5–28.

Baddeley, A. D. (2001). Is working memory still working? *American Psychologist, 56,* 849–864.

Baddeley, A. D., & Logie, R. H. (1999). Working memory: The multiple component model. In A. Miyake & P. Shah (Eds.), *Models of working memory: Mechanisms of active maintenance and executive control* (pp. 28–61). Cambridge, UK: Cambridge University Press.

Baddeley, A. D., & Scott, D. (1971). Short-term forgetting in the absence of pro-active interference. *Quarterly Journal of Experimental Psychology, 23,* 275–283.

Baddeley, A. D., & Warrington, E. K. (1970). Amnesia and the distinction between long-term and short-term memory. *Journal of Verbal Learning and Verbal Behavior, 9,* 176–189.

Bahrick, H. P. (1983). The cognitive map of a city: Fifty years of learning and memory. In G. H. Bower (Ed.), *The psychology of learning and motivation: Advances in research and theory* (Vol. 17, pp. 125–163). New York: Academic Press.

Bahrick, H. P. (1984). Semantic memory content in permastore: Fifty years of memory for Spanish learned in school. *Journal of Experimental Psychology: General, 113,* 1–29.

Bahrick, H. P., Bahrick, P. C., & Wittlinger, R. P. (1975). Fifty years of memories for names and faces: A cross-sectional approach. *Journal of Experimental Psychology: General, 104,* 54–75.

Bar-Hillel, M. (1980). What features make samples seem representative? *Journal of Experimental Psychology: Human Perception and Performance, 6,* 578–589.

Baron-Cohen, S. (1995). *Mindblindness: An essay on autism and theory of mind.* Cambridge, MA: MIT Press.

Baron-Cohen, S., Leslie, A. M., & Frith, U. (1985). Does the the autistic child have a "theory of mind"? *Cognition, 21,* 37–46.

Barret, L. F., & Wager, T. D. (2006). The structure of emotion: Evidence from neuroimaging studies. *Current Directions in Psychological Science, 15,* 79–83.

Barsalou, L. W. (1983). Ad hoc categories. *Memory & Cognition, 11,* 211–227.

Barsalou, L. W., & Sewell, D. R. (1985). Contrasting the representation of scripts and categories. *Journal of Memory and Language, 24,* 646–665.

Bartlett, F. C. (1932). *Remembering: A study in experimental and social psychology.* Cambridge, UK: Cambridge University Press.

Bartlett, J. C., & Searcy, J. (1993). Inversion and configuration of faces. *Cognitive Psychology, 25,* 281–316.

Barton, M. E., & Komatsu, L. K. (1989). Defining features of natural kinds and artifacts. *Journal of Psycholinguistic Research, 18,* 433–447.

Begg, I., & Denny, J. P. (1969). Empirical reconciliation of atmosphere and conversion interpretations of syllogistic reasoning errors. *Journal of Experimental Psychology, 81,* 351–354.

Begg, I., & White, P. (1985). Encoding specificity in interpersonal communication. *Canadian Journal of Psychology, 39,* 70–87.

Bellezza, F. S. (1986). A mnemonic based on arranging words on visual patterns. *Journal of Educational Psychology, 78,* 217–224.

Bergman, E. T., & Roediger, H. L., III. (1999). Can Bartlett's repeated reproduction experiments be replicated? *Memory & Cognition, 27,* 937–947.

Berlyne, D. E. (1965). *Structure and direction in thinking.* New York: John Wiley.

Bertoncini, J., Bijeljac-Babic, R., Jusczyk, P. W., Kennedy, L. J., & Mehler, J. (1988). An investigation of young infants' perceptual representations of speech sounds. *Journal of Experimental Psychology: General, 117,* 21–33.

Biederman, I. (1985). Human image understanding: Recent research and a theory. *Computer Vision, Graphics, and Image Processing, 32,* 29–73.

Biederman, I. (1987). Recognition-by-components: A theory of human understanding. *Psychological Review, 94,* 115–147.

Biederman, I., Glass, A. L., & Stacy, E. W. (1973). Searching for objects in real world scenes. *Journal of Experimental Psychology, 97,* 22–27.

Biederman, I., & Ju, G. (1988). Surface vs. edge-based determinants of visual recognition. *Cognitive Psychology, 20,* 38–64.

Bishop, K., & Curran, H. V. (1995). Psychopharmacological analysis of implicit and explicit memory: A study with lorazepam and the benzodiazepine antagonist, flumazenil. *Psychopharmacology, 121,* 267–278.

Blakemore, C., & Cooper, G. F. (1970). Development of the brain depends on the visual environment. *Nature, 228,* 477–478.

Blaney, P. H. (1986). Affect and memory: A review. *Psychological Bulletin, 99,* 229–246.

Boden, M. (1992). *The creative mind: Myths and mechanisms.* New York: Basic Books.

Bond, C. F., & Omar, A. S. (1990). Social anxiety, state dependence, and the next-in-line effect. *Journal of Experimental Social Psychology, 26,* 185–198.

Boring, E. G. (1957). *A history of experimental psychology.* Englewood Cliffs, NJ: Prentice Hall.

Bourne, L. E., Jr. (1970). Knowing and using concepts. *Psychological Review, 77,* 546–556.

Bourne, L. E., Jr., Dominowski, R. L., Loftus, E. F., & Healy, A. F. (1986). *Cognitive processes* (2nd ed.). Englewood Cliffs, NJ: Prentice Hall.

Bousfield, W. A. (1953). The occurrence of clustering in the recall of randomly arranged associates. *Journal of General Psychology, 49,* 229–240.

Bower, G. H. (1970). Analysis of a mnemonic device. *American Psychologist, 36,* 129–148.

Bower, G. H. (1972). Mental imagery and associative learning. In L. W. Gregg (Ed.), *Cognition in learning and memory* (pp. 51–88). New York: John Wiley.

Bower, G. H. (1981). Mood and memory. *American Psychologist, 36,* 129–148.

Bower, G. H., Black, J. B., & Turner, T. J. (1979). Scripts in memory for text. *Cognitive Psychology, 11,* 177–220.

Bransford, J. D., & Franks, J. J. (1971). Abstraction of linguistic ideas. *Cognitive Psychology, 2,* 331–350.

Bransford, J. D., & Johnson, M. K. (1972). Contextual prerequisites for understanding: Some investigations of comprehension and recall. *Journal of Verbal Learning and Verbal Behavior, 11,* 717–726.

Brewer, W. F., & Treyens, J. C. (1981). Role of schemata in memory for places. *Cognitive Psychology, 13,* 207–230.

Broadbent, D. E. (1957). A mechanical model for human attention and immediate memory. *Psychological Review, 64,* 205–215.

Broadbent, D. E. (1958). *Perception and communication.* New York: Pergamon.

Broadbent, D. E. (1975). The magic number seven after fifteen years. In A. Kennedy & A. Wilkes (Eds.), *Studies in long-term memory* (pp. 3–18). London: Wiley.

Brooks, L. R. (1968). Spatial and verbal components of the act of recall. *Canadian Journal of Psychology, 22,* 349–368.

Brown, A. S. (1991). A review of the tip-of-the-tongue experience. *Psychological Bulletin, 109,* 204–223.

Brown, J. A. (1958). Some tests of the decay theory of immediate memory. *Quarterly Journal of Experimental Psychology, 10,* 12–21.

Brown, R., & Kulik, J. (1977). Flashbulb memories. *Cognition, 5,* 73–99.

Brown, R., & McNeill, D. (1966). The "tip-of-the tongue" phenomenon. *Journal of Verbal Learning and Verbal Behavior, 5,* 325–337.

Bruner, J. S. (1990). *Acts of meaning.* Cambridge, MA: Harvard University Press.

Bruner, J. S., Goodnow, J. J., & Austin, G. A. (1956). *A study of thinking.* New York: John Wiley.

Buckhout, R. (1974). Eyewitness testimony. *Scientific American, 231,* 23–31.

Buckner, R. L. (1996). Beyond HERA: Contributions of specific prefrontal brain areas to long-term memory retrieval. *Psychonomic Bulletin & Review, 3,* 149–158.

Buckner, R., Goodman, J., Burock, M., Rotte, M., Loutstaal, W., Schacter, D., et al. (1998). Functional-anatomic correlates of object priming in humans revealed by rapid presentation event-related fMRI. *Neuron, 20,* 285–296.

Buckner, R. L., Koutstaal, W., Schacter, D. L., Dale, A. M., Rotte, M., & Rosen, B. R. (1998). Functional-anatomic study of episodic retrieval: Selective averaging of event-related fMRI trials to test the retrieval success hypothesis. *NeuroImage, 7,* 151–162.

Buckner, R. L., & Petersen, S. E. (2000). Neuroimaging of functional recovery. In H. S. Levin & J. Grafman (Eds.), *Cerebral organization of function after brain damage* (pp. 318–330). New York: Oxford University Press.

Cantor, N., Mischel, W., & Schwartz, J. C. (1982). A prototype analysis of psychological situations. *Cognitive Psychology, 14,* 45–77.

Caramazza, A. (1991). *Issues in reading, writing, and speaking: A neuropsychological perspective.* Dordrecht, Netherlands: Kluwer.

Carey, S. (1978). The child as word learner. In M. Halle, J. Bresnan, & G. Miller (Eds.), *Linguistic theory and psychological reality* (pp. 264–293). Cambridge, MA: MIT Press.

Cavanagh, J. P. (1972). Relation between the immediate memory span and the memory search rate. *Psychological Review, 79,* 525–530.

Ceci, S. J., & Bruck, M. (1993). Suggestibility of the child witness: A historical review and synthesis. *Psychological Bulletin, 113,* 403–439.

Ceci, S. J., & Bruck, M. (1995). *Jeopardy in the coutroom: A scientific analysis of children's testimony.* Washington, DC: American Psychological Association.

Ceci, S. J., Crossman, A. M., Gilstrap, L. L., & Scullin, M. H. (1998). Social and cognitive factors in children's testimony. In C. P. Thompson, D. J. Hermann, D. J. Read, D. Bruce, D. G. Payne, & M. P. Toglia (Eds.), *Eyewitness memory: Theoretical and applied perspectives* (pp. 15–30). Mahwah, NJ: Lawrence Erlbaum.

Ceci, S. J., Leichtman, M., Putnick, M., & Nightingale, N. (1993). Age differences in suggestibility. In D. Cicchetti & S. Toth (Eds.), *Child abuse, child development, and social policy* (pp. 117–137). Norwood, NJ: Ablex.

Ceraso, J., & Provitera, A. (1971). Sources of error in syllogistic reasoning. *Cognitive Psychology, 2,* 400–410.

Chase, W. G., & Simon, H. A. (1973). Perception in chess. *Cognitive Psychology, 4,* 55–81.

Chance, J. E., & Goldstein, A. G. (1981). Depth of processing in response to own and other-race faces. *Personality and Social Psychology Bulletin, 7,* 475–480.

Chang, T. M. (1986). Semantic memory: Facts and models. *Psychological Bulletin, 99,* 199–220.

Cheesman, I., & Merikle, P. M. (1984). Priming with and without awareness. *Perception and Psychophysics, 36,* 387–395.

Cheng, P. W., & Holyoak, K. J. (1985). Pragmatic reasoning schemas. *Cognitive Psychology, 17,* 391–416.

Cheng, P. W., Holyoak, K. J., Nisbett, R. E., & Oliver, L. M. (1986). Pragmatic versus syntactic approaches to training deductive reasoning. *Cognitive Psychology, 18,* 293–328.

Cherry, C. (1953). Some experiments on the recognition of speech with one and with two ears. *Journal of the Acoustical Society of America, 25,* 975–979.

Chi, M. T. H. (1978). Knowledge structures and memory development. In R. S. Siegler (Ed.), *Children's thinking: What develops?* (pp. 73–96). Hillsdale, NJ: Lawrence Erlbaum.

Chi, M. T. H., Feltovich, P. J., & Glaser, R. (1981). Categorization and representation of physics problems by experts and novices. *Cognitive Science, 5,* 121–152.

Chomsky, N. (1965). *Aspects of the theory of syntax.* Cambridge, MA: MIT Press.

Chomsky, N. (1986). *Knowledge of language: Its nature, origin, and use.* New York: Praeger.

Christianson, S. A. (1992). Emotional stress and eyewitness memory: A critical review. *Psychological Bulletin, 112,* 284–309.

Cirilo, R. K. (1981). Referential coherence and text structure in story comprehension. *Journal of Verbal Learning and Verbal Behavior, 20,* 358–367.

Cirilo, R. K., & Foss, D. J. (1980). Text structure and reading time for sentences. *Journal of Verbal Learning and Verbal Behavior, 19,* 96–109.

Clark, H. H. (1977). Inferences in comprehension. In D. LaBerge & S. J. Samuels (Eds.), *Basic processes in reading: Perception and comprehension* (pp. 243–263). Hillsdale, NJ: Lawrence Erlbaum.

Clark, H. H., & Chase, W. G. (1972). On the process of comparing sentences against pictures. *Cognitive Psychology, 3,* 472–517.

Clark, H. H., & Clark, E. V. (1977). *Psychology and language.* New York: Harcourt Brace Jovanovich.

Cohen, J. D., Barch, D. M., Carter, C., & Servan-Schreiber, D. (1999). Context-processing deficits in schizophrenia: Converging evidence from three theoretically motivated cognitive tasks. *Journal of Abnormal Psychology, 108,* 120–133.

Cole, M., & Scribner, S. (1974). *Culture and thought: A psychological introduction.* New York: John Wiley.

Cole, R. A., & Jakimik, J. (1980). A model of speech perception. In R. A. Cole (Ed.), *Perception and production of fluent speech* (pp. 133–163). Hillsdale, NJ: Lawrence Erlbaum.

Collins, A. M., & Loftus, E. F. (1975). A spreading activation theory of semantic processing. *Psychological Review, 82,* 85–88.

Collins, A. M., & Quillian, M. R. (1969). Retrieval time from semantic memory. *Journal of Verbal Learning and Verbal Behavior, 8,* 240–247.

Conrad, C. (1972). Cognitive economy in semantic memory. *Journal of Experimental Psychology, 92,* 49–54.

Conrad, R. (1964). Acoustic confusions in immediate memory. *British Journal of Psychology, 55,* 77–84.

Conway, M. A. (1992). A structural model of autobiographical memory. In M. A. Conway, D. C. Rubin, H. Spinnler, & W. A. Wagenaar (Eds.), *Theoretical perspectives on autobiographical memory* (pp. 167–193). Dordrecht, Netherlands: Kluwer.

Conway, M. A., Anderson, S. J., Larsen, S. F., Donnelly, C. M., McDaniel, M. A., McClelland, A. G. R., et al. (1994). The formation of flashbulb memories. *Memory & Cognition, 22,* 326–343.

Conway, M. A., Cohen, G., & Stanhope, N. (1991). On the very long-term retention of knowledge acquired through formal education: Twelve years of cognitive psychology. *Journal of Experimental Psychology: General, 120,* 395–409.

Corballis, M. C. (1989). Laterality and human evolution. *Psychological Review, 96,* 492–505.

Coren, S. (1984). Subliminal perception. In R. J. Corsini (Ed.), *Encyclopedia of psychology* (Vol. 3, p. 382). New York: John Wiley.

Cosmides, L., & Tooby, J. (1992). Cognitive adaptations for social exchange. In J. H. Barkow, L. Cosmides, & J. Tooby (Eds.), *The adapted mind: Evolutionary psychology and the generation of culture* (pp. 163–228). New York: Oxford University Press.

Cowan, N. (1988). Evolving conceptions of memory storage, selective attention, and their mutual constraints within the human information-processing system. *Psychological Bulletin, 104,* 163–191.

Cowan, N. (2000). The magical number 4 in short-term memory: Reconsideration of mental storage capacity. *Behavioral and Brain Sciences, 24,* 87–185.

Craik, F. I. M., Govoni, R., Naveh-Benjamin, M., & Anderson, N. C. (1996). The effects of divided attention on encoding and retrieval processes in human memory. *Journal of Experimental Psychology: General, 125,* 159–180.

Craik, F. I. M., & Lockhart, R. S. (1972). Levels of processing: A framework for memory research. *Journal of Verbal Learning and Verbal Behavior, 11,* 671–684.

Craik, F. I. M., & Tulving, E. (1975). Depth of processing and the retention of words in episodic memory. *Journal of Experimental Psychology: General, 104,* 268–294.

Craik, F. I. M., & Watkins, M. J. (1973). The role of rehearsal in short-term memory. *Journal of Verbal Learning and Verbal Behavior, 12,* 599–607.

Crick, F. H. C. (1994). *The astonishing hypothesis: The scientific search for the soul.* New York: Scribner.

Crowder, R. G. (1982). Decay of auditory memory in vowel discrimination. *Journal of Experimental Psychology: Learning, Memory, and Cognition, 8,* 153–162.

Crowder, R. G. (1993). Short-term memory: Where do we stand? *Memory & Cognition, 21,* 142–146.

Croyle, R. T., Loftus, E. G., Klinger, M. R., & Smith, K. D. (1992). Reducing errors in health-related memory: Progress and prospects. In J. R. Schement & B. D. Ruben (Eds.), *Information and behavior: Between communication and information* (Vol. 4, pp. 255–268). New Brunswick, NJ: Transaction.

Curran, H. V. (2000). Psychopharmacological perspectives on memory. In E. Tulving & F. I. M. Craik (Eds.), *The Oxford handbook of memory* (pp. 539–554) New York: Oxford University Press.

Curran, H. V., & Hildebrandt, M. (in press). Dissociative effects of alcohol on recollective experience. *Consciousness & Cognition.*

Curran, T., Schacter, D. L., Johnson, M. K., & Spinks, R. (2001). Brain potentials reflect behavioral differences in true and false recognition. *Journal of Cognitive Neuroscience, 13,* 201–216.

Curtiss, S. (1977). *Genie: A psycholinguistic study of a modern day "wild child."* New York: Academic Press.

Damasio, A. R. (1994). *Descartes' error: Emotion, reason, and the human brain.* New York: Avon.

Damasio, H., Grabowski, T. J., Tranel, D., Hichwa, R. D., & Damasio, A. R. (1996). A neural basis for lexical retrieval. *Nature, 380,* 499–505.

Daneman, M., & Carpenter, P. A. (1980). Individual differences in working memory and reading. *Journal of Verbal Learning and Verbal Behavior, 18,* 450–466.

Darley, C. F., & Glass, A. L. (1975). Effects of rehearsal and serial list position on recall. *Journal of Experimental Psychology: Learning, Memory, and Cognition, 104,* 453–458.

Darwin, C. J., Turvey, M. T., & Crowder, R. G. (1972). An auditory analogue of the Sperling partial report procedure: Evidence for brief auditory storage. *Cognitive Psychology, 3,* 255–267.

David, A. S. (1993). Spatial and selective attention in the cerebral hemispheres in depression, mania, and schizophrenia. *Brain & Cognition, 23,* 166–180.

Deacon, T. W. (1997). *The symbolic species: The co-evolution of language and the brain.* New York: Norton.

Deese, J. (1959). On the prediction of occurrence of particular verbal intrusions in immediate recall. *Journal of Experimental Psychology, 58,* 17–22.

Della Sala, S., Gray, C., Baddeley, A. D., Allamano, N., & Wilson, L. (2000). A means of unwelding visuo-spatial memory. *Neuropsychologia, 20,* 626–646.

Deutsch, J. A., & Deutsch, D. (1963). Attention: Some theoretical considerations. *Psychological Review, 70,* 80–90.

de Villiers, J. G., & de Villiers, P. A. (1978). *Language acquisition.* Cambridge, MA: Harvard University Press.

Dickstein, L. S. (1978). Error processes in syllogistic reasoning. *Memory & Cognition, 6,* 537–543.

Dominowski, R. L. (1977). Reasoning. *Interamerican Journal of Psychology, 11,* 68–77.

Dooling, D. J., & Christiansen, R. E. (1977). Episodic and semantic aspects of memory for prose. *Journal of Experimental Psychology: Human Learning and Memory, 3,* 428–436.

Drews, F. A., Johnston, W. A., & Strayer, D. L. (2003). Cell phone-induced failures of visual attention during simulated driving. *Journal of Experimental Psychology: Applied, 9,* 23–32.

Dronkers, N. F., Redfern, B. B., & Knight, R. T. (2000). The neural architecture of language disorders. In M. S. Gazzaniga (Ed.), *The new cognitive neurosciences* (pp. 949–958). Cambridge, MA: MIT Press.

Duncker, K. (1945). On problem-solving. *Psychological Monographs, 58*(Whole No. 270).

D'Ydewalle, G., Delhaye, P., & Goessens, L. (1985). Structural, semantic, and self-reference processing of pictorial advertisements. *Human Learning, 4,* 29–38.

Eakin, D. K., Schreiber, T. A., & Sergent-Marshall, S. (2003). Misinformation effects in eyewitness memory: The presence and absence of memory impairment as a function of warning and misinformation accessibility. *Journal of Experimental Psychology: Learning, Memory, and Cognition, 29,* 813–825.

Ebbinghaus, H. (1964). *Uber das Gedächtnis: Intersuchungen zur experimentellen psychologie* (H. A. Ruger & C. D. Bussenius, Trans.). New York: Dover. (Original work published 1885)

Eich, J. E. (1980). The cue-dependent nature of state-dependent retrieval. *Memory & Cognition, 8,* 157–173.

Eich, J. E. (1989). Theoretical issues in state-dependent memory. In H. L. Roediger, III, & F. I. M. Craik (Eds.), *Varieties of memory and consciousness: Essays in honour of Endel Tulving* (pp. 331–354). Hillsdale, NJ: Lawrence Erlbaum.

Eimas, P. D. (1974). Auditory and linguistic processing of cues for place of articulation by infants. *Perception and Psychophysics, 16,* 531–521.

Eimas, P. D., & Miller, J. L. (1992). Organization in the perception of speech by young infants. *Psychological Science, 3,* 340–344.

Eimas, P. D., Miller, J. L., & Jusczyk, P. W. (1987). On infant speech perception and the acquisition of language. In S. Harnad (Ed.), *Categorical perception* (pp. 161–195). New York: Cambridge University Press.

Ekman, P. (1972). Universals and cultural differences in facial expressions of emotion. In J. Cole (Ed.), *Nebraska symposium on motivation* (pp. 207–283). Lincoln: University of Nebraska Press.

Engle, R. W., Cantor, J., & Carullo, J. J. (1992). Individual differences in working memory and comprehension: A test of four hypotheses. *Journal of Experimental Psychology: Learning, Memory, and Cognition, 18,* 972–992.

Engle, R. W., Tuholski, S. W., Laughlin, J. E., & Conway, A. R. A. (1999). Working memory, short-term memory, and general fluid intelligence: A latent variable approach. *Journal of Experimental Psychology: General, 12,* 309–331.

Erdelyi, M. (2001). Defense processes can be conscious or unconscious. *American Psychologist, 56,* 761–762.

Ericsson, K. A., & Simon, H. A. (1980). Verbal reports as data. *Psychological Review, 87,* 215–251.

Ernst, G. W., & Newell, A. (1969). *GPS: A case study in generality and problem solving.* Orlando, FL: Academic Press.

Estes, W. K. (1976). The cognitive side of probability learning. *Psychological Review, 83,* 37–64.

Estes, W. K. (1988). Human learning and memory. In R. C. Atkinson, R. J. Herrnstein, G. Lindsay, & R. D. Luce (Eds.), *Stevens' handbook of experimental psychology* (2nd ed., Vol. 2, pp. 351–415). New York: John Wiley.

Evans, J. St. B. T., Barston, J. L., & Pollard, P. (1983). On the conflict between logic and belief in syllogistic reasoning. *Memory & Cognition, 11,* 295–306.

Evans, J. St. B. T., & Over, D. E. (1996). *Rationality and reasoning.* Hove, UK: Psychology Press.

Evans, L. (1991). *Traffic safety and the driver.* New York: Van Nostrand Reinhold.

Eysenck, H. J. (1979). *The structure and measurement of intelligence.* New York: Springer.

Farah, M. J. (1988). Is visual imagery really visual? Overlooked evidence from neuropsychology. *Psychological Review, 95,* 307–317.

Farah, M. J. (1990). *Visual agnosia: Disorders of object recognition and what they tell us about normal vision.* Cambridge, MA: MIT Press.

Farah, M. J. (1998). What is "special" about face perception? *Psychological Review, 105,* 482–498.

Farah, M. J., Peronnet, F., Gonon, M. A., & Girard, M. H. (1988). Electro-physiological evidence for a shared representational medium for visual images and visual percepts. *Journal of Experimental Psychology: General, 117,* 248–257.

Fink, G. R., Markowitsch, H. J., Reinkemeier, M., Bruckbauer, J., Kessler, J., & Heiss, W. D. (1996). Cerebral representation of one's own past: Neural networks involved in autobiographical memory. *Journal of Neuroscience, 16,* 4275–4282.

Finke, R. A. (1989). *Principles of mental imagery.* Cambridge, MA: MIT Press.

Fischhoff, B. (1975). Hindsight foresight: The effect of outcome knowledge on judgment under uncertainty. *Journal of Experimental Psychology: Human Perception and Performance, 1,* 288–299.

Fischhoff, B. (1977). Perceived informativeness of facts. *Journal of Experimental Psychology: Human Perception and Performance, 3,* 349–358.

Fischhoff, B., Slovic, P., Lichtenstein, S., Reid, S., & Combs, B. (1978). How safe is safe enough? A psychometric study of attitudes towards technological risks and benefits. *Policy Science, 9,* 127–52.

Fischler, I. (1998). Attention and language. In R. Parasuraman (Ed.), *The attentive brain* (pp. 381–400). Cambridge, MA: MIT Press.

Fisher, R. P., & Geiselman, R. E. (1992). *Memory-enhancing techniques for investigative interviewing: The cognitive interview.* Springfield, IL: Charles C Thomas.

Fivush, R., Gray, J. T., & Fromhoff, F. A. (1987). Two-year-olds talk about the past. *Cognitive Development, 2,* 393–409.

Flavell, J. H., Miller, P. H., & Miller, S. A. (1993). *Cognitive development* (2nd ed.). Englewood Cliffs, NJ: Prentice Hall.

Fodor, J. A. (1983). *The modularity of mind.* Cambridge, MA: MIT Press.

Foss, D. J. (1988). Experimental psycholinguistics. *Annual Review of Psychology, 39,* 301–348.

Foss, D. J., & Hakes, D. T. (1978). *Psycholinguistics: An introduction to the psychology of language.* Englewood Cliffs, NJ: Prentice Hall.

Foulke, E., & Sticht, T. (1969). Review of research on the intelligibility and comprehension of accelerated speech. *Psychological Bulletin, 72,* 50–62.

Freud, S. (1953). The interpretation of dreams. In J. Strachey (Ed.), *The standard edition of the complete psychological works of Sigmund Freud* (Vols. 4–5). London: Hogarth. (Original work published 1900)

Friedman, A. (1979). Framing pictures: The role of knowledge in automatized encoding and memory for gist. *Journal of Experimental Psychology: General, 108,* 316–355.

Gabrieli, J.D.E. (1998). Cognitive neuroscience of human memory. *Annual Review of Psychology, 49,* 87–115.

Gallahue, D. L. (1989). *Understanding motor development: Infants, children, adolescents* (2nd ed.). Indianapolis, IN: Benchmark Press.

Gardiner, J. M., & Richardson-Klavehn, A. (2000). Remembering and knowing. In E. Tulving & F. I. M. Craik (Eds.), *The Oxford handbook of memory* (pp. 229–244). New York: Oxford University Press.

Gardner, B. T., & Gardner, R. A. (1975). Evidence for sentence constituents in the early utterances of child and chimpanzee. *Journal of Experimental Psychology: General, 104,* 244–267.

Gardner, R. A., & Gardner, B. T. (1969). Teaching sign language to a chimpanzee. *Science, 165,* 644–672.

Garrett, M., Bever, T., & Fodor, J. (1966). The active use of grammar in speech perception. *Perception & Psychophysics, 1,* 30–32.

Gazzaniga, M. S. (1970). *The bisected brain.* New York: Appleton-Century-Crofts.

Gazzaniga, M. S. (1995). Principles of human brain organization derived from split-brain studies. *Neuron, 14,* 217–228.

Gazzaniga, M. S., Bogen, J. E., & Sperry, R. W. (1965). Observations on visual perception after disconnection of the cerebral hemispheres on man. *Brain, 88,* 221–236.

Gazzaniga, M. S., Ivry, R. B., & Mangun, G. R. (1998). *Cognitive neuroscience: The biology of mind.* New York: Norton.

Geis, M. L., & Zwicky, A. M. (1971). On invited inferences. *Linguistic Inquiry, 2,* 561–566.

Geiselman, R. E., Fisher, R. P., MacKinnon, D. P., & Holland, H. L. (1986). Enhancement of eyewitness memory with the cognitive interview. *American Journal of Psychology, 99,* 385–401.

Gelman, S. A. (1988). The development of induction within natural kind and artifact categories. *Cognitive Psychology, 20,* 65–95.

Gentner, D., & Stevens, A. L. (1983). *Mental models.* Hillsdale, NJ: Lawrence Erlbaum.

Gernsbacher, M. A. (1990). *Language comprehension as structure building.* Hillsdale, NJ: Lawrence Erlbaum.

Gernsbacher, M. A., & Faust, M. (1991). The role of suppression in sentence comprehension. In G. B. Simpson (Ed.), *Understanding word and sentence* (Advances in Psychology, No. 77, pp. 97–128). Amsterdam: North-Holland.

Gernsbacher, M. A., & Kaschak, M. P. (2003). Neuroimaging studies of language production and comprehension. *Annual Review of Psychology, 54,* 91–114.

Gibson, E. J. (1969). *Principles of perceptual learning and development.* New York: Prentice Hall.

Gick, M. L., & Holyoak, K. J. (1980). Analogical problem solving. *Cognitive Psychology, 12,* 306–355.

Gigerenzer, G., Hoffrage, U., & Kleinbölting, H. (1991). Probabilistic mental models: A Brunswikean theory of confidence. *Psychological Review, 98,* 506–528.

Gilhooly, J. J. (1982). *Thinking: Directed, undirected, and creative.* New York: Academic Press.

Glanzer, M., & Cunitz, A. R. (1966). Two storage mechanisms in free recall. *Journal of Verbal Learning and Verbal Behavior, 5,* 351–360.

Glaser, R. (1984). Education and thinking: The role of knowledge. *American Psychologist, 39,* 93–104.

Glaser, R., & Chi, M.T.H. (1988) Overview. In M. T. H. Chi, R. Glaser, & M. J. Farr (Eds.), *The nature of expertise* (pp. xv–xxxvi). Hillsdale, NJ: Lawrence Erlbaum.

Glass, A. L., & Holyoak, K. J. (1975). Alternative concepts of semantic memory. *Cognition, 3,* 313–339.

Glucksberg, S., Gildea, P., & Bookin, H. B. (1982). On understanding nonliteral speech: Can people ignore metaphors? *Journal of Verbal Learning and Verbal Behavior, 21,* 85–98.

Godden, D. R., & Baddeley, A. D. (1975). Context-dependent memory in two natural environments: On land and underwater. *British Journal of Psychology, 66,* 325–331.

Goldin-Meadow, S., McNeill, D., & Singleton, J. (1996). Silence is liberating: Removing the handcuffs on grammatical expression in the manual modality. *Psychological Review, 103,* 34–55.

Goldin-Meadow, S., & Mylander, C. (1990). Beyond the input given: The child's role in the acquisition of language. *Language, 66,* 323–355.

Goldman-Rakic, P. S. (1995). Cellular basis of working memory. *Neuron, 14,* 477–485.

Goodglass, H. (1993). *Understanding aphasia.* San Diego: Academic Press.

Goodman, R., & Aman, C. (1990). Children's use of anatomically detailed dolls to recount an event. *Child Development, 61,* 1859–1871.

Gould, S. J., & Lewontin, R. C. (1979). The spandrels of San Marco and the Panglossian paradigm: A critique of the adaptionist programme. *Proceedings of the Royal Society of London, 205,* 281–288.

Graesser, A. C., Hoffman, N., & Clark, L. F. (1980). Structural components of reading time. *Journal of Verbal Learning and Verbal Behavior, 19,* 135–151.

Graf, P., Squire, L. R., & Mandler, G. (1984). The information that amnesic patients do not forget. *Journal of Experimental Psychology: Learning, Memory, and Cognition, 10,* 164–178.

Greenberg, J. H. (1966). *Language universals.* The Hague, Netherlands: Mouton.

Greene, R. L. (1986). Sources of recency effects in free recall. *Psychological Bulletin, 99,* 221–228.

Greene, R. L. (1987). Effects of maintenance rehearsal on human memory. *Psychological Bulletin, 102,* 403–413.

Greene, R. L. (1992). Unitary and modular approaches to human memory. In D. K. Detterman (Ed.), *Is mind modular or unitary? Current topics in human intelligence* (Vol. 2, pp. 229–250). Norwood, NJ: Ablex.

Grice, H. P. (1975). Logic and conversation. In P. Cole & J. L. Morgan (Eds.), *Syntax and semantics: Speech acts* (Vol. 3, pp. 41–48). New York: Seminar Press.

Griffin, D. R. (1984). *Animal thinking.* Cambridge, MA: Harvard University Press.

Griggs, R. A., & Cox, J. R. (1982). The elusive thematic-materials effect in Wason's selection task. *British Journal of Psychology, 73,* 407–420.

Halliday, M.A.K., & Hasan, R. (1976). *Cohesion in English.* London: Longman.

Hasher, L., & Zacks, R. T. (1979). Automatic and effortful processes in memory. *Journal of Experimental Psychology: General, 108,* 356–388.

Hasher, L., & Zacks, R. T. (1984). Automatic processing of fundmental information: The case of frequency of occurrence. *American Psychologist, 39,* 1372–1388.

Hashtroudi, S., Parker, E. S., DeLisi, L. E., Wyatt, R. J., & Mutter, S. A. (1984). Intact retention in acute alcohol amnesia. *Journal of Experimental Psychology: Learning, Memory, and Cognition, 10,* 156–163.

Hastie, R. (2001). Problems for judgment and decision making. *Annual Review of Psychology, 52,* 653–683.

Haviland, S. E., & Clark, H. H. (1974). What's new? Acquiring new information as a process in comprehension. *Journal of Verbal Learning and Verbal Behavior, 13,* 512–521.

Haxby, J. V., Clark, V. P., & Courtney, S. M. (1997). Distributed hierarchical neural systems for visual memory in the human cortex. In B. Hyman, C. Duyckaerts, & Y. Christen (Eds.), *Connections, cognition, and Alzheimer's disease* (pp. 167–180). New York: Springer.

Hayes, J. R. (1989). *The complete problem solver* (2nd ed.). Hillsdale, NJ: Lawrence Erlbaum.

Healy, A. F., & McNamara, D. S. (1996). Verbal learning and memory: Does the modal model still work? *Annual Review of Psychology, 47,* 143–172.

Hebb, D. O. (1949). *The organization of behavior: A neuropsychological theory.* New York: John Wiley.

Hell, W., Gigerenzer, G., Gauggel, S., Mall, M., & Muller, M. (1988). Hindsight bias: An interaction of automatic and motivational factors? *Memory & Cognition, 16,* 533–538.

Henle, M. (1962). On the relation between logic and thinking. *Psychological Review, 69,* 366–378.

Hilgard, E. R. (1986). *Divided consciousness: Multiple controls in human thought and action.* New York: John Wiley.

Hintzman, S. L. (1990). Human learning and memory: Connections and dissociations. *Annual Review of Psychology, 41,* 109–139.

Hoch, S. J., & Lowenstein, G. F. (1989). Outcome feedback: Hindsight and information. *Journal of Experimental Psychology: Learning, Memory, and Cognition, 15,* 605–619.

Holender, D. (1986). Semantic activation without conscious identification in dichotic listening, parafoveal vision, and visual masking: A survey and appraisal. *Behavioral and Brain Sciences, 9,* 1–23.

Holzner, B., Kopp, M., Langer, P., & Magnet, W. (2005). Hands-free mobile conversation impairs the peripheral visual system to an extent comparable to an alcohol level of 4-5 g 100 ml, *Human psychopharmacology: Clinical and experimental, 20,* 65–66.

Howe, M. L., & Courage, M. L. (1993). On resolving the enigma of infantile amnesia. *Psychological Bulletin, 113,* 305–326.

Hubel, D. H., & Wiesel, T. N. (1959). Receptive fields of single neurones in the cat's striate cortex. *Journal of Physiology, 148,* 574–591.

Hubel, D. H., & Wiesel, T. N. (1963). Receptive fields of cells in the striate cortex of very young, visually inexperienced kittens. *Journal of Neurophysiology, 26,* 994–1002.

Hummel, J. E., & Biederman, I. (1992). Dynamic binding in a neural network for shape recognition. *Psychological Review, 99,* 480–517.

Hunt, E. B. (1989). Cognitive science: Definition, status, and questions. *Annual Review of Psychology, 40,* 603–629.

Hunt, E. B., & Love, T. (1972). How good can memory be? In A. W. Melton & E. Martin (Eds.), *Coding processes in human memory* (pp. 237–260). Washington, DC: V. H. Winston & Sons.

Hunt, R. R., & Einstein, G. O. (1981). Relational item-specific information in memory. *Journal of Verbal Learning and Verbal Behavior, 19,* 497–514.

Hunt, R. R., & McDaniel, M. A. (1993). The enigma of organization and distinctiveness. *Journal of Memory and Language, 32,* 421–445.

Imada, T., Zhang, Y., Cheour, M., Taulu, S., Ahonen, A., & Kuhl, P. K. (2006). Infant speech perception activates Broca's area: A developmental magnetoencephalography study. *NeuroReport, 17,* 957–962.

Inhoff, A. W., Lima, S. D., & Carroll, P. J. (1984). Contextual effects on metaphor comprehension in reading. *Memory & Cognition, 12,* 558–567.

Isen, A. M., Nygren, T. E., & Ashby, F. G. (1988). The influence of positive affect on the subjective utility of gains and losses: Its just not worth the risk. *Journal of Personality and Social Psychology, 55,* 710–717.

Jacoby, L. L. (1974). The role of mental contiguity in memory: Registration and retrieval effects. *Journal of Verbal Learning and Verbal Behavior, 13,* 483–496.

Jacoby, L. L. (1983). Perceptual enhancement: Persistent effects of an experience. *Journal of Experimental Psychology: Learning, Memory, and Cognition, 9,* 21–38.

Jacoby, L. L. (1991). A process dissociation framework: Separating automatic from intentional uses of memory. *Journal of Memory and Language, 30,* 513–514.

Jacoby, L. L., & Dallas, M. (1981). On the relationship between autobiographical memory and perceptual learning. *Journal of Experimental Psychology: General, 110,* 306–340.

Jacoby, L. L., Woloshyn, V., & Kelley, C. M. (1989). Becoming famous without being recognized: Unconscious influences of memory produced by dividing attention. *Journal of Experimental Psychology: General, 118,* 115–125.

James, W. (1890). *The principles of psychology* (Vol. 1). New York: Holt.

Jenkins, J. J. (1974). Remember that old theory of memory? Well, forget it! *American Psychologist, 29,* 785–795.

Johnson, M. K. (1988). Discriminating the origin of information. In T. F. Oltmans & B. A. Maher (Eds.), *Delusional beliefs: Interdisciplinary perspectives* (pp. 34–65). New York: John Wiley.

Johnson, M. K., Bransford, J. D., & Solomon, S. K. (1973). Memory for tacit implications of sentences. *Journal of Experimental Psychology, 98,* 203–205.

Johnson, M. K., & Hasher, L. (1987). Human learning and memory. *Annual Review of Psychology, 38,* 631–668.

Johnson, M. K., Hastroudi, S., & Lindsay, D. S. (1993). Source monitoring. *Psychological Bulletin, 114,* 3–28.

Johnson-Laird, P. N. (1983). *Mental models: Towards a cognitive science of language, inference, and consciousness.* Cambridge, MA: Harvard University Press.

Johnson-Laird, P. N., & Bara, B. G. (1984). Syllogistic inference. *Cognition, 16,* 1–61.

Johnson-Laird, P. N., & Steedman, M. (1978). The psychology of syllogisms. *Cognitive Psychology, 10,* 64–99.

Johnston, W. A., & Heinz, S. P. (1978). Flexibility and capacity demands of attention. *Journal of Experimental Psychology: General, 107,* 420–435.

Jonides, J., Lacey, S. C., & Evan Nee, D. (2005). Processes of working memory in mind and brain. *Current Directions in Psychological Science, 14,* 2–5.

Just, M. A., & Carpenter, P. A. (1980). A theory of reading: From eye fixations to comprehension. *Psychological Review, 87,* 329–354.

Just, M. A., & Carpenter, P. A. (1992). A capacity theory of comprehension: Individual differences in working memory. *Psychological Review, 99,* 122–149.

Just, M. A., Carpenter, P. A., Keller, T. A., Eddy, W. F., & Thulborn, K. R. (1996). Brain activation modulated by sentence comprehension. *Science, 274,* 114–116.

Kahneman, D. (1973). *Attention and effort.* Englewood Cliffs, NJ: Prentice Hall.

Kahneman, D., & Tversky, A. (1972). Subjective probability: A judgment of representativeness. *Cognitive Psychology, 3,* 430–454.

Kahneman, D., & Tversky, A. (1973). On the psychology of prediction. *Psychological Review, 80,* 237–251.

Kahneman, D., & Tversky, A. (1982a). On the study of statistical intuitions. *Cognition, 11,* 123–141.

Kahneman, D., & Tversky, A. (1982b). The simulation heuristic. In D. Kahneman, P. Slovic, & A. Tversky (Eds.), *Judgment under uncertainty: Heuristics and biases* (pp. 201–208). Cambridge, UK: Cambridge University Press.

Kahneman, D., & Tversky, A. (1984). Choices, values, and frames. *American Psychologist, 39,* 341–350.

Kail, R. (1984). *The development of memory in children* (2nd ed.). New York: Freeman.

Kaplan, G. A., & Simon, H. A. (1990). In search of insight. *Cognitive Psychology, 22,* 374–419.

Kassin, S. M., & Gudjonsson, G. H. (2004). The psychology of confessions: A review of the literature and issues. *Psychological Science in the Public Interest, 5,* 33–67.

Katz, A. (1997). Creativity in the cerebral hemispheres. In M. A. Runco (Ed.), *Creativity research handbook* (pp. 203–236). Cresskill, NJ: Hampton Press.

Keil, F. C. (1989). *Concepts, kinds, and cognitive development.* Cambridge, MA: MIT Press.

Kieras, D. E. (1978). Good and bad structure in simple paragraphs: Effects on apparent theme, reading time, and recall. *Journal of Verbal Learning and Verbal Behavior, 17,* 13–28.

Kihlstrom, J. F., Schacter, D. L., Cork, R. C., Hunt, L. A., & Bahr, S. E. (1990). Implicit and explicit memory following surgical anesthesia. *Psychological Science, 1,* 303–306.

Kinchla, R. A. (1992). Attention. *Annual Review of Psychology, 43,* 711–742.

Kintsch, W. (1970). *Learning, memory, and conceptual processes.* New York: John Wiley.

Kintsch, W. (1974). *The representation of meaning in memory.* Hillsdale, NJ: Lawrence Erlbaum.

Kintsch, W. (1998). *Comprehension: A paradigm for cognition.* Cambridge, UK: Cambridge University Press.

Kintsch, W., & Keenan, J. M. (1973). Reading rate as a function of the number of propositions in the base structure of sentences. *Cognitive Psychology, 5,* 257–274.

Kintsch, W., & van Dijk, T. A. (1978). Toward a model of text comprehension and production. *Psychological Review, 85,* 363–394.

Klass, P. J. (1989). *UFO abductions: A dangerous game.* Buffalo, NY: Prometheus.

Klayman, J., & Ha, Y. W. (1987). Confirmation, disconfirmation, and information in hypothesis testing. *Psychological Review, 94,* 211–228.

Knight, R. T. (1996). Contribution of human hippocampal region to novelty detection. *Nature, 383,* 256–259.

Koffka, K. (1935). *Principles of Gestalt psychology.* New York: Harcourt, Brace.

Köhler, W. (1925). *The mentality of apes.* London: Routledge & Kegan Paul.

Kolers, P. A. (1983). Perception and representation. *Annual Review of Psychology, 34,* 129–166.

Kopelman, M. D. (1999). Varieties of false memory. *Cognitive Neuropsychology, 16,* 197–214.

Kosslyn, S. M. (1973). Scanning visual images: Some structural implications. *Perception and Psychophysics, 14,* 90–94.

Kosslyn, S. M. (1975). Information representation in visual images. *Cognitive Psychology, 7,* 341–370.

Kosslyn, S. M. (1980). *Image and mind.* Cambridge, MA: Harvard University Press.

Kosslyn, S. M. (1981). The medium and the message in mental imagery. *Psychological Review, 88,* 46–66.

Kosslyn, S. M., Ball, T. M., & Reiser, B. J. (1978). Visual images preserve metric spatial information: Evidence from studies of visual scanning. *Journal of Experimental Psychology: Human Perception and Performance, 4,* 47–60.

Kotovsky, K., & Fallside, D. (1989). Representation and transfer in problem solving. In D. Klahr & K. Kotovsky (Eds.), *Complex information processing: The impact of Herbert A. Simon* (pp. 69–108). Hillsdale, NJ: Lawrence Erlbaum.

Krauth, J. (1982). Formulation and experimental verification of models in propositional reasoning. *Quarterly Journal of Experimental Psychology, 34,* 285–298.

Kreiman, G., Koch, C., & Fried, I. (2000). Imagery neurons in the human brain. *Nature, 408,* 357–361.

Kroll, N.E.A., Knight, R. T., Metcalfe, J., Wolf, E., & Tulving, E. (1996). Cohesion failure as a source of memory illusions. *Journal of Memory and Language, 35,* 176–196.

Kucera, H., & Francis, W. N. (1967). *A computational analysis of present day American English.* Providence, RI: Brown University Press.

Kunst-Wilson, W. R., & Zajonc, R. B. (1980). Affective discrimination of stimuli that cannot be recognized. *Science, 207,* 557–558.

Kutas, M., & Hillyard, S. A. (1980). Reading senseless sentences: Brain potentials reflect semantic incongruity. *Science, 207,* 203–205.

Kutas, M., & Hillyard, S. A. (1984). Brain potentials during reading reflect word expectancy and semantic association. *Nature, 307,* 161–163.

Kutas, M., Van Petten, C., & Besson, M. (1988). Event-related potential asymmetries during the reading of sentences. *Electroencephalography and Clinical Neurophysiology, 69,* 218–233.

LaBerge, D., & Buchsbaum, M. S. (1990). Positron emission tomographic measurements of pulvinar activity during an attention task. *Journal of Neuroscience, 10,* 613–619.

Labov, W. (1973). The boundaries of words and their meanings. In C. J. N. Bailey & R. W. Shuy (Eds.), *New ways of analyzing variations in English* (pp. 340–373). Washington, DC: Georgetown University Press.

Ladefoged, P. (1975). *A course in phonetics.* New York: Harcourt Brace Jovanovich.

Lakoff, G. (1987). *Women, fire, and dangerous things.* Chicago: University of Chicago Press.

Lakoff, G., & Johnson, M. (1980). The metaphorical structure of the human conceptual system. *Cognitive Science, 4,* 195–298.

Landauer, T. K., & Dumais, S. T. (1997). A solution to Plato's problem: The latent semantic analysis theory of the acquisition, induction, and representation. *Psychological Review, 104,* 211–240.

Langer, E. J. (1989). *Mindfulness.* Reading, MA: Addison-Wesley.

Larkin, J. H., McDermott, J., Simon, D. P., & Simon, H. A. (1980). Expert and novice performance in solving physics problems. *Science, 208,* 1335–1342.

LeDoux, J. E. (2000). Emotion circuits in the brain. *Annual Review of Neuroscience, 23,* 155–184.

Lee, G., & Oakhill, J. (1984). The effects of externalization on syllogistic reasoning. *Quarterly Journal of Experimental Psychology, 36A,* 519–530.

Lenneberg, E. H. (1967). *Biological foundations of language.* New York: John Wiley.

Leslie, A. M. (1987). Pretense and representation: The origins of "theory of mind." *Psychological Review, 94,* 412–426.

Liberman, A. M., Cooper, F., Shankweiler, D., & Studdert-Kennedy, M. (1967). Perception of the speech code. *Psychological Review, 74,* 431–459.

Lieberman, P. (1984). *The biology and evolution of language.* Cambridge, MA: Harvard University Press.

Light, L. L., & Carter-Sobell, L. (1970). Effects of changed semantic context on recognition memory. *Journal of Verbal Learning and Verbal Behavior, 9,* 1–11.

Lindsay, D. S., & Read, J. D. (1994). Psychotherapy and memories of childhood sexual abuse: A cognitive perspective. *Applied Cognitive Psychology, 8,* 281–338.

Lindsay, P. H., & Norman, D. A. (1977). *Human information processing: An introduction to psychology* (2nd ed.). New York: Academic Press.

Lisker, L. (1986). "Voicing" in English: A catalog of acoustic features signalling lb/ versus/pl in trochees. *Language & Speech, 29,* 3–11.

Lisker, L., & Abramson, A. (1970). The voicing dimension: Some experiments in comparative phonetics. In *Proceedings of Sixth International Congress of Phonetic Sciences, Prague, 1967* (pp. 563–567). Prague, Czechoslovakia: Academia.

Livingston, M. S., & Hubel, D. H. (1987). Psychological evidence for separate channels for the perception of form, color, movement, and depth. *Journal of Neuroscience, 7,* 3416–3468.

Loftus, E. F. (1979). *Eyewitness testimony.* Cambridge, MA: Harvard University Press.

Loftus, E. F. (1986). Ten years in the life of an expert witness. *Law and Human Behavior, 10,* 241–263.

Loftus, E. F. (1993). The reality of repressed memories. *American Psychologist, 48,* 518–537.

Loftus, E. F., & Ketcham, K. (1994). *The myth of repressed memory.* New York: St. Martin's.

Loftus, E. F., & Loftus, G. R. (1980). On the permanence of stored information in the human brain. *American Psychologist, 35,* 409–420.

Loftus, E. F., Miller, D. G., & Burns, H. J. (1978). Semantic integration of verbal information into a visual memory. *Journal of Experimental Psychology: Human Learning and Memory, 4,* 19–31.

Loftus, E. F., & Palmer, J. C. (1974). Reconstruction of automobile destruction: An example of the interaction between language and memory. *Journal of Verbal Learning and Verbal Behavior, 13,* 585–589.

Loftus, E. F., & Pickrell, J. E. (1995). The formation of false memories. *Psychiatric Annals, 25,* 720–725.

Logan, G. D. (1988). Toward an instance theory of automatization. *Psychological Review, 95,* 492–527.

Luchins, A. S. (1942). Mechanization in problem solving. *Psychological Monographs, 54*(Whole No. 248).

Luria, A. R. (1968). *The mind of a mnemonist.* New York: Basic Books.

Luria, A. R. (1976). *Cognitive development: Its cultural and social foundations* (M. Cole, Ed., M. Lopez-Morillas, & L. Solotaroff, Trans.). Cambridge, MA: Harvard University Press.

Mack, A., & Rock, I. (1998). *Inattentional blindness.* Cambridge, MA: MIT Press.

MacKay, D. G. (1973). Aspects of the theory of comprehension, memory, and attention. *Quarterly Journal of Experimental Psychology, 25,* 22–40.

MacKinnon, D. W. (1978). *In search of human effectiveness.* New York: Creative Education Foundation.

MacLean, H. N. (1993). *Once upon a time: A true story of memory, murder, and the law.* New York: HarperCollins.

MacLean, P. D. (1973). *A triune concept of the brain and behaviour.* Toronto: University of Toronto Press.

MacLeod, C. M. (1991). Half a century of research on the Stroop effect: An integrative review. *Psychological Bulletin, 109,* 163–203.

MacNeil, J. E., & Warrington, E. K. (1993). Prosopagnosia: A face-specific disorder. *Quarterly Journal of Experimental Psychology, 46,* 1–10.

Mandler, G. (1979). Organization and repetition: Organizational principles with special reference to rote learning. In L. G. Nilsson (Ed.), *Perspectives on memory research: Essays in honor of Uppsala University's 500th anniversary* (pp. 293–328). Hillsdale, NJ: Lawrence Erlbaum.

Mandler, G. (1980). Recognizing: The judgment of previous occurrence. *Psychological Review, 87,* 252–271.

Mandler, G., Pearlstone, Z., & Koopmans, H. J. (1969). Effects of organization and semantic similarity on recall and recognition. *Journal of Verbal Learning and Verbal Behavior, 8,* 410–423.

Mandler, J. M. (1984). *Stories, scripts, and scenes: Aspects of schema theory.* Hillsdale, NJ: Lawrence Erlbaum.

Mandler, J. M., & Ritchey, G. H. (1977). Long-term memory for pictures. *Journal of Experimental Psychology: Human Learning and Memory, 3,* 386–396.

Mantyla, T. (1986). Optimizing cue effectiveness: Recall of 500 and 600 incidentally learned words. *Journal of Experimental Psychology: Learning, Memory, and Cognition, 12,* 66–71.

Marcel, A. J. (1983). Conscious and unconscious perception: Experiments on visual masking and word recognition. *Cognitive Psychology, 15,* 197–237.

Marcus, S. L., & Rips, L. J. (1979). Conditional reasoning. *Journal of Verbal Learning and Verbal Behavior, 18,* 199–223.

Markman, A. B., & Gentner, D. (2001). Thinking. *Annual Review of Psychology, 52,* 223–247.

Marks, L. E. (1987). On cross-modal similarity: Auditory-visual interactions in speeded discrimination. *Journal of Experimental Psychology: Human Perception and Performance, 13,* 384–394.

Marschark, M., Richman, C. L., Yuille, J. C., & Hunt, R. R. (1987). The role of imagery in memory: On shared and distinctive information. *Psychological Bulletin, 102,* 28–41.

Martin, A., Wiggs, C. L., & Weisberg, J. A. (1997). Modulation of human temporal lobe activity by form, meaning, and experience. *Hippocampus, 7,* 587–593.

Martin, R. C., Shelton, J. R., & Yaffee, L. S. (1994). Language processing and working memory: Neuropsychological evidence for separate phonological and semantic capacities. *Journal of Memory and Language, 33,* 83–111.

Massaro, D. W. (1970). Preperceptual auditory images. *Journal of Experimental Psychology, 85,* 411–417.

Massaro, D. W. (1994). Psychological aspects of speech production. In M. A. Gernsbacher (Ed.), *Handbook of psycholinguistics* (pp. 219–263). San Diego: Academic Press.

Massaro, D. W., & Cowan, N. (1993). Information processing models: Microscopes of the mind. *Annual Review of Psychology, 44,* 383–425.

Masson, M. E. (1983). Conceptual processing of text during skimming and rapid sequential reading. *Memory & Cognition, 11,* 262–274.

McCarthy, R. A., & Warrington, E. K. (1990). *Cognitive neuropsychology: A clinical introduction.* San Diego: Academic Press.

McClelland, J. L., & Elman, J. L. (1986). The TRACE model of speech perception. *Cognitive Psychology, 18,* 1–86.

McClelland, J. L., McNaughton, B. L., & O'Reilly, R. C. (1995). Why there are complementary learning systems in the hippocampus and neocortex: Insights from the successes and failures of connectionist models of learning and memory. *Psychological Review, 102,* 419–457.

McClelland, J. L., & Rumelhart, D. E. (Eds.). (1981). An interactive model of context effects in letter perception: I. An account of basic findings. *Psychological Review, 88,* 375–407.

McCloskey, M., Wible, C. G., & Cohen, N. J. (1988). Is there a special flashbulb-memory mechanism? *Journal of Experimental Psychology: General, 117,* 171–181.

McConkie, G. W., & Rayner, K. (1975). The effective stimulus during a fixation in reading. *Perception and Psychophysics, 17,* 578–586.

McCulloch, W. S., & Pitts, W. (1943). A logical calculus of the ideas immanent in nervous activity. *Bulletin of Mathematical Biophysics, 5,* 115–133.

McDaniel, M. A., & Einstein, G. O. (1986). Bizarre imagery as an effective memory aid: The importance of distinctiveness. *Journal of Experimental Psychology: Learning, Memory, and Cognition, 12,* 54–65.

McDaniel, M., & Pressley, M. (Eds.). (1987). *Imagery and related processes.* New York: Springer-Verlag.

McDonald, J. L. (1997). Language acquisition: The acquisition of linguistic structure in normal and special populations. *Annual Review of Psychology, 48,* 215–241.

McGaugh, J. L. (2004). The amygdala modulates the consolidation of memories of emotionally arousing experiences. *Annual Review of Neuroscience, 27,* 1–28.

McGeoch, J. A. (1942). *The psychology of human learning: An introduction.* New York: Longmans, Green.

McGlone, R. E. (1998). Deciphering memory: John Adams and the authorship of the *Declaration of Independence. Journal of American History, 85,* 411–438.

Medin, D. L., & Ortony, A. (1989). Psychological essentialism. In S. Vosniadou & A. Ortony (Eds.), *Similarity and analogical reasoning.* New York: Cambridge University Press.

Melo, B., Winocur, G., & Moscovitch, M. (1999). False recall and false recognition: An examination of the effects of selective and combined lesions to the medial temporal lobe/diencephalon and frontal lobe structures. *Cognitive Neuropsychology, 16,* 343–359.

Merikle, P. M. (1980). Selection from visual persistence by perceptual groups and category membership. *Journal of Experimental Psychology: General, 109,* 279–295.

Merikle, P. M., & Reingold, E. M. (1992). Measuring unconscious perceptual processes. In R. F. Bornstein & T. S. Pittman (Eds.), *Perception without awareness: Cognitive, clinical, and social perspectives* (pp. 55–80). New York: Guilford.

Metzler, J., & Shepard, R. N. (1974). Transformational studies of the internal representations of three dimensional objects. In R. L. Solso (Ed.), *Information processing and cognition: The Loyola Symposium* (pp. 147–201). Hillsdale, NJ: Lawrence Erlbaum.

Meyer, B.J.F. (1975). *The organization of prose and its effect on memory.* Amsterdam: North-Holland.

Meyer, D. E. (1970). On the representation and retrieval of stored semantic information. *Cognitive Psychology, 1,* 242–300.

Michel, C., Rossion, B., Han, J., Chung, C., & Caldara, R. (2006). Holistic processing is finely tuned for faces of one's own race. *Psychological Science, 17,* 608–615.

Miller, G. A. (1956). The magical number seven, plus or minus two: Some limits on our capacity for processing information. *Psychological Review, 63,* 81–97.

Miller, G. H. (1999). On knowing a word. *Annual Review of Psychology, 50,* 1–19.

Miller, J. L., & Eimas, P. D. (1983). Studies on the categorization of speech by infants. *Cognition, 13,* 135–165.

Miller, J. R., & Kintsch, W. (1980). Readability and recall of short prose passages: A theoretical analysis. *Journal of Experimental Psychology: Human Learning and Memory, 6,* 335–354.

Milner, B. (1965). Visually-guided maze learning in man: Effects of bilateral hippocampal, bilateral frontal, and unilateral cerebral lesions. *Neuropsychologia, 3,* 317–338.

Milner, B. (1966). Amnesia following operations on the temporal lobes. In C. W. M. Whitney & O. L. Zangwill (Eds.), *Amnesia* (pp. 109–133). London: Butterworth.

Minsky, M. L. (1977). Frame-system theory. In P. N. Johnson-Laird & P. C. Wason (Eds.), *Thinking: Readings in cognitive science* (pp. 355–376). Cambridge, UK: Cambridge University Press.

Mishkin, M. (1978). Memory in monkeys severely impaired by combined but not separate removal of the amygdala and hippocampus. *Nature, 273,* 297–298.

Monahan, J. L., Murphy, S. T., & Zajonc, R. B. (2000). Subliminal mere exposure: Specific, general, and diffuse effects. *Psychological Science, 11,* 462–466.

Moran, J., & Desimone, R. (1985). Selective attention gates visual processing in the extrastriate cortex. *Science, 229,* 782–784.

Moray, N. (1959). Attention in dichotic listening: Affective cues and the influence of instructions. *Quarterly Journal of Experimental Psychology, 11,* 56–60.

Moray, N., Bates, A., & Barnett, T. (1965). Experiments on the four-eared man. *Journal of the Acoustical Society of America, 42,* 196–201.

Morris, C. D., Bransford, J. D., & Franks, J. J. (1977). Levels of processing versus transfer appropriate processing. *Journal of Verbal Learning and Verbal Behavior, 16,* 519–533.

Moscovitch, M. (1982). Multiple dissociations of function in amnesia. In L. S. Cermak (Ed.), *Human memory and amnesia* (pp. 337–370). Hillsdale, NJ: Lawrence Erlbaum.

Moscovitch, M. (1992). Memory and working-with-memory: A component process model based on modules and central systems. *Journal of Cognitive Neuroscience, 4,* 257–266.

Mumford, M. D., & Gustafson, S. B. (1988). Creativity syndrome: Integration, application, and innovation. *Psychological Bulletin, 103,* 27–43.

Murdock, B. B. (1974). *Human memory: Theory and data.* Hillsdale, NJ: Lawrence Erlbaum.

Murphy, G. L., & Medin, D. L. (1985). The role of theories in conceptual coherence. *Psychological Review, 92,* 289–316.

Murphy, T. D., & Eriksen, C. W. (1987). Temporal changes in the distribution of attention in the visual field in response to precues. *Perceptions and Psychophysics, 42,* 576–586.

Murray, J. E., Yong, E., & Rhodes, G. (2000). Revisiting the perception of upside-down faces. *Psychological Science, 11,* 492–496.

Naka, M., Itsukushima, Y., & Itoh, Y. (1996). Eyewitness testimony after three months: A field study on memory for an incident in everyday life. *Japanese Psychological Research, 38,* 14–24.

Nash, M. (1987). What, if anything, is regressed about hypnotic age regression? A review of the empirical literature. *Psychological Bulletin, 102,* 42–52.

Navon, D., & Gopher, D. (1979). On the economy of the human-processing system. *Psychological Review, 86,* 214–255.

Neisser, U. (1963). Decision time without reaction time: Experiments in visual scanning. *American Journal of Psychology, 76,* 376–385.

Neisser, U. (1967). *Cognitive psychology.* New York: Appleton.

Neisser, U. (1976). *Cognition and reality.* San Francisco: Freeman.

Neisser, U. (1981). John Dean's memory: A case study. *Cognition, 9,* 1–22.

Neisser, U., & Harsch, N. (1992). Phantom flashbulbs: False recollections of hearing the news about Challenger. In E. Winograd & U. Neisser (Eds.), *Affect and accuracy in recall: Studies of "flashbulb memories"* (pp. 9–31). Cambridge, UK: Cambridge University Press.

Neisser, U., & Libby, L. K. (2000). Remembering life experiences. In E. Tulving & F. I. M. Craik (Eds.), *The Oxford handbook of memory* (pp. 315–332). New York: Oxford University Press.

Neisser, U., Winograd, E., Bergman, E. T., Schreiber, C. A., Palmer, S. E., & Weldon, M. S. (1996). Remembering the earthquake: Direct experience vs. hearing the news. *Memory, 4,* 337–357.

Nelson, K. (1990). Remembering, forgetting, and childhood amnesia. In R. Fivush & J. A. Hudson (Eds.), *Knowing and remembering in young children* (pp. 301–316). New York: Cambridge University Press.

Nespor, M. (1999). Acquisition of phonology. In R. A. Wilson & F. C. Keil (Eds.), *The MIT encyclopedia of the cognitive sciences* (pp. 642–643). Cambridge, MA: MIT Press.

Neville, H. J., & Bavelier, D. (2000). Specificity and plasticity in neurocognitive development in humans. In M. S. Gazzaniga (Ed.), *The new cognitive neurosciences* (pp. 83–98). Cambridge, MA: MIT Press.

Newell, A., & Simon, H. A. (1972). *Human problem solving.* Englewood Cliffs, NJ: Prentice Hall.

Nickerson, R. S., & Adams, M. J. (1979). Long-term memory for a common object. *Cognitive Psychology, 11,* 287–307.

Nipher, F. E. (1878). On the distribution of errors of numbers written from memory. *Transactions of the Academy of Sciences of St. Louis, 3,* ccx–ccxi.

Nissen, M. J., Knopman, D., & Schacter, D. L. (1987). Neurochemical dissociation of memory systems, *Neurology, 37,* 789–794.

Norman, D. A. (1968). Toward a theory of memory and attention. *Psychological Review, 75,* 522–536.

Norman, D. A., & Shallice, T. (1986). Attention to action: Willed and automatic control of behaviour. In R. J. Davidson, G. E. Schwarts, & D. Shapiro (Eds.),

Consciousness and self-regulation: Advances in research and theory (pp. 1–18). New York: Plenum.

Nyberg, L., & Cabeza, R. (2000). Brain imaging of memory. In E. Tulving & F. I. M. Craik (Eds.), *The Oxford handbook of memory* (pp. 501–519). New York: Oxford University Press.

Ochse, R. (1990). *Before the gates of excellence.* New York: Cambridge University Press.

Odean, T. (1998). Are investors reluctant to realize their losses? *Journal of Finance, 53,* 1775–1798.

Olio, K. A. (1989). Memory retrieval in the treatment of adult survivors of sexual abuse. *Transactional Analysis Journal, 19,* 93–100.

Ornstein, R. E. (1997). *The right mind: Making sense of the hemispheres.* New York: Harcourt Brace.

Osherson, D. N., Smith, E. E., Wilkie, O., Lopez, A., & Shafir, E. (1990). Category-based induction. *Psychological Review, 97,* 185–200.

Overton, D. A. (1971). State-dependent learning produced by alcohol and its relevance to alcoholism. In B. Kissin & H. Begleiter (Eds.), *The biology of alcoholism: Physiology and behavior* (Vol. 2, pp. 193–217). New York: Plenum.

Paivio, A. (1971). *Imagery and verbal processes.* New York: Holt, Rinehart & Winston.

Paivio, A. (1983). The empirical case for dual coding. In J. Yuille (Ed.), *Imagery, memory, and cognition: Essays in honor of Allen Paivio* (pp. 307–332). Hillsdale, NJ: Lawrence Erlbaum.

Paivio, A. (1986). *Mental representations: A dual coding approach.* New York: Oxford University Press.

Paivio, A. (1991). Dual coding theory: Retrospect and current status. *Canadian Journal of Psychology, 45,* 255–287.

Palmer, J., MacLeod, C. M., Hunt, E., & Davidson, J. E. (1985). Information processing correlates of reading. *Journal of Memory and Language, 24,* 59–88.

Palmer, S. E. (1975). The effects of contextual scenes on the identification of objects. *Memory & Cognition, 3,* 519–526.

Parker, E. S., Cahill, L., & McGaugh, J. L. (2006). A case of unusual autobiographical remembering. *Neurocase, 12,* 35–49.

Parkin, A. J., & Russo, R. (1993). On the origin of functional differences in recollective experience. *Memory, 1,* 231–237.

Penney, C. G. (1975). Modality effects in short-term verbal memory. *Psychological Bulletin, 82,* 68–84.

Penney, C. G. (1989). Modality effects and the structure of short-term verbal memory. *Memory & Cognition, 17,* 398–422.

Perfetti, C. A. (1985). *Reading ability.* New York: Oxford University Press.

Perris, E. E., Myers, N. A., & Clifton, R. K. (1990). Long-term memory for a single infancy experience. *Child Development, 61,* 1796–1807.

Peterson, C. R., & Beach, L. R. (1967). Man as an intuitive statistician. *Psychological Bulletin, 68,* 29–46.

Peterson, L. R., & Peterson, M. J. (1959). Short-term retention of individual verbal items. *Journal of Experimental Psychology, 58,* 193–198.

Petersen, S. E., Fox, P. T., Snyder, A. Z., & Raichle, M. E. (1990). Activation of extrastriate and frontal cortical areas by visual words and word-like stimuli. *Science, 249,* 1041–1044.

Petty, R. E., & Cacioppo, J. T. (1981). *Attitudes and persuasion: Classic and contemporary approaches.* Dubuque, IA: William C. Brown.

Phelps, E. A. (2006). Emotion and cognition: Insights from studies of the human amygdala. *Annual Review of Psychology, 57,* 27–53.

Pillemer, D. B. (1984). Flashbulb memories of the assassination attempt on President Reagan. *Cognition, 16,* 63–80.

Pinker, S. (1990). Language acquisition. In D. N. Osherson & H. Lasaik (Eds.), *An invitation to cognitive science: Language* (Vol. 1, pp. 199–241). Cambridge MA: MIT Press.

Pinker, S. (1994). *The language instinct.* New York: Harper Collins.

Pinker, S. (1999). *How the mind works.* New York: Norton.

Place, E. J. S., & Gilmore, G. C. (1980). Perceptual organization in schizophrenia. *Journal of Abnormal Psychology, 89,* 125–144.

Poizner, H., Bellugi, U., & Klima, E. S. (1990). Biological foundations of language: Clues from sign language. *Annual Review of Neuroscience, 13,* 283–307.

Pollatsek, A., & Rayner, K. (1989). Reading. In M. I. Posner (Ed.), *The foundations of cognitive science* (pp. 401–436). Cambridge, MA: MIT Press.

Polya, G. (1957). *How to solve it: A new aspect of mathematical method* (2nd ed.). Garden City, NY: Doubleday.

Posner, M. I. (1980). Orienting of attention. *Quarterly Journal of Experimental Psychology, 32,* 3–25.

Posner, M. I., Cohen, Y., & Rafal, R. D. (1982). Neural systems control of spatial orienting. *Philosophical Transactions of the Royal Society of London, 298B,* 187–198.

Posner, M. I., & DiGirolamo, G. J. (1998). Executive attention: Conflict, target detection, and cognitive control. In R. Parasuraman (Ed.), *The attentive brain* (pp. 401–424). Cambridge, MA: MIT Press.

Posner, M. I., & Petersen, S. E. (1990). The attention system of the human brain. *Annual Review of Neuroscience, 13,* 25–42.

Posner, M. I., Petersen, S. E., Fox, P. T., & Raichle, M. E. (1988). Localization of cognitive operations in the brain. *Science, 240,* 1627–1631.

Posner, M. I., & Raichle, M. E. (1994). *Images of mind.* New York: Scientific American Library.

Posner, M. I., & Snyder, C.R.R. (1974). Attention and cognitive control. In R. L. Solso (Ed.), *Information processing and cognition: The Loyola Symposium* (pp. 55–85). Hillsdale, NJ: Lawrence Erlbaum.

Posner, M. I., & Snyder, C.R.R. (1975). Facilitation and inhibition in the processing of signals. In P.M.A. Rabbit & S. Dornic (Eds.), *Attention and performance* (Vol. 5, pp. 669–682). New York: Academic Press.

Premack, D., & Woodruff, G. (1978). Chimpanzee problem solving: A test for comprehension. *Science, 202,* 532–535.

Pylyshyn, Z. W. (1981). The imagery debate: Analogue media versus tacit knowledge. *Psychological Review, 88,* 16–45.

Rafal, R. D., & Posner, M. I. (1987). Deficits in human visual spatial attention following thalamic lesions. *Proceedings of the National Academy of Science USA, 84,* 7349–7353.

Rajaram, S., & Roediger, H. L., III. (1997). Remembering and knowing as states of consciousness during recollection. In J. D. Cohen & J. W. Schooler (Eds.), *Scientific approaches to the questions of consciousness* (pp. 213–240). Hillsdale, NJ: Lawrence Erlbaum.

Reed, S. K. (1973). *Psychological processes in pattern recognition.* New York: Academic Press.

Reed, S. K. (1974). Structural descriptions and the limitations of visual images. *Memory & Cognition, 2,* 329–336.

Reed, S. K., & Johnson, J. A. (1975). Detection of parts in patterns and images. *Memory & Cognition, 3,* 569–575.

Reicher, G. M. (1969). Perceptual recognition as a function of meaningfulness of stimulus material. *Journal of Experimental Psychology, 81,* 275–280.

Reichle, E. D., Pollatsek, A., Fisher, D. L., & Rayner, K. (1998). Toward a model of eye movement control in reading. *Psychological Review, 105,* 125–157.

Reitman, J. S. (1974). Without surreptitious rehearsal, information in short-term memory decays. *Journal of Verbal Learning and Verbal Behavior, 13,* 365–377.

Repp, B. H., & Liberman, A. M. (1987). Phonetic boundaries are flexible. In S. Harnad (Ed.), *Categorical perception: The groundwork of cognition* (pp. 89–112). Cambridge, UK: Cambridge University Press.

Revlis, R. (1975). Two models of syllogistic reasoning: Feature selection and conversion. *Journal of Verbal Learning and Verbal Behavior, 14,* 180–195.

Richardson-Klavehn, A., & Bjork, R. A. (1988). Measures of memory. *Annual Review of Psychology, 39,* 475–543.

Rips, L. J. (1990). Reasoning. *Annual Review of Psychology, 41,* 321–353.

Rips, L. J., & Marcus, S. L. (1977). Supposition and the analysis of conditional sentences. In M. A. Just & P. A. Carpenter (Eds.), *Cognitive processes in comprehension* (pp. 185–220). Hillsdale, NJ: Lawrence Erlbaum.

Rips, L. J., Shoben, E. J., & Smith, E. E. (1973). Semantic distance and the verification of semantic relations. *Journal of Verbal Learning and Verbal Behavior, 12,* 1–20.

Rodriguez, H. S., Porjesz, B., Chorlian, D. B., Polich, J., & Begleiter, H. (1999). Visual P3a in male subjects at high risk for alcoholism. *Biological Psychiatry, 46,* 281–291.

Roediger, H. L., III. (1984). Does current evidence from dissociation experiments favor the episodic/semantic distinction? *Behavioral and Brain Sciences, 7,* 252–254.

Roediger, H. L., III. (1996). Memory illusions. *Journal of Memory and Language, 35,* 76–100.

Roediger, H. L., III, & Blaxton, T. A. (1987). Retrieval modes produce dissociations in memory for surface information. In D. S. Gorfein & R. R. Hoffman (Eds.), *Memory and cognitive processes: The Ebbinghaus Centennial Conference* (pp. 349–379). Hillsdale, NJ: Lawrence Erlbaum.

Roediger, H. L., III, & McDermott, K. (1995). Creating false memories: Remembering words not presented in lists. *Journal of Experimental Psychology: Learning, Memory, and Cognition, 21,* 300–318.

Rogers, T. B., Kuiper, N. A., & Kirker, W. S. (1977). Self-reference and the encoding of personal information. *Journal of Personality and Social Psychology, 35,* 677–688.

Rosch, E. H. (1973). Natural categories. *Cognitive Psychology, 4,* 328–350.

Rosch, E. H. (1975). Cognitive representations of semantic categories. *Journal of Experimental Psychology: General, 104,* 192–233.

Rosch, E. H., & Mervis, C. B. (1975). Family resemblances: Studies in the internal structure of categories. *Cognitive Psychology, 7,* 573–605.

Rosch, E. H., Mervis, C. B., Gray, W. D., Johnson, D. M., & Boyes-Braem, P. (1976). Basic objects in natural categories. *Cognitive Psychology, 8,* 382–439.

Ross, B. H. (1987). This is like that: The use of earlier problems and the separation of similarity effects. *Journal of Experimental Psychology: Learning, Memory, and Cognition, 13,* 629–639.

Ross, D. F., Read, J. D., & Toglia, M. P. (1994). *Adult eyewitness testimony: Current trends and developments.* Cambridge, UK: Cambridge University Press.

Rubin, D. C., & Wenzel, A. E. (1996). One hundred years of forgetting: A quantitative description. *Psychological Review, 103,* 734–760.

Rubinstein, M. F. (1975). *Patterns of problem solving.* Englewood Cliffs, NJ: Prentice Hall.

Rubinstein, M. F. (1986). *Tools for thinking and problem solving.* Englewood Cliffs, NJ: Prentice Hall.

Runco, M. A. (2004). Creativity. *Annual Review of Psychology, 55,* 657–687.

Rundus, D. (1971). Analysis of rehearsal processes in free recall. *Journal of Experimental Psychology, 89,* 63–77.

Russo, J. E., Johnson, E. J., & Stephens, D. L. (1989). The validity of verbal protocols. *Memory & Cognition, 17,* 759–769.

Sacks, O. (1970). *The man who mistook his wife for a hat and other clinical tales.* New York: HarperCollins.

Salasoo, A., & Pisoni, D. (1985). Interaction of knowledge sources in spoken word identification. *Journal of Memory and Language, 24,* 210–231.

Sanders, R. E., Gonzalez, E. G., Murphy, M. D., Liddle, C. L., & Vitina, J. R. (1987). Frequency of occurrence and the criteria for automatic processing. *Journal of Experimental Psychology: Learning, Memory, and Cognition, 13,* 241–250.

Savage-Rumbaugh, E. S., McDonald, K., Sevcik, R., Hopkins, B., & Rupert, E. (1986). Spontaneous symbol acquisition and communicative use in pygmy chimpanzees (Pan paniscus). *Journal of Experimental Psychology: General, 115,* 21–35.

Savage-Rumbaugh, E. S., & Rumbaugh, D. M. (1993). The emergence of language. In K. R. Gibson & T. Ingold (Eds.), *Tools, language, and cognition in human evolution* (pp. 86–108). Cambridge, UK: Cambridge University Press.

Schacter, D. L. (1987). Implicit memory: History and current status. *Journal of Experimental Psychology: Learning, Memory, and Cognition, 13,* 501–518.

Schacter, D. L. (2001). *The seven sins of memory: How the mind forgets and remembers.* Boston: Houghton Mifflin.

Schacter, D. L., Israel, L., & Racine, C. (1999). Suppressing false recognition in younger and older adults: The distinctiveness heuristic. *Journal of Memory and Language, 40,* 1–24.

Schacter, D. L., & Kihlstrom, J. F. (1989). Functional amnesia. In F. Boller & J. Grafman (Eds.), *Handbook of neuropsychology* (Vol. 3, pp. 209–231). New York: Elsevier Science.

Schacter, D. L., & Tulving, E. (1994). What are the memory systems of 1994? In D. L. Schacter & E. Tulving (Eds.), *Memory systems* (pp. 1–38). Cambridge, MA: MIT Press.

Schacter, D. L., Wagner, A. D., & Buckner, R. L. (2000). Memory systems of 1999. In E. Tulving & F. I. M. Craik (Eds.), *The Oxford handbook of memory* (pp. 627–643). New York: Oxford University Press.

Schank, R. C., & Abelson, R. (1977). *Scripts, plans, goals, and understanding.* Hillsdale, NJ: Lawrence Erlbaum.

Schiffman, H. R. (2000). *Sensation and perception: An integrated approach* (5th ed.). New York: John Wiley.

Schneider, W., & Shiffrin, R. M. (1977). Controlled and automatic human information processing: Detection, search, and attention. *Psychological Review, 84,* 1–66.

Schooler, J. W., Bendiksen, M., & Ambadar, A. (1997). Taking the middle line: Can we accommodate both fabricated and recovered memories of sexual abuse? In M. A. Conway (Ed.), *Recovered memories and false memories* (pp. 251–292). New York: Oxford University Press.

Seamon, J. G., Marsh, R. L., & Brody, N. (1984). Critical importance of exposure duration for affective discrimination of stimuli that are not recognized. *Journal of Experimental Psychology: Learning, Memory, and Cognition, 10,* 465–469.

Searcy, J. H., & Bartlett, J. C. (1996). Inversion and processing of component and spatial relational information in faces. *Journal of Experimental Psychology: Human Perception and Performance, 22,* 904–915.

Sejnowski, T. J., & Churchland, P. S. (1989). Brain and cognition. In M. I. Posner (Ed.), *Foundations of cognitive science* (pp. 301–356). Cambridge, MA: MIT Press.

Seyfarth, R. M., & Cheney, D. L. (2003). Signalers and receivers in animal communication. *Annual Review of Psychology, 54,* 145–173.

Shafir, E., & LeBoeuf, R. A. (2002). Rationality. *Annual Review of Psychology, 53,* 491–517.

Shah, P., & Miyake, A. (1999). Models of working memory: An introduction. In A. Miyake & P. Shah (Eds.), *Models of working memory: Mechanisms of active* *maintenance and executive control* (pp. 1–27). Cambridge, UK: Cambridge University Press.

Shapiro, K. L. (1994). The attentional blink: The brain's "eyeblink." *Current Directions in Psychological Science, 3,* 86–89.

Shaywitz, B. A., Fletcher, J. M., & Shaywitz, S. E. (1995). Defining and classifying learning disabilities and attention-deficit/hyperactivity disorder. *Journal of Child Neurology, 10*(Suppl. 1), S50–S57.

Shepard, R. N. (1967). Recognition memory for words, sentences, and pictures. *Journal of Verbal Learning and Verbal Behavior, 6,* 156–163.

Shepard, R. N. (1984). Ecological constraints on internal representation: Resonant kinematics of perceiving, imagining, thinking, and dreaming. *Psychological Review, 91,* 417–447.

Shepard, R. N. (1990). *Mind sights.* New York: Freeman.

Shepard, R. N., & Cooper, L. A. (1983). *Mental images and their transformations.* Cambridge, MA: MIT Press.

Shepard, R. N., & Metzler, J. (1971). Mental rotation of three-dimensional objects. *Science, 171,* 701–703.

Sherry, D. F., & Schacter, D. L. (1987). The evolution of multiple memory systems. *Psychological Review, 94,* 439–454.

Shiffrin, R., & Schneider, W. (1977). Controlled and automatic human information processing: II. Perceptual learning, automatic attending, and a general theory. *Psychological Review, 84,* 127–190.

Shimamura, A. P. (1986). Priming effects in amnesia: Evidence for dissociable memory function. *Quarterly Journal of Experimental Psychology, 38A,* 619–644.

Shimamura, A. P. (1997). Neuropsychological factors associated with memory recollection: What can science tell us about reinstated memories? In J. D. Read & D. S. Lindsay (Eds.), *Recollections of trauma: Scientific research and clinical practice* (pp. 253–272). New York: Plenum.

Simon, H. A. (1969). *The sciences of the artificial.* Cambridge, MA: MIT Press.

Simon, H. A. (1990). Invariants of human behavior. *Annual Review of Psychology, 41,* 1–19.

Simon, H. A., & Chase, W. G. (1973). Skill in chess. *American Scientist, 61,* 394–403.

Simon, H. A., & Hayes, J. R. (1976). The understanding process: Problem isomorphs. *Cognitive Psychology, 8,* 165–190.

Simons, D. J., & Ambinder, M. S. (2005). Change blindness: Theory and consequences. *Currrent Directions in Psychological Science, 14,* 44–48.

Simonton, D. K. (1988). *Scientific genius: A psychology of science.* Cambridge, UK: Cambridge University Press.

Simonton, D. K. (1997). Creative productivity: A predictive and explanatory model of career trajectories and landmarks. *Psychological Review, 104,* 66–89.

Sloman, S. A. (1996). The empirical case for two systems of reasoning. *Psychological Bulletin, 119,* 3–22.

Slovic, P., Fischhoff, B., & Lichtenstein, S. (1982). Facts versus fears: Understanding perceived risk. In D. Kahneman, P. Slovic, & A. Tversky (Eds.),

Judgment under uncertainty: Heuristics and biases (pp. 463–489). New York: Cambridge University Press.

Smith, E. E., & Jonides, J. (1997). Working memory: A view from neuroimaging. *Cognitive Psychology, 33,* 5–42.

Smith, E. E., & Medin, D. L. (1981). *Categories and concepts.* Cambridge, MA: Harvard University Press.

Smith, E. E., Shoben, E. J., & Rips, L. J. (1974). Structure and process in semantic memory: A featural model for semantic decisions. *Psychological Review, 81,* 214–241.

Smith, R. E., & Hunt, R. R. (1998). Presentation modality affects false memory. *Psychonomic Bulletin & Review, 5,* 710–715.

Smith, S. M., Glenberg, A., & Bjork, R. A. (1978). Environmental context and human memory. *Memory & Cognition, 6,* 342–353.

Smith, S. M., Ward, T. B., & Schumacher, J. S. (1993). Constraining effects of examples in a creative generation task. *Memory & Cognition, 21,* 837–845.

Spanos, N. P. (1996). *Multiple identities and false memories: A sociocognitive perspective.* Washington, DC: American Psychological Association.

Spear, N. E. (1979). Experimental analysis of infantile amnesia. In J. F. Kihlstrom & F. J. Evans (Eds.), *Functional disorders of memory* (pp. 75–102). Hillsdale, NJ: Lawrence Erlbaum.

Spelke, E., Hirst, W., & Neisser, U. (1976). Skills of divided attention. *Cognition, 4,* 215–230.

Sperling, G. (1960). The information available in brief visual presentation. *Psychological Monographs, 74*(Whole No. 498).

Spiro, R. J. (1980). Accommodative reconstruction in prose recall. *Journal of Verbal Learning and Verbal Behavior, 19,* 84–95.

Spitzer, H., Desimone, R., & Moran, J. (1988). Increased attention enhances both behavioral and neuronal performance. *Science, 240,* 338–340.

Squire, L. R. (1992). Declarative and nondeclarative memory: Multiple brain systems supporting learning and memory. *Journal of Cognitive Neuroscience, 4,* 232–243.

Squire, L. R., Amaral, D. G., & Press, G. A. (1990). Magnetic resonance measurements of hippocampal formation and mammillary nuclei distinguish medial temporal lobe and diencephalic amnesia. *Journal of Neuroscience, 10,* 3106–3117.

Squire, L. R., Haist, F., & Shimamura, A. P. (1989). The neurology of memory: Quantitative assessment of retrograde amnesia in two groups of amnesic men. *Journal of Neuroscience, 9,* 828–839.

Standing, L. (1973). Learning 10,000 pictures. *Quarterly Journal of Experimental Psychology, 25,* 207–222.

Stanovich, K. E. (1999). *Who is rational: Studies of individual differences in reasoning.* Mahwah, NJ: Lawrence Erlbaum.

Stanovich, K. E., Cunningham, A. E., & Feeman, D. J. (1984). Intelligence, cognitive skills, and early reading progress. *Reading Research Quarterly, 19,* 278–303.

Sternberg, R. J. (1988). *The nature of creativity: Contemporary psychological perspectives*. Cambridge, UK: Cambridge University Press.

Sternberg, S. (1966). High-speed scanning in human memory. *Science, 153,* 652–654.

Sternberg, S. (1969). Memory scanning: Mental processes revealed by reaction time experiments. *American Scientist, 57,* 421–457.

Sternberg, S. (1995). Inferring mental operations from reaction-time data: How we compare objects. In D. Scarborough & S. Sternberg (Eds.), *An invitation to cognitive science: Methods, models, and conceptual issues* (Vol. 4, pp. 365–454). Cambridge, MA: MIT Press.

Stevens, A., & Coupe, P. (1978). Distortions in judged spatial relations. *Cognitive Psychology, 10,* 422–437.

Stillings, N. A., Feinstein, M. H., Garfield, J. L., Rissland, E. L., Rosenbaum, D. A., Weisler, S. E., et al. (1987). *Cognitive science: An introduction.* Cambridge, MA: MIT Press.

Stromeyer, C. F., & Psotka, J. (1970). The detailed texture of eidetic images. *Nature, 225,* 346–349.

Stroop, J. R. (1935). Studies of interference in serial verbal reactions. *Psychological Monographs, 50,* 38–48.

Sutherland, N. S. (1968). Outlines of a theory of visual pattern recognition in animals and man. *Proceedings of the Royal Society of London, 171,* 297–317.

Talarico, J. M., & Rubin, D. C. (2003). Confidence, not consistency, characterizes flashbulb memories. *Psychological Science, 14,* 455–461.

Talmi, D., Grady, C. L., Goshen-Gottstein, Y., & Moscovitch, M. (2005). Neuroimaging the serial position curve: A test of single-store versus dual store models. *Psychological Science, 16,* 716–723.

Taplin, J. E., & Staudenmeyer, H. (1973). Interpretation of abstract conditional sentences in deductive reasoning. *Journal of Verbal Learning and Verbal Behavior, 12,* 530–542.

Taylor, C. W., & Sacks, D. (1981). Facilitating lifetime creative processes: A think piece. *Gifted Child Quarterly, 25,* 116–118.

Terrace, H. S., Petitto, L. A., Sanders, R. J., & Bever, T. G. (1979). Can an ape create a sentence? *Science, 206,* 891–902.

Thomas, L. (1992). *The fragile species.* New York: Maxwell Macmillan International.

Thompson, C. P., Hermann, D. J., Read, D. J., Bruce, D., Payne, D. G., & Toglia, M. P. (Eds.). (1998). *Eyewitness memory: Theoretical and applied perspectives.* Mahwah, NJ: Lawrence Erlbaum.

Thompson, P. G. (1980). Margaret Thatcher: A new illusion. *Perception, 9,* 483–484.

Thompson, R. F. (2000). *The brain: A neuroscience primer* (3rd ed.). New York: Worth.

Thorndike, E. L. (1898). Animal intelligence: An experimental study of associative processes in animals. *Psychological Monographs, 2*(Whole No. 8).

Thorndike, R. L. (1973-1974). Reading as reasoning. *Reading Research Quarterly, 9,* 135–147.

Thorndyke, P. W. (1977). Cognitive structures in comprehension and memory of narrative discourse. *Cognitive Psychology, 9,* 77–110.

Tobias, P. V. (1987). The brain of *Homo habilis:* A new level of organization. *Journal of Human Evolution, 16,* 741–761.

Treisman, A. M. (1960). Contextual cues in encoding listening. *Quarterly Journal of Experimental Psychology, 12,* 242–248.

Treisman, A. M. (1970). Contextual cues in selective listening. *Quarterly Journal of Experimental Psychology, 12,* 242–248.

Treisman, A. M. (1987). Properties, parts, and objects. In K. Boff, L. Kaufman, & J. Thomas (Eds.), *Handbook of perception and performance* (pp. 159–198). New York: John Wiley.

Treisman, A. M., & Gelade, G. (1980). A feature-integration theory of attention. *Cognitive Psychology, 12,* 97–136.

Treisman, A. M., & Sato, S. (1990). Conjunction search revisited. *Journal of Experimental Psychology: Human Perceptual Performance, 16,* 459–478.

Tulving, E. (1962). Subjective organization in free recall of "unrelated" words. *Psychological Review, 69,* 344–354.

Tulving, E. (1983). *Elements of episodic memory.* New York: Oxford University Press.

Tulving, E. (1985). How many memory systems are there? *American Psychologist, 40,* 385–398.

Tulving, E., Kapur, S., Craik, F. I. M., Moscovitch, M., & Houle, S. (1994). Hemispheric encoding/retrieval asymmetry in episodic memory: Positron emission tomography findings. *Proceedings of the National Academy of Science, 91,* 2012–2015.

Tulving, E., Mandler, G., & Baumal, R. (1964). Interaction of two sources of information in tachistoscopic word recognition. *Canadian Journal of Psychology, 18,* 62–71.

Tulving, E., & Pearlstone, Z. (1966). Availability versus accessibility of information in memory for words. *Journal of Verbal Learning and Verbal Behavior, 5,* 381–391.

Tulving, E., & Schacter, D. L. (1990). Priming and human memory systems. *Science, 247,* 301–306.

Tulving, E., & Thomson, D. M. (1973). Encoding specificity and retrieval processes in episodic memory. *Psychological Review, 80,* 352–373.

Tversky, A., & Kahneman, D. (1971). Belief in the law of small numbers. *Psychological Bulletin, 76,* 105–110.

Tversky, A., & Kahneman, D. (1973). Availability: A heuristic for judging frequency and probability. *Cognitive Psychology, 5,* 207–232.

Tversky, B. (1981). Distortions in memory for maps. *Cognitive Psychology, 13,* 407–433.

Tversky, B. (1991). Spatial mental models. *Psychology of Learning and Motivation, 27,* 109–145.

Valentine, T. (1988). Upside-down faces: A review of the effect of inversion upon face recognition. *British Journal of Psychology, 79,* 471–491.

Vokey, J. R., & Read, J. D. (1985). Subliminal messages: Between the devil and the media. *American Psychologist, 40,* 1231–1239.

von Frisch, K. (1950). *Bees: Their vision, chemical senses, and language.* Ithaca, NY: Cornell University Press.

von Neumann, J. (1958). *The computer and the brain.* New Haven, CT: Yale University Press.

Wallas, G. (1926). *The art of thought.* New York: Harcourt Brace.

Warren, R. M. (1970). Perceptual restoration of missing speech sounds. *Science, 167,* 392–393.

Warrington, E. K. (1985). Agnosia: The impairment of object recognition. In P. J. Vinken, G. W. Bruyn, & H. L. Klawans (Eds.), *Handbook of clinical neurology* (pp. 333–349). New York: Elsevier Science.

Warrington, E. K., & Shallice, T. (1972). Neuropsychological evidence of visual storage in short-term memory tasks. *Quarterly Journal of Experimental Psychology, 24,* 30–40.

Warrington, E. K., & Shallice, T. (1984). Category specific semantic impairments. *Brain, 107,* 829–854.

Warrington, E. K., & Weiskrantz, L. (1970). Amnesia: Consolidation or retrieval? *Nature, 228,* 628–630.

Warrington, K. K. (1982). Neuropsychological studies of object recognition. *Philosophical Transactions of the Royal Society of London, 298B,* 13–33.

Wason, P. C. (1968). On the failure to eliminate hypotheses: A second look. In P. C. Wason & P. N. Johnson-Laird (Eds.), *Thinking and reasoning* (pp. 44–75). New York: Penguin.

Wason, P. C., & Johnson-Laird, P. N. (1972). *Psychology of reasoning: Structure and content.* Cambridge, MA: Harvard University Press.

Waters, G. S., Rochon, E., & Caplan, D. (1992). The role of high-level speech planning in rehearsal: Evidence from patients with apraxia of speech. *Journal of Memory and Language, 31,* 54–73.

Waugh, N. C., & Norman, D. A. (1965). Primary memory. *Psychological Review, 72,* 89–104.

Weisberg, R. W. (1986). *Creativity: Genius and other myths.* New York: Freeman.

Weisberg, R. W., & Alba, J. W. (1981). An examination of the alleged role of "fixation" in the solution of several "insight" problems. *Journal of Experimental Psychology: General, 110,* 169–192.

Weiskrantz, L. (1986). *Blindsight: A case study and its implications.* Oxford, UK: Oxford University Press.

Weiskrantz, L., & Warrington, E. K. (1979). Conditioning in amnesic patients. *Neuropsychologia, 17,* 187–194.

Wells, G. L. (1993). What do we know about eyewitness identification? *American Psychologist, 48,* 553–571.

Wells, G. L., & Olson, E. A. (2001). The other-race effect in eyewitness identification: What do we do about it? *Psychology, Public Policy, and Law, 7,* 230–246.

Wertheimer, M. (1959). *Productive thinking.* New York: Harper & Row.

Wickelgren, W. A. (1974). *How to solve problems: Elements of a theory of problems and problem solving.* San Francisco: Freeman.

Wickens, C. D. (1980). The structure of attentional resources. In R. Nickerson (Ed.), *Attention and performance* (Vol. 8, pp. 239–257). Hillsdale, NJ: Lawrence Erlbaum.

Wickens, D. D. (1972). Characteristics of word encoding. In A. W. Melton & E. Martin (Eds.), *Coding processes in human memory* (pp. 191–215). New York: Winston.

Wickens, D. D., Dalezman, R. E., & Eggemeier, F. T. (1976). Multiple encoding of word attributes in memory. *Memory & Cognition, 4,* 307–310.

Willis, J., & Todorov, A. (2006). First impressions: Making up your mind after a 100-ms exposure to a face. *Psychological Science, 17,* 592–598.

Winston, J. S., Strange, B. A., O'Doherty, J., & Dolan, R. J. (2002). Automatic and intentional responses during the evaluation of trustworthiness of faces. *Nature Neuroscience, 5,* 277–283.

Woodworth, R., & Sells, S. (1935). An atmosphere effect in formal syllogistic reasoning. *Journal of Experimental Psychology, 18,* 451–460.

Yarbus, A. L. (1967). *Eye movements and vision* (B. Haigh, Trans.). New York: Plenum.

Yuille, J. C., & Daylen, J. (1998). The impact of traumatic events on eyewitness memory. In C. P. Thompson, D. J. Hermann., D. J. Read, D. Bruce, D. G. Payne, & M. P. Toglia (Eds.), *Eyewitness memory: Theoretical and applied perspectives* (pp. 155–178). Mahwah, NJ: Lawrence Erlbaum.

Zaragoza, M. S., & Mitchell, K. J. (1996). Repeated exposure to suggestion and the creation of false memories. *Psychological Science, 7,* 294–300.

Zola, S. M., & Squire, L. R. (2000). The medial temporal lobe and the hippocampus. In E. Tulving & F. I. M. Craik (Eds.), *The Oxford handbook of memory* (pp. 485–500). Oxford, UK: Oxford University Press.

Zola-Morgan, S., & Squire, L. R. (1990). Neurophysiological investigations of memory and amnesia: Findings from humans and nonhuman primates. In A. Diamond (Ed.), *The development and neural bases of higher cognitive functions* (pp. 434–456). New York: New York Academy of Sciences.

Zola-Morgan, S., Squire, L. R., & Amaral, D. G. (1986). Human amnesia and the medial temporal region: Enduring memory impairment following a bilateral lesion limited to field CA1 of the hippocampus. *Journal of Neuroscience, 6,* 2950–2967.

INDEX

Abelson, R., 191

Abramson, A., 59

Absent-mindedness, 94

Academic American Encyclopedia (Grolier's), 204

Acquired dyslexia, 52

Adams, John, 159–160

ADHD (Attention deficit/hyperactivity disorder), 64

Affect. *See* Emotion

Affirming the antecedent, 289, 291 (figure)

Affirming the consequent, 289

Agnosia, 39–42
  appreciative, 40, 42
  associative, 41, 190

AI. *See* Artificial intelligence

Airport drive problem, 305 (box)

Alba, J. W., 271

Algorithm, 80, 255–257, 277

Alignment heuristic, 202

Alzheimer's disease, 2, 27

American Sign Language (ASL), 221, 229, color plate #7

Amnesia
  anterograde, 102–104, 106, 123, 129, 169
  infantile, 110
  retrograde, 102–106, 123
  trauma-induced, 179

Amygdala, 13–14, 17, 53, 138–139, 171, 172

Analog properties, mental imagery, 197–198

Analytic processing, 49–51

Anaphora, 234–235

Anderson, A. K., 87–88

Animals, communication among, 220–222

Anterior cingulate gyrus, 83

Anterograde amnesia, 102–104, 106, 123, 129, 169

Appreciative agnosia, 40, 42

Apraxia, 121

Archimedes, 273

Artificial intelligence (AI), 6, 252

ASL. *See* American Sign Language

Assimilation, 156

Associative agnosia, 41, 190

Assumption of pure insertion, 24–25

Atchison, J., 215

Atkinson, R. C., 9–11, 95, 99, 101

Atmosphere hypothesis, 285

Attention, 63–92
  automatic processes, 76–81
  capacity model of, 73 (figure)
  capacity theories, 72–76
  divided, 65
  executive, 83–84, 118
  filter theories, 65–72
  late selection model of, 71 (figure)
  selective, 65
  visual, 81–89

Attention deficit/hyperactivity disorder (ADHD), 64

Attentional blink, 86–88
  study of, 88 (figure)

Attenuation, filter theory, 69–71, 70 (figure), 90

Atwood, M. E., 262

Auditory cortex, 27
Autobiographical events, reconstruct-
    ing, 158–160
Automatic processes, 77
Automatic search, 79 (figure)
Automaticity, 77–80
Autonomic nervous system, 21
Availability heuristic, 303–306, 309
Axon, 14, 36

Backward chaining, 267
Backward masking, 72
Baddeley, A. D., 118, 147
Baddeley's model, 120–121, 124
Bahrick, H. P., 108
Ball, T. M., 197
Bank teller problem, 303 (box)
Baron-Cohen, S., 193
Barsalou, L. W., 192
Bartlett, F. C., 155–157, 161
Barton, M. E., 190
Basic geometric features (geons),
    47, 47 (figure)
Baumal, R., 44
Begg, I., 285
Behavioral measures, 20–21
Behaviorism, 2
Bever, T., 218, 222
Bias
    belief, 286, 288, 309
    memory and, 95
Biederman, I., 47–49
Binding
    perceptual, 84–88
    problem, 85–86
Biology, evolutionary, 5
Bjork, R. A., 146
Blakemore, C., 36
Blindness, inattentional, 86
Blindsight, 37, 38 (figure)
Blocking, memory and, 94
Boden, M., 268, 273, 275
BOLD signal, 24
Bottom-up processes, 43. See also
    data-driven processes

Boundary of the object concept,
    186 (figure)
Bower, G. H., 147
Brain
    cerebral cortex, 14–18
    hemisphere activation,
        color plate #7
    language zone of, 229 (figure)
    lateralization, 227
    lesions, 27–28
    mammalian. See Limbic system
    parallel processing, 18–19
    pathways, ventral versus dorsal,
        18 (figure)
    posterior left hemisphere,
        color plate #8
    regions, color plate #1
    reptilian. See Cerebellum
    structures involved in emotion,
        17 (figure)
Brainstem, 17
Bransford, J. D., 136, 160–161,
    163, 203
Brewer, W. F., 154
Bridging inferences, 235–236
Broadbent, D. E., 67–71
Broca, Paul, 27, 225–226
Broca's aphasia, 226, 243
Broca's area, 27, 121, 214, 226 (figure),
    227, 229–230, 234, 243
Brown, J. A., 107
Brown-Peterson procedure, 107
Bruck, M., 175
Burns, H. J., 174

Cantor, N., 192
Capacity, of memory, 106–107
Capacity theories, 72–76
    mental effort, 73–75
    resources, multiple, 75–76
Carpenter, P. A., 234, 241
Carter-Sobell, L., 144
Categorical perception, 58–61
Categorize, time required to,
    207 (figure)

Category
  cues, 140
  size effect, 208–209
Ceci, S. J., 175
Cell body, 14
Central executive, working memory
    and, 119
Ceraso, J., 284–286
Cerebellum, 17, 128
Cerebral cortex, 14–18
  views of the lobes, 16 (figure)
Change blindness, 44
Chase, W. G., 233–234
Cherry, C., 66, 68
Chi, M. T. H., 263, 265–266
Christianson, S. A., 171
Chunking, 106–107
Cingulate gyrus, 17, 84 (figure)
Clark, H. H., 233–236
Clifton, R. K., 110
Clinical neuropsychology, 27
Coarticulation, 55–58, 56 (figure)
Coding, memory and, 111–114
Cognitive architecture, 9–11
Cognitive economy assumption, 206
Cognitive interview, 149–150
Cognitive neuroscience, 27
Cognitive psychologist, 30
Cognitive psychology,
  core concepts, 7–14
  historical perspective, 2–3
  research in, 6 (figure)
  research methods, 19–28
  scope of, 2–6
Cognitive science, 1, 5, 6 (figure)
Cohen, G., 108
Cole, M., 287
Collins, A. M., 206–209
Combs, B., 299
Communication, among animals,
    220–222
Components, multiple, of working
    memory, 118–120
Comprehension
  discourse, 237–239

eye movements and, 240–242
  of language, 230–241
  of sentences, 233–236
  task, 233 (figure)
Concept(s)
  boundary of the object, 186 (figure)
  hierarchical network representation,
      205 (figure)
  object, 185–192
  representing, 184–193
  rule-governed, 184–185
  theory, as 189–190
Conceptually driven processes,
    43–44, 58
Conclusion, valid deductive, 281
Conditional reasoning, 294, 309
  four-card selection task, 291 (figure)
Conditional syllogism, evaluation of the
    eight forms, 291 (table)
Confabulation, 169–170, 177, 181
Confirmation bias, 294–295
Conjunction error, 168
Conjunctive fallacy, 303
Conjunctive search task, color plate #4
Connectionist models, 10
  example of, 11 (figure)
Conrad, C., 207–208
Consciousness, 12–13
  visual, 33–37
Consolidation, long-term memory and,
    104–105
Constraints, cognitive
  conditional reasoning, 290–295
  syllogistic reasoning, 285–288
Controlled processes, 77
Conway, M. A., 108–109, 158
Cooper, G. F., 36
Cooperative principle, 220
Coren, S., 89
Cornea (eye), 34
Corpus callosum, 228
Cortex, primary visual, 36
Cold pressor method, 65
Cosmides, L., 293
Courage, M. L., 110

Cowan, N., 98
Cox, J. R., 293
Craik, F. I. M., 111, 133–135, 142, 144
Creativity, 267–276
   blocks, 270–274
   historical, 268, 277
   sources of, 274–275
   stages of, 268–270
Crossman, A. M., 175

Dalezman, R. E., 112
Damasio, A. R., 300
Darwin, C. J., 98
Data-driven processes, 43–44
Daylen, J., 179
Decision making, 295–308
Decision
   payoff matrix, 296 (table)
   theory, 295
   types of, 295–296
   under certainty, 295–296
   under risk, 296
   under uncertainty, 295–296
Declarative memory, 126–130
Deliberate practice, 269
Delusional false memory, 176
Denny, J. P., 285
Denying the antecedent, 289
Denying the consequent, 289
Descriptions, structural, 46–49
Detection time, automatic pop-out
   search, 85 (figure)
Deutsch, D., 71
Deutsch, J. A., 71
Dichotic listening, 65–66
DiGirolamo, G. J., 83
Directed thinking, 246
Discourse comprehension, 237–240
Dissociations, neurological, 102–106
Distinctive features, perceptual
   concepts and, 46
Distinctiveness, memory and, 137–140
Distortions, of memory, 153–182
Divided attention, 65

Dolan, R. J., 53
Double dissociation, 28, 28 (figure)
Dronkers, N. F., 226–227
Dual coding theory, 112
Dual process theory, 14
Duncker, K., 258, 273
Duration, of memory, 107–110
Dyslexia, 1, 52
Dyspraxia, 121

Eakin, D. K., 174
Early selection, 67, 67 (figure),
   68 (figure)
   filter theory, 67–69
   theory, 90
Ebbinghaus, Hermann, 3, 93
Echoic memory, 98–99, 112
Ecological validity, 180–181
Eddy, W. F., 234
Edison, Thomas, 275
EEG, 21, 23
Eggemeier, F. T., 112
Eidetic memory, 97–98. See also
   Photographic memory
Eimas, P. D., 60
Elaborative rehearsal, 133–134
Electroencephalogram (EEG), 21, 23
Electromagnetic radiation spectrum,
   34 (figure)
Emotion, 13–14
   decision making and, 299–300
   brain structures involved in,
      17 (figure)
Encoding
   memory and, 94
   selective, 171–172
   specificity, 148–150
Environmental context, learning
   and, 146–147
Episodic buffer, working memory
   and, 119, 124
Episodic memory, 125, 130–132,
   color plate #6
Eriksen, C. W., 81

Ernst, G. W., 251

ERP. *See* Event-related potential

Error(s)

common in conditional
reasoning, 290

common in syllogistic
reasoning, 284–285

proportion of, 20

Estes, W. K., 307

Euler circles, 281, 283 (figure), 286

Evans, J. St. B. T., 288, 292

Event-related potential (ERP),
21–23, 30, 200, 232

idealized P3a, 22 (figure)

Events

encoding, 133–141

remembering, 125–151

storing, 133–141

Evoked potential, 21. *See also*
Event-related potential (ERP)

Evolutionary biology, 5

Executive attention, 83–84, 118

Exhaustive search, 115

Expected utility theory, 297

Eye-mind assumption, 241

Eye movements, and comprehension,
240–241

Eyewitness testimony, 170–180

Eysenck, H. J., 137

Face

matching task, color plate #2

perception, 51–53

False memories, 178

prefrontal cortex and, 168

verbal, 167

Family resemblance structure, 189

Farah, M. J., 51–52

Faust, M., 236

Feature Comparison Model, The,
208–209

Feature detectors, 46

Feature integration theory, 84, 91

Features, basic geometric (geons), 47

Field, visual, 33

Filter theories, 65–72, 76

Fischhoff, B., 299, 304, 306

Fisher, R. P., 149

Fixation, 271–273, 277

problem solving, in, 272 (figure)

Flashbulb memory, 138–139, 159

fMRI. *See* Functional magnetic
resonance imaging

Fodor, J., 218

Folk theories, 189

Forgetting, 114–115

Forgetting curve, 108 (figure)

Formants, 54–55, 57

Forms, syllogistic, 281–284

Forward chaining, 267

Fragile Species, The (Thomas), 258

Frames, 191–192

Framing effect, 298

Franks, J. J., 136, 163, 203

Frequency heuristic, 306–307

Freud, S., 110, 177, 246

Fried, I., 200

Frith, U., 193

Frontal cortex, 300

Frontal lobe, 16, 29, 83,
color plate #6

Functional equivalence hypothesis, 199

Functional fixedness, 273–274, 277

Functional magnetic resonance imaging
(fMRI), 24, 30, 103, 128, 142, 200,
229, 234, color plate #2,
color plate #5

scanner, 25 (figure)

Functionalism, 3

Gambler's fallacy, 302

Gardner, B. T., 221

Gardner, R. A., 221

Garrett, M., 218

Geiselman, R. E., 149

Gelade, G., 84

General Problem Solver (GPS),
251–252, 260–262, 277

Generative capacity, human
    language of, 222
Genetics, maturation and, 80–81
Gentner, D., 294
Geons. *See* Basic geometric features
Gernsbacher, M. A., 236
Gestalt psychology, 249, 277
Gick, M. L., 258
Gilstrap, L. L., 175
Given-new strategy, 235
Glass, A. L., 209
Glenberg, A., 146
Global frameworks, 238–240
Goal state, of problem, 246, 277
Goldman-Rakic, P. S., 122
Gooden, D. R., 147
GPS. *See* General Problem Solver
Grammatical structure, 219 (figure)
Grammar, universal, 223–225
Graphemes, 231
Gray matter, 15
Greenberg, J. H., 224
Grice, H. P., 220
Griggs, R. A., 293
Gudjonsson, G. H., 176

Hadamard, Jacques, 274
Haist, F., 105
Hasher, L, 81
Haviland, S. E., 235–236
Hayes, J. R., 252–254, 268
Hebb, D. O., 10
Heinz, S. P., 74
Hemispheric encoding/retrieval
    asymmetry (HERA), 142
Heuristic, 255–257, 277
    alignment, 202
    problem solving for, 257–263
    probability, 300–307
Hilgard, E. R., 65
Hillyard, S. A., 232
Hindsight bias, 306
Hippocampus, 17, 123, 143,
    color plate #5

lesions in, 168
loss of function of, 102 (figure)
memory and, 104
Hirst, W., 79
Historical creativity, 268, 277
Holender, D., 89
Holistic processing, 49–51,
    50 (figure), 62
Holyoak, K. J., 209, 258
Homo habilis, 214
Homo sapiens sapiens, 215
Hopkins, B., 222
Houle, S., 142
Howe, M. L., 110
Hunt, R. R., 168

Iconic memory, 96–98
Ill-defined problems, 248
Illicit conversion, 286, 308
Illumination, creativity and, 269, 278
Illusions, memory, 166–168
Imagery, versus perception, 199–200
Images, 193–204
Imaginal code, 194, 195 (figure), 210
Immediacy assumption, 241
Inattentional blindness,
    86, 87 (figure)
Incubation, creativity and, 269, 278
Inductive reasoning, 294
Infantile amnesia, 110
Information
    access, 12–13
    processing approach, 4
Inhoff, A. W., 237
Initial state, of problem, 246, 277
Insertion, assumption of pure, 24–25
Integration
    encoding and, 162–163
    memory distortion and, 160
Interference, forgetting and, 114
Interpretation
    encoding and, 161–162
    memory distortion and, 160
Isomorphic problems, 254

Jacoby, L. L., 132
James, William, 2, 3, 63, 99
Jefferson, Thomas, 160
Johnson-Laird, P. N., 237–238, 285, 290, 293
Johnson, M. K., 160–162
Johnston, W. A., 74
Ju, G., 49
Just, M. A., 234, 241

Kahneman, D., 72, 298, 301–305
Kahneman's capacity theory, 75
Kaplan, G. A., 251, 254–255
Kassin, S. M., 176
Keller, T. A., 234
Kinchla, R. A., 82
Kintsch, W., 237–239
Kirker, W. S., 135
Knight, R. T., 226
Knowing, 131
Knowledge
    domain-specific, 263–267
    power and, 263–264
    representation, 183–211
Koch, C., 200
Koffka, K., 137
Köhler, W., 249–250
Komatsu, L. K., 190
Kopelman, M. D., 169
Korsakoff's syndrome, 169, 181
Kosslyn, S. M., 197
Kreiman, G., 200
Kroll, N. E. A., 168
Kuiper, N. A., 135
Kutas, M., 232

Laboratory events,
    reconstructing, 155–158
Labov, W., 185–186
Lakoff, G., 183
Langer, E. J., 272
Language
    comprehension of, 230–242
    defining, 213–223
    meaningful units of, 216 (figure)

origins of, 214–215
    representations of, 223–230
    tasks, color plate #1
Language acquisition device (LAD),
    223–225
Latent semantic analysis (LSA), 204
Lateral geniculate nucleus, 34
Law of small numbers, 302
Learning
    drug-induced state and,
        149 (figure)
    free-recall demonstration, 99 (box)
    state-dependent, 148
Learning environment, word
    recollection and, 147 (figure)
Leichtman, M., 175
Lens (eye), 34
Lesions, brain, 27–28
Leslie, A. M., 192–193
Leveling, 156, 181
Lexigrams, 222
Liberman, A. M., 60
Lichenstein, S., 299, 304
Light, L. L., 144
Limbic lobe, 16
Limbic system, 15, 17–18, 29, 300
Linguistic universals, 223
Lisker, L., 59
Listening, dichotic, 65–66
Location matching task,
    color plate #2
Loci
    demonstration of, 134 (box)
    method of, 134, 150
Lockhart, R. S., 111, 133–134
Loftus, E. F., 172–174
Logan, G. D., 80
Long-term memory, 9, 38
    multiple systems of, 132, 150
    types of, 126–133
Lopez, A., 209
LSA (Latent semantic analysis), 204
Luchins, A. S., 261, 271
Luria, A. R., 139–140, 286–287

Mack, A., 86
MacKay, D. G., 72
Macropropositions, 239
Magnetic resonance imaging (MRI), 103
Maintenance rehearsal, 133–134
Mammalian brain. *See* Limbic system
Mandler, G., 44
Mantyla, T., 145
Marcel, A. J., 72
Martin, A., 103
Martin, R. C., 120
Masking, backward, 72
Maturation, genetics and, 80–81
MC Problem, 254–255
McClelland, J. L., 10
McCulloch, W. S., 10
McDonald, K., 222
McGlone, R. E., 160
Meaning, knowledge and,
    286–288, 292–294
Means-end analysis, 260–263
Medulla oblongata, 17
Memory
    capacity of, 106–107
    characteristics of, 111 (figure)
    coding and, 111–114
    cognitive function of, 4 (figure)
    declarative, 126–130, 127–128
    demonstration, 167 (box)
    distortions, 153–182
    duration of, 107–110
    echoic, 98–99, 112
    episodic, 130–132
    experiment, Part 1, 164 (figure)
    experiment, Part 2, 165 (figure)
    false, 167, 176, 178
    flashbulb, 138–139, 159
    free-recall demonstration, 99 (box)
    iconic, 96–98, 96 (figure)
    illusions, 166–168
    impaired short-term, 106
    implanted, 174–176
    long-term, 9, 38, 126–133,
        127 (figure), 150

malfunctions of, 94–95
    nondeclarative, 127–128
    photographic, 97
    picture, 137–138
    procedural, 126–130
    recovered, 176–180
    semantic, 127, 130–132, 205–209
    sensory, 67, 95–99
    serial position effects and,
        100 (figure)
    seven sins of, 94–95
    short-term, 9, 106 (box),
        109, 113 (figure)
    short-term versus long-term, 99–117
    storage and, 94
    stores, 11
    systems, 93–124, 94 (figure),
        95 (figure)
    tests, 128–129
    three-store model of, 93, 101,
        117, 123
    visual sensory. *See* Iconic memory
    working, 117–124, 285–286
Mental effort, capacity theory, 73–75
Mental images, study of, 199 (figure)
Mental lexicon, 217
Mental maps, versus real maps,
    202 (figure)
Mental representation, 7
Merikle, P. M., 111
Mervis, C. B., 187, 189
Meta-representations, 192–193,
    194 (figure)
Metacognition, 29, 263–267, 264
Method of loci, 134, 134 (box), 150
Method of subtraction, 24–26,
    26 (figure), 121
Meyer, D. E., 208
Micropropositions, 239
Miller, D. G., 174
Miller, G. A., 106
Milner, B., 103, 129
Mind, 9
Mind-body problem, 12–13

Mindblindness, 193
Minsky, M. L., 191
Misattribution, memory and, 94
Mischel, W., 192
Misinformation effect, 172–174
   demonstration of, 173 (figure)
Mitchell, K. J., 175
Mnemonic techniques, 133–135, 150
Mode, of retrieval, 142–144
Modularity, perception and, 49–61
Module, 9
Modus ponens, 290. *See also* Affirming
   the antecedent
Modus tollens, 289–290, 292–294. *See
   also* Denying the consequent
Monahan, J. L., 89
Monster problem, 253 (figure)
Mood congruence effect, 147
Moray, N., 69, 70
Morpheme, 216, 217, 242
Morris, C. D., 136
Moscovitch, M., 142
MRI (Magnetic resonance imaging), 103
Multiple capacity theory, 90
Multiple resource theories, 75
Murphy, S. T., 89
Murphy, T. D., 81
Murray, J. E., 51
Mutilated checkerboard problem,
   250 (figure)
Myers, N. A., 110

Neisser, U., 46, 79, 98, 170
Neocortex, 15–16, 18–19. *See also*
   Cortex, primary visual
Neural activation, color plate #1
Neural basis of selection, 81–82
Neural systems, 225–230
Neuroimaging techniques,
   23 (figure), 23–27
Neuroimages, 30
Neurological dissociations, 102–106
Neuron, 14, 15 (figure)
Neurophysiology, 5

Neuropsychology, clinical, 27
Neuroscience, cognitive, 27
Neuroscientist, 6, 19
Newell, A., 251, 261
Nightingale, N., 175
Nine-dot problem, 249 (figure),
   270 (figure)
Nondeclarative memory, 127–128
Norman, D. A., 71
Nucleus, lateral genticulate, 34

Object
   concepts, 185–192, 210
   matching, 196 (figure), 198 (figure)
   perception, 48 (figure)
   representations, 45–49
Occipital cortex, 27, 36–37, 40, 46
Occipital lobe, 16, 19, 29
Odean, T., 298–299
O'Doherty, J., 53
Operator, problem states, 247, 277
Optic chiasm, 36
Optic nerve, 36
Organization, subjective, 140–141
Osherson, D. N., 209
Over, D. E., 292

Paivio, A., 112
Palmer, J. C., 173
Parallel processing, 8, 18–19
Parallel search, 115
Parietal lobe, 16, 19, 29, 85
Parity, checkerboard representation of,
   256 (figure)
Parkinson's disease, 27
Partial report condition, 97
Pathways, visual, 35 (figure)
Patients, amnesiac, and recall of
   events, 105 (figure)
Pattern recognition, 37–49,
   39 (figure), 46, 90
   bottom-up processes, 42–45
   object representations, 45–49
   top-down processes, 42–45

Pearlstone, Z., 140
Perception, 31–62, 52, 277
  categorical, 58–61
  constructive nature of, 32 (figure)
  modularity, 49–61
  of objects, 48 (figure)
  pattern recognition, 37–49
  subliminal, 88–89
  versus imagery, 199–200
  visual consciousness, 33–37
Perceptual
  binding, 84–88
  categorization, 41 (figure)
  priming, 128
Perris, E. E., 110
Persistence, memory and, 95
PET. See Positron emission tomography
Petersen, S. E., 82
Peterson, L. R., 107
Peterson, M. J., 107
Petitto, L. A., 222
Phoneme, 53–54, 56–58, 60, 62, 216, 242
Phonemic similarity effect, 112
Phonological loop, working memory
    and, 119–121, 124
Photographic memory, 97
Physics, problem solving, 264–267,
    265 (figure), 266 (figure)
Physiological measures, 21–29
Pickering, Thomas, 160
Pickrell, J. E., 174
Picture memory, 137–138
Pillemer, D. B., 138
Pinker, S., 12, 224
Pitts, W., 10
Poincaré, Henri, 274
Political poll problem, 307 (box)
Polson, P. G., 262
Polya, G., 258
Polysemy, 236–237
Pons, 17
Pop-out search task, color plate #4
Positron emission tomography (PET),
    24, 27, 30, 82–83, 128, 142, 200,
    232, color plate #1, color plate #6

Posner, M. I., 77, 82–83
Power, knowledge and, 263–264
Practice, automaticity and, 77–80
Pragmatics, 219–220, 242
Preattentive processes. See Automatic
    processes
Prefrontal cortex, 83
  confabulation and, 169
  episodic encoding and, 143 (figure)
  false memories and, 168
Premack, D., 193
Premises, major and minor,
    284 (figure)
Preparation, creativity and, 268–269
Primacy effect, 100
Primary visual cortex, 36
Priming, 72
Principles of Psychology, The (James),
    2–3, 99
Proactive interference, 114
Probability, actual versus subjective,
    301 (figure)
Probability heuristic, 306–307
Problem solving, 245, 276–278
  creativity in, 267–275
  general model of, 251–267
  knowledge, domain specific,
    263–267
  metacognition, 263–267
  methods, 255–257
  types of thinking and, 246–250
Problem
  ill-defined, 246–250, 248
  isomorphic, 254
  representing, 252–255
  space, searching, 255–263
  well-defined, 246–250
Procedural memory, 126–130
Procedures, encoding and
    retrieval, 149 (box)
Processes
  automatic, 76–81
  bottom-up, 42–45. See also
    Data-driven processes
  controlled, 77

of retrieval, 141–150
top-down, 42–45. *See also*
    Conceptually driven processes
Processing
    analytic, 50
    holistic, 49
    levels of, 135–136, 136 (figure)
    parallel, 8
    relational, 140–141
    serial, 8
    stages of, 8
    transfer-appropriate, 136–137
Production, creative, 275–276
Productive thinking, 249, 277
Productivity, of human language, 222
Properties, analog, mental imagery,
    197–198
Proportion of errors, 20
Propositional code, 195,
    195 (figure), 210
Propositional representations,
    203 (figure)
Propositions, 193–204
Prosopagnosia, 51–52
Prototype, categories, 187–189, 210
Provitera, A., 284–286
Psychological context, memory retrieval
    cue, 147–148
Psychologist, cognitive, 30
Psychosurgery, 27
Pulvinar thalamic nucleus, 82, 91
Putnick, M., 175

Quillian, M. R., 206–209

Radiation problem, 259 (figure),
    260 (figure)
Rapid eye movement (REM), 163
Reaction time, 20
Read, J. D., 89
Reading, requirements, 239 (figure)
Reasoning
    conditional, 288–295, 309
    constraints, cognitive,
        285–288, 290–295

errors, common, 284–285, 290
inductive, 294
invalid, 289
syllogistic, 279–288, 294
syllogistic forms, 281–284
valid, 289
Recency effect, 100
Recognition judgment, confidence
    in, 166 (figure)
Reconstructing
    autobiographical events, 158–160
    laboratory events, 155–158
Reconstructive retrieval, 154–160,
    155 (figure), 170–171
Recovered memory, 178
Redfern, B. B., 226
Reed, S. K., 200
Referential coherence, 237–238
Rehearsal, 133–134
Reicher, G. M., 43
Reid, S., 299
Reiser, B. J., 197
Relational processing, 140
REM (Rapid eye movement), 163
Remembering, 125–151
Repp, B. H., 60
Representation, of knowledge, 183–212
Representativeness heuristic, 302–303,
    306, 309
Repression, 177–179
Reproductive thinking, 249
Reptilian brain. *See* Cerebellum
Research methods, in cognitive
    psychology, 19–28
Resources, multiple, capacity
    theory, 75–76
Retention, long-term, 109 (figure)
Retrieval
    memory and, 94, 115–117
    mode, 142, 142–144
    process, 141–150
    reconstructive, 154–160
    specificity, encoding, 144–150
Retroactive interference, 114
Retrograde amnesia, 102–106, 123

Rhodes, G., 51
Rips, L. J., 207–208
Rock, I., 86
Roediger, H. L. III, 132
Rogers, T. B., 135
Rosch, E. H., 187, 189
Ross, B. H., 259
Rotation heuristic, 202
Rubenstein, M. F., 295
Rubin, D. C., 115
Rule-governed concepts, 184–185
Rumelhart, D. E., 10
Rundus, D., 101
Rupert, E., 222

Saccade, 240
Sacks, O., 40
Sanders, R. J., 222
Savage-Rumbaugh, E. S., 222
Schacter, D. L., 94–95, 97, 129
Schank, R. C., 191
Schema, 42, 61, 154–155, 160, 170,
    178, 180–181, 210
Schizophrenia, 83
Schneider, W., 77–78
Schumacher, J. S., 272
Schwartz, J. C., 192
Scribner, S., 287
Scripts, 191–192
Scullin, M. H., 175
Search, 115–116
Selection
    early, 67–69
    encoding and, 160–161
    late, filter theory, 71–72
    memory distortion and, 160
    neural basis of, 81–82
Selective attention, 65
Selective encoding, 171–172
Self-knowledge, 12–13
Self-reference effect, 135
Self-terminating search, 115–116
Sells, S., 285
Semantic memory,
    127, 130–132, 205–209

Semantic network model, 205–208
Semantics, 215–217, 218 (box), 242
Sensory memory, 67, 95–99
    echoic memory, 98–99
    iconic memory, 96–98
Sentence comprehension, 233–237
Sentience, 12
Serial exhaustive search, 116
Serial position effects, memory
    and, 100–101
Serial processing, 8
Serial search, 115–116
Sevcik, R., 222
Sewell, D. R., 192
Shadowing, 66, 66 (figure)
Shafir, E., 209
Shallice, T., 106
Sharpening, 156
Shelton, J. R., 120
Shepard, R. N., 196, 197
Shiffrin, R. M., 9–11, 77, 78,
    95, 99, 101
Shimamura, A. P., 105
Shoben, E. J., 207–208
Short-term memory
    semantic coding in, 113 (figure)
    serial exhaustive search in,
        116 (figure)
Simon, H. A., 251–255, 261
Simonton, D. K., 275–276
Simulation heuristic, 305–306, 309
Single capacity theory, 90
Single dissociation, 28 (figure)
Slovic, P., 299, 304
Smith, E. E., 207–209
Smith, R. E., 168
Smith, S. M., 146, 272
Snyder, C. R. R., 77
Solomon, S. K., 161
Somatic marker hypothesis, 300
Source monitoring, 181
    memory and, 163–170
Spanos, N. P., 176
Spatial neglect, 82
Specificity, encoding, 144–150

Spectrogram, speech, 54, 55 (figure), 57 (figure), 59 (figure)
Speech
  act, 219
  perception, 53–61, 62
Spelke, E., 79
Sperling, G., 96–98, 111
Squire, L. R., 104–105
Stages of processing, 8
Stanhope, N., 108
State-dependent learning, 148
Steedman, M., 285
Sternberg, R. J., 268
Sternberg, S., 115–116
Stevens, A. L., 294
Stillings, N. A., 5
Storage, memory and, 94
Strange, B. A., 53
Stroop effect, 76, 81, 83, 90, color plate #3
Stroop, J. R., 76
Structural descriptions, 46–49
Structuralism, 2
Subgoals, of problem, 246
Subjective organization, 140–141
Subjective utility, 298
Subliminal perception, 88, 88–89
Subtraction, method of, 24–26, 26 (figure)
Suggestibility, memory and, 94–95
Sulci, 15
Superior colliculus, 36–37
Syllogisms, valid and invalid, 282 (table)
Syllogistic reasoning, 279, 294, 308
Symbolic logic, 279
Symbolic models, 9, 10 (figure)
Synaptic connection, 14
Synesthesia, 139–140
Synset, 206
Syntax, 217–219, 218 (box), 242
Systems, memory, 93–124
Systems, multiple, of long-term memory, 132–133

Tachistoscope, 96
Temporal cortex, 27

Temporal lobe, 16, 19, 27, 29, 85, 104, 190, 191 (figure), color plate #6
Temporal medial lobe, color plate #5
Terms, relations among, 250–251
Terrace, H. S., 222
Test dissociations, interpreting, 129–130
Testimony
  eyewitness, 170–180
  memories, 174–180
  misinformation effect, 172–174
  selective encoding, 171–172
Tests, memory, 128–129
Thalamus, 34, 82
Theories, dual process, 307–308
Theory of mind, 193, 194 (figure)
Thinking
  decision making and, 299–300
  directed, 246
  productive, 249
  reproductive, 249
  types of, 246–251
  undirected, 246
Thomas, L., 258
Thomson, D. M., 145
Thorndike, E. L., 249–250, 257
Three-store model, 93, 101, 117, 123
Thulborn, K. R., 234
Tip of the tongue (TOT) states, 145–146, 146 (box), 148, 150
Titchener, Edward B., 2
Todorov, A., 53
Tooby, J., 293
Top-down processes, 43, 58. *See also* Conceptually driven processes
TOT. *See* Tip of the tongue states
Tower of Hanoi problem, 247 (figure), 247–248, 260
Transduction, 31
Transfer-appropriate processing, 136
Transience, memory and, 94
Trauma-induced amnesia, 179

Traumatic event, recollection of, 180 (figure)
Treisman, A. M., 69, 70, 71, 84
Treyens, J. C., 154
Tulving, E., 44, 129, 131, 135, 140–142, 144–145
Tversky, A., 298, 301–305
Tversky, B., 200, 202
Typicality effect, 187 (figure), 188 (table), 189

UNDERSTAND (computer program), 252–254
Undirected thinking, 246
Universal grammar, 223–225, 243
    bridging inferences, 234–235
    given-new strategy, 235–236
    global frameworks, 238–240
    input, absence of, 224–225
    laterality, 227–230
    parameter setting, 224
    polysemy, 236–237
    referential coherence, 237–238
Utilities, decision maker and, 295–296
Utility, subjective, 296–299, 297 (figure)

Valid deductive conclusion, 281
van Dijk, T. A., 237–239
Venn diagrams, 286
Verbal protocols, 20
Verification
    creativity and, 269, 278
    time required, 207 (figure)
Visual attention, 81–89
Visual consciousness, 33–37
Visual cortex, 36–37, color plate #8
Visual field, 33
Visual imagery, limitations of, 201 (figure)
Visual pathways, 34–36
Visual perception, 19

Visual search task, 78 (figure)
Visual sensory memory.
    See Iconic memory
Visual-spatial sketch pad, working memory and, 119–120, 124
Vokey, J. R., 89
von Frisch, K., 221
von Kekulé, Friedrich, 274
von Neumann, J., 9

"War of the Ghosts" (folk tale), 155, 156 (box), 157 (box), 158 (box)
Ward, T. B., 272
Warren, R. M., 54
Warrington, E. K., 106, 129
Warrington, K. K., 40, 42
Wason, P. C., 290, 293–295
Water jar problem, 262 (figure)
Waugh, N. C., 114
Weisberg, J. A., 103
Weisberg, R. W., 271
Weiskrantz, L., 129
Well-defined problem, 246, 248
Wenzel, A. E., 115
Wernicke, Karl, 227
Wernicke's aphasia, 227, 243
Wernicke's area, 226 (figure), 229–230, 234, 243
Whole report condition, 96–97
Wickens, C. D., 75
Wickens, D. D., 112
Wiggs, C. L., 103
Wilkie, O., 209
Willis, J., 53
Winston, J. S., 53
Wittgenstein, Ludwig, 185
Woloshyn, V., 132
Woodruff, G., 193
Woodsworth, R., 285
Word recognition, 45 (figure), 230–233
Word superiority effect, 43–44

WordNet (dictionary), 206–207
Words, comprehension, features
    activated, 231 (figure)
Working memory, 93, 117–123,
    118 (figure), 120 (figure), 122
    (figure), 285–286. *See also*
    Short-term memory
Wundt, Wilhelm, 2

Yaffee, L. S., 120
Yong, E., 51
Yuille, J. C., 179

Zacks, R. T., 81
Zajonc, R. B., 89
Zaragoza, M. S., 175

ABOUT THE AUTHOR

Ronald T. Kellogg is Professor of Psychology in the Department of Psychology at Saint Louis University. He holds degrees from the University of Iowa (B.S., psychology) and the University of Colorado (M.A. and Ph.D., experimental psychology) and held a National Science Foundation Postdoctoral Fellowship at Stanford University. His past research has examined attention, long-term memory, concept learning, and cognitive processes in writing. His current work concerns the role of working memory in thought and text production and the effects of writing on memory retrieval. He has authored three previous books and over 50 scientific publications. His teaching includes courses in cognitive psychology, cognitive neuroscience, perception, and language.